THE HISTORY
OF COMMUNICATION

Robert W. McChesney
and John C. Nerone, editors

A list of books in the series appears
at the end of this book.

Radio's Hidden Voice

The Origins of

Public Broadcasting in the

United States

HUGH RICHARD SLOTTEN

University of Illinois Press

URBANA AND CHICAGO

Library of Congress Cataloging-in-Publication Data
Slotten, Hugh Richard.
Radio's hidden voice : the origins of public broadcasting
in the United States / Hugh Richard Slotten.
p. cm. — (The history of communication)
Includes bibliographical references and index.
ISBN 978-0-252-03447-3 (cloth : alk. paper)
1. Broadcasting—United States—History—20th century.
I. Title.
HE8689.8.S567   2009
384.540973—dc22   2008046796

Contents

Illustrations

Acknowledgments

I would particularly like to thank colleagues at four institutions for their valuable advice with this project: the History of Science Department at Harvard University; the Science, Society, and Technology Program at the Massachusetts Institute of Technology; the Media, Film, and Communication Studies Department at the University of Otago; and the Journalism and Mass Communications Department at the University of Wisconsin–Madison. I am also grateful to the numerous archivists and librarians that facilitated research in some very large collections across the United States and to Carol Moser for her expert assistance at a crucial stage of this project. The research for this book was supported by generous grants from the National Science Foundation, the Spencer Foundation, and the University of Otago.

Different versions of sections of this book were previously published in three journals: *Technology and Culture; The Historical Journal of Film, Radio, and Television;* and *Media History.* I am extremely grateful for the advice I received from staff and referees with these journals as well as with the University of Illinois Press.

Radio's Hidden Voice

Prologue

A few days after Christmas in 1929, Ralph Goddard died while regulating equipment in the generator room of the radio station at New Mexico State Agricultural and Mechanical College. Goddard, a professor in the school's engineering department, was forty-two years old. The circumstances of his death remain unclear—no one witnessed the accident—but he seems to have been electrocuted after walking from the studio in a drizzle to the building that housed the generator. The fatal spark could have been conducted by moisture on his shoes and on the wooden stick he used to adjust the generator.[1]

This event marked the end of an era for the radio station KOB. Licensed in 1922, eight years after Goddard moved to New Mexico from New England, it had become one of the most powerful stations in the Southwest under his direction, broadcasting market and weather reports, news, music by local artists, as well as talks on agriculture and other subjects by faculty. It remained noncommercial throughout the 1920s, but when it was no longer able to compete with stations that accepted advertising, the college was forced to consider sponsored programming or selling the station to a commercial interest. During the 1930s, the station was first leased to a newspaper in Albuquerque and then sold to a commercial broadcasting company.[2]

The early history of KOB is paradigmatic of a transformation in American radio during the 1920s: the change from a largely amateur, nonprofit, and local activity conducted by a diverse range of institutions and individuals to a predominantly professional and commercial pursuit dominated by national networks interested in selling audiences to advertisers. The diversity of stations at the end of 1922, about twelve months into the radio boom that began nearly a year after the first regularly scheduled broadcasts from the station KDKA and other pioneers, is clear in the ownership pattern at that time. On December 1, 1922, 230 of the 570 American stations were licensed by radio and electrical manufacturers and dealers primarily interested in selling receivers and related electrical components to the public. The rest included seventy stations operated by newspapers, sixty-five owned by educational institutions, thirty established by department stores, and ten operated by churches and YMCAs.[3] Before the mid-1920s, the majority of stations in the country did not accept sponsored advertising.[4] By the 1930s, however, many local stations that survived had adopted advertising and become oriented toward national service. As Lizabeth Cohen has pointed out, "Where once radio had provided a voice for community groups, by the 1930s it treated these constituencies as potential markets for advertisers' products."[5]

Because historians generally focus on analyzing winners, we know a great deal about "mainstream, hegemonic practices" of large commercial stations connected to networks during the late 1920s and 1930s. Largely unexplored have been the early experiences of stations that provided an alternative model for broadcasting.[6] The focus on the development of network-dominated, commercial broadcasting (popularly known as the American System) as a master narrative has obscured the historical importance of alternative meanings for radio broadcasting and their complex interaction with dominant trends. That few of the primary documents necessary to such a study have survived complicates the historian's task; however, archival sources do exist for stations such as the one Goddard organized in New Mexico—radio stations operated by institutions of higher education. These were especially important for two reasons: they helped pioneer the idea and practice of broadcasting, and they provided a noncommercial alternative to the emerging commercial broadcast system. It is true that during this early period other independent, local stations owned by small businesses were operated more to generate goodwill among their listeners (and possible customers) than to enrich their owners, but when advertising became more acceptable in the late 1920s, many of these stations adopted the new practice. Those operated by institutions of higher learning, however, remained both noncommercial and nonprofit. As Robert McChesney has argued, the "existence" of these stations "constitutes what could almost be termed a 'hidden history' of American radio."[7] This book, using extensive research in archives across the United States, examines the origins of alternative constructions of radio based especially on a commitment to providing noncommercial service with diverse forms of programming not merely meant to entertain but also to educate, inform, enlighten, and uplift local citizens.

Since the 1960s, the existence of a largely noncommercial public broadcasting system providing an alternative to the dominant American System of commercial broadcasting has become a familiar feature of American cultural and social life. Congress established the Public Broadcasting System (PBS) for television in 1969 and National Public Radio (NPR) in 1970. The two national networks have institutionalized the concept of public broadcasting for radio and television. NPR uses public funds to support advertising-free programming meant to entertain, inform, and enlighten.

By focusing on developments since the 1960s, however, historians have not sufficiently recognized crucial early patterns. The tension between public-service and commercial ideals has existed since the first experiments with radio early in the century. Decisions made by government officials during the 1920s were especially important. During this period, the federal government decided that because the radio spectrum was a public resource, to retain a license, broadcasters needed to demonstrate that they served the public interest. Partly because some of the first radio stations in the United States were developed by land-grant universities such as Goddard's institution in New Mexico, a commitment to education became a central means for defining the public-interest standard. Stations operated by agriculturally oriented land-grant schools played a crucial role defining the character of public-service broadcasting in the United States. But in the face of the rise of commercial broadcasting, these early noncommercial public-service broadcasters barely managed to survive. Many did not. Whereas in 1924, there were nearly forty stations operated by land-grant universities, by 1930, less than twenty land-grant stations continued to operate.[8] Overall, the number of stations operated by universities and colleges dropped from 124 in 1925 to less than thirty in 1932.[9] These stations were not only important for providing an alternative model for broadcasting during this crucial period when commercial radio became dominant; they remain important today because many of the surviving university stations provided a foundation for the establishment of NPR during the 1970s. The licenses of most NPR stations remain in the hands of universities. Despite this continuity with the past, the early history of educational and public radio stations in the United States reflected specific historical conditions. The objectives and practices of stations during the 1920s and 1930s need to be analyzed in their proper historical context.

The first chapter examines early developments, especially during the period before World War I, that established a foundation for different understandings of radio broadcasting in the United States. When broadcasting emerged during the early 1920s, many observers believed that they were witnessing a revolutionary new form of communications. But broadcasting was not simply created after 1920 as a completely new innovation. It came into existence as the result of a complex process of interaction among different institutions and individuals during the previous two decades. The resulting precedents established a powerful framework that would shape the emergence of radio broadcasting in the United States.[10]

Just as it is important to understand how the dominant commercial system was shaped by processes that occurred during the period before the First World War, it is also important to understand how earlier patterns shaped the alternative system of noncommercial public-service broadcasting that emerged during the 1920s. In analyzing these complex patterns, the first chapter focuses on the crucial involvement of universities for the emergence of wireless before 1920. Since specific individuals often played central roles at universities and colleges, the involvement of key faculty members and students needs to be examined in detail. The focus then shifts to an analysis of the interaction among universities, amateur hobbyists, and government agencies. An examination of this interplay is crucial for understanding the unique role of institutions of higher education, especially land-grant agricultural colleges, in shaping an alternative understanding and an alternative organizational framework for radio broadcasting in the United States.

The second chapter analyzes the policies and practices of radio stations operated by universities and colleges during the 1920s. What characteristics distinguished these stations from broadcasters that represented the emerging dominant system of commercial, network radio? A detailed analysis using archival sources is essential because of the existence of a number of partially unexamined assumptions about noncommercial stations during this period. A number of scholars have correctly recognized that university stations were particularly interested in broadcasting programs that would reform or uplift audiences.[11] But the exact relationship between broadcasters and audiences has not been clearly explored. By analyzing detailed practices based especially on archival sources, this study provides a complex and nuanced understanding of radio during the 1920s. University stations did not simply treat audiences as passive recipients of messages; practices were diverse, and motives were mixed.

The use of radio for informational talks and educational programming was a distinct aspect of stations operated by universities during the 1920s; however, most stations also provided a variety of programs, including music and other forms of entertainment. Although university stations emphasized especially their important role in extending educational benefits to all citizens, they increasingly also stressed their nonprofit commitment during the 1920s. In the face of the rise of commercial broadcasting, stations operated by universities underscored how the commercial goals of advertisers were incompatible with the public-service obligations of extension education. While commercial networks beginning in the late 1920s served national advertisers promoting a homogenized ethic of consumption, educational stations committed to noncommercial ideals affirmed connections to local and regional communities.

Chapter 3 explores the development of public policy for radio from early in the century until the passage by Congress of the 1927 Radio Act. The federal government made crucial decisions about such issues as whether the radio spectrum should be considered a public resource or a private commodity, whether broadcasting is a right or a privilege, and who should have priority of access to different frequencies. As the secretary of commerce during the 1920s, Herbert Hoover played a particularly important role in the development of radio broadcasting in the United States. Despite publicly criticizing the development of commercial broadcasting and speaking out in favor of educational or public-service broadcasting, Hoover generally preferred industrial self-regulation. This chapter examines key decisions by the Department of Commerce that affected the development of noncommercial radio stations. It also explores political developments leading to the passage of the 1927 Radio Act, which for the first time gave the federal government authority to regulate radio stations by withholding licenses and by actively reassigning stations to different frequencies. The congressional debates leading to the passage of the 1927 legislation established an important framework for delineating the role of public-service ideals in broadcasting.

Chapter 4 analyzes the Federal Radio Commission (FRC), the independent regulatory agency established by the 1927 legislation. During the late 1920s and early 1930s, the FRC played a crucial role in establishing the dominant system of commercial broadcasting in the United States. The chapter explores key decisions made by the commission that helped lead to the demise of many noncommercial stations. The commission forced stations to invest in new equipment, a hardship for university stations especially during the Depression. It also ruled that stations could compete for the use of scarce frequencies on the radio spectrum by arguing their cases in front of the commission. Commercial stations seeking better frequency assignments took advantage of this policy, which forced university stations (as well as other commercial stations) to hire expensive lawyers and spend limited resources on lengthy legal proceedings. A number of universities decided to accept offers from eager commercial operators to buy their facilities rather than accept these difficulties. The radio commission also tended to lump college stations together with special-interest or "propaganda" stations, including especially religious broadcasters. The commission preferred allocating the use of a limited band of frequencies for "general purpose" broadcasters providing entertainment, education, and other types of programs. This policy tended to favor large commercial stations and stations connected by telephone wires to networks. The rise of the National Broadcasting Company (NBC) beginning in 1926 and the Columbia Broadcasting System (CBS) one year later led to a consolidation in the industry that placed stations serving local regions—such as the land-grant college radio stations—at a disadvantage.

Although the policies and decisions adopted by the FRC are important for understanding the reasons stations operated by institutions of higher education declined during the late 1920s and early 1930s, other significant factors also need to be taken into account. Archival records are especially important for revealing the crucial role of specific policies adopted by university administrations and state governments and of commercial stations and the commercial networks that actively pressured noncommercial stations to accept commercial broadcasting as an inevitable development.

Chapter 5 analyzes the attempt by noncommercial radio stations and their supporters to organize a movement for the reform of radio broadcasting, mainly during the early 1930s. Supporters of public-service broadcasting were upset with the growing dominance of commercial, network radio and the decline of noncommercial stations during the period when the FRC oversaw the organization of broadcasting. Radio stations at universities played a key role in mobilizing support for individual stations and lobbying Congress to reexamine policies. The chapter focuses especially on how advocates of public-service or educational broadcasting dealt with the tension between commercial and public-service principles. The meaning of public-service and educational broadcasting became a central focus of debates during this period. A major question for advocates of noncommercial radio was whether to cooperate with commercial networks or to continue to try to build support for a separate, alternative system.

Chapter 6 investigates the practices and policies of radio stations operated by universities during the 1930s. University stations that survived into the 1930s adapted to the realities of commercial dominance by emphasizing their unique role in providing alternative noncommercial programming. But they also developed new hybrid forms of programming that finessed the tension between the demands of professional education and the practices of commercial showmanship. University stations also increasingly relied on public funding from state governments during the Depression. This practice raised important questions about the need for independence from government influence.

Chapter 7 uses a detailed study of one of the most significant public-affairs programs broadcast by NBC during the 1930s and 1940s, the *University of Chicago Round Table*, to explore how commercial, network radio dealt with public-service obligations. A study of the *Round Table* provides a unique opportunity to explore basic tensions in the organization of broadcasting during a crucial period when commercial broadcasting dominated the airwaves. The *Round Table* faced a fundamental tension in attempting to use a commercial medium to extend the benefits of the university to the general public. The program had to deal with pressure to treat listeners as consumers rather than citizens and to expand the number of listeners by adopting radio techniques based on traditions of showmanship. An analysis of the *Round Table* is also important for evaluating the predictions made by advocates of a separate system of public-service or educational broadcasting during the late 1920s and early 1930s that commercial broadcasters could not be trusted to uphold promises to ignore the demands of advertisers.

The epilogue explores postwar developments that led to the establishment of NPR during the 1970s. The Public Broadcasting Act of 1967, which authorized funding for public radio and television systems, marked a new era in the history of noncommercial broadcasting in the United States. The old system was dominated by state-funded, locally oriented noncommercial stations licensed to state universities. The new system used federal funds to construct a national system concerned especially with public-affairs programming. Although NPR was a product of the social and political concerns of the 1950s and 1960s, earlier patterns and developments provided an important framework for the establishment of the new federally defined form of noncommercial broadcasting. A detailed analysis of this early "hidden history" is essential for revealing the complex patterns that shaped broadcasting in the United States.

1. Public-Service Experimentation, Land-Grant Universities, and the Development of Broadcasting in the United States, 1900–1925

Early in 1922, during the initial period of the "radio boom" that would sweep the country within a year after the first scheduled broadcast transmissions in November 1920 by the Westinghouse Company from its Pittsburgh station KDKA, Cyril M. Jansky, an engineer interested in radio broadcasting at the University of Minnesota, surveyed the state of the new public technology and declared that radio stations "established for the sake of creating a market for apparatus or for advertising purposes should not be granted . . . privileges at the expense of stations which broadcast educational information where there is no monetary interest involved."[1] Four years later, the official in charge of licensing radio stations in the United States, Secretary of Commerce Herbert Hoover, also emphasized the central role of education in broadcasting when he praised radio stations at universities and colleges as "a step towards the realization of the true mission of radio."[2]

These statements underscore the fact that during the early years of radio broadcasting, before the stabilization that occurred beginning in the late 1920s with the triumph of commercial, network forces, the character of the new public technology remained in flux as a diverse collection of individuals and institutions competed over its different meanings and institutional arrangements. Radio stations at universities were particularly important because they pioneered some of the earliest experiments with radio in the United States, and they played a key role in the establishment of an alternative, noncommercial, public-service model for broadcasting. These stations had a number of goals and objectives as they experimented with different uses for the new technology, not only with serious informational and educational broadcasting but also with entertainment programming. Although the 1920s is the key decade for the development of radio broadcasting, to understand the competing traditions that existed during this period, it is essential to first understand earlier processes. Institutions serving agricultural interests played an especially important role in the early history of noncommercial public-service broadcasting. The rural link reflects the crucial involvement of noncommercial experimentation by state universities, especially land-grant colleges in the Midwest. Public-service ideals for broadcasting in the United States were grounded in traditions of agricultural extension pioneered by state universities, especially land-grant colleges.

Wireless and the Early Involvement of Universities

Why did universities first become involved with radio? Investigating Hertzian waves involved fundamental scientific knowledge and practical engineering innovation. Faculty members in physics and electrical engineering were interested in gaining a deeper understanding of the complex nature of radio propagation for different regions of the electromagnetic spectrum and in developing new electronic components and circuitry for wireless communication, both wireless telegraphy (the exchange of coded messages) and wireless telephony (the transmission of voice communication and music). One of the most important problems for researchers before World War I was the development of high-quality transmitters. The discovery by 1914 of the full potential of the vacuum tube as a receiver and transmitter capable of reproducing the human voice—six years after Lee De Forest patented his three-plate audion in 1908—was a crucial development that stimulated extensive research in universities and private industry.[3]

Before the rise of radio broadcasting after World War I using vacuum-tube technology, wireless communication was dominated by a point-to-point model pioneered by the Italian inventor Gugliemo Marconi. For Marconi and most other institutional early users of wireless before World War I (mainly military services, especially naval forces), the new technology was not a revolutionary form of communication but primarily an extension of the telegraph. After his first successful transatlantic transmission in 1901, Marconi established a global company based in Great Britain that dominated civilian ship-to-shore, ship-to-ship, and transoceanic wireless telegraphy before the First World War.[4]

Although Marconi did not have an extensive college-level education in advanced science, mathematics, and engineering, he relied heavily on the work of other, better-educated researchers. University research and training were particularly important for developments in continuous wave transmission. Intermittent transmission was fine for broadcasting coded messages (dots and dashes), but transmitting speech and music required continuous wave generators. The inventor best known for developing an early system of continuous wave transmission using large high-frequency dynamos, Reginald Fessenden, taught for eight years in research universities, first at Purdue University and then, from 1893 to 1900, at the University of Pittsburgh. John Stone, an innovator best known for developing a system for tuning wireless transmissions (patented in 1900), studied high-level mathematics at Columbia and the Johns Hopkins University. De Forest primarily conducted his initial research and development of the audion in private laboratories; however, his university training was crucial. After completing an undergraduate degree at the Yale Sheffield Scientific School, he wrote one of the first Ph.D. dissertations specifically focusing on technical issues related to wireless communication. De Forest's audion was based on the earlier work of John Fleming, who developed a two-element vacuum tube that functioned as a superior detector of radio waves—the "Fleming valve." Before he entered private industry, Fleming was trained by James Clerk Maxwell and held a position as professor of electrical engineering at University College, London. In 1912, Edwin Armstrong, while a student at Columbia University working under the famous electrical engineer Michael Pupin, discovered the ability of the audion to generate waves when the output signal was "fed back" to the input in a "feedback circuit."[5]

Physicists and engineers at universities in the United States used experimental radio stations to conduct research and provide hands-on "laboratory" experience for students. Especially because of their important role in laying a foundation for the development of radio broadcasting, universities served as a third significant type of institution using wireless in the United States (in addition to the federal government, mainly the navy, and private companies, mainly the Marconi Company). Records documenting the existence and early work of many university stations are incomplete, particularly for the period before the federal government began to license all stations in 1912. Some research relating to wireless transmission and reception was conducted with the new technology as early as the late 1890s, soon after the news of Marconi's initial success with wireless signaling.[6] During the approximately four-year period before the United States entered World War I, the Department of Commerce issued special experimental licenses (or, in a few cases, special instructional licenses) to at least twenty major public universities in sixteen states and to at least fifteen private colleges and universities.[7] The special experimental license was especially important because it allowed a station to experiment with transmissions over a wide range of wavelengths and power levels.

In many cases, students at these and other universities, excited by the potential of the new technology for revolutionizing communications, played important roles assisting key faculty members in building and operating wireless stations. This was particularly true at the University of Wisconsin. Earle Terry, a faculty member in the physics department, received vital help from a number of students for work he conducted with wireless. Terry first became seriously interested in problems related to radio transmission as a graduate student while working with a young faculty member interested in applied physics, A. Hoyt Taylor, who left Wisconsin in 1909 to head the physics department at the University of North Dakota. By 1915, Terry became particularly interested in exploring the recently recognized potential use of the audion as a receiver and a transmitter, especially for voice communications. Most of the students he directed during the next decade conducted research and wrote theses involving the design, construction, and operation of this new development in electrical engineering and applied physics. As a first step toward building a radiotelephone station to test the performance of vacuum tubes he constructed in his laboratory, Terry decided to build a radiotelegraph station in the spring of 1915.[8] The students in charge of operating the experimental station 9XM during 1915 and 1916 became known as the "wireless squad."[9] The most important of these students was Malcolm Hanson, who later became famous as the radio engineer on Adm. Richard E. Byrd's first Antarctic expedition. Hanson, who also helped Terry construct the station, and other students became enthusiastic radio operators, often staying up late into the night to operate the station or to work on technical problems with Terry.[10]

After experimenting with the use of vacuum tubes on the first transmitter, Terry and another student, C. M. Jansky Jr., built the university's first radiotelephone station in 1917 (also licensed as 9XM).[11] Jansky claimed later that he "did most of the work involved in designing and building the radiotelephone transmitter." The research connected with the development of the station served as the basis for Jansky's thesis. When Jansky took a position at the University of Minnesota, he also constructed a radio station at that university.[12]

9XM was one of the few civilian stations allowed to continue to operate during the war. Terry received special permission to participate in experimental radiotelephone transmissions with the navy. His students continued

Earle M. Terry, professor of physics at the University of Wisconsin–Madison and founder of the radio station WHA. Courtesy of the University of Wisconsin–Madison Archives.

to play a major role supporting this activity. A number of them, including Hanson, were drafted directly into the naval wireless service to assist Terry. The University of Wisconsin station also participated in similar war-related radiotelephone experiments with the U.S. Army Signal Corps. One of Terry's students who participated in these tests recalled, "[W]e would work with an officer from various parts of the surrounding states. He would contact Professor Terry regarding reception. Then Professor Terry would make rearrangements of the transmitter or insert new tubes in an effort to increase the range and clarity of transmission."[13]

Because of this extensive experimentation during the war, when the ban on civilian transmissions was lifted in 1919, 9XM was much better prepared than other university stations to pursue radio broadcasting. In 1920, Malcolm Hanson, who returned to the university to finish his studies after the war, assisted Terry in designing and constructing a new transmitter using improved tubes manufactured in the department's laboratory. Another one of Terry's students later claimed that "many of the undergraduate and graduate students in the Physics Department assisted in the actual construction" of the new station. The Department of Commerce assigned this station the call letters WHA in January 1922, one year after the station initiated a regular radio-broadcasting program.[14]

Another important early experimenter, Ralph Goddard, the head of the electrical engineering department at New Mexico Agricultural College, shared Terry's passion for applied electronics. Goddard first became fascinated with electronics as a boy. His early experiments, including a short-range transmission of a wireless telegraph signal when he was sixteen years old, resulted in newspaper stories proclaiming him a "wizard when doing things with electricity." Goddard moved to New Mexico in 1914 after earning an undergraduate degree from Worcester Polytechnic Institute in Massachusetts. During the war, Goddard's department was chosen by the Signal Corps to train wireless operators for the army and assist with the operation of a "listening post" established on campus by the wartime Intelligence Department. After the war, Goddard not only established a wireless station on campus, constructed partly from leftover army training apparatus, but also convinced a group of students to get involved and form a campus radio club. Goddard arranged to locate the station in a small building on campus, which also served as the living quarters for the chief operator, a student named Earl Kiernan. The first experimental voice transmitter was installed in 1920; two years later the university received a license for the radio broadcasting station KOB.[15]

In a number of cases, university students who helped build and operate stations had, like Goddard, first become interested in wireless when they were much younger. Two students, Ernest Lawrence at the University of South Dakota and Herbert McClelland at Kansas State Agricultural College (Kansas State University), used their previous experiences with wireless telegraphy to build up support at their respective schools. Lawrence, who later became famous as an experimental particle physicist, convinced the engineering department to acquire wireless equipment late in 1919, when he was a sophomore. The following year, the dean appointed him as the chief operator of the university's new wireless station. Lawrence also played a key role in the development of wireless telephony at the university in 1922. He was the chief operator of the station 9YAM, which broadcast music and conversation. The station received a regular broadcasting license in 1923 (first known as WEAJ and, after October 1925, as WUSD).[16]

Ralph W. Goddard (bottom right) and members of the New Mexico College of Agriculture radio club meet at the "Radio Shack." Hobson-Huntsinger University Photograph Collection, courtesy of the New Mexico State University Library, Archives and Special Collections.

Unlike Lawrence, Herbert McClelland, who graduated from Kansas State in 1922, became involved with the university wireless station before he entered the school as a student. Herbert and his brother Harold, the sons of the local Methodist minister, first became interested in wireless while growing up in Iowa. They used their knowledge and experience to build a telegraphic station at the university in 1912 (the station was assigned the call letters 9YV). Herbert McClelland later recalled that the head of the physics department "provided the money, and my brother and I did all the work." After the war, the two brothers also helped bring wireless telephony to the university. As an officer in the army during the war, Harold served in France, where he acquired a voice transmitter. Upon his return to campus, he helped his brother use the French transmitter to construct the first wireless telephone station at the college.[17]

The student who played a key role in the development of wireless at the Alabama Polytechnic Institute (Auburn University), Victor Caryl McIlvaine,

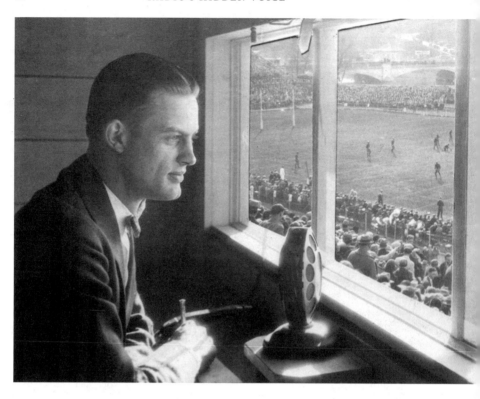

first became interested in wireless at the age of fourteen. As a teenager, he constructed his own wireless receiver and taught himself to translate code. In 1918, after working for the Marconi Company as a wireless operator on ships in the Gulf of Mexico for a year, McIlvaine contributed to the war effort by teaching wireless telegraphy to military personnel at the Alabama Polytechnic Institute. The university's first wireless transmitter was donated in 1912 by a graduate of the school who became an assistant to the famous inventor Thomas Edison. After the war, McIlvaine decided to matriculate as a student at the university. When the government lifted the ban on the nonmilitary use of radio in 1919, he constructed a new wireless telegraph station for the university partly by using his own equipment. The Department of Commerce licensed the station as an experimental transmitter with the call letters 5XA. McIlvaine and other student operators formed the "I Tappa Key" wireless club in 1920. Two years later, when the university decided to follow the example of other universities and use school funds to construct a radio broadcasting station, McIlvaine and other students volunteered to as-

Carl Menzer, the director of the radio station WSUI, announcing a State University of Iowa football game. Frederick W. Kent Collection of Photographs, courtesy of the University of Iowa Archives, Department of Special Collections, University of Iowa Libraries.

semble the station, which was assigned the broadcasting call letters WMAV (after 1926 a new university station adopted the call letters WAPI).[18]

Carl Menzer, who entered the University of Iowa as a student in 1917, played a similar key role at his school. Like McIlvaine, Menzer first became interested in wireless as a teenager. Before enrolling at the university, he received training in wireless telegraphy while a high school student in Lone Tree, Iowa. The wartime ban on civilian use of wireless kept him from pursuing work during the war. When the federal government lifted the ban in 1919, Menzer quickly assumed a leading role promoting wireless at the university. Earlier experiments before the war, dating back to at least 1912, had only involved the transmission of coded messages. After the war, Menzer built a wireless telephone transmitter, licensed as 9YA, using vacuum tubes he received from a friend who worked at one of the large manufacturers. Menzer continued to work with the station until he graduated in 1922. A year later, he returned to the university to become station director of the newly licensed radio broadcasting station WSUI, a post he held for the next forty-five years.[19]

University Stations and Amateurs

The involvement of Menzer, McIlvaine, McClelland, and Lawrence underscores the close connection between university wireless stations operated
by academic departments of physics and electrical engineering and groups
of young amateur radio enthusiasts operating homemade transmitters and
receivers. Amateurs played a key role in the development of wireless during
the formative period before the rise of radio broadcasting. Most important,
the amateurs helped provide an alternative "broadcasting" model for wireless
during the period before 1920, when the point-to-point model of communications promoted by Marconi was dominant. Quantitatively, there were more
amateur stations in the country than any other type. Of the total number
of wireless stations in the country in 1910, only 15 to 20 percent were operated by institutions (mainly the navy and commercial users); the rest were
largely owned by amateurs. Partly because amateurs were less concerned
about infringing patent rights, in some cases they had better equipment
than institutional users. By 1912, especially after the introduction of low-cost
crystal detectors six years earlier, there were 120 groups of amateurs across
the country. The amateurs—mainly, although not exclusively, composed of
boys and young men—used their homemade receivers and transmitters to
exchange coded messages and to experiment with sending voice communications and music using the new vacuum-tube technology. The amateurs used
wireless to form their own "imagined community," based on a shared passion
for technical expertise and technical knowledge. As wireless clubs became
more important, the amateurs focused their activities on relaying messages
to distant points beyond the limited range of individual stations.[20]

The amateurs organized into clubs and emphasized their ability to serve
the public by relaying messages, especially during emergencies, partly to
counteract the bad publicity created by the irresponsible actions of a few
operators who interfered with official wireless transmissions of the navy and
commercial stations. But the amateurs were not able to halt congressional
efforts to discipline their activities. The 1912 Radio Act reserved the most
desirable frequencies in the radio spectrum for the federal government and
commercial users (effectively this meant the navy and the Marconi Company). The amateurs were relegated to frequencies considered undesirable
(two hundred meters or less). In response, amateur groups intensified their
efforts to serve the public. The most important leader of the amateurs was
Hiram Percy Maxim, an engineer and businessman with a degree from the
Massachusetts Institute of Technology. In 1914, Maxim organized the American Radio Relay League, a national organization linking the different ama-

teur groups in a coast-to-coast relay network. He was able to convince the Department of Commerce to allow members contributing to the national relay network the use of a more desirable radio wavelength. Maxim's efforts to discipline amateurs did not limit their growth, but it probably helped to increase the number that decided to officially register with federal authorities. The number of amateurs licensed by the Department of Commerce increased from 322 in 1912 to 10,279 in 1916.[21]

The relationship between university experimenters and amateurs was complex. Universities often provided amateurs with technical advice, but amateurs also participated directly in the construction or operation of university stations in their home towns.[22] Kansas State was not the only university where this type of involvement occurred. In 1909 a local high school student provided many of the electrical components for the first wireless transmitting and receiving station at the University of Nebraska. A high school student and amateur enthusiast who was the son of William Lighty, a professor in the Extension Division at the University of Wisconsin, actively participated in the operation of the wireless station at that university.[23] Amateur operators outside of universities also provided university researchers essential information about the technical quality and character of experimental transmissions over a wide area.[24]

Faculty members who were supporting wireless at their schools often identified with the activities of amateurs either because they were licensed as amateurs or because they worked closely with amateurs. Professors at the University of Minnesota, Purdue University, and the University of Wisconsin attended meetings of the American Radio Relay League.[25] At the University of Wisconsin, Terry and his student enthusiasts used their experimental station, 9XM, as a "key station" cooperating with the work of the league.[26] Some faculty members likely also had their own amateur transmitters at home. This was the case with Goddard at New Mexico State, who often stayed up late into the night listening to coded messages on his home station (licensed as 5ZJ).[27] Also, in some cases, stations at universities were licensed as regular amateur stations. For example, the station established by Lawrence at the University of South Dakota was first licensed as the amateur station 9APC.[28] The radio club Goddard organized at his institution held three separate licenses for amateur equipment, in addition to the experimental radio license (5XD) the university received in 1920 for a different transmitter.[29]

An experimental license was one of the three kinds of "special" licenses authorized by the 1912 Radio Act. The other two special types of stations were "technical and training school stations" and "special amateur stations." Other licenses authorized by the 1912 law were for regular amateur stations

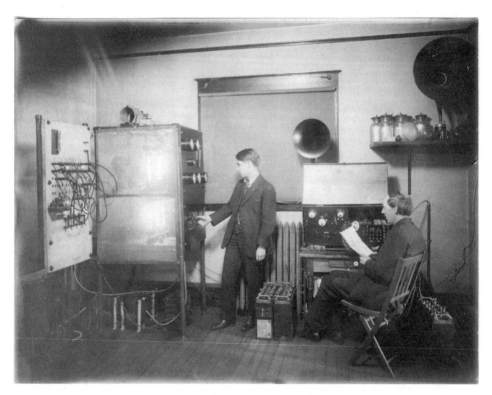

Working with early radio apparatus at the University of Illinois, ca. 1924.
Photographic Subject File, Record Series 39/2/20, courtesy of the University of
Illinois Archives.

limited to frequencies below two hundred meters and commercial stations
transmitting wireless messages over the most desirable wavelengths. The
Department of Commerce issued licenses for experimental stations "for the
purpose of conducting experiments for the development of the science of
radio communication . . . using any amount of power or any wave lengths, at
such hours and under such conditions as will insure the least interference."
These licenses were particularly important because they allowed universities to experiment with the type of activity that would establish important
precedents for radio broadcasting.[30]

Historians of broadcasting have emphasized the key role of individual inventors and amateurs in promoting a "broadcasting" model for radio before
1920. The main users of wireless in the United States during this period, the
navy and the Marconi Company, took advantage of their dominant position
to promote a "point-to-point" model as the only viable model for wireless.

This did not mean, however, that early inventors never considered the possible use of wireless for broadcasting. As early as 1898, several inventors speculated about establishing a commercial service using radio waves to broadcast to the public, but decided that it would be impractical. "As to the practical applications," argued one observer, "no one wants to pay for shouting to the world on a system by which it would be impossible to prevent non-subscribers from benefitting gratuitously."[31]

Most scholars agree that the earliest broadcast of an audio transmission was made by Reginald Fessenden on Christmas Eve 1906 using a high-frequency alternator built by Ernst F. W. Alexanderson at General Electric. But Fessenden was committed to point-to-point communications—radio telephony, not radio broadcasting.[32] By contrast, Lee De Forest's early experiments broadcasting especially to amateur wireless operators, which began in early 1907, were motivated by the possibility of establishing a commercial service providing entertainment to individual homes from a central transmitter. Although De Forest's experiments using an arc transmitter represented one of the earliest efforts to introduce the idea of broadcasting, the equipment available was not capable of high-quality audio transmissions. His early work also did not help the cause of broadcasting because of the way he used sensational publicity stunts to sell stock to potential investors. By 1910, De Forest's company was bankrupt, and the federal government had decided to aggressively crack down on wireless stock-promotion schemes. As Susan Douglas has argued, "De Forest imprinted radio with the possibilities and excesses capitalism allows."[33]

Amateur radio enthusiasts following De Forest's example also experimented with radio broadcasting during this early period. But unlike De Forest, they were mainly motivated by noncommercial considerations, especially a desire to promote their new hobby. One of the most important was Charles Herrold of San Jose, California, who began to experiment with voice transmissions in 1909. By 1912, amateurs were tuning in every Wednesday night for music and talks broadcast from his popular station.[34] But like De Forest, Herrold became increasingly interested in the commercial possibilities of broadcasting. His broadcasts to amateurs and other listeners were not simply a public service. His main interest was in using radio as a means to attract potential students to his private wireless technical school. Also like De Forest, he mainly viewed radio broadcasting as a form of entertainment. Early experimenters such as Herrold and De Forest usually referred to early broadcasts as "wireless phone concerts" or "radio concerts."[35]

When the capacity of the audion to transmit high-quality voice messages and music was recognized around 1914, De Forest and other wireless enthusiasts reintensified their efforts to experiment with broadcasting. Although he probably still hoped to eventually create a commercial broadcast service, De Forest mainly used his experimental broadcasts to stimulate a market among amateurs for his apparatus. He established a regular schedule of evening half-hour concerts of phonograph music in 1915 from his factory in Highbridge, New Jersey. In 1916, he broadcast the Yale-Harvard football game and, later in the year, broadcast the results of the presidential elections. Perhaps most important, he used the radio station to promote the sale of his apparatus to amateur operators.[36]

Herrold also continued his earlier broadcast experiments, especially after 1915, using the experimental station 6XF. During the 1915 Panama-Pacific International Exposition or "World's Fair" at San Francisco, he broadcast special programs for the benefit of listeners using receivers located at the fair. These broadcasts were particularly important because they were specifically aimed at a general audience. Around the same time, Herrold also worked to build an audience by helping local residents construct receivers and by encouraging them to invite friends and relatives to hear his concerts. Attracting students to his school continued to be his major motivation. Herrold's assistant during this period, Ray Newby, later recalled that "Herrold used to build these little receiving sets for the kids and get 'em interested to come and learn code and then come to the school. . . . That's the only way he made his money, was his school. He charged for his tuition."[37]

Compared to independent inventors such as De Forest and Herrold, universities played a distinct role in developing radio broadcasting in the United States. Universities conducted early experiments broadcasting coded messages and audio transmissions to networks of listeners, especially amateurs. But unlike inventors such as De Forest or Herrold, university researchers like Terry were not motivated by commercial gain. They promoted a noncommercial public-service ideal of broadcasting. Further, although universities and individual amateurs used wireless along similar lines to promote the idea of radio broadcasting (especially the broadcast of telegraphic messages), their activities differed in significant ways. Most important was the fact that amateurs generally operated as individuals; they were suspicious of institutions and systems of authority. By involving amateurs in early wireless broadcast experiments, universities helped discipline amateurs and give legitimacy to their activities. Universities also played an important role linking amateurs to established traditions of public service. The amateurs felt a need to participate in public-service activities to demonstrate, especially to the federal government, that they were not simply using wireless for personal amusement. Although the relay networks operated by amateurs served a public function, they were ad hoc arrangements in comparison to publicly supported universities committed to established public-service principles.

University Stations, Weather Reports, and Public-Service Broadcasting

Increasingly, university officials, including engineers such as Terry and Goddard, viewed radio as an instrument to extend the public-service mission of educational institutions. During the period before World War I, state universities, especially land-grant schools, began to use wireless stations to disseminate information and useful knowledge to citizens not enrolled as students. This practice established a crucial early model for broadcasting. In cooperation with the United States Department of Agriculture (USDA), pioneer radio stations at land-grant colleges sent out weather reports and, especially after 1920, market information to amateur radio receivers, especially to farmers in rural areas.

Federal officials organized the USDA and state-college experiment stations during the nineteenth century to pursue scientific research and disseminate findings to rural populations. They supported scientific experimentation through a conviction that research would yield innovations that would engender economic and social development. By the beginning of the twentieth century, key members of Congress became concerned that the USDA was not doing enough to disseminate its agricultural research and used the Smith-Hughes Act and subsequent initiatives to establish state extension services across the country. The extension services were mandated to keep farmers informed of current agricultural research by all available means. This included technological innovations such as radio broadcasting.[38]

Engineers such as Terry and Goddard shared this vision of the importance of extending the benefits of state universities to all citizens. They were progressive engineers in the sense that they believed that new technologies should be used to benefit the public rather than simply enrich commercial interests. Specifically, they promoted the use of radio in the service of the social and economic reform of rural America. Radio would help bring modern agricultural practices to rural households by giving farmers access to useful knowledge. Rural reformers such as Terry and Goddard sought to harness radio's ability to transcend time and space to give farmers and ranchers equal access to agricultural information freely available in cities and towns. This would help put a stop to the exodus of rural people to urban areas, a trend that greatly concerned social reformers during the early 1920s. The economic depression in agriculture that occurred during this period in many regions of the country, following the "golden age of agriculture" before the war, also played an important role in inspiring the work of men such as Terry and Goddard.[39] Goddard believed that engineers needed to "broaden out socially and display his talent to his neighbors; assert his rights as a citizen . . . to zealously guard the public welfare."[40] The engineers who played key roles establishing radio stations at state institutions of higher education first recognized the new technology's potential use for university extension. Terry, for example, was responsible for convincing extension faculty at the school to participate in the new public service.[41]

Universities first experimented with the wireless transmission of weather reports to amateur operators. Receiving and disseminating weather information from the government provided an opportunity for amateurs to serve their communities. University radio experts encouraged amateurs to participate in their experimental agricultural broadcasts to demonstrate to the public that wireless was not simply a hobby or "a mere plaything" but a serious technology with important public-service implications.[42] Even at this early date, the tension between entertainment and education was apparent.

Land-grant universities in the Midwest conducted the earliest experiments with wireless weather broadcasting in cooperation with the Weather Bureau. Iowa State Agricultural College sent out coded weather information to amateurs at least as early as 1913.[43] A. Hoyt Taylor at the University of North Dakota made similar efforts beginning in 1914.[44] Kansas State may have started broadcasting weather information to amateurs as early as 1912.[45] These early experimental transmissions were intended to benefit rural farmers who were not able to receive weather information more quickly using other techniques, such as newspapers and the rural postal service. The general idea for using wireless stations to transmit official weather reports originated earlier in the century as part of naval efforts to serve maritime interests. Beginning in 1905, the navy received storm warnings from the Weather Bureau and used its wireless shore stations to transmit the information to ships at sea or "to other places where the information can be made useful."[46]

Although many participants seemed to consider early experiments broadcasting weather information to amateurs in the Midwest successful, USDA officials in Washington initially withheld full support. In the fall of 1915, the chief of the Weather Bureau rejected a request from the University of Wisconsin to cooperate in a regular wireless service. The main drawback, he believed, was that "most of the amateur operators are located in towns and cities" where other methods existed to disseminate information. According to the annual report for that year, the Weather Bureau was already sending out forecasts by mail to more than one hundred thousand homes and by a special phone service to more than five million subscribers.[47] At least compared to mail delivery in this early period, the wireless transmission of weather forecasts might provide faster service, but mainly for small towns and rural areas.

By 1916 the Weather Bureau was willing to establish a wireless program. The annual report for 1916 announced that four wireless telegraph stations were distributing forecasts for nine midwestern states. Three of the stations were located at the University of North Dakota, Ohio State University, and at a naval installation near Chicago.[48] Apparently in an independent development, Iowa State reported that "more than 250 amateur wireless stations" were receiving weather reports sent out twice daily from its wireless telegraph station.[49] And as part of the new commitment by the Weather Bureau, the University of Wisconsin began its own program in December 1916.[50] Eric Miller, one of Terry's former students in charge of the local weather bureau, stressed the existence of a close connection between the university wireless station and amateurs. He believed that the use of the station for weather reporting would stimulate the establishment of new receiving stations, which would help justify the practice.[51] "Any boy can set up a receiving out-fit," Miller argued. "The apparatus will cost about $10 so that there is no reason why the forecast can not be received in every Village and on every farm where there is an intelligent boy, by 11 AM."[52] Terry's "wireless squad" took responsibility for the new public service at the university.[53]

University officials understood that they were dealing with a different understanding of wireless. While the old model of point-to-point communication for wireless built on traditions established for the telegraph, the new broadcasting model drew on specific uses connected with the telephone. Miller used the analogy of a rural "party line" telephone to explain the new concept of a wireless audience composed of multiple listeners simultaneously receiving a message broadcast from one source. "You understand that wireless telegraphy is just like talking over a rural telephone," Miller explained, "you can't tell how many are listening, only more so, since there is not a chorus of clicks when the receivers are put up."[54] Since the university station was transmitting coded messages, the audience was not a true broadcast audience made up of all potential listeners owning a receiver and living within the range of the broadcast signal. The audience was composed of amateurs with the technical skills to translate the coded message. Nevertheless, the University of Wisconsin and other universities pioneered a new model for wireless involving the idea of a single source and multiple listeners. Most important, they also established the idea of broadcasting as a public service, extending the mission of the university to all citizens.

On at least one occasion before the war, the idea for using wireless to extend the educational benefits of the university to the public was even more closely tied to the traditional teaching role of the university. Beginning on November 22, 1916, the University of Iowa transmitted seventy-five classroom-type lessons on wireless telegraphy to amateur operators. The professor who taught the course encouraged students to mail him any questions they might have about any of the lessons. This series of lectures was one of the earliest efforts to extend the educational benefits of universities to citizens not able to attend classes on campus.[55]

Although the concept of using wireless to support the public-service mission of universities was an important reason for educational institutions to establish radio stations, we also need to recognize additional uses, in particular during the postwar period, when stations broadcast voice transmissions and music. Most important, radio stations were often used to publicize or "advertise" universities. The publicity role of radio stations was especially clear with the broadcast of campus news and the results of major college sporting events. During the winter of 1915, for example, the station at the University of Iowa sent out basketball scores at the conclusion of games using a general QST code signal (meaning "everybody listen"). The practice became more regular during 1916. The sports scores of all athletic events were broadcast on Saturdays. On Mondays the university also sent out bulletins describing the general news of events at the university.[56] Although during this early period stations were mainly operated by electrical engineering or physics departments, the use of wireless to publicize university events and news was similar to the function of press offices responsible for publishing university bulletins.

The publicity role of university radio stations was explicitly stated by some of the men responsible for the operation of the stations, especially after the war, when radio telephony allowed stations to broadcast to a general audience. In September 1920, Malcolm Hanson told his mother in a letter discussing the station he helped construct at the University of Wisconsin that wireless telephony will be "very interesting, and, if successful, . . . will give us a name over the whole country."[57] In 1924, an official in charge of the station KSAC argued that although the "primary function" of the station was "to give instruction and information to the people of Kansas," a secondary objective was to take advantage of the free publicity for the school: "A public institution such as ours, you can understand, will derive much from the advertising received."[58] Goddard, at New Mexico State, proposed having the station announcer always use a catchy phrase after the call sign—for example, "State College, in the Land of Eternal Sunshine"—that would leave a favorable impression about the university.[59] Along similar lines, in August 1921, H. O. Peterson, the operator of the wireless station 9YY at the University of Nebraska, sent out messages to other amateurs requesting that they inform major wireless magazines about the university's transmissions. He pointed out that this would "be good advertising for our work here at the Department of Electrical Engineering at the University of Nebraska."[60] Specifically, Hanson, Peterson, and other engineers in charge of wireless stations valued wireless for its ability to reach the kind of person they hoped would apply for admission to their departments: technically competent teenagers. Undoubtedly, many students were drawn to these disciplines because of their early interest in amateur radio.[61]

By the early 1920s, some universities specifically viewed the publicity created by the enthusiasm for radio as a useful way to convince state legislatures to allocate special funding for improvements to broadcast stations. In a letter to another radio enthusiast, Peterson first discussed the difficulties the station faced finding funding for the development of radio telephony, then suggested as a possible solution that his friend write a letter to Omaha newspapers telling about receiving a talk broadcast on the previous night. "Such publicity," according to Peterson, "will help interest the public in the radiofone work here which will be a boon to us."[62] Hanson at the University of Wisconsin was even more explicit about this motivation in a letter to a friend in January 1922: "It looks as tho[ugh] I will have to devote my entire time to radio development work, at least during the next year or so, until we can get our special radio appropriation out of the legislature when they meet a year from now." Until that time, according to Hanson, "constant development and publicity work is necessary, in order to bring home the possibilities of radio phone broadcasting to the people of the state."[63] Some university stations also specifically chose programs, especially radiophone concerts, primarily to attract an audience rather than to educate or inform. For example, in February 1922, the radio station operated by the University of Minnesota broadcast music and entertainment because officials believed such programs were "of great value in stimulating public interest in [the] University."[64] The use of radio to publicize university activities was consistent with the practices of other early radio stations during the early 1920s. Before commercial advertising became a standard practice, stations were used to create goodwill for institutions.

Agriculture, Postwar Broadcasting, and the Federal Government

Although before the war the federal government hesitated to become involved in cooperative activities involving radio at universities, after the war officials actively engaged with the new technology. The federal government became convinced of the importance of radio and supported efforts to promote its use to serve the public. Thus, to understand the role of radio at universities, it is crucial to understand the interaction with the federal government, especially with the Department of Agriculture. The USDA decided to expand the wireless weather-reporting program after the war by also promoting the use of radio for the dissemination of agricultural information, especially market reports. The public-service function of radio became closely identified with service to farm families. This dominant trend was also consistent with the special role of land-grant universities in establishing important traditions for public-service broadcasting in the United States.

World War I stimulated a number of agencies of the federal government—including the Post Office Department, the navy, and the Department of Commerce—to expand use of radio telegraph stations across the country. William Wheeler, the government official with the USDA's Bureau of Markets who spearheaded efforts to use radio to disseminate market information, was inspired not only by the growth of government-run stations but especially by his son's activities as an amateur radio enthusiast, communicating from coast to coast with other hobbyists.[65] The Bureau of Markets began experimenting with a radio-market information service in December 1920, one month after the first regularly scheduled broadcast from KDKA, using a radio telegraph station operated by the Bureau of Standards of the Department of Commerce in Washington, D.C. During the next two years, the bureau expanded the project using other stations operated by the federal government, including initially four stations owned by the Air Mail Radio Service of the Post Office Department (located in Omaha, St. Louis, Washington, and Bellefonte, Pennsylvania) and then two of the navy's radio stations (in Arlington, Virginia, and Chicago). During 1922, the two naval stations broadcast information for farmers over ten different times during the day, from 8:00 AM to 11:00 PM, including weather forecasts and reports on the status of markets in major cities of commodities such as livestock, fruit and vegetables, hay and feed, and dairy and poultry. The Arlington station received market news by telegraph from the navy's headquarters in Potomac Park after a messenger delivered the information from the Bieber Building of the Department of Agriculture.[66]

The USDA's radio network supplemented a leased-wire telegraph network established before World War I to connect the department's many field offices. Before the development of local radio stations—including stations operated by land-grant universities—the USDA offices relayed the market and weather information received through the telegraph network using press releases and telegrams sent to newspapers, farm organizations, and the central offices of local telephone exchanges. Arrangements were often made for farmers to receive calls from the central telephone exchanges at specified times for official daily bulletins. But the USDA was not entirely satisfied with these methods. An agriculture official reported in 1922 that these arrangements alone only connected the service to "a small percentage of the people interested." Officials also complained that telegrams were expensive and did not always provide timely information.[67]

The USDA decided to promote the use of radio to expand the market and weather service, potentially save money, and provide up-to-date information. As a new technology identified with modernity and progress, radio seemed an ideal tool for diffusing market information, which would reform rural society by providing a "basis for quick, uniform, satisfactory settlement between buyers and sellers of the commodities." As a technology known for breaking down distances and eliminating time constraints, radio seemed ideal not only for empowering individuals through education (especially once receivers became widely available) but also for rationalizing and stabilizing market forces by placing farmers on an equal level with producers, consumers, shippers, traders, and dealers.[68]

Amateur radio enthusiasts licensed by the Department of Commerce continued to play a key role in supporting the new technology. The war stimulated interest in radio for government institutions and a new generation of amateurs. The military helped train new hobbyists during the war by sponsoring special radio courses at universities for military personnel. Purdue University, for example, trained over three hundred men for the Army Signal Corps during 1918.[69]

The USDA took advantage of the expanded ranks of amateurs during the postwar period to facilitate the distribution of market reports not only directly to farmers but also to county agents, farm bureaus and other farm organizations, banks, newspapers, post offices, and the central offices of local telephone exchanges. The institutions usually posted the reports on bulletin boards for the public. The amateurs' role during this early period was crucial; they had the necessary expertise to decipher the telegraph code used by government stations. One authority reported that 2,500 amateur operators were available during the spring of 1921 in the vicinity of the four stations operated by the Post Office Department.[70]

Radio-Telephony and Market Service

The broadcasting boom of the 1920s provided the USDA with hundreds of potential new links in its market-news and weather-forecast network. Importantly, the department decided that instead of giving noncommercial radio stations at agricultural colleges preferential treatment, it would work closely with all stations, especially commercial stations using advertising. The department likely believed this was necessary partly because the radio stations operated by the federal government did not receive funding for expansion. By using all radio-broadcasting stations, the USDA could maximize the number of citizens able to tune in. But the decision to work actively with commercial stations underscored a central tension: whether to restrict public-service broadcasting to the domain of university radio stations or to try to carve out an ideal noncommercial space on commercial stations. The decision to work directly with commercial stations meant that the department had to face the potential problem that advertisers or commercial forces would try to control or influence programs.

The number of radio stations cooperating with the USDA swelled from nine at the beginning of 1922 to approximately one hundred in 1924. New stations felt subtle pressure to cooperate with the Department of Agriculture; when the Department of Commerce received an application for a broadcast license, it immediately informed the Bureau of Markets and the Weather Bureau, which then promptly wrote the station to request participation in the market-news and weather-forecast service.[71]

Because of the key role of agricultural colleges and the USDA, rural households played an especially important part in the early development of public-service broadcasting in the United States. Estimates by county agents of the number of receivers on farms increased dramatically during the 1920s. The total jumped from 145,000 receivers in 1923 to 365,000 in 1924; from July 1925 to April 1927, the estimated number grew from approximately 553,000 to 1,252,000. Across the nation as a whole, the percentage of farms that owned radios went from roughly 8 percent in 1925 to at least 21 percent in 1930. Southern states had the lowest percentages; in July 1925, only about 1 percent of farm households in Alabama and Georgia owned radios. States in the Northeast and the Midwest had the highest numbers; according to the 1925 estimate, 40 percent of Massachusetts farms, 30 percent of Rhode Island farms, 27 percent of Nebraska farms, and 21 percent of Kansas farms owned radios (the top four states).[72]

The USDA and agricultural universities operating radio stations encouraged farmers to construct their own relatively inexpensive receivers. Officials such as Terry at the University of Wisconsin recognized the importance of creating a radio audience. As early as 1916, the University of Wisconsin sent diagrams of simple receivers to farmers and answered questions submitted to the radio station about their operation. After the war, staff at the university's station WHA distributed crystals and wires for the construction of crystal sets and arranged to have a local company manufacture a quality receiver based on the university's own design that could be purchased for forty dollars. Similarly, during the early 1920s, the USDA collaborated with the Bureau of Standards to circulate detailed instructions for building crystal sets (at a total equipment cost of ten dollars) and more sensitive receivers using vacuum tubes. Special USDA instructional bulletins were specifically directed to boys and girls affiliated with the club work of the extension service. Electrical engineers at Ohio State University during the early 1920s printed twenty thousand copies of a bulletin they wrote providing information for farmers interested in purchasing a receiver; fifteen-thousand copies were sent to farmers across the state.[73]

Although poorly funded, Ralph Goddard's station at the New Mexico College of Agriculture and Mechanical Arts, located near the Mexican border in Las Cruces, still managed to distribute lengthy, detailed instructions for constructing a receiver appropriate for the region and then offered to sell partially constructed sets to farmers and ranchers based on the wholesale cost to the university. Goddard informed readers of his 1923 engineering extension bulletin that he had "carefully studied and experimented with . . . many types of receiving sets, . . . in an attempt to find one suitable to the needs of the ranchman and others living in isolated places." He limited his offer to partially assembled receivers to avoid infringing on basic patents.[74] Goddard was able to keep the cost down by using students to help with the construction.[75]

At an average price well over one hundred dollars in 1923, commercially manufactured high-quality receivers able to pick up stations hundreds of miles away would have been considered luxury items by many farm families suffering from the effects of the agricultural depression of the early 1920s. Writing in 1924, a county agent in Chattanooga, Tennessee, speculated that an obvious reason why only a few farmers in his county had acquired radios was "that for the last few years, excluding last year, farmers have made very little money." A few individuals questioned whether the service radio could provide was worth the investment. An agent in Jackson County, Wisconsin, observed "that the Radio is a wonderful invention and that farmers are buying them whether or not they can afford them"; however, he felt it was "not the duty of an agricultural agent to urge the purchase of such commodities, when they are now selling far above their values."[76] Other county agents did not specifically encourage farmers to buy receivers, but they did attempt to steer them away from purchasing sets that were "cheaply made and of inferior quality." In an extreme case, an agent in Nelson County, Missouri, encouraged a local radio dealer to set up an example of a quality receiver and demonstrate its operation to farmers at one of their meetings.[77]

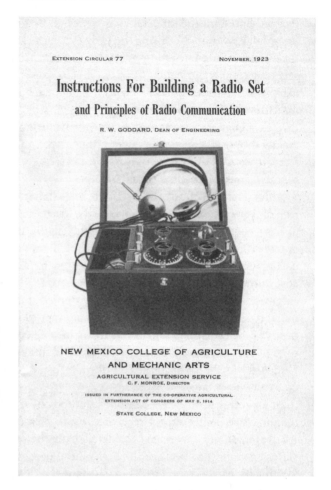

Instructional booklet for
building a radio receiver
written and distributed
by Ralph Goddard at
the New Mexico College
of Agriculture, 1923.
Courtesy of the New
Mexico State University
Library, Archives and
Special Collections.

Some farm families were willing to pay over four hundred dollars for
high-quality sets during the early 1920s. A survey of over ten thousand midwestern farmers conducted during the first half of 1925 found that over 60
percent had purchased relatively expensive radios with three or more tubes.
Secretary of Agriculture William Jardine, who had overseen the early development of radio at Kansas State College as the school's president, believed
that even high-priced receivers were worth the investment. Some reports
from farmers supported this view. A 1925 letter from Washington County,
Indiana, for example, reported that "generally farmers in this county think
of the radio now in terms of an investment that will return a profit directly
through more intelligent selling of livestock." According to this writer, before

the availability of radio market reports, farmers "took chances on what the market was before" leaving the farm. "Now," he reported, "he could put his hogs on the city market in two or three hours and know what the market was before he left the farm." Otto Nan from Henry county, Iowa, wrote in 1925 that his family "purchased a five-tube set last September"; he figured it had "paid for itself twice since then on market reports alone."[78]

Undoubtedly, all farmers did not receive the same economic benefits from the purchase of radios. The official policy of encouraging farmers to purchase radios probably made more sense for wealthy farmers able to purchase high-quality receivers. But it is important to recognize that state and federal government officials were not simply motivated by rational economic calculations; the promotion of radio was part of a broader movement seeking to reform rural society through the introduction of modern technologies and modern industrial business practices. Radio would form an important component linking producers to consumers and to agricultural experts. These developments were guided by an ideology Deborah Fitzgerald has called an "industrial logic or ideal in agriculture." Experts such as Terry and Goddard served as "agents of industrialism" helping to develop a more "rational" and efficient system.[79]

Land-Grant Stations, Public-Service Information, and Commercialism

Like the USDA, state agricultural bureaus also used radio to disseminate market reports. In many cases, they worked closely with the USDA, using market information from the department's telegraph network. Coordination of radio activities between state and federal agencies built on cooperative efforts developed by the Federal Bureau of Markets with about twenty state marketing agencies before the rise of broadcasting.[80]

In states with land-grant universities that operated radio stations, state market bureaus worked especially closely with college outlets. Enthusiasm and optimism for the great potential to use radio to extend university service to the public on a large scale—including the dissemination of market and weather information—lay behind much of the effort in many states to build and maintain publicly owned radio-broadcasting stations. Organizers believed that at the very least, experimentation was worth pursuing because of radio's great potential. Electrical engineers and physicists at state colleges played a key role because their prewar work communicating with amateurs on a large scale led them to foresee the possibilities of using radio for broadcasting to the public well before other individuals or groups, including commercial interests who continued to view radio as exclusively a means for point-to-point communication even as late as the summer of 1920.[81] University experimenters committed to academic research were also more likely to want to see their invention used for serious ends instead of as a mere plaything or profit-making enterprise.

At land-grant universities, there was also a general sense that if universities built stations and helped create an audience by assisting with the construction of receivers, farm families would quickly recognize the benefits of the new public technology. Eric Lyon, a physics instructor at Kansas State College and one of the school's most important promoters of radio, argued in 1921 that once a university station was "established on a permanent working basis in any district, it will not be any trouble to get a large number of the more progressive farmers to install receiving sets and listen for the broadcasts." Despite the depression in agriculture, he believed that there were still "many farmers who have the money, the interest, and the time to install and to devote to a receiver for radiophone broadcasts."[82]

But by 1923, competition with commercial stations was inhibiting the establishment of university stations, especially in urban areas or in regions such as the Northeast, where companies set up a number of high-power stations. As early as 1922, President Jardine at Kansas State College wrote to a colleague about his fears that commercial interests were actively "trying to eliminate" college radio stations. These fears were not unfounded. Commercial stations aggressively worked to convince colleges that private stations would provide all the airtime they needed free of charge. During the spring of 1924, the General Electric Company made an attractive offer to establish a remote-control station at the University of California for the free use of its new high-power station (KGO), eight miles away in Oakland. The university officials who accepted the company's proposal did not seem to worry about the potential loss of control over their official activities. They were mainly interested in being able to reach more farmers without having to maintain their own proposed station.[83]

University stations that did succeed in becoming established often had difficulty convincing university administrators to provide funding for new equipment. In 1922, the president of the University of Minnesota refused to spend "six or seven thousand dollars for equipment" to improve the school's radio station so it could provide better and more extensive service. A radio advisory committee at the University of Illinois actually recommended terminating the operation of its station in 1924 "in view of the competition with commercial broadcasting stations," rather than purchase a more powerful transmitter less susceptible to interference from powerful stations one hundred miles north in Chicago. The university continued to operate its radio station thanks partly to a wealthy philanthropist who donated a new transmitter, but the presence of large stations nearby in Chicago—especially WLS (call letters that stood for "World's Largest Store"), operated during the mid-1920s by the Sears, Roebuck Agricultural Foundation—kept the station from developing its full potential until well into the 1930s.[84]

Although thirty-eight agricultural colleges and universities across the country were officially licensed to operate radio stations in 1924, most stations only broadcast a few hours per week. Many did not survive to the end of the decade. In 1930, nineteen land-grant institutions continued to operate radio stations.[85] The majority were located in the Midwest. Four of the most innovative stations with consistent support during most of the 1920s were WHA at the University of Wisconsin, WOI at the Iowa State College of Agriculture and Mechanic Arts, WEAO ("Willing Energetic Athletic Ohio") at Ohio State University, and KSAC at Kansas State. By far the most important university station in the western United States serving the needs of agriculture during this decade, especially after 1925, was KOAC at Oregon State Agricultural College. In the Southwest, KOB in New Mexico managed to stand out in a poor region. Only a few universities in the South established and maintained radio stations during the 1920s. The two most significant were WRUF at the University of Florida (beginning in 1928) and WAPI at the Alabama Polytechnic University (Auburn University). WEAI, at Cornell University, was the most important land-grant station in the Northeast. Other land-grant stations in the Midwest that operated for different periods during the 1920s included WKAR at Michigan Agricultural College, KFDY at the South Dakota State College of Agriculture, WILL at the University of Illinois, WLB at the University of Minnesota, and WBAA at Purdue University. Land-grant stations in other regions that operated during the 1920s included KWSC at the Washington State College, WCAC at Connecticut Agricultural College, WPSC at the Pennsylvania State University, WTAW at Texas A&M University, and KUOA at the University of Arkansas.[86]

The range of these stations depended on a number of factors, including power levels, interference from other stations operating on the same or nearby frequencies, environmental conditions, and the time of day or night. Broadcasts during the night through ionospheric propagation could extend for thousands of miles. Daytime broadcasts limited to propagation through ground waves generally had a reliable range from fifty to two hundred miles. As the number of new commercial stations grew dramatically during the mid-1920s, interference increasingly limited the range of many college stations. During the period when WOI transmitted at a power of 500 to 750

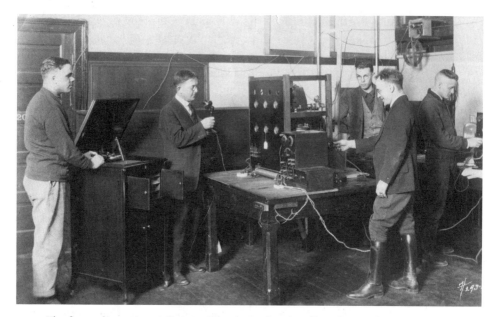

The first radio station at Oregon State Agricultural College (licensed as KFDJ; later known as KOAC) built by a professor of physics, Jacob Jordan (second from left), 1922. Harriet's Photographic Collection (HC05981), courtesy of the Oregon State University Archives.

watts, the reliable daytime range went from 150 miles in 1923 "under good atmospheric conditions" to not much more than seventy-five miles in 1926; however, during most of this period at least a weak signal could be picked up throughout most of Iowa. Through the end of 1923, the greatest range attained by the WOI transmitter during the night was 2,600 miles. WEAO at Ohio State reported remarkable coverage in 1925: the daylight range of WEAO "consistently" covered "all of Ohio and most of the states of Kentucky, Indiana, Michigan, West Virginia, and western Pennsylvania. . . . The night range covers consistently the eastern half of the United States and Canada."[87]

When the main "trunk" line of the USDA telegraph network ran through towns with university radio stations—such as Ames, Iowa (Iowa State), and Corvallis, Oregon (Oregon State)—the federal government generally took care of lease charges and operator costs. Other universities with radio stations that wanted a leased-wire connection had to pay for the cost or convince state representatives to lobby for a special appropriation from Congress.[88] In 1926, Iowa State received a yearly appropriation of $6,500 from the USDA to cover lease charges and telegraph-operator expenses required to connect WOI to the USDA network. The university also supplied listeners with a preprinted form for recording market quotations heard over the radio station. The station supplemented information obtained over the leased wire from the USDA with information about local markets in Iowa gathered through telephone calls and local telegrams. In a number of cases, Iowa grain and livestock dealers decided to cancel their private subscription to Western Union market reports, relying instead on the detailed and reliable reports from WOI.[89]

The college stations obtaining information from the telegraph network continued practices developed before the war to disseminate agricultural information. During the mid-1920s, the Butler-Bremer Mutual Telephone Company in Plainfield, Iowa, spent approximately thirty minutes every day ringing up 675 patrons who did not have radio receivers to convey the market and weather reports picked up from the Iowa State station. In 1921, the state department of markets in Wisconsin supplied special forms and metal receptacles to over three hundred amateur operators so they could more easily post the market and weather information received over the university station in Madison. The weather reports, in particular, attracted the interest of a wide range of people. A firefighter in Freeport, Illinois, reported that "every noon after we receive the weather report it is put out in front of the station in the receptacle I got from you and you would be surprised to see the number of people that stop to read it." The idea for the use of receptacles for reports originated with the Weather Bureau. The local forecaster in Wisconsin, Eric Miller, secured the receptacles for the station.[90]

Such practices as the use of amateurs indicate that many agricultural officials were trying to diffuse information widely, not simply to serve the wealthy farmers who could afford receivers. Farmers without receivers were also encouraged to listen to market reports at the offices of county agents. The Alabama Department of Agriculture made special funds available during the late 1920s to help county agents purchase radios to receive broadcasts from the university station WAPI. Some agents placed loudspeakers connected to the sets outside their offices. As many as seventy-five patrons were reported to have gathered in the street listening to reports from one of these receivers.[91]

In three states—Nebraska, Wisconsin, and Missouri—market-information bureaus operated their own stations for different periods of time during the 1920s. The Wisconsin Department of Markets decided to construct a station of its own near the center of the state—WLBL (the call letters stood for "Wisconsin, Land of Beautiful Lakes")—after realizing that broadcasts from WHA could not reach farmers in the northern part of the state. By broadcasting information adapted from the USDA eight times per day, within ten to fifteen minutes after coming over the federal leased-wire network, WLBL claimed in 1924 that farmers in the state were able to get market reports "in less than an hour, in most cases, from the time that the market is quoted." The state official in Wisconsin in charge of the radio service argued that unlike his station, the private stations in Chicago and Minneapolis with signals that could be heard in Wisconsin were "putting out a lot of information that is absolutely of no interest to us in Wisconsin—cotton markets, or something about any of the other crops that we are not greatly interested in."[92]

But most state market agencies did not operate their own stations and, following the example of the USDA, did not want to exclusively rely on existing university stations. Instead, a number of state market bureaus worked to coordinate efforts to ensure that the growing number of private stations broadcast accurate and unbiased reports reflecting local conditions. Like the college stations, state market agencies were committed to a noncommercial ideal of public service; however, they believed that they could work with commercial stations by carving out a separate space protected from commercial forces.[93]

* * *

Although a separate tradition of noncommercial public-service broadcasting has existed since the emergence of broadcasting after 1920, precedents were established before this date that played a fundamental role shaping the emergence of alternative traditions. The interaction between universities and amateurs was especially important in shaping an alternative, disciplined view of broadcasting. Without the institutional connection provided by universities, amateurs tended to treat broadcasting as primarily a form of entertainment. When amateurs worked with institutions of higher education, their contribution was transformed into a serious pursuit serving public functions valued by government agencies. Established traditions of public service at universities, especially land-grant colleges in the Midwest, provided a robust framework for public involvement. The interaction between amateurs and public universities also reinforced noncommercial ideals. Amateurs, by definition, were not motivated by commercial considerations but by the enjoyment they received from pursuing a hobby for its own sake. This noncommercial orientation became greatly enhanced when combined with the traditional nonprofit commitment of universities. We see this especially in the case of engineers such as Terry at the University of Wisconsin or Goddard at New Mexico State, who not only served as university teachers and researchers but also identified with the activities of amateurs. This precedent played a crucial role shaping alternative traditions of public-service broadcasting in the United States. By contrast, the origins of the dominant model of commercial broadcasting also was rooted in the work of amateurs, but the crucial interaction was with independent inventors like De Forest and Herrold, who were primarily motivated by commercial considerations. Their involvement with amateurs stressed the entertainment value of wireless, especially radio concerts. This early work provided a framework for corporations after 1920, when they recognized the potential commercial benefits of radio broadcasting.

An analysis of the early history of radio also underscores the existence of fundamental tensions in the new technology's organization and practice. An especially important tension was manifest in the relationship between public-service or educational broadcasting and commercial interests. Educators needed to decide whether to cooperate with commercial stations in the presentation of public-service or educational programming or set up a separate system insulated from commercial forces. The USDA provided an early precedent for the cooperative model. State universities, especially land-grant schools, championed the alternative tradition. These stations played a crucial role in the development of noncommercial broadcasting. Because of the institutional connection of these noncommercial stations, education became a central element of public-service broadcasting. The terms, however, were open for negotiation. To understand what educational or public-service broadcasting meant in practice, we need to explore in detail the policies and practices of radio stations operated by institutions of higher education, in particular stations licensed to state universities.

2. University Stations, Extension Ideals, and Broadcast Practices during the 1920s

In 1924, the Ohio State University radio station WEAO broadcast an unusual program by a faculty member in the psychology department. Professor Harold B. Burtt used the college radio station to test a hypothesis about the ability of a postulated "ether" to transmit thoughts to a radio audience. Burtt, alone in the studio, began his fifteen-minute broadcast by explaining the goal of the experiment. He then proceeded to think hard about the suit and number of a playing card and also concentrated on the results from a roll of two dice. Next, he adjusted the time on his watch and tried to project his thoughts about the new time to the radio audience. Finally, he attempted to transmit the idea of a cigarette brand name chosen randomly from one of three packages. The local newspaper in Columbus reported that at the conclusion of the broadcast, "the microphone was given over [to] the more prosaic duties such as shouting out 'If I Can't Get the One I Want,' by an orchestra." No records exist indicating whether the university made an effort to determine the results of this early radio experiment. But this program underscores, in an especially dramatic way, the experimental and wide-ranging character of programs broadcast by radio stations operated by universities.[1]

In many ways, stations such as WEAO were representative of the majority of stations operating in the United States during this early period in the history of broadcasting. Most radio stations provided local or regional communities with an eclectic range of programming. Although local businesses interested in publicity established many stations that operated during this early period, hundreds of stations were also established by educational institutions, churches, and local nonprofit community organizations. Most stations relied on the participation of local amateur artists for music and other entertainment features, but stations operated by universities also used faculty and staff for programming. This was a significant difference from other local stations that could not rely on in-house talent. The wide-ranging and experimental nature of broadcasting by college radio stations is clear in the case of WHA at the University of Wisconsin. A 1926 account reported that the station broadcast a variety of addresses by faculty and students representing "all colleges, schools, courses, departments, and undertakings in the University." In addition, the school broadcast music and dramatic performances, athletic events, baccalaureate addresses, forensics, and convocations. The programming sought to reflect "both the work-a-day and recreational life of the University."[2]

Although stations such as WEAO and WHA followed practices representative of many local radio stations during the 1920s, university stations were especially distinctive in helping to establish public-service ideals that would provide a robust alternative to commercial practices. What were the major characteristics of stations operated by universities during the 1920s? How did these stations differ from stations representative of the emerging system of commercial, network broadcasting?

The number of incompletely examined assumptions about university-operated stations renders a detailed analysis based on archival sources essential. It has been widely supposed, for example, that these stations were contributing to a wider movement, that of using radio to reform or "uplift" audiences by imposing genteel, urban, middle-class values. Through this top-down agenda, all regions of the country, especially rural areas, would be not only modernized but homogenized into a national culture based on the values of the "educated bourgeoisie." According to this view, university stations were giving listeners not so much what they wanted but what experts and elites believed they should have.[3]

Analysis of archival and other primary sources, however, challenges this received wisdom and reveals a more complex picture of the practice of university stations and the relationship between broadcasters and audiences in the 1920s. Stations operated by state universities did not treat audiences simply as passive recipients. They tried to take the views of their audience into account and to build a sense of community among listeners, staff, and students. The noncommercial activities of university radio stations pointed to the possibility of an alternative model for broadcasting in the United States that involved nonprofit institutions committed to public service. Importantly, this potential alternative model was based on the state-supported public-service traditions pioneered by extension services connected with state universities and serving local communities. To understand the work of these stations, we need to cast our nets widely by engaging not only scholarship in the history of broadcasting but also the work of historians of education, agricultural extension, and home economics.

Early Experimentation and the Development of Extension Broadcasting

The most important radio stations operated by institutions of higher education were at land-grant agricultural colleges. Extension officials at land-grant schools had two primary goals for their broadcasts. The more important was to improve the rural economy by transmitting information about markets and weather as well as the latest information derived from scientific research in agriculture and home economics. Ideally, rural people would be persuaded to change their everyday practices based on this new knowledge. The second goal was to enrich the cultural and social lives of farmers and their families through programs that featured university offerings in general education, liberal arts, music, and art.

Land-grant schools were not the only educational institutions that built and operated radio stations during the 1920s. State universities without agricultural colleges did so as well. Especially important were the State University of Iowa (WSUI), the University of Kansas (KFKU), the University of North Dakota (KFJM), and the University of Oklahoma (WNAD). Private schools such as Marquette University, St. Lawrence University, and Rensselaer Polytechnic Institution also operated radio stations and broadcast educational programs. Although major schools such as Harvard University, Yale University, and Columbia University were interested in extension education, they did not build their own stations. Schools such as these, especially Columbia, used commercial stations for educational radio programs partly because of the availability of a large number of commercial outlets in the Northeast interested in broadcasting university programs.[4] This chapter specifically examines the policies and practices during the 1920s of radio stations operated by state universities and colleges, which drew on traditions of extension education to establish the idea of broadcasting as a noncommercial public service.

Five stations at state agricultural colleges played a particularly important role in the development of extension broadcasting for farming communities during the early and mid-1920s: KSAC (Kansas State), KOAC (Oregon State), WEAO (Ohio State), WOI (Iowa State), and WHA (University of Wisconsin). By 1926, the first four stations were broadcasting fifteen to twenty-two hours every week, WHA between four and six. KOAC's official slogan, "Science for

Service," nicely captures a primary objective of radio stations at agricultural colleges. Broadcasting was viewed as the newest method available to agricultural extension personnel, supplementing or replacing such older tools as posters, circulars, bulletins, newspapers, and the telephone. Some advocates went so far as to argue that radio might make it "unnecessary to send out field representatives from the agricultural colleges, because they could do their jobs of educating and organizing from a seat in front of the microphone." One of the most important early promoters of extension broadcasting, Harry Umberger, the extension-service director at Kansas State Agricultural College, argued more specifically that one of the major advantages of radio was its capacity to give specialists at agricultural colleges direct access to farm families in their homes, without having to work through intermediaries.[5]

Beginning in the early 1920s, schools with radio stations supplemented market and weather reports with occasional lectures by college faculty, including faculty connected with agricultural extension. But faculty members in general and extension personnel in particular were not always enthusiastic about organizing and participating in systematic programming. The scripts of the first lectures at the University of Wisconsin (WHA) were read by station announcers because the faculty did not consider speaking into a microphone a dignified practice. In 1923, the general extension division at the University of Florida had an opportunity to get involved in radio, but the director "became convinced that radio extension work would not be satisfactory because of the great cost in proportion to the results secured and the constant attention the work would require." Extension personnel at the University of Illinois resisted getting involved in a new activity because "there were so many other demands for their services." In a revealing remark, a professor of zoology at the University of Wisconsin sarcastically referred to other "victims" who could be asked to speak over the radio. The president of at least one university, Ohio State, apparently did not believe faculty would willingly volunteer; he felt it was necessary to specifically order all faculty members to "cooperate with the broadcasting station and to prepare programs when requested."[6] Goddard at KOB found that he had to offer faculty "special compensation" to get them to "work up really good material for broadcasting."[7]

Speaking to an invisible audience of unknown size during the early days of broadcasting was especially disconcerting. In 1925, several faculty who spoke over KOB at New Mexico State "expressed doubts as to their messages being received by many or doing much good." The director of extension at the university wrote Goddard that he realized extension staff needed to adjust to radio, in which "the one who broadcasts must forego the inspiration that comes from a receptive audience." He encouraged Goddard to send him

Oregon Agricultural College
Extension Service
PAUL V. MARIS
Director

Broadcasting Schedule
Radio Station KFDJ
Wave Length 254 Meters

1925-26

Apperson Hall, Home of O. A. C. Radio Station

SCIENCE FOR SERVICE

CORVALLIS, OREGON

Cooperative Extension Work in Agriculture
and Home Economics
United States Department of Agriculture and Oregon Agricultural College cooperating. Printed and distributed in
furtherance of the Acts of Congress of
May 8 and June 30, 1914

Radio program schedule 1925–26, Oregon State Agricultural College station KFDJ (later KOAC). Courtesy of the Oregon State University Archives.

the acknowledgment cards sent in by listeners to "encourage the speakers." Faculty who had to give talks in cramped studios with walls covered in non-descript soundproof cloth felt especially removed from listeners. A faculty member at the University of Wisconsin suggested that the station director decorate WHA's studio with "a large number of snapshot pictures of home where the radio is operating." He thought this "would give the speaker some idea of his audience, and offset to a degree the flatness that comes from not seeing whom one is speaking to." A similar frustration with not being able to interact directly with people was expressed by an official in charge of agricultural extension work in the western United States, who pointed out that the federal government established the cooperative extension service primarily to support hands-on demonstration activities, not detached broadcasting bereft of physical contact.[8]

Despite the lack of interest on the part of some faculty, key extension personnel and college administrators believed that the great potential of radio justified extensive experimentation.[9] The five most important stations that experimented with systematic programming for farm families beginning in the early and mid-1920s (WOI, KSAC, KOAC, WHA, and WEAO) developed similar patterns. They generally had a special farm program around the noon dinner hour that included talks supplementing market and weather reports by faculty members in such fields as animal husbandry and plant pathology. WHA established a noontime farm program broadcasting weather reports and agricultural information supplied by the College of Agriculture as early as the spring of 1921. All five stations also developed a special homemaker program organized by faculty in home economics. KSAC started its *Housewives' Half Hour* in 1925. Amy Kelly, a state home-demonstration leader with a "sparkling Irish personality," tried to give listeners a sense of being part of the university by informing the audience when classes were changing and other campus events were occurring.[10] Talks broadcast during WOI's *Homemakers' Half Hour* included "Improving One's Appearance," "What Makes Me So Tired When I Sew?" and "This Reminds Me—Suggestions for Timely Foods."[11] KOAC broadcast its homemaker program, the *Women's Forum,* from 2:00 to 2:45 PM; the other four stations used the 10:00 AM time slot. WHA's separate morning program for women was split off from the noontime farm program in 1929. WEAO began its morning program for women in 1925. Instead of developing a regular noon farm program, the Ohio State station broadcast farm material throughout the day.[12]

Some of the stations also broadcast programs for children during the 1920s. WOI scheduled a 4–H Girls' Club program and a Boy Scout program.[13] A staff member at WEAO, Allen McNaningal, broadcast bedtime stories to children

Gustave Y. Hagglund in the announcer's room of KOAC, Oregon State
Agricultural College, 1929. Harriet's Photographic Collection (HC0598), courtesy
of the Oregon State University Archives.

in Ohio as the radio personality "Uncle Al."[14] Further, a number of university
stations developed programs for rural schools during the 1920s. In 1925, two
stations, WOI and KSAC, started broadcasting school programs regularly
at nine in the morning. Both stations presented similar material, including
music lessons and a calisthenics program as well as "a short, inspirational
talk, carefully planned to give those plastic, young minds a broader vision
of life and to stimulate their interest in the value of education."[15]

In general, the land-grant college stations at first tried to serve different
groups of listeners during distinct blocks of time. This was especially true
for KSAC. During the station's first year, programmers decided to meet the
needs of school children from 9:00 to 9:25 AM; housewives from 9:55 to 10:25
AM; and the "farm menfolk" from 12:30 to 1:30 PM. Only the period in the
evening from 7:20 to 8:00 was set aside for a general audience.[16]

Faculty committees helped oversee the management and organization of
most stations at universities. In practice, usually one person played a key

role. At the University of Wisconsin, for example, the president appointed a committee to determine station policy. But Earle Terry reported in March 1925 that the committee "held only a few meetings, and the work has finally settled down to the state where" one person "does it."[17] That person was William Lighty, the head of the extension department, who played a crucial role organizing station programming.

In addition to short, relatively informal talks with other types of programming, some stations also attempted to offer "home study courses," "short courses," or "radio-correspondence courses." Experiments with this type of programming sought to test the theory that radio could provide the kind of formal education normally presented in the classroom and represent "a partial solution to the problem of overcrowded class rooms in our colleges and universities," since "there is practically no limit to the number of students a professor can reach through the microphone."[18] Agricultural colleges that

WHY BOYS STAY ON THE FARM.

—Thomas in the Detroit *News*.

This early cartoon not only depicts radio's educational possibilities but also its potential for keeping farmers' sons from moving to cities. *Literary Digest*, September 23, 1922, p. 28.

experimented with giving agricultural courses over the radio during the early and mid-1920s included Kansas State, Iowa State, Ohio State, Michigan State, and the University of Minnesota. Farmers enrolled in radio courses received course material through the mail and then earned certification after passing a final examination.[19]

The extension service at Kansas State Agricultural College broadcast the most important series of agricultural radio courses beginning in February 1924. Success with initial work over a nearby commercial station led the extension director, Umberger, to support extensive programming over the college's own new transmitter. During the broadcast season 1924–25, twenty-seven courses were broadcast over a thirty-two-week period: twelve in general science, five in agriculture, six in engineering, and four in home economics. The extension division sent out 78,850 copies of lectures to a total of 850 people enrolled in the courses. The material in all of the courses was selected based on its "practical application in the home on the farm and in business."[20]

Umberger convinced the Kansas State administration of the value of these and other radio programs. During the period when radio courses were broadcast, the general correspondence of the extension division increased 50 percent. Umberger calculated that the cost per farmer contacted was much lower for radio than for traditional extension methods—about ten cents per lecture using radio, as opposed to 35.5 cents per contact using extension specialists in the field. He also emphasized the value of radio for getting information to farmers quickly during emergencies such as grasshopper plagues.[21] Surveys of farmers conducted by extension staff in two Kansas counties during 1927 indicated that radio contributed to farmers adopting specific practices. But these studies also indicated that radio worked best when used in conjunction with a full range of extension practices.[22]

University of Iowa was the most important state university not involved with agriculture that experimented extensively with radio correspondence courses during the 1920s. Officials wanted to use the courses not only to provide access to the university for all citizens but, ideally, to also help convince students to formally enroll at the university. The Bureau of Correspondence Study, part of University Extension, promoted the courses by distributing thousands of flyers to other institutions and mailing bulletins to potential listeners using an extensive mailing list compiled with the assistance of radio dealers who were willing to give the names and addresses of customers. The bureau also helped organize and manage the program. Eighty students enrolled for the first semester; sixty-four completed the course work through correspondence and received college credit; many more simply listened to the lectures without bothering to register.[23] Registering for a radio course cost ten

IOWA STATE COLLEGE OF AGRICULTURE AND MECHANIC ARTS
OFFICIAL PUBLICATION

| Vol. XXIV | November 25, 1925 | No. 26 |

Broadcasting Schedule WOI
Wave Length 270 Meters

General View of Operating Room

Published weekly by Iowa State College of Agriculture and Mechanic Arts, Ames, Iowa. Entered as Second-class matter, and accepted for mailing at the special rate of postage provided for in Section 429, P. L. & R., Act August 24, 1912, authorized April 12, 1920.

Radio program schedule, Iowa State College of Agriculture, November 25, 1925. Courtesy of the University Archives, Iowa State University Library.

dollars; a single course included twelve lectures, each lasting approximately twenty minutes. The station broadcast the lectures during the evening, when people who worked during the day could listen. Students enrolled in courses received syllabi with detailed instructions for completing written work. They could also obtain copies of lectures they were not able to hear.[24]

Despite initial success with the radio courses at the University of Iowa, problems during the next two years led to a reevaluation of the program. University officials initially were convinced of the effectiveness of this use of radio for education. A relatively small but important segment of the population appreciated being able to listen to college courses over the radio. The decline in this use of radio by the late 1920s resulted not simply from lack of listener interest but also from the competitive demands of commercial radio. Especially important was the interference with commercial stations that increased dramatically after the mid-1920s. In 1925 listeners to WSUI from as far away as Oklahoma and Saskatchewan were able to complete the course work because they were able to receive radio broadcasts with little trouble. However, by the late 1920s, satisfactory reception was reduced to about one hundred miles. Federal regulators forced the station to shift its frequency six different times between 1925 and 1929 and to divide time with three different stations assigned to the same frequency.[25] The novelty factor connected with extension education by radio also became less important as a motivation for listeners during this period. A further problem was that some faculty members objected to having to work during the evening for little additional pay. In a reevaluation in 1929, the university decided to continue to broadcast college courses but to play down the credit aspect and to reduce the additional preparation time for faculty by transmitting regular courses directly from specially equipped classrooms. A series of microphones located in the classroom broadcast the lecture and the class discussion.[26] The university reported that "professors doing the actual teaching of such courses reported that their lectures were greatly improved by having to be prepared with a radio audience in mind and that the effect upon the classes was most favorable."[27] Nevertheless, despite these benefits, in the context of the rise of commercial broadcasting where stations needed to maximize audiences to please advertisers, a program mainly serving a small audience was at a great disadvantage.

Experts and Reform

The use of talks and lectures by university radio stations was in part intended to uplift farm families by exposing them to the broader culture. It was also intended to persuade rural listeners to modernize their occupational and domestic practices to reflect the latest scientific research. University broadcasters avoided sounding dictatorial by presenting material in a straightforward, noncoercive way. In analyzing these station practices, it is important to consider not only studies in the history of broadcasting that emphasize the "uplift" objective of the period but also recent work in the history of agriculture, agricultural extension, and home economics. Scholars in these fields emphasize that extension staff with state universities did not devise top-down educational projects. While they hoped farm families would adopt the modern techniques and ideas developed by land-grant universities and the USDA, they also learned the views of farmers and housewives through individual and group meetings and took these into account. In her study of home economics and the parent-education movement of the 1920s, for example, Julia Grant argues that home economists who conducted classes for groups of mothers in rural New York "assumed that adult homemakers needed an opportunity to connect learning with living and encouraged group members to integrate their experiences as mothers with course materials." Extension experts helped to mediate between the government institutions producing new knowledge and consumers who were expected to use the innovations. Radio stations operated by state universities drew on these traditions when they used the new technology to educate the public.[28]

One technique that state university stations adapted from extension work was that of using a question-and-answer format to foster interaction with individual listeners. Kansas State's KSAC included a *Noon-day Question Box* on its dinner-hour farm program, in which specialists "concisely answered" as many as twenty-five questions mailed in by listeners. Interaction with listeners through letters also helped faculty appreciate the educational possibilities of radio. A professor of poultry husbandry at the University of Wisconsin College of Agriculture who was originally "skeptical" about the new medium became convinced that "radio offers a wonderful opportunity" to give information to citizens after receiving a number of appreciative letters from listeners.[29] The Extension Division at New Mexico State not only answered specific questions over the air but, in 1925, also directed heads to forward letters "which seem to be of state-wide interest," marking the answers "radio" so that they "may be broadcast, with the question, the name of the person asking it, and the name of the one who gives the answer."[30]

A technique known as "group listening" was adopted, not only because it re-created the shared experience typical of the first years of radio but also because it dovetailed with the extension-service view that the best adult education involved "learning from others and seeking the stimulation and guidance of others." Rural women were especially encouraged to listen to and discuss educational broadcasts. In 1922, Spokane County, Washington, organized a club "devoted to the study of radio, and only members of the agricultural home economics clubs" were eligible for membership. Home-demonstration agents in a number of California counties organized "radio parties" during the mid-1920s; the state home-demonstration leader reported in 1926 that these had been attended by "over 100 men and women." Extension staff at Iowa State organized similar radio clubs for homemakers and used feedback from these groups to organize programs broadcast by WOI.[31]

Another important tradition at radio stations at state universities inherited from extension work was to distinguish clearly between hard-sell salesman-ship and enlightened education. This distinction was especially important for extension agents because many accepted employment with companies that expected them to convince consumers to purchase specific products. Carolyn Goldstein has argued that home economists who worked with cor-

Thalia Bell, home extension agent, demonstrating radio in rural Alabama, February 4, 1926. Courtesy of Special Collections, Extension Records, Auburn University.

porations that sold domestic products incorporated this distinction into their professional ethic and saw their mission as that of educating the public to be rational consumers. This tradition of public service was grounded in the academy, which taught its future extension experts and home economists what might be called an enlightened distrust of advertisers' manipulative and exploitative techniques.[32]

In their work with radio, extension personnel also rejected the practices of commercial broadcasters. Most important, their information-based broadcasting technique specifically avoided the more sensational entertainment-based formats used by commercial stations using "special stunts or tricks." An example of the kind of program college stations did not want to emulate was the premier agricultural program, in April 1924, carried by the Sears, Roebuck Agricultural Foundation station WLS. Despite talks by agricultural officials such as the dean of the University of Illinois College of Agriculture, it was promoted in newspapers as more vaudeville show than educational event: "It will be the most witch-ing, sump-tu-ous, glo-ri-ous, ear-gladdening and im-press-ive three-ring radio circus ever staged on this or any other con-ti-nent, lad-eez and gentle-men."[33]

College stations also criticized commercial broadcasters for their close ties to not only station owners but the economic interests of program sponsors. Beginning in the mid-1920s, for example, KQW, a commercial station in San Jose slanted toward farm families, regularly presented professionals employed by advertisers, including a cooking expert with the Sperry Flour Company. Some universities did not approve of extension staff appearing even on unsponsored programs carried by commercial stations, fearing that their recommendations might conflict with policies advocated by advertisers underwriting other programs. Extension staff at the University of Florida, which was unusual in having a radio station that accepted advertising, were extremely critical of station officials for broadcasting a commercial message promoting the use of Morton's "smoked salt" for curing meat, a direct contradiction of their own on-air recommendation against this practice.[34] In short, extension officials at universities committed to noncommercial values generally promoted broadcasting meant to inform and uplift the public and worked to distinguish these goals from commercial interests, while commercial stations, even those serving agricultural regions, became increasingly committed to selling audiences to national advertisers, even if this meant short-changing efforts to bring modern practices to rural households.

The Oregon Agricultural College band performing on KFDJ (later KOAC), 1923. Photograph P095:284, courtesy of the Oregon State University Archives.

University Stations, Entertainment, and Audiences

University broadcasts of campus activities and events did more than generate publicity for their home institutions. They also provided a public service through the cultural enrichment offered by transmissions of public lectures, musical recitals, and even athletic contests.[35] Historical evidence suggests that musical programming drew the particular attention of extension officers and that decisions about the types of music broadcast from university stations were based partly on a desire to uplift or reform audiences. By exposing listeners to "choruses, orchestras, bands, and soloists," stations such as WEAO at Ohio State sought to give listeners "an opportunity to study

and unconsciously acquire a taste for music of the highest quality." Generally, this meant classical or semiclassical music rather than jazz or what was then called "hillbilly music." Goddard at New Mexico State informed a letter writer that the orchestral pieces played on KOB were selected by the schools' music director, who was "not favorably inclined to jazz music." The station operated by the University of Nebraska also refused to "indulge the 'jazz craze.'" At the University of South Dakota, the Board of Regents prohibited the college station, KUSD, from playing jazz. The director of WOI made his personal views clear in an annual report for 1926 when he complained about commercial stations that "served the so-called 'farmer' music—old time fiddlin', harmonica, and jew's harp duets, and all the cheap clap trap that was calculated to please the yokels."[36] As an alternative to either jazz or "heavy classical music," WSUI at the University of Iowa specialized in "light classical numbers and the better grade of popular music that has stood the test of time . . . the songs of Schubert, Schumann, and Brahms, and some of the modern American composers," as well as "Chadwick, MacDowan, and the older Foster songs, old English folk songs and the like."[37]

Some stations did try to accommodate the diverse interests of their listeners. Despite the personal preferences of New Mexico State's music director, KOB included programs by the College Jazz Orchestra, while WAPI at Auburn University broadcast jazz performed by the "Auburn Collegians." (It is likely that these groups did not play African American jazz but only the less radical variety considered appropriate for white audiences.)[38] A few stations also broadcast programs for specific ethnic groups. KOB broadcast Mexican music and programs in Spanish for the benefit of the local Mexican American population.[39] Similarly, KUSD at the University of South Dakota ran a program featuring "low German and other German dialects." Its sta-

Oregon Agricultural College Small Orchestra in the KOAC studio, 1925. Harriet's Photographic Collection (HC0598), courtesy of the Oregon State University Archives.

tion manager wrote that as far as he knew, it was "the only broadcast of the kind on the air" and later reported that "very great appreciation is shown by those in our territory who once used this language [low German] but in many cases have not heard it spoken for a very long time."[40]

As the above two examples make clear, a number of stations were not simply interested in uplifting the masses because they did not believe they should be serving a mass audience; some university stations began to view their role as serving the public by broadcasting programs not offered by commercial stations. This tendency became more important during the 1930s; however, we already see evidence of this theme during the 1920s. WOI, for example, endeavored to broadcast programs that were "distinctive of a state college and worthy of an educational institution."[41] The station specifically avoided trying "to compete with the paid programs from commercial stations."[42] In 1924, officials at the University of Iowa decided that the university station should not try to compete with commercial stations offering popular entertainment. Officials warned that this would simply result in the institution becoming "a poor act in a highly competitive vaudeville show."[43] In 1925, the director of WEAO at Ohio State reported that the station "furnishes types of entertainment which are not furnished by other agencies."[44] The director of WILL did not discount the value of "certain types" of popular music, including jazz, but he also believed that there were "enough stations on the air which send out jazz to meet the requirements of the average listener."[45] WILL also decided to only broadcast entertainment by artists or musicians enrolled at or employed by the University of Illinois; "outsiders" were not permitted to use the station. The station director, Josef Wright, argued that taxpayers "would resent our spending money for this sort of thing."[46]

Wright correctly recognized that taxpayers would not support state-owned institutions paying for radio performances by expensive professional musicians. When radio was still a novelty before the mid-1920s, professional musicians gave performances in exchange for the free publicity. But with advertisers willing to pay stations large amounts of money for high-quality entertainment, professional artists expected compensation. They also increasingly viewed radio as a potential threat that could cut into concert attendance. Early in the 1920s, WHA was able to broadcast campus concerts by a number of famous artists, including the cellist Pablo Casals, the soprano Mabel Garrison, and the pianist Josef Levine. But a year later, at least one of the artists had adopted a new policy. Malcolm Hanson recalled that when Casals returned, "[B]roadcasting had become more popular and was considered a menace to concert artists with the result that Casals had been enjoined by his manager from appearing for broadcasts."[47]

Dick Mote Band in the KOAC studio, Oregon State Agricultural College, 1935.
Harriet's Photographic Collection (HC0598), courtesy of the Oregon State
University Archives.

Kansas State avoided such problems by largely rejecting the inclusion of
entertainment on its radio station. The president informed a state senator that
the school was "not particularly interested in the field of entertainment as
there are hundreds of commercial stations who devote their entire attention
to that field."[48] The extension director, Umberger, agreed—radio should be
used by universities to support university extension, not to entertain. "The
extension work done by this institution," according to Umberger, received
support "not because it has entertained people, but because it has given them
something which has helped them to make their business more profitable
or to make the home a better place."[49]

William Lighty, the extension director and head of WHA programming at
the University of Wisconsin, as well as an influential figure in adult education, spoke out specifically against "uplift" objectives. Wanting, he said, "to
disabuse people's minds of the important conception that adult education is
some kind of an uplift movement," he emphasized that "modern democratic

civilization is based upon the assumption that men and women not only have developed their intelligence" but also "keep themselves intelligent and discriminatingly poised and abreast of the times throughout life."[50] One of his colleagues at the University of Wisconsin described Lighty as a "delight-ful character and a colorful one—with his neatly trimmed goatee, a flowing Windsor tie, and his twinkling eyes and merry laugh." For many years, he was well known around campus for his habit of riding horseback to and from his home. After he bought a car, he was a familiar figure "driving about town perched high in an old-fashioned Franklin air-cooled automobile long after other cars of that make had disappeared from the streets."[51]

Under Lighty's direction, WHA broadcast an eclectic schedule, organized in part based on letters for listeners. On one December evening in 1926, the station broadcast a music program by faculty in the school of music, *Keep the Hens Healthy* by a professor of veterinary science, and *Readings from Irish Poets* by a professor of romance languages. In addition to classical music, the station also played recordings that included not only "American Folk Dances" and "American Folk Songs" but also "Songs of the American Indians," featur-ing chants by Hopi Indians and members of other tribes. Lighty's views about the place of radio in adult education were reflected in the varied nature of the programming: a schedule that "arouses and stimulates curiosity," whose goal was that of "breaking down error, prejudices, and other evils through the broadening and illumination of men's horizons."[52]

The University of Wisconsin was unique partly because it had a general extension service separate from agricultural extension. Although he thought isolated farm families would especially benefit from radio, Lighty did not believe specialized agricultural programs were crucial. The extension division of the College of Agriculture did present programs over WHA, but Lighty made sure they never dominated the schedule. He encouraged all radio pro-grams, especially agricultural programs, to appeal to a broad audience and to avoid being "too bookish." A course of radio lectures on home economics, for example, was "designed to be of interest and of value to boys and to girls, to men and to women, to all who would be happy and efficient in that large way in which food and nutrition contributes to happiness and efficiency."[53]

Lighty's desire to use radio to expose citizens to a wide range of issues and programs was shared by at least some other land-grant stations during the 1920s. KOAC's *Women's Forum,* for example, included public-affairs lectures on issues "known to be of interest to women, but not dealing with house-wifery duties," such as "China and Her Present Troubles," "Is the League of Nations a Success?" and "Eugenics and Social Welfare." WOI's *Homemak-ers' Half Hour* also sought "to broaden" homemakers' "interests by having homemaking in other lands discussed by the several members of the faculty who had been abroad."[54]

The earliest efforts by radio stations to evaluate the reaction of the public to programming relied on letters sent to stations by members of the listening audience. Although listeners' views varied, certainly there is no clear consensus that the station broadcast music and other programming they did not want to hear. This is not to say that no one had a strong opinion. After hearing one of WHA's "'classic' concerts" in February 1925, a listener suggested that if the station would give "us something with a melody . . . you will git the applause." Saying his pigs were capable of "more melody" than what he had "been forced to listen to from station WHA," he offered to "load them up and put them before the 'Mike' some night and if the Applause cards don't come in next day I'll buy the Oyster stew."[55] Somewhat surprisingly, the station's director was sympathetic: "I think perhaps your criticism that our musical programs are too much of a classical nature is perhaps justified, and we will attempt to include some of the lighter type of music with simpler melodies in the future."[56]

Many listeners valued classical music, however, and did not resent being exposed to "high culture." Public reaction to a music program broadcast by WOI indicated that a large number of families preferred classical or semiclassical music, or at least appreciated being able to find a station broadcasting this genre. In 1929, when listeners were asked to vote whether "so-called 'popular' music" should be included in the programming, the vast majority of three thousand cards and letters expressed opposition.[57]

In assessing audience satisfaction or dissatisfaction with programming, it is important to understand that the transmitters used by universities were sometimes so powerful that they interfered with reception of neighboring stations and thus limited the variety of programs available. In April 1923, for example, five residents of Darlington, Wisconsin, wrote WHA to complain about the lectures broadcast nightly by the extension division. "After our day spent about our business," they desired "in the evening, to listen to musical programs, news items, weather, market reports etc." They did not oppose WHA's policy of broadcasting lectures; in fact, they appreciated "many of your broadcasts." The main problem was that no receiver in town seemed able to tune out the university station, so listeners had no choice but to listen to lectures.[58] While the authors of this letter avoided vituperative language, others did not. "Radio Mike" wrote WHA in January 1924 that "if a prize were hung up to be awarded to the rottenest broadcasting station in the North American continent, you would win it by miles." While he preferred entertainment programs to lectures, his main problem was that interference limited his ability to choose. Radio Mike "just gave up the ghost" when the university speaker "bumped" the *Detroit News* concert with "pointless remarks on 'visual instruction' as he covered the whole range of my set. . . . For gosh sake, quit and give us [a] chance to use our radios."[59]

University-operated stations that did not cause interference were more likely to receive positive letters from listeners. During the mid-1920s, WEAO received as many as five thousand replies from listeners in response to a single program.[60] The faculty member in charge of WSUI reported in 1924 that the station had received only "three unfavorable communications out of several thousand."[61] Interference of another kind could rouse even generally supportive listeners, however—and this occurred when the broadcasts of sporting events were preempted by lectures. WHA received a number of complaints from angry listeners in January 1927 when the basketball game between Ohio State and the University of Wisconsin was replaced with "a talk and then the Orchestra."[62] "The farm programs are all right," one listener wrote, "but why be so inconsiderate as to disappoint a great many Wisconsin people?"[63] Sports broadcasts formed a genuine connection between listeners,

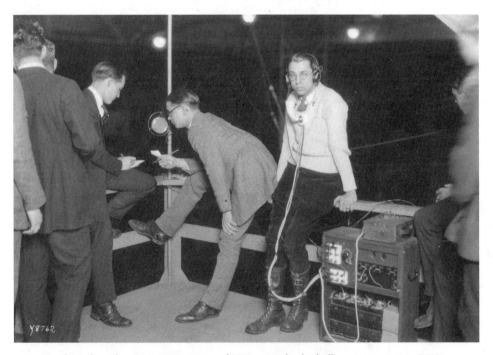

Students broadcasting a University of Wisconsin basketball game on station WHA in 1923. Courtesy of the University of Wisconsin–Madison Archives.

an opportunity to forge ties not only with the state university but also with other like-minded fans. In other words, the shared experience of tuning in created a virtual community.[64]

An experiment in 1922 that underscores the power of radio to create this sense of union occurred when Lighty at WHA organized a special transmission to celebrate Independence Day. The program included not only short patriotic addresses but also a music professor in the extension division, Edgar B. Gordon, leading listeners in the singing of the first and last stanzas of "America." "To stimulate the imagination of the listeners," Gordon asked them to "become part of a great unseen chorus."[65] The response was dramatic.

Professor Edgar B. "Pop" Gordon, music program host on the University of Wisconsin station WHA during the 1920s and 1930s. Courtesy of the University of Wisconsin–Madison Archives.

WHA received hundreds of letters from listeners thrilled to take part in the station's imagined community. A listener in Belleville, Wisconsin, wrote that although he had sung "America" hundreds of times in the past, he had never "experienced such real pleasure and inspiration from it as when it came . . . on the 'ether waves.'" When "you close your eyes and imagine that you look into hundreds of homes where people join in the song," he said, "with their leader ever so far away, one is ready to admit that in this age of wonders, radio is the greatest."[66]

Amateur Traditions and Student Involvement

An important characteristic that distinguished stations at universities from their commercial (and generally more urban) counterparts was their quasi-amateur status. This was a legacy of the early preprofessional years of radio, which—in the university context—involved students from the local community in the various phases of broadcasting and used equipment constructed or assembled by students and professors in physics and electrical engineering. The radio station at the University of Wisconsin is an excellent example. Beginning in 1917, Earle Terry and his student assistant, C. M. Jansky Jr., constructed one of the first "broadcasting" stations using vacuum tubes, whose manufacture involved fabricating the grids, plates, lead-ins, filaments, and casings; operating the pumps to create a vacuum; and sealing the components in the tubes. Although Terry eventually hired a professional glass blower, for the first tubes, he and Jansky took care of all the necessary glass blowing.[67] "If there ever was a technique to try the patience of Job," Jansky later recalled, "it is glassblowing. Many were the tubes I carried through various stages of construction only to have a crack develop somewhere. That would end several weeks' work and I would have nothing to show for it." Pumping the air out of tubes was also a long and involved process. Terry and Jansky spent many hours exhausting the first tubes.[68] After World War I, another student, Malcolm Hanson, helped Jansky construct all the components—including five vacuum tubes—for the station known as 9XM, which would later become WHA. This new transmitter was tested in 1920.[69]

The homemade character of many radio stations at universities, using the labor of faculty and students, meant that they were generally much cheaper to construct and operate than most commercial stations. An engineering student at Michigan State Agricultural College, F. I. Phippeny, saved the university thousands of dollars in 1923 by assembling a new transmitter instead of purchasing one from a major commercial manufacturer.[70] Instead of spending eighteen thousand dollars to purchase a new 750–watt transmitter from the Western Electric Company in 1924, members of the electrical engineering department at Iowa State took apart WOI's old transmitter and constructed a new 750–watt transmitter for only $3,432.[71] When the University of Illinois investigated the costs of a new transmitter for WILL, Wright argued that the "conditions involving [the] costs are somewhat different at the University than they would be where the ordinary commercial station would be installed." He pointed out, for example, that the university already had "available the testing equipment and batteries." And the office furniture "which we would need to secure is less than would be required in a commercial station." Furthermore, Wright contended that the operating charges for a university would be lower than for a commercial station. For instance, "[T]here would be no direct charge for rent, taxes, insurance, interest, [and] power." And because a university station would use students and faculty, often on a part-time basis, it would not need the same number of full-time employees.[72]

Students gained valuable experience helping to design and operate stations, but for at least one student, Malcolm Hanson at the University of Wisconsin, overzealousness with station operations undermined academic goals. In the fall of 1923, he promised his mother that he would avoid the station and concentrate on his studies, but his mother reported that he was unable to resist the station's attraction. His passion for radio kept him from receiving a diploma from the University of Wisconsin.[73]

Hanson designed the University of Wisconsin's first studio in 1921, located in the basement of the Physics Building. By isolating speakers and performers from the station operator, this separate facility eliminated the earlier acoustical problems that occurred when the transmitter and the microphone shared the same space. Hanson's studio was modeled on a telephone booth and lined with "multi-colored 'crazy quilts'" to reduce sound reverberations. Inside the studio, the speaker faced a row of eight or nine electric lights mounted in separate compartments within a rectangular box. Instructions for speakers were posted on the frosted glass that covered each light, which were individually illuminated by the operator at the adjacent transmitter. One indicated that everything was "OK." Others signaled the speaker to talk faster, slower, or louder, wait "one minute please," or stand further from the microphone. "[O]ccasionally our speakers would suffer from a case of microphone fright or become disgusted with the relentless flashing of the signs," according to Hanson, "in which case it was usually my job to complete the talk with as good an imitation of the speaker's voice as I could muster."[74]

A speaker who participated in early broadcasts, Charles E. Brown, the curator of the State Historical Museum, later recalled how he could "never forget the little box into which I was asked to enter." Brown vividly remembered feeling disoriented and claustrophobic inside Hanson's homemade studio: "Heavy curtains were draped on all sides of this 'telephone booth,' no air, no sound, no hope was available for him who entered here." Once inside, the lights signaled multiple commands "until the poor mortal who had thought he was reading a well prepared script was not sure whether he had read in an intelligent fashion or mumbled it to an unseen friend or foe." According to Brown's dramatic account, he left the studio "limply from the ordeal" and "weak with nervous exhaustion and heavy perspiration, . . . hoping that never again would I be called upon to participate in this strange new field of broadcasting."[75]

Professors and students also constructed local networks on campuses to broadcast college events. During the mid-1920s, the University of Wisconsin established a telephone-cable network using heating tunnels to link the station with a number of other locations on campus, including the gymnasium, Science Hall, Music Hall, Agricultural Hall, the football field, and the open-air theater on campus.[76] In addition to sporting events, the university broadcast concerts, recitals, lectures, addresses, and other events from many places across campus. Similarly, WOI had permanent cables connecting the station to microphone outlets in the Agricultural Assembly, the stadium, the gymnasium, and the Campanile.[77] At Ohio State University, the station maintained cables connecting the radio station to the university chapel, the stadium, the Campbell Hall Auditorium, and the chimes tower.[78]

The use of campus cable networks to broadcast sporting events was especially important. The University of Nebraska conducted its first broadcast of a sports contest using a university transmitter in August 1921. During a football game, an engineering student phoned in the plays to other students at the station, who then broadcast the action in code over the university transmitter.[79] The New Mexico station KOB occasionally had to use telegraph cables to relay games to station transmitters. When this was necessary, the station developed a special code; for instance, the possession of the ball was indicated by "V.B." or "A.B.," and the number of downs was indicated by "Four D" or "Two D."[80] To broadcast baseball games at the University of Iowa, Menzer and other WSUI staff transported heavy transmission equipment from the station to the roof of the grandstand at the baseball field.[81] "Andy" Woolfries, the popular announcer at Iowa State, strung a telephone cable between the station transmitter and the football field by crawling nearly seventeen hundred feet through the underground campus steam tunnels.[82]

Early broadcasts from sporting events used soundproof booths to shield announcers from the noise of the game. Starting in January 1922, WKAR at

Michigan State broadcast basketball games using a telephone booth set up on the balcony of the gymnasium.[83] During the halftime break at University of South Dakota football games, the station broadcast a musical quartet that it managed to crowd into the announcer's booth.[84] But by the mid-1920s a number of university stations attempted to also include in their broadcasts the sounds of the game, including the audience and the players. WEAO at Ohio State reported in 1925 that when it transmitted football games, the station was able to "broadcast clearly the music from a band marching on the field, two hundred feet from the microphone, and pick up with the same microphone the cheering during the progress of the game."[85] This was accomplished using eight microphones located around the upper part of the stadium.[86]

While university stations could find ways to reduce costs, they sometimes did so by operating in less-than-ideal conditions. Until its first studio was constructed in 1928, KUSD at the University of South Dakota had to use a classroom on the third floor of Science Hall. Sliding, dark-green burlap drapes, said to have had a "pungent odor," were hung in front of the blackboards "so that they could be made available for class use" during the daytime.[87] Michigan State's early studio facilities in the Home Economics Building were similarly inadequate. Not only were rooms too small for the university band and orchestra, but the noise from the adjacent elevator disrupted broadcast transmissions and had to be shut down during broadcast hours, inconveniencing everyone who used the building.[88]

Even after WHA replaced Hanson's studio with a new one, faculty at the university participating in broadcasts still complained about the facilities. In 1925, Terry appealed to the business manager of the university for funds to rent a high-quality grand piano for the studio on the grounds that the station had been "repeatedly embarrassed during the past year because artists of the first rank have refused to play on the upright piano which we now have."[89] Two years later, performers were still complaining about WHA's piano. The director of the university's School of Music, Charles Mills, requested that "the piano be more carefully tuned and that the action of the instrument be overhauled." Mills also pointed out that the lighting in the studio was "terrible. . . . I have been requested to send the string quartet for the next program and I hope that something can be done about the lighting before that time." Mills's comments indicate that he was trying to introduce professional standards of studio quality. He suggested that "experiments should be conducted to determine if the present position of the piano is the best" and that "chalk marks" be used to indicate the ideal location for "vocalists, violinists, quartets, etc." He also suggested that the station maintain a constant temperature in the studio, "since change of temperature always changes pitch," and arrange the

Two performers in the Iowa State College of Agriculture radio station WOI in 1925. Courtesy of the University Archives, Iowa State University Library.

studio "in such a manner as to allow the players to sit in a half circle around the microphone as is done by the quartets when making Victor records."[90]

Station equipment at universities not built by faculty and students in electrical engineering and physics was often donated by local businesses. This represented another major difference between major commercial stations and stations operated by institutions of higher education. During the early 1920s, when tubes were still not widely available from commercial manufacturers, F. B. Jewett of the Western Electric Company loaned transmitting tubes to the University of South Dakota for an early radio telephone station. At the University of Wisconsin, WHA's early studio was constructed using donations from local companies. Burgess Laboratories, for example, supplied the station with a special wood product for soundproofing the studio. The Taylor Electric Company gave the station an amplifier and other electrical equipment. Another business donated curtains and rugs.[91] In 1925, KOAC at Oregon State was loaned a Chickering grand piano from the G. F. Johnson Piano Company.[92] When the Detroit station WWJ (owned by the *Detroit News*) installed a new transmitter in 1924, it donated its old transmitter—

reportedly worth thirty-five thousand dollars—to the Michigan State station WKAR in East Lansing. During that same year, WKAR received a new 182–foot tower from another local outfit, Consumer's Power Company.[93]

Stations that did purchase equipment in some cases were able to receive a discount because of their nonprofit status. Auburn University, for example, bought equipment for an early transmitter "at a discount" from a local electrical-supply company in Birmingham.[94] The station also received special permission from the American Society of Composers, Authors, and Publishers (ASCAP) to use copyrighted material at a special low rate reserved for educational institutions. Although the society decided to reconsider the rate offer, in 1929, when it recognized the commercial nature of most of the programming on the station, the ASCAP was still willing to "allow a discount of 50 percent upon the premise that WAPI, although operating commercially and selling the performance of our copyrighted music to advertisers, is sponsored by an educational institution."[95] Ohio State University was able to purchase furnishings for its offices and studio—including furniture, rugs, and burlap curtains—using money donated by a nonprofit institution, the Franklin County Ohio State University Association.[96]

Student involvement in broadcasting was typical of university-operated radio stations in the 1920s. Although faculty were in charge of overall management and planning, students often played a key role in day-to-day operations. Some, as at the University of Wisconsin, received university credit for their work. Others were employed as operators, engineers, and announcers. In 1925, WHA employed a number of students, including a chief operator, two assistant operators, a secretary, and a part-time stenographer. The chief operator, who replaced Hanson when he left the university during the previous year, was a junior. The university budgeted thirty-six hundred dollars for this work.[97]

New Mexico State also hired students to operate KOB. As a fringe benefit, the university allowed the student operator to use one of the rooms connected with the station for his living quarters. In 1923, the student operator was "a Federal Board Vocational Training man," with a salary coming directly from the federal government.[98] By 1928, KOB employed three student operators with first-class licenses for fifty cents per hour (approximately twenty dollars a month). A fourth operator was a faculty member who did not receive compensation. The station also paid fifty cents per hour to three students to announce programs. Students and faculty were members of the orchestra that KOB carried on its payroll.[99]

The University of South Dakota station KUSD employed a student with a broadcast license as a station operator for forty cents an hour. The director of the station argued that the student's work was "a sustaining job that enables that particular student to remain in school, when he could not meet his expenses without this job." Following a policy commonly practiced by other schools, all other work for KUSD was "contributed by persons employed for other lines of work."[100]

Student involvement did not always result in "high-quality" work, at least as defined by large commercial stations with professional announcers, engineers, and artists. Brackett at the University of South Dakota reported that the policy of using students made it possible to construct frequency-control equipment at "perhaps one-fourth what an equivalent outfit would cost if purchased in the usual way," but he admitted that "these young men . . . made some very absurd mistakes that got our frequency temporarily incorrect through using too high a temperature for the crystal." The mistake resulted in "various reprimands" from the Secretary of Commerce in charge of regulating radio broadcasting. In a revealing statement that signaled the distinct nature of university-operated radio stations, Brackett noted that "of course in regular commercial broadcasting we should have discharged this operator upon his first bad mistake." They did not because an important objective of the station was to give students "experience in broadcasting and also to help them through college by means of the little that they can earn in this way."[101]

In a number of cases, the engineering involvement of students and faculty in a less-than-ideal working environment resulted in some serious accidents as well as near misses. Malcolm Hanson barely escaped serious injury in the fall of 1920 during an early test of the university's transmitter. Although he thought he had taken the necessary precaution to avoid electrocution by standing on an insulated stool before touching a high-voltage wire, Hanson forgot to first put down a "grounded microphone transmitter" he was holding in his other hand. "As I touched the high voltage wires with my right hand," Hanson recalled, "my muscles doubled up so that I was unable to remove my hands, and apparently was caught while the current burned some gashes into my fingers." Fortunately, he was able to interrupt the circuit by kicking himself over backwards. A night watchman found him a few minutes later, "partly dazed on the floor but not much the worse for the experience."[102] Goddard at New Mexico State University was less fortunate. His death by electrocution in 1929 resulted partly from carelessness and from working under compromised conditions.[103]

Listener Complaints and Authenticity

Audiences complained about the poor quality of some student performances, especially when compared to broadcasts by professional artists and announcers at large commercial stations. In a letter to WHA in May 1926, a listener grumbled that the concerts presented by students at the School of Music were inferior to the professional performances available from major commercial stations in New York City: "I have listened . . . to the programs presented by pupils of the School of Music and I can see no reason why this radio hour should be used for practice purposes." One number was "excruciatingly bad," according to the writer: "If we want good music, we can get it from WJZ or WEAF or one-half dozen other places."[104] Compared to announcers on the eastern stations, with their "perfect enunciation," the WHA announcers' "jerky, uneven manner" was "particularly annoying. . . . There are long waits between numbers, words are frequently mispronounced, especially musical terms and names of composers, and bad phrasing is the rule."[105]

KOB announcers received a similarly harsh critique from a listener at a rural camp near Black Rock, New Mexico. "As a suggestion," he wrote the station, "would it not be much better to employ someone to do your broadcasting who is able to pronounce ordinary English words; who has at least a rudimentary knowledge of geography; . . . and can make a stab at the correct pronunciation of the common Mexican proper names so commonly in use in this country?" Because the listener lived in an isolated camp seventy-five miles from the closest post office, he was especially concerned about the quality of radio programs. Radio was "about our only source of enjoyment, recreation, and means of keeping in touch with the outside." The New Mexico listener was especially upset when instead of reporting the results of the 1928 presidential election, "the prune who was broadcasting your so-called news and reports, read us the prices of cows and hogs and cotton for half an hour before he even mentioned the election."[106]

An embarrassed Goddard admitted that the announcers were college students. He argued that lack of funds meant that the station had no choice but to use students rather than professional announcers. "It is a handicap we have to endure," according to Goddard, "for the funds available for the operation of the station KOB are ridiculously inadequate so that it is utterly impossible to employ as you suggest 'A first class announcer.'" As soon as they trained one up, he complained, "they are immediately offered positions with other stations with greater financial support."[107]

University staff who participated in radio programs sometimes also complained about student operators. In December 1925, the extension director at New Mexico State informed Goddard that "several of the people who have been broadcasting for the Monday evening program have complained . . . that they were frequently disturbed by thoughtless young people who talked and laughed" during the program. Their behavior not only interfered with the broadcast, he pointed out, "but also has the effect of disconcerting the speaker."[108] This critique of university stations repeated some of the earlier criticisms leveled at amateur radio operators in the years before the rise of broadcasting. Although the point should not be overstated, there were good reasons not to trust college students with the operation of radio stations. Radio broadcasting was almost killed off at Michigan State University in 1922 when a group of students played a prank by broadcasting "several ribald songs" over a transmitter they thought only had a limited range within the campus. A public protest resulted when the students found that their broadcast had been heard up to fifteen miles away.[109]

Despite complaints about the less-than-polished nature of programming on university stations during the 1920s, some listeners appreciated the local and authentic character of broadcasts. They were not impressed by elitist definitions of professionalism as defined by stations in large, primarily eastern, cities. This was the experience of F. R. Calvert, the manager of WLBL, the agriculturally oriented station in Stevens Point operated by the Wisconsin Department of Agriculture, which had a strong connection to WHA in Madison. Although he regularly broadcast performances and talks by local citizens, Calvert had a low opinion of the quality of their broadcasts, stating that "the greater portion of them . . . have very poor talent." Nevertheless, he found that "even when the music is flat and out of tune the calls come in like a flood." So far as he could tell, "[T]he people who listen to them and send in phone calls and telegrams" were mainly "people from their home town and relatives." (It is important to recognize that Calvert's personal views about the quality of local talent were related to his negative views of immigrants or, to use his term, the "foreign element." In a letter to a state official, he pointed out that more than 50 percent of the residents of Stevens Point were Polish-Americans, and that "for the most part, they are not the type you would care to bring your children up with in the schools.")[110]

Lighty at the University of Wisconsin also found that the authentic and familiar nature of broadcasts by local citizens was more important to many listeners than the fact that performances did not always meet the standards of education professionals. In a letter to the person supervising radio at the University of Florida, he argued that "as a matter of fact, the contributions that come out of the student body are always acceptable, wherever there is merit, because the local papers are very glad to make announcement of the fact that some boy or girl from the home town is broadcasting over the university radio station on a given night." In short, the use of students "guarantees you a definite constituency in your listening audience."[111]

Student announcers did not always draw listener complaints. Especially at universities committed to radio, some became extremely popular, not only for their polished presentation style but also for their local appeal. The best example from the 1920s was Iowa State's Andrew G. Woolfries. As a student in electrical engineering, he helped construct WOI's first broadcast station in 1921. Like many of his peers, he also tried his hand as an announcer; unlike most of them, he had a natural ability to connect with the Iowa audience. For some twenty years, "Andy" served as the station's chief announcer. That WOI found him valuable is proved by the university's willingness to increase his salary by 12 percent when a commercial station tried to lure him away with a generous offer in the middle of the Depression. One observer argued that "necessity, combined with a natural talent, found him introducing entertainment programs, reading the news, giving play-by-play accounts of sports, and delivering farm market reports." He did it "all with an ease and confidence that made him seem like a personal friend to many Iowans who were regular listeners." During the mid-1920s, Woolfries broadcast a number of sporting events, including basketball, indoor track competitions, wrestling, boxing, and swimming.[112] Popular announcers such as Woolfries helped university stations create a virtual community for listeners, allowing them to transcend geography and participate in the extended social network centered on their local stations.

Woolfries was responsible for two of the most popular programs at WOI, the *Music Shop* and an innovative book-reading program. The *Music Shop* began in 1925 as a way to fill the time between morning market reports with music from phonograph records. The station initially solicited requests from listeners; within a short time, the station was receiving more than one thousand requests per day from listeners interested in dedicating musical selections for special occasions such as birthdays and anniversaries. Woolfries then decided that the program needed to be better structured using musical selections more appropriate for a university. He halted the practice of soliciting listener requests and created instead a program dedicated to classical music. To help educate the audience, he included short biographical discussions about individual composers. The program received large numbers of letters from appreciative listeners, and surveys conducted during the following decade also indicated that the program was popular with large numbers of Iowans.[113]

The second important program introduced by Woolfries that helped endear him to Iowans was a book program, started in 1925. Librarians worried that radio would take the place of book reading. Initially, Iowa State librarians discussed the book collections at the university. The intent was to "acquaint listeners with entertaining and worthwhile books and to awaken in them a

Andrew Woolfries, the beloved WOI announcer, Iowa State College of Agriculture. Courtesy of the University Archives, Iowa State University Library.

desire to read for themselves." Because letters seemed to indicate that listeners were not thrilled with the program, Woolfries came up with a new, innovative program. Inspired by a newsreel that showed someone reading aloud to assembly-line workers at a factory, he decided to try something similar on the radio. Starting in February 1927, he broadcast a daily half-hour book-reading program at 9:00 AM. The station received many appreciative letters from listeners, especially women. One analyst has argued that this program "quickly became the 'alternative' soap opera for women who either found them too improbable and repetitious or disliked the constant interruptions for commercials."[114] It also provided a model for other university stations, especially after 1930, when Woolfries combined the book program with a book-lending service.[115] A three-dollar membership fee entitled listeners to borrow twenty books. Over two hundred listeners joined within a few days of the announcement of the program in 1930. A committee of state librarians helped compile a list of books for Woolfries to purchase for the *Radio Book Club*. Having books delivered directly through the mail was an especially valuable service for rural and urban listeners.[116]

The homemade character of university stations did not necessarily mean that they were always viewed as technically inferior to major commercial stations. Despite the complaints expressed by staff at the university about WHA's studio facilities in 1925, the station still received a "first class" rating (Class B) from the Department of Commerce. Of the approximately six hundred stations operating in the country, only about 150 were given this rating based mainly on the technical quality of station equipment.[117] The studio facilities at a number of stations at educational institutions included components comparable to equipment used by some of the top-quality commercial stations. The University of Iowa's new station, opened in 1924, was equipped with a heating and ventilation system consisting of "an electrically driven fan drawing fresh air from above the roof, from which it escapes through registers properly placed in the side-wall."[118] In 1927, Iowa State's studio was large enough for the 160–member college orchestra or the largest glee clubs.[119]

Broadcast Dilemmas: Commercial Tensions, Independence, and Sectarianism

Radio stations operated by institutions of higher education also broadcast programs that dealt with timely political, social, and economic public issues. This type of programming became increasingly important as educators recognized that broadcasting could serve as an ideal tool for sustaining a healthy democracy through the maintenance of an informed and educated citizenry. But noncommercial university stations receiving public support needed to deal with a distinct set of problems; they had to avoid practices that would leave them open to the same type of criticism leveled at commercial stations. This meant that they needed to maintain independence from public officials who made decisions about funding. Specifically, the need to avoid political sectarianism while providing a form of public-affairs programming was a major problem faced by radio stations at state universities.

Stations responded to this dilemma during the 1920s in different ways. The Iowa State station WOI adopted a rigid policy against partisan broadcasts of controversial political issues. In practice, this meant that outside groups with axes to grind were not allowed on the air. Faculty were expected to give dispassionate analyses based on scholarly research.[120] Academic expertise would thus assure station independence. KSAC at Kansas State adopted a rigid policy against allowing outside groups to use the station to broadcast "propaganda." Umberger argued in 1924 that broadcasting material "in any way propagandistic . . . would discredit the institution." But he was willing to broadcast "educational" material submitted by government officials, including a representative of the governor's office. Thus, stations were not all able to maintain complete political independence.[121]

KOB at New Mexico State at first adopted a similarly rigid policy banning any broadcasts by political parties. In response to a request for information about the station's plans for the 1922 election campaign, Goddard wrote that it was "absolutely refraining from entering into the political field in any shape or form."[122] He thought that this was necessary because the station was located at a state college that received federal aid. However, in 1928, the Board of Regents of the college changed this policy, deciding that the station could broadcast speeches connected to the presidential campaign, but only if "it entails no charges to us." Instead of refusing requests from the two political parties to broadcast the acceptance speeches of each party's nominee for president, Goddard announced that the station would broadcast both speeches, but only if the parties paid the telephone-cable charges.[123]

Religion was another tricky subject for state-supported institutions. During the 1920s, some university radio stations did not have to deal with the problem of religious sectarianism because they did not broadcast on Sundays. Although WHA reported in 1926 that it did not broadcast regular religious services, programs involving religion were allowed, but only as "incidental features" of other programs. For example, the station broadcast "special occasions like campus religious meetings, campus convocations, baccalaureate services and sermons, at such times as they occur on the campus."[124] Goddard at New Mexico State introduced a more extreme policy in 1922, banning the broadcast of "church services of any kind." According to Goddard, KOB was "purely educational, maintained by government funds, and could not according to law be utilized to the broadcasting of any religious service."[125] WOI adopted a similar official policy of not broadcasting "political, religious, fraternal, or other propaganda."[126] But like WHA, the Iowa station did not avoid religion altogether. In practice, the station remained nonsectarian by allowing a wide variety of groups and individuals to present chapel talks from the station, including Catholics and different Protestant groups.[127]

This issue became a major public concern at Kansas State. In 1924, a professor of rural sociology, Walter Burr, convinced the administration to allow him to broadcast a *Rural Radio Church Service* on Sundays. He argued that the program would "not attempt to duplicate the work of the church, or keep people away from the church, but to supplement that work." Lay leaders in rural churches without pastors would be able to use the university's radio service temporarily until pastors became available. The radio church service would also be a great benefit to "vast numbers of country people" not able to attend churches because of isolation or infirmity. Burr intentionally chose hymns that would be "accepted without question by all branches of the church" and prayers that would "be the sincere expression of any well-minded person toward any conception of Deity he may have." The sermon, he assured the administration, "will be always on themes of the common individual virtues and social duties in the community where one lives." Burr thought that the Catholic church would be the main possible source of criticism for his religious program, but he believed that Catholics would support him because of his close ties to the Catholic director of rural work.[128]

In fact, the main group that objected to Burr's broadcasts were Protestant ministers who did not approve of a state university encroaching on their territory, especially a department of sociology rather than a department of theology or religion.[129] In 1926, the president discontinued Burr's program, arguing reluctantly that there was "real merit" in the objections of the ministers. He commented that "history seems to prove that it is inadvisable for church and state not to be kept distinctly separate." Nevertheless, he did approve of the radio station broadcasting a program for young people dealing with "some such subject as 'The Old-fashioned Virtues.'"[130]

Commercial pressure on stations also resulted in a related set of tensions. The early history of the University of North Dakota radio station KFJM, located in Grand Forks, provides an excellent example of the conflicting demands on educational stations trying to negotiate a noncommercial public-service understanding of broadcasting in the context of commercial imperatives. The station was established in 1923 to promote the university and extend its educational mission to the larger community. But as the radio station's connections to the community grew, it increasingly drifted away from its original mission. The first broadcasts mainly included faculty talks and live music programs. Gradually the station also began to schedule programs of a local and regional character. A faculty member in the history department, for example, developed a half-hour program discussing myths and legends of local Native American tribes, including the Mandan, Chippewa, and Hidatsa. The secretary for the Bureau of Public Information at the university broadcast a weekly review of local and regional as well as national news.[131]

Since KFJM was the only station serving the city of Grand Forks and nearby communities during this early period, local citizens encouraged it to fill out its schedule by taking advantage of local talent and local programming. The university not only broadcast programs presented by local organizations but agreed to broadcast dinner-hour orchestra concerts presented every night during the week at two of the city's hotels. The hotels made arrangements with the local telephone company to provide line connections directly to the radio building on campus. By 1926, telephone connections were extended to other establishments in town, including a Piano Company, the Elks Club, local churches, and the Grand Theatre. This expanded schedule resulted in increased expenses for the university. In response, the university decided it had to charge organizations for the use of the radio station. The station sold more and more airtime to commercial organizations until, by 1928, it was effectively operating as a business. A year later, in response to pressure from local community and business leaders who felt that the university was still not taking advantage of the radio station's full potential, the university agreed to turn over the day-to-day operation of the station to a commercial manager. A Faculty Radio Committee retained control of programs presented by students and staff at the university, but this distinction was difficult to maintain in practice. University organizations would often participate in sponsored programs. Thus what started out as an attempt to serve the public interest by maintaining links to the community became commercially defined.[132]

Some early university radio stations potentially compromised noncommercial ideals with the policy of borrowing records from local companies in exchange for free publicity over the air. In some cases, stations publicized the local businesses over university stations in exchange for the loan. University stations adopting this practice during the early 1920s did not seem to realize its implications because they did not imagine the degree to which radio could be used by advertisers. Some of the earliest broadcasts from Purdue University used phonograph records "which were begged for and borrowed at downtown stores."[133] In Madison, Wisconsin, Malcolm Hanson borrowed records from the Albert E. Smith Music Company for a special Friday-night program over the station 9XM. He reported that "recognition was given to the music store by the announcement that it had provided the records."[134] Around 1922, after the station was licensed as WHA, it used another local business, the Hook Brothers Piano Company, for the "latest and best Edison phonograph records."[135] A staff member at the University of Florida station WRUF, which was unusual in accepting advertising, recalled that during the late 1920s, "[E]very day, somebody would make a trip to [the] Gainesville Furniture Company. . . . We'd go down and get a stack of records, and of course we'd give him credit for [lending] them."[136] The Tri-State Talking

Machine Company in El Paso, Texas, loaned batches of thirty or forty records through the mail to KOB at New Mexico State throughout most of the 1920s. Goddard wrote in 1922 that he was "instructing the [station] operator to announce the call and also the source of supply of records between each piece."[137] But by 1928, he was forced to conclude that the "scheme did not work out practically for the reason that we have many telephone calls and letters requesting us to play certain numbers."[138] Iowa State avoided compromising its noncommercial ideals by obtaining support from individuals in the local community. At first, Carl Menzer, the engineer in charge of the station, relied on his own supply of seven records as well as his own windup phonograph, but "after a period of weeks," loyal listeners sent in their own personal collections of records to be played over the air.[139]

Although most radio stations at universities in the Midwest worked hard to maintain a noncommercial status, at least one station, WEAO at Ohio State, also for a time adopted general practices that crossed the line into the commercial realm. In 1926, a commercial station in Columbus, WAIU, accused WEAO of broadcasting music performed by groups indirectly supporting commercial establishments, including "The May Furniture Company Orchestra." Although the university was not charging the May Furniture Company a commercial fee for the use of the station to advertise its products, the station was indirectly publicizing commercial institutions. WAIU was mainly upset because its economic survival depended on selling airtime to commercial establishments. The insurance company that operated the station argued that it was unfair for a station supported by public funds to publicize commercial organizations. Company officials insisted that WEAO only use talent from the university campus. The university countered that it "would find this much easier to do, if the commercial station . . . would not continually try to get a large part of their program material from the campus."[140] WEAO broadcast sponsored musical groups from a studio at a hotel in downtown Columbus. The hotel had agreed to construct the studio for WEAO to allow the university to take advantage of talent located in the center of the city. The hotel benefitted from this arrangement because it received free publicity from the station, partly through the regular use of the orchestra sponsored by the hotel.[141]

This arrangement linking WEAO to sponsored performers ended in 1929 in response to a formal complaint from the ASCAP, which argued that the station could not claim special exemption from licensing fees as a nonprofit educational institution because it was effectively broadcasting commercial programs. The group specifically complained about a series of programs that included an announcement stating that "the program during the past half-hour was sponsored by the Union Building and Savings Co. now located at 48 W. Gay St. but soon to be located in their new building [at an address included in the announcement]." The ASCAP argued that the station was benefitting from commercial sponsorship of programming without paying the required commercial royalties on the copyrighted material. After lengthy negotiations, the station agreed to terminate the arrangement with the hotel and to stop providing publicity for musical groups supported by commercial organizations.[142]

* * *

Like other stations in the years before the 1930s, when the commercial network system became dominant in the United States, university stations were closely tied to local regions and communities. Although the rhetoric of uplift expressed by reformers during the 1920s may give the impression that radio stations operated by universities were interested solely in imposing a certain kind of programming on all listeners, the actual practice was more complex. While the stations generally sought to use radio to uplift citizens and modernize practices and sensibilities, they also recognized the need to adapt these goals to local circumstances. If, beginning in the late 1920s, commercial networks worked to standardize American society to better serve national advertisers promoting a homogenized ethic of consumption, educational stations committed to noncommercial ideals affirmed connections to local communities with targeted programming, personnel, and listening practices.[143] Unlike those small independent stations that effectively operated as nonprofit entities in this period, university stations could and did draw on extension education to frame their commitment to noncommercial as well as nonprofit status. Some of the fundamental tensions explored in this chapter, especially the dilemma of how to use public funds to provide nonpartisan political education while remaining nonsectarian, were grounded in some of these earlier public-service traditions.

The commitment to noncommercial public-service broadcasting was rooted in the work of state universities, especially extension services at land-grant colleges. By extending the mission of state universities to all citizens in individual states, educational radio stations helped build an electronic public culture that linked state public-service agencies, state universities, and local listening practices. Community building was based on the noncommercial principles of extension work that provided an alternative to the public culture resulting from the dominance of a centralized broadcasting system primarily serving advertisers and national markets.

3. Public-Service Broadcasting and the Development of Radio Policy, 1900–1927

The experience of noncommercial radio stations operated by institutions of higher education during the 1920s points to fundamental tensions in the history of broadcasting in the United States. What was the relationship between private stations operated for profit and publicly supported stations operated by nonprofit institutions? Should radio service primarily provide entertainment or programming meant to educate, inform, and enlighten? More fundamentally, how should the country view the radio spectrum? Should the government allow private interests to exploit it for commercial purposes, or should the spectrum be viewed as a public resource that private companies could only use in a clearly circumscribed way as a privilege rather than a right? Since the radio spectrum was a finite resource limited to a discrete number of useable frequencies, what criteria would be used to determine who would have access? By the end of the 1920s, what became known as the American System of broadcasting, with its commitment to entertainment supported by advertisers mainly interested in selling commercial products to urban listeners, was becoming the dominant model in the United States, but stations owned by institutions of higher education and committed to nonprofit programming continued to serve as an alternative model. A deeper social, economic, and political understanding of the alternative public-service model for broadcasting in the United States demands an analysis of how educational and public-interest broadcasting interacted with the rise of the commercial system in the context of key decisions by government institutions.

Public Policy for Radio before 1920

Important precedents that would help determine public policy for the future of broadcasting were established well before the 1920s with point-to-point wireless telegraphy and telephony. Guglielmo Marconi's activities symbolized the potential for private interests to carve up and dominate the radio spectrum. Instead of establishing a company that would manufacture or sell wireless apparatus, Marconi set up the Marconi International Marine Communications Company to sell access to a communications network. To keep down competitors and to maintain monopoly control, he formulated a "non-inter-communication rule," which meant that Marconi operators were not allowed to communicate with wireless stations that were not part of his system.[1]

To Marconi, the radio spectrum was akin to new territory that pioneers had a right to claim and exploit. Since traditional notions of property rights were not obviously appropriate for something as invisible and intangible as the radio spectrum, or "ether" (the term commonly used during the early twentieth century), Marconi sought to assert private-property rights through control of the technology necessary for access. He clearly did not view the radio spectrum as primarily a public or common-property resource. Responding to a draft of a 1903 directors' report for his company, Marconi had the phrases "the general public" and "a public service" replaced with the phrase "commercial purposes."[2]

Marconi sought to establish a wireless communications system that would support Britain's global empire through monopoly control. In response to these efforts, other governments also began to recognize the geopolitical implications of control of the radio spectrum. They did not want to allow the British to expand control of the majority of the world's submarine telegraph cables by also controlling the airwaves. An incident in 1902—when Marconi stations refused to communicate with a ship carrying the German Prince Henry, the brother of Kaiser Wilhelm II—led the Germans to organize the first international wireless conference to work out agreements for the use of wireless. The seven-nation conference adopted a statement encouraging coastal stations to receive and transmit wireless messages from ships "without distinction as to the system of wireless telegraphy employed"; however, the resolution lacked the force of law. Great Britain and Italy, which had contracts with the Marconi Company to support the use of wireless by their navies, refused to sign the agreement. But an important precedent was established at the conference; for the first time nations officially acknowledged the public value of the ether for securing the safety of ships at sea.[3]

During this early period, the United States, because of its relative isolation, was less concerned than European nations about developing international agreements or an overall national policy for wireless. Three government agencies—the Weather Bureau at the Department of Agriculture, the Army Signal Corps, and the navy—had begun to experiment with wireless, but they did not attempt to coordinate their activities. The navy, in particular, intensely disliked Marconi's efforts to monopolize the ether; however, bureaucratic conservatism hampered efforts to introduce wireless effectively into naval operations.[4]

President Theodore Roosevelt initiated the first effort to develop a national policy for wireless, mainly after observing its important role during the 1904 Russo-Japanese War. Japanese naval forces defeated Russia partly because of superior wireless equipment. A second lesson from the war was the need to police the airwaves in the name of national security to keep commercial interests from interfering in military operations. A number of press correspondents covering the war also used wireless to dispatch news accounts. Roosevelt and other observers gained a new appreciation of questions involving the issue of who should have priority of access to the radio spectrum. The war underscored the importance of not simply treating the radio spectrum as an economic resource to be privately exploited.[5]

In June 1904, Roosevelt appointed an Interdepartmental Board of Wireless Telegraphy to examine the need for coordination among government users of wireless and to analyze the relationship between government and private users of the radio spectrum. Roosevelt's preference for naval control was clear in his choice of three naval officers versus one representative from the army and another from the Weather Bureau. Although the board reassured private companies that the government would continue to allow private use of the radio spectrum, it also clearly favored giving preference to the military. It recommended against allowing the construction of private stations near the coast that would interfere with nearby naval stations.[6]

The Roosevelt Board placed the United States strongly on the side of Germany and other European countries striving to prevent Marconi from gaining monopoly control of the radio spectrum. Specific recommendations by the board that sought to restrict access of private stations to the ether would need congressional authorization. A group of naval officers enthusiastic about wireless began to push for legislation, giving the navy authority over wireless. Although these legislative efforts were not successful, naval enthusiasts did begin to work towards building an extensive coastal network that would provide an alternative to the Marconi system.[7]

Partly because of the strong support of the United States, delegates representing twenty-seven countries at a second International Wireless Conference in 1906 agreed to international rules mandating that all shore stations agree to communicate with any ships irrespective of wireless systems. By this date, a number of events involving shipping emergencies had demonstrated the value of the ether for public safety. The Marconi Company's strongest supporter, Great Britain, was now prepared to support the conference resolution against the non-intercommunication rule. Other rules relating to safety adopted by the conference included the licensing of ship stations and operators to ensure high-quality communications and the requirement that operators always give the highest priority to distress messages. Most countries, including Great Britain, ratified the treaty by 1908.[8]

The other major result of the conference was an agreement for the first time to divide the spectrum among different users. Commercial services, notably the Marconi Company, were limited to useable frequencies above 499.7 kHz (below 600 meters). Government users, including the military services, were directed to use the band of frequencies between 187.4 kHz (1,600 meters) and 499.7 kHz (600 meters), a band considered most desirable because of its greater range.[9]

Although the U.S. delegates at the conference strongly supported the international treaty, the Senate delayed ratifying the agreement, mainly because of fears about giving the navy too much authority over wireless. Unlike most European countries, which gave control of telegraph communications to post office departments or military agencies, the United States had a tradition of allowing private companies to largely control cable traffic.[10]

In addition to commercial users, a second influential group also opposed legislative efforts that might lead to government control: the amateurs. By 1910, amateurs represented the largest group of wireless users and in many cases had the best equipment. They provided an alternative tradition in the prehistory of radio broadcasting, opposed to commercial interests and government operators. Using democratic language and imagery, amateurs viewed the ether as a common resource ideally open to all users. They believed that at the very least their early wireless experiments, which had been crucial for opening up new territory in the radio spectrum, gave them unique rights.

The amateurs also provided an alternative tradition in the way that they used the ether: instead of treating wireless as a serious pursuit important for national security or economic development, the amateurs generally viewed it as a hobby pursued for amusement and entertainment. Naval operators, in particular, increasingly rejected this side of amateur radio. They especially disapproved of amateurs who interfered with official communications or in extreme cases sent out false messages to navy ships. Naval officials used such incidents to support their calls for legislation, acknowledging that stations

serving the national-security interests of the country should have priority
of access to the ether.[11]

The 1910 Wireless Ship Act ratified key regulations dealing with maritime safety recommended by the 1906 International Conference. Congress
acted at this time after the organizers of the next international conference
informed government officials that they would not invite representatives
from the United States to participate unless they acted to support the earlier
agreements. The Wireless Ship Act placed the United States in compliance
with the international requirement that oceangoing ships carrying at least fifty
people and traveling between coastal stations separated by a distance of two
hundred or more miles have trained wireless operators and "efficient" wireless
equipment capable of communicating over distances of at least one hundred
miles. By defining "efficient" equipment in terms of the ability to communicate with other wireless systems, the law effectively put an end to efforts by
the Marconi Company to push its "non-intercommunication" rule. Congress
placed responsibility to carry out the new legislation with the Department of
Commerce and Labor. The department, in turn, set up a new radio-inspection
service in its Bureau of Navigation to enforce regulations.[12]

But the Wireless Ship Act did not deal with one of the key agreements at
the 1906 Berlin Convention: the decision to divide the radio spectrum among
different users. Implementation of this policy in the United States required
more fundamental legislation. Congress passed the Radio Act of 1912 in August to provide regulatory guidance for the overall domestic control of radio.
Although the immediate incentive for passing the law was the need to ratify
the international agreements, the *Titanic* disaster in April 1912, which underscored the importance of wireless for shipping, helped convince members of
Congress to vote in favor of the new law. It remained the major law guiding
regulators until Congress passed a new Radio Act in 1927.[13] The 1912 law
required operators of transmitters to obtain a license from the Department
of Commerce and Labor for the use of particular frequencies. All operators
had to give priority to distress calls. Significantly, the 1912 law also effectively
gave preferential treatment to the navy by allocating the desirable band of
frequencies from 187.4 to 499.7 kHz to government users. And although it
placed commercial users on frequencies above and below this band, the act
allowed the navy to continue operating on specific commercial frequencies.
Because members of Congress were particularly interested in ensuring that
all ships have access to wireless communications, the law required the navy
to transmit and receive commercial messages in cases where commercial
stations were not available. This regulation provided ambitious officers with
a justification for expanding the navy's large-scale wireless system. The im-

portance of the radio spectrum to national security was clear. In time of war or national emergency the Radio Act authorized the government to take over all radio stations.[14]

Although the 1912 Radio Act favored government users—especially the navy but also the Weather Bureau, the Army Signal Corps, and eventually the Air Mail Radio Service of the Post Office Department—the Marconi Company was not completely opposed to the new legislation. By 1912, the company had succeeded in gaining dominance over commercial maritime wireless by taking over or driving out of business rival companies. Because of its near monopoly control, Marconi did not mind abandoning the non-intercommunication policy. The company shared the navy's desire for regulation of wireless that would bring order to the airwaves. The navy and the Marconi Company shared a desire to discipline amateurs.[15] The act allowed amateurs to use frequencies above 1500 kHz (below 200 meters), a region generally considered useless at the time. Thus, the major result of the 1912 Radio Act was to uphold serious uses of the airwaves. Hobbyists mainly interested in using wireless for entertainment purposes were sidelined. The other major tradition arising from the act was an intensification of the tension between viewing the radio spectrum as primarily an economic resource to be exploited for profit and considering the spectrum as an important public resource that ideally should support commonly held, noncommercial values such as public safety and national security.

Building on the favorable policies of the 1912 act, the navy continued to expand wireless operations before and during World War I. Secretary of the Navy Josephus Daniels worked to integrate wireless into everyday operations and lobbied Congress to establish a government monopoly supervised by his department. During the period before the entry of the United States into the war, Daniels took control of major German and British (Marconi) coastal radio stations based on accusations that they were violating neutrality rules. When the United States entered the war, Daniels convinced the president to either close down or assume control of all wireless transmitters in the country not already operated by the federal government. The navy was able to add an additional fifty-three commercial stations to its growing international system.[16]

Unlike the Marconi Company, other companies recognized the need to support the development of transmitters and receivers using new continuous-wave technology able to transmit human speech and other complex sounds over the airwaves. Communication using earlier spark-gap transmitters could not be modulated to reproduce the human voice; transmissions were either "on" or "off." Between 1912 and 1917, key patents for innovations crucial to the new technology passed from individual inventors to new potential rivals of the Marconi Company. AT&T bought the patents for the audion from Lee De Forest and turned it into the vacuum tube; General Electric acquired control of the alternator originally developed by Reginald Fessenden and perfected by E. F. W. Alexanderson; and the Federal Telegraph Company acquired the patents for Valdemar Poulsen's arc transmitter. The navy developed a close relationship with these companies, especially during the war, when they supplied essential wireless equipment. A patent moratorium imposed by Daniels during the war stimulated new innovations in continuous wave technology, especially in the development of the vacuum tube. During May 1918, the navy acquired the patent rights to Poulsen's arc transmitter when it bought out Federal Telegraph.[17]

After the war, Daniels believed that Congress would sanction his plan to maintain the navy's de facto control of radio. He thought members of Congress would especially appreciate the need to keep foreign companies, notably the Marconi Company, from acquiring the new American innovations in radio. Although government control of radio during the war clearly supported innovations and efficiencies, Congress was critical of the record of government involvement with other industries, notably with the telephone system and the railroads. By the spring of 1919, it was clear that Congress would not accept complete government control of radio by the navy or any other department.[18]

Daniels was motivated to seek naval control not only to avoid having to give back to the Marconi Company its high-power coastal stations but also to prevent the company from acquiring the new American innovations in continuous wave technology that would allow it to reassert and maintain monopoly control. Of particular concern were Marconi's efforts to purchase alternators from GE. Since Daniels could not get congressional backing for the navy, he convinced other members of the Woodrow Wilson administration to help establish an all-American company that would purchase the U.S. subsidiary of the Marconi Company. The new company would control the country's long-distance point-to-point wireless-communications network. GE worked out an agreement with Marconi to form the Radio Corporation of America (RCA) and officially incorporated the new company in October 1919. The navy also convinced the other electrical and communications companies that held patents for radio technology to arrive at cross-licensing agreements with RCA and GE, in order to effectively duplicate the war-imposed patent moratorium. During the next eighteen months, RCA worked out agreements with GE, AT&T, Westinghouse, and the United Fruit Company for cross-licensing patent rights as well as for dividing up different aspects of the radio industry. RCA had the exclusive right to use the necessary patents for transoceanic radio telegraphy and ship-to-shore transmissions. The company also had nonexclusive rights for transoceanic radio telephony. AT&T largely retained control of radio telephony over land, including the exclusive right for toll purposes. GE agreed to manufacture 60 percent of the equipment sold by RCA; Westinghouse would produce the other 40 percent. AT&T, GE, and Westinghouse owned stock in RCA, and their representatives served on the board of directors.[19]

RCA was established to promote point-to-point wireless transmission; the cross-licensing and other agreements establishing the company did not take into account the possibility of using radio to broadcast to the general public. Although RCA's birth underscored the important tradition of using the radio spectrum to promote commercial business, some of the early experiments with broadcasting before 1920 reinforced a legacy that strongly questioned the legitimacy of treating the public airwaves as a private resource. Beginning as early as 1907, Lee De Forest, the inventor of the audion, attempted to set up a company that would fulfill his dream of using the nascent radio telephone technology to broadcast music and speech to the public. Although his dream may have been noble, his business activities proved to be little more than a stock-market scam. Among a number of major problems with his scheme, the most important was the fact that the technology still needed years of development before it could broadcast music and speech of acceptable quality. Nevertheless, De Forest and his business partners dreamed up various stunts and promotional schemes to convince gullible investors to buy stock in their company. For instance, they convinced hundreds of Christian Scientists to buy stock by arguing that radio fulfilled a prophesy of the founder of their movement, Mary Baker Eddy, who predicted that "Spirit needs no wires or electricity to carry messages." The government eventually cracked down on this and a number of other wireless-stock scams. De Forest's early efforts demonstrated the potential problems and contradictions in trying to make a profit from the use of the public airwaves for transmitting information and entertainment.[20]

Another important tradition during the pre-1920 period that helped shape the political and social context for public-service and educational radio was the wartime role of wireless for disseminating propaganda. Radio became especially important for the Germans after the British cut their cable connections to the United States at the outbreak of the war. Both sides tried to use their high-power trans-Atlantic wireless stations to communicate their versions of the war. Sensing the new importance of wireless for political propaganda and psychological warfare, President Wilson directed countries to only transmit neutral messages. The navy shut down stations that seemed to violate this rule.[21]

But after the United States entered the war, the government sought to follow the example of England and Germany by using trans-Atlantic wireless to transmit official news and information, especially for American troops overseas. With the assistance of the State Department and the Committee on Public Information, the navy sent a daily evening-news program titled *Home Stuff*. During 1918, naval coastal stations transmitted speeches by Woodrow Wilson criticizing Germany's undemocratic political system and encouraging the adoption of an American style of government.[22] The use of radio during the war for propaganda underscored the potentially powerful role of the new technology for influencing public opinion. The wartime experience served as a warning for individuals concerned about government control. But other forces in society were also interested in manipulating public opinion for less-than-noble ends. Wartime propaganda pointed to the potential problem of commercial propaganda and efforts to link the public airwaves to private commercial interests.

Herbert Hoover and the First Radio Conference

The initial boom in radio broadcasting, during 1921 and especially 1922, surprised many individuals and led to the development of a new relationship between commercial wireless companies and the federal government. The informal broadcasts of live and recorded music by the amateur operator and Westinghouse employee Frank Conrad—especially beginning in May 1920, eight months after the navy lifted the wartime ban on radio transmitters— demonstrated to company officials the potential value of broadcasting for stimulating the sale of the company's new radio receivers. Company officials recognized the value of Conrad's station (licensed later as KDKA) for stimulating enthusiasm for radio broadcasting among the general public. The company began regularly scheduled programming beginning with the broadcast of the presidential-election returns in November 1920.[23] The Department of Commerce established a new radio license category in September 1921 for "limited commercial stations." Before this date, stations experimenting with broadcasting, including especially the engineering departments at state universities, were given experimental licenses.[24] The number of licensed broadcasting stations in the United States grew from twenty-eight on January 1, 1922, to 570 on December 1, 1922.[25] Estimates of the number of radio receivers owned by citizens at the end of 1922 range from five hundred thousand to one million.[26]

The first broadcast stations licensed by the Department of Commerce were placed on one frequency, 833.3 kHz (360 meters). In December 1921, the department added a second frequency, 618.6 kHz (485 meters), for stations broadcasting government reports, including weather reports and agricultural information. As the number of stations expanded dramatically during the spring and summer of 1922, government officials realized that more frequency bands were needed to prevent interference.[27] But the 1912 Radio Act set aside most useable frequencies in the radio spectrum for the use of the federal government, especially the navy, and commercial point-to-point wireless companies.

After his appointment in March 1921, the new secretary of the Department of Commerce, Herbert Hoover, used the agency to protect broadcasters from efforts to push for government ownership or complete government control. Hoover learned to appreciate radio from his son, who was an amateur operator, and radio fit well into his vision of harnessing his department's resources to encourage new industries.[28] As with the navy, the Post Office Department sought to maintain or gain control over radio after the war. Congress appropriated $850,000 to the post office in 1919 for the operation of radio stations in support of the new airmail service. The department began to construct a series of stations across the country at airports beginning in August 1920. Postmaster General Will Hays was particularly interested in using the stations to support farmers by providing weather and crop information. During 1922 and 1923, Hays lobbied Congress for legislation, giving the department general oversight and control over radio. Although these efforts were unsuccessful, Hays's activities did reinforce the general political belief that radio should be treated as a public-service activity with a strong role for the federal government.[29]

Hoover successfully maneuvered to give his department a key role in the development of broadcasting, especially by working to gain more frequencies for stations and by taking steps to reduce interference. But initially he had a problem; he lacked clear legal authority to take meaningful action. In an opinion written immediately after passage of the 1912 Radio Act, the U.S. attorney general advised the secretary of commerce that Congress had only given his department guidance to follow the nineteen specific regulations listed in the act. The 1912 Radio Act did not give the secretary the general authority to take actions deemed necessary based on such new developments as the rise of broadcasting. None of the nineteen regulations, for example, explicitly gave the secretary authority to direct radio stations to use specific frequencies.[30]

Soon after Hoover became secretary, the chief of the department's radio service advised him that they should seek new legislation from Congress giving the department clear legal authority to regulate radio broadcasting. Beginning in the spring of 1921, Hoover worked with like-minded members

WHEN UNCLE SAM WANTS TO TALK TO ALL HIS PEOPLE

"When Uncle Sam Wants to Talk to All of His People." As this
cartoon shows, the federal government, especially the Department of Agriculture, used all radio stations across the country,
including a number of stations operated by government agencies, to broadcast useful information during the early 1920s.
Radio Broadcast, May 1922.

of Congress to introduce legislation authorizing the department to oversee
the rational development of broadcasting. But attempts to introduce different bills in Congress by various representatives all failed. Congress was
preoccupied with issues during this period that seemed more pressing, and
many members of Congress probably did not understand the technical issues
connected with the regulation of radio. The major radio companies also did
not entirely approve of specific aspects of the proposed legislation.[31]

Hoover responded to these legislative failures by working to gain support from participants involved in radio broadcasting for actions he believed were necessary. During the early and mid-1920s, he sponsored a series of conferences to bring together broadcasters, government officials, technical experts, and other interested parties. Hoover believed that the section of the 1912 Radio Act directing the department to license stations for the "least possible interference" provided at least minimal legal justification for actions by his department to bring order to broadcasting.[32]

Hoover's views about radio developed during the early 1920s as he prodded Congress to pass new legislation. Although he supported the use of radio broadcasting by private interests, he viewed the radio spectrum as a national resource that businesses should not monopolize for commercial ends. Licensing was necessary to ensure that stations provided a service for the public good. He feared the creation of "a situation where vested interest has been created" and a system where "a sort of national resource will have been parted with which will come to have ultimately a commercial and monopolistic value."[33] Hoover and most other officials came to believe that radio broadcasting was different from traditional print media. Unlike newspapers or other media of public opinion that were protected from state intervention by the First Amendment right of free speech, radio seemed to demand different rules because of its uniquely powerful capacity to broadcast messages directly into citizens' homes. Intrusive propaganda could go directly to children as well as adults, without their obvious voluntary consent. Government regulation seemed necessary to ensure the almost utopian predictions for radio's role in education and public affairs. And perhaps most important, unlike newspapers, which anyone with the necessary desire and resources could operate, only a finite number of radio stations could operate using a limited number of frequencies in the broadcast spectrum.[34]

Hoover organized the first national radio conference in February 1922. Participants agreed that radio should be considered "a public utility and as such should be regulated and controlled by the Federal Government in the public interest."[35] Hoover seriously considered allowing one of the "public service corporations to set up a broadcast system to be used generally by all sections of the government and to be under the control of monopolies."[36] He seemed to have in mind a proposal by AT&T that the Department of Commerce give it a monopoly over broadcasting, to complement its monopoly control of the telephone system. The company still believed the cross-licensing agreements it had with the other companies involved in radio gave it exclusive rights to toll broadcasting. Viewing radio along the same lines as the telephone, AT&T argued that the government could establish a regulated monopoly

Secretary of Commerce Herbert Hoover listening to a radio installed in his office, March 9, 1922. Courtesy of the Library of Congress.

open to all parties willing to pay toll charges. A regulated monopoly could also more effectively and efficiently deal with interference, since it would control all stations.[37]

But Hoover realized that AT&T's proposal was politically unrealistic and impractical, given the number of separately owned stations already broadcasting and the growing hostility in the country and in Congress to AT&T's monopoly control of communications. He also concluded that although radio ought to be treated as a public utility, the analogy with traditional public-utility regulation was not exact. Requiring stations to open up to anyone able to pay for programs—consistent with the "common carrier" principle of public-utility regulation—seemed to invite chaos and the debasement of broadcasting by propagandists, hucksters, and subversives. Hoover also believed that the federal government should not apply the traditional practice of public-utility regulation, involving the control of pricing and service standards. Thus, general principles of public-utility regulation were central to

Hoover's vision for radio broadcasting, but the specific practices developed for nineteenth-century industries, such as telephone service and electricity production and distribution, were not entirely appropriate.

Faced with the major problem of trying to license an increasing number of stations using a limited part of the radio spectrum, the First National Radio Conference focused on determining which stations should have priority of access to the airwaves to avoid interference. At least one delegate, Representative Wallace H. White of Maine, questioned whether making decisions about priority of access would amount to censorship by the government, which he strongly opposed.[38] But Hoover and the majority of representatives decided that a hierarchy should be established, with priority given to government stations such as the ones operated by the post office and the navy as well as "public" broadcasters, including the stations operated by state universities. A lower priority should be given to private broadcasters, especially stations experimenting with advertising or the use of toll broadcasting, a practice in which companies or individuals paid stations for the privilege of broadcasting their own programs. Toll broadcasting, developed by AT&T in 1922, was based originally on the idea that the company would provide access to all users on a system it owned as a public utility, irrespective of content.[39]

A greater value was placed on government and public stations mainly because they provided a distinct public service. While the private broadcasters specialized in providing entertainment, the public broadcasters supplied informational and educational service. Hoover praised radio stations at universities and colleges as "a step towards the realization of the true mission of radio."[40] In introductory remarks at the first national radio conference, he warned against allowing radio service "to be drowned in advertising chatter." By this date, only a few stations had begun to experiment with the use of radio for advertising goods and services using commercial messages, but the line between using radio to create goodwill among potential consumers and using it to sell directly was becoming blurred.[41] For example, some early stations accepted the participation of singers known as "song pluggers" who worked for music publishers interested in publicizing their product. As early as November 1922, the monthly magazine *Radio Broadcast* complained that "driblets of advertising, indirect but unmistakable, are floating through the ether every day. The woods are full of opportunists who are restrained by no scruples when the scent of profit comes down the wind."[42]

Participants at the 1922 conference generally preferred the establishment of two systems of broadcasting: one consisting of private commercial stations mainly providing entertainment, and a second consisting of public and government stations broadcasting useful information, news, and educational

"Advertising by Radio: Can It and Should It Be Done?" This cartoon shows that advertising was a controversial practice when first introduced during the early 1920s. *Radio News,* August 1922, p. 232.

programs. If arrangements could be made with the navy to give up the use of frequencies, participants at the conference preferred placing the two types of stations on separate bands in the spectrum.[43] Participants felt confident that the meeting of national experts had "expressed its opinion that broadcasts of crop and market information, weather forecasts, news, etc., from government and public stations are of greater importance and consequently deserve greater consideration than broadcasts from private stations."[44] The conference recommended that the Department of Commerce allow public and government stations to broadcast using higher power to serve a greater area: five hundred miles for government stations and 250 miles for public stations. Private commercial broadcasters, by contrast, should be limited to a fifty-mile range.[45] The faculty member in charge of the station at the University of Wisconsin commented approvingly in a May 1922 letter to the president of the university that "the Conference was quite liberal to the educational institutions in granting the use of much larger power than is allowed the commercial companies."[46]

The conference also recommended that the Department of Commerce decide about licensing private commercial broadcasters based on how well they demonstrated a commitment to the public interest. A private station's "character, quality, and value to the public" should be taken into account. Finally, the conference recommended that "direct advertising in radio broadcasting service be absolutely prohibited and that indirect advertising be limited to a statement of the call letters of the station and of the name of the concern responsible for the matter broadcasted."[47] As with the distinction between using radio to create goodwill and using it to sell products, the boundary between direct and indirect advertising was never entirely clear. But the conference was primarily concerned that companies not use radio to sell products directly, by advertising prices and presenting sales pitches on the air.

Hoover appreciated stations operated by public universities, but his support for government stations was not as clear, mainly because government stations of all types, especially those operated by the navy, continued to hold a monopoly on some of the most desirable regions in the radio spectrum. For private and public broadcasting stations to expand and provide interference-free service, government stations would need to agree to give up frequencies. Hoover did not seem to support efforts by the navy and post office to establish a permanent system of broadcast stations committed to serving the public. Further, he opposed adoption in the United States of the method of funding government-operated broadcast stations developed in England during the early 1920s: the collection of fees from owners of broadcast receivers. Governments that established this policy only allowed citizens who paid the fee to own receivers.[48]

Despite the clear preference of the first radio conference to have the Department of Commerce decide licensing issues based on applicants' commitment to specific types of public service, Hoover concluded that without new legislation he had no choice but to give licenses to all applicants. One applicant, the Intercity Radio Company, had already challenged Hoover about the department's authority to deny a license. The courts had ruled against Hoover during the spring and fall of 1921, and he likely expected to continue to lose on appeal. Indeed, the Court of Appeals ruled in favor of the Intercity Company in February 1923.[49]

Instead of denying licenses to stations, Hoover's department attempted to solve interference problems by convincing broadcast stations using the same frequency (there were still only two available) and located in the same city or region to work out time-sharing arrangements to avoid operating during overlapping periods. The department had already established this policy for amateur stations, ship stations, and stations transmitting telegraphic messages. Although Hoover believed he had the legal authority to fix hours of operation for stations, he generally tried to use his department to facilitate voluntary cooperation.[50]

If stations refused to cooperate, staff at the department referred them to the license, which stated that "a division of time may be required whenever in the opinion of the Secretary of Commerce such action is necessary." Radio inspectors assigned to different regions of the country met with station owners to "act as mediator or referee." In May 1922, for example, the radio inspector overseeing the New York City region helped negotiate time-sharing arrangements for fourteen stations. Significantly, Hoover and his staff did not seem to think the department had the authority to decide that certain stations were more deserving of time assignments than others. During a meeting with station owners in Detroit in the spring of 1922, the acting secretary of commerce informed the stations that "the matter of priority could not be considered in the allocation of time as each station would have equal right under the existing law."[51] In practice, this meant that despite the recommendations of the first radio conference, public stations committed to education and the dissemination of useful information were not given preferential treatment when deciding how to divide time with commercial stations.

As the main frequency band (833.3 kHz) became increasingly congested during the summer of 1922, the Department of Commerce decided to open up a second general frequency for broadcasters (749.6 kHz or 400 meters). With this decision, the department articulated its policy for determining priority of access to the spectrum. Instead of following the recommendation of the first radio conference and emphasizing priority in terms of public versus commercial or education and information versus entertainment, the department decided to primarily use technical standards. The new category of stations, which were given Class B licenses, had to demonstrate that they had a dependable and steady source of power, superior modulation controls, spare parts available to maintain constant service, an antenna sufficiently rigid to withstand wind effects, and studio facilities properly soundproofed to avoid reverberations. But additionally, to gain a Class B license, stations needed to demonstrate a commitment to higher-quality programming, defined mainly in terms of not using phonograph records.[52]

Although stations in the new category were considered of "a better grade" than stations in the Class A category, the Department of Commerce did not want to leave the impression that it was making judgments based on program quality.[53] Hoover and his staff tried to avoid decisions that critics could label as censorship. Commissioner David B. Carson, who was in charge of the day-to-day regulation of radio as the head of the Bureau of Navigation, informed a radio inspector in Boston that "under existing law the broadcasting of advertisements cannot be prohibited."[54] But as Carson later admitted during testimony to a congressional committee, the decision that the new class of stations should use live talent instead of phonograph records did place restrictions on programming and program policy; judged on this basis, the decision could be considered censorship.[55] And in a somewhat contradictory way, Carson used language that clearly assumed a hierarchy in types of programming; he emphasized that he placed a higher value on radio stations that supplied "first class programs."[56] Critics worried that the decision to establish a second class of stations might also establish a hierarchy benefitting the large electrical manufacturers, which could effectively wield a particular form of censorship based on control of superior economic resources. During 1921, Westinghouse established other important stations besides KDKA: WBZ in Springfield, Massachusetts; WJZ in Newark, New Jersey; and KYW in Chicago. Two other major stations established by companies involved in radio manufacturing during the earliest period of broadcasting were GE's WGY in Schenectady, New York, and AT&T's WEAF in New York City.

The reason for wanting to restrict the use of phonograph records is not entirely clear. The Department of Commerce may have been motivated by a rejection of jazz music by cultural elites and the close link between jazz and phonograph records during this period. A common complaint during the 1920s was that too many commercial stations were playing jazz music. As a number of scholars have pointed out, the hostility toward jazz was racially inspired, based on its identification with African Americans.[57] But the antipathy towards phonograph records by the Department of Commerce seems to have been more closely linked to the effort by the department to make a clear distinction between amateur stations and broadcast stations. In January 1922, the department ordered amateurs not to use their stations for broadcasting.[58] Amateurs had conducted some of the first experiments with broadcasting using phonograph records. The earliest experiments by the amateurs who helped establish KDKA and other pioneer stations had also mainly used phonograph records. By limiting the use of phonograph records, the Department of Commerce sought to limit the total number of stations broadcasting and to establish a professional class of stations using live talent. Initially, many musicians participated in broadcast programs to gain publicity rather than to receive compensation, but by the end of the 1920s, participants generally expected to be paid as professionals.[59]

A vivid example at Purdue University in 1922 illustrates why federal regulators were justified in being suspicious about the use of phonograph records, linking their use not only to amateurism but also fraudulent behavior. Faculty tried to interest the public in radio during that year by putting on a demonstration of the reception of music broadcast from an early transmitter to a receiver positioned in a large auditorium "jammed" with people anxious to hear the new communication medium. The university employee who helped conduct this early experiment later recalled that "every square foot was occupied and some people were leaning in the windows from the outside." But the receiver failed to operate. The faculty member later told how he "turned on the tubes, put on the headphone, adjusted the coils and turned the dials, but there wasn't a sound." He recalled that after working "there for some time trying to get something out of that receiver, . . . the people knew we were in trouble and their remarks didn't help. There was no use to try any longer, the set was as dead as the table it was setting on." In desperation, they then "faked a program, operating a phonograph upstairs and presenting the music through the speaker to the crowd in the room."[60]

Spectrum Management and Industry Experimentation

By the fall of 1922, the Department of Commerce had to admit that its decision to open up another frequency was not sufficient to eliminate problems with congestion in the airwaves. Listeners and broadcasters in large urban areas again complained of intolerable interference. After Congress failed to pass new legislation during February 1923, giving the Department of Commerce more authority to take drastic measures, Hoover decided that the only solution was to try to convince the navy to give up control of some of the frequencies assigned to it and other government users by the 1912 Radio Act. He first held discussions with other government institutions involved in radio and then organized a second radio conference. The second conference was more focused than the first. In a letter to the chief radio inspector of the department, Hoover argued that the new radio conference was necessary solely "to consider what should be done by way of invasion of the Naval Reserve."[61]

Hoover succeeded in convincing the navy to open up frequencies for the general use of radio broadcasters. The navy mainly agreed to move some of its activities to other frequencies because this would help convince Congress to authorize necessary funding for the modernization of its radio equipment. Everyone involved in radio was pleased to rid the ether of the old spark transmitters designed and built for the older frequencies; they were notorious for creating interference.[62]

By March 1923, at the time of the Second Radio Conference, the number of broadcasting stations had grown from approximately sixty, a year earlier, to 588.[63] To accommodate these new stations, the navy agreed to allow broadcasting on the band from 550 kHz to 1350 kHz. The other major result of the second conference was the establishment of three classes of stations. The department authorized a Class C category for broadcasters who wanted to continue transmitting on 833.3 kHz. The two new classes sought to institutionalize two kinds of stations: powerful stations located in major urban areas serving large sections of the country, and less powerful, local stations serving smaller regions. The conference set up Class A stations to use up to five hundred watts power on the band from 999.4 to 1365 kHz. Class B stations could use five hundred to one thousand watts power on the band from 870 to 999.4 kHz.[64] Conference participants recommended that Class A stations provide "programmes of local interest." Class B stations should continue to set high technical standards, including the requirement that the "quality of reproduction" of broadcasts should "be high."[65] Gaining Class B status had its rewards, especially in terms of increased publicity. Daily newspapers and magazines generally only published schedules of radio programs for Class B stations.[66]

The second conference did not follow the tradition of the first by making a clear distinction between stations based on programming or ownership. It could have allocated different bands in the spectrum among different users, drawing a distinction most importantly between commercial broadcasters and "public" broadcasters, represented especially by state universities. Alternatively, the conference could have recommended that the department set aside frequencies for a separate category of nonprofit organizations operating radio stations, including churches and local governments as well as universities. Instead, the status of nonprofit or educational stations was not taken into account. Although the first conference used the term "public" radio stations to refer to university broadcasters and publicly owned stations, during the second conference Hoover used the term to refer to the broadcasting industry in general.[67]

By the time of the second conference, powerful stations mainly broadcasting entertainment and music were becoming much more important, especially those operated by the large manufacturers. In May 1923, RCA bought WJZ from Westinghouse; the company also operated WJY in New York and was in the process of building a new station, WRC, in Washington, D.C. General Electric planned to establish a new station, KGO, in San Francisco and another station, KOA, in Denver. Hoover looked out for the interests of these broadcasters not because he wanted them to become the dominant force in radio but mainly because he needed the support of the large electrical and radio manufacturers to prevent overall control of radio by the navy.

But Hoover also worried about RCA, AT&T, and the other major companies gaining monopoly control over broadcasting; he tried to make sure proposed legislation took these concerns into account. By contrast, some of the members of his department were less critical of the large corporations and their ambitions in radio broadcasting. In January 1923, the radio inspector based in New York City, Arthur Batcheller, recommended that the department not be "influenced too greatly by individuals who are forever bringing

up the subject of monopoly."[68] Batcheller approved of AT&T's plan to establish
a system of broadcast stations across the country supported through the sale
of airtime. He wrote the department that "generally speaking, I am not in
favor of a monopoly, . . . but there is one thing sure that a monopoly on both
radio telephony and telegraphy . . . is absolutely necessary before the public
can be served." Batcheller thought that monopoly control by AT&T and RCA
was inevitable: "It is further my opinion and belief that the American Bell
Telephone Company will control the radio telephone communications on
land in this country in the future, and the Radio Corporation of America
will control the telegraph [radio] communications on land."[69]

Despite the rejection by Hoover of AT&T's proposal to operate radio
broadcasting as a regulated monopoly, this general belief in the inevitability of
corporate dominance helps explain the role of the Department of Commerce
in the development of the dominant system of commercial broadcasting in
the United States based on entertainment. In January 1923, another radio
inspector wrote that "the primary object of broadcasting is to serve the radio
public with enjoyable music and entertainment."[70] A sense of the inevitability
of commercial broadcasting also provided an incentive for the navy to give
up ambitions to control radio broadcasting. Sanford Hooper, one of the most
important naval officers involved in radio, argued that "the number of long-
distance radio broadcasting stations . . . would be reduced in a short time
from the hundreds then in existence to perhaps two, and that these would
be owned by the Telephone Corp. [AT&T] and Radio Corp. [RCA]."[71] Along
with the navy, the post office had put aside its ambitions to control radio by
1923. This loss of support from federal agencies for the cause of giving special
status to government-operated radio stations also led to the loss of influence
in Washington of universities or other nonprofit organizations operating
radio stations. In October 1923, James G. Harbord, the president of RCA,
proudly asserted that the "heresy of government ownership, especially in
radio matters," no longer existed among federal employees.[72]

By 1923, advertising, or the selling of airtime to sponsors, was becoming
an important means of economic support for a number of stations, despite
the negative comments against the practice by Hoover. The earliest stations,
broadcasting programs to create goodwill among listeners, largely functioned
as nonprofit institutions. At first they were able to convince performers to
participate in broadcasts based on the free publicity they would receive,
but as stations became established and competition arose for professional
involvement, performers increasingly demanded compensation. In February
1924, the ASCAP, which controlled the rights to the performance of music,
demanded that stations pay license fees. As radio became professionalized,

stations became more expensive to operate. In response, station owners increasingly turned to advertising as a significant source of funding.[73]

Following the Second Radio Conference, Hoover continued to work with likeminded members of Congress for new legislation that would give the Department of Commerce general authority to oversee radio, including the power to deny licenses. When it became clear that Congress was not going to act during 1924, he decided to call another radio conference. Following in the tradition of the other meetings, the Third Radio Conference, which met in October, presented Hoover with a united front supporting his actions. One of the most important issues Hoover wanted the conference to support was further experimentation, with new technological developments facilitating national service. By interconnecting local stations with broadcasters in large cities serving a national audience, he hoped to retain the best aspects of local and national radio. Hoover believed that "the local stations must be able to deliver every important national event with regularity." This could only be accomplished "by regularly organized interconnection on a national basis with nationally organized and directed programs for some part of the day in supplement to local programs." AT&T began experimenting with the use of telephone wires to interconnect stations during 1923. General Electric experimented with using short-wave radio relays for interconnection. Before the third conference, the major companies involved in radio met with Hoover and his staff and decided to support wire interconnection rather than further experimentation with radio relays. All the major companies involved in broadcasting also wanted to experiment with the use of higher power levels. Hoover supported requests for experimentation with moderate power increases, but not large increases that would overwhelm local stations.[74]

By the end of 1924, as the dominant patterns in the commercial system of radio broadcasting were beginning to become established, Hoover publicly clarified his own views about some of these developing practices. Rejecting the Marconi tradition of effectively treating the spectrum as a private resource, he reiterated strong support for the dominant tradition of government ownership of the ether and the utilization of some form of the public-utility model for broadcasting. During testimony at a congressional hearing in March 1924, Hoover emphasized that "radio communication is not to be considered as merely a business carried on for private gain, for private advertisement or for entertainment of the curious. It is a public concern impressed with the public trust and to be considered primarily from the standpoint of public interest to the same extent and upon the basis of the same general principles as our other public utilities."[75] Hoover also specifically reaffirmed a commitment to the kind of programming sponsored by land-grant universities. He hoped that broadcasters, instead of exclusively specializing in entertainment programs, would recognize that "the public, especially our people on farms and in isolated communities," were "coming to rely" on educational programs "for the information necessary to the conduct of their daily activities."[76]

Despite this commitment to defining the public interest based on how well broadcasters provided education and useful information to listeners, Hoover did not want to intervene directly in decisions about programming, including the commercial decisions of broadcasters who were increasingly relying on advertising for economic support. Hoover was critical of the use of advertising, but he also publicly opposed the major alternative, government license fees. He did not believe his department had the legal authority to oppose advertising, and he was unwilling to challenge the major companies supporting broadcasting. Instead of actively supporting alternatives to advertising, Hoover believed "we must leave this question to further experience."[77]

This position in favor of industry experimentation was Hoover's main solution to the most difficult issues in broadcasting. He opposed government involvement in programming based on his opposition to censorship; however, his belief that the public would best decide issues of programming based on a free competition among different stations ignored difficult problems. He argued that "stations naturally are endeavoring to please their listeners and thus there is an indirect censorship by the public," but this did not take into account the fact that many stations were more interested in responding to the needs of sponsors. And increasingly the public's interest was being shaped by advertisers to fit the economics of product marketing.[78]

Despite the official public position against censorship, the Department of Commerce's practices were more complex. The department directly influenced the content of broadcasts by requiring stations regularly to identify their call letters and their locations. Further, regulators at the Department of Commerce held clear views about types of programming. In July 1922, the department encouraged broadcasters to avoid "transmission of all political, religious, labor, or class propaganda, which would tend to engender factional controversy and strife." In January 1925, Commissioner Carson complained that there was "too much trashy material filling the air at present." Although the degree to which Carson and other staff members made decisions based on these views remains unclear, at least one radio inspector admitted that he decided about whether to allow stations to move to the Class B category based on whether they would "severely lower" the "standard and dignity of Class B stations as a whole."[79]

Following the Third Radio Conference, the Department of Commerce attempted to reallocate stations to reduce interference for all broadcasters in the three major classes, relying again on time-sharing arrangements. At least in one case, instead of seeking voluntary cooperation, Hoover imposed a time-sharing schedule on two stations located in the same city that were sharing a wavelength. He also tried to crack down on stations using inferior equipment not capable of ensuring constant transmission on an assigned frequency.[80] But despite these attempts to take a more forceful role, in May 1925 Hoover admitted that his department did not have any "intention whatever of making any radical change in wavelength assignments."[81] Interference persisted as new stations sought licenses. In February 1925, 557 stations held licenses, including 454 Class A, 85 Class B, and 16 Class C stations.[82] Hoover did make one notable minor change after the Third Radio Conference; he eliminated Class C stations by moving them to the Class A category.[83]

University Stations and Network Radio

Stations operated by universities believed that they faced special problems trying to adjust to rigid arrangements for time sharing. The University of Wisconsin station WHA complained about inflexible schedules that did not allow for "special programs such as lectures and concerts by distinguished visitors at the university."[84] The Department of Commerce assigned WHA to share a frequency with the Westinghouse station KYW in Chicago. Westinghouse opposed dividing time for its stations but told WHA in October 1925 that "because of your position as an educational institution, we will make certain exceptions in your case."[85] Officials at WHA resented this patronizing view and complained that the "attitude assumed" by KYW "acknowledges no rights on our part to any broadcasting time, but merely permits us to operate by your permission."[86] WHA reminded KYW that the university "held a broadcasting license that is in all respects the equivalent of yours."[87]

Partly because of this position of having to accept the crumbs of time not wanted by Westinghouse, WHA faced difficulties trying to grow and develop during the mid-1920s. Despite limited funds, the station had received a Class B rating from the Department of Commerce after making necessary changes, including the construction of a soundproof studio and a more efficient transmitter. During the approximately three hours every week when KYW was off the air, WHA had exclusive use of its frequency assignment. In March 1925, the business manager reported that the station "had very gratifying reports by postcards, letters, and telegrams, demonstrating that our broadcasts are easily and satisfactorily heard from coast to coast."[88] But because of the problems with Westinghouse that developed especially during the fall, the station sought a different frequency assignment.[89]

The difficulties with Westinghouse also exacerbated problems between WHA and the administration at the University of Wisconsin, which refused to provide regular operating funds for the station. While three other state universities—the University of Kansas, the University of Iowa, and the University of Illinois—were reportedly spending up to one hundred thousand dollars to upgrade station equipment during 1925, the president of the University of Wisconsin only authorized $1,601 for capital improvement. Professor William Lighty, who supervised much of the programming over WHA, complained that the university president during this period "did not seem to visualize the potentialities of the radio station. He seemed reluctant to give it any support from the President's office."[90]

Problems with interference between stations intensified during 1925 and 1926 as new stations began broadcasting and more stations increased power. During the period from the fall of 1924 through the spring of 1925, the University of South Dakota station KUSD reported having had "the most wonderful year . . . ever heard of for a set rated at only 100 watts." Listeners "from nearly every state in the Union and from all of northwest Canada" reported receiving the station. But for the same period a year later, the station complained of "broadcasting conditions so bad here that the same equipment which gave such wonderful results the year before was now almost useless."[91]

With nearly six hundred stations trying to broadcast (increasingly at higher power levels) over approximately eighty-eight available frequencies and with nearly two hundred new applications for licenses in the pipeline, Hoover realized that he had to find a way to limit the number of stations broadcasting.[92] During 1925, he began to notify applicants that all available frequencies for Class A and Class B stations were entirely filled.[93] To gain support for restricting further growth and for decisively dealing with the problem of interference, Hoover called a Fourth Radio Conference in November.

The conference made a number of recommendations supporting an active role for Hoover's department in combating interference. Perhaps most important, it recommended that Congress give Hoover the legal authority to place limits on stations.[94] But the conference was also significant because it underscored for the first time Hoover's acceptance of the emerging American System of broadcasting. His introductory remarks at the conference echoed commercial broadcasters' arguments about the superiority of their system based on private enterprise with minimal regulation by the federal government. A crucial aspect was the importance of a number of high-power stations serving a national audience and the interconnection of these stations with local outlets. Hoover sanctioned both of these developments at the conference. Despite earlier worries about high power leading to monopoly control, he now believed that experiments demonstrated that it was "not only harmless . . . but advantageous." "Power increase," according to Hoover, "has meant a general rise in broadcasting efficiency; it has meant clearer reception; it has helped greatly to overcome static and other difficulties."[95]

Hoover also believed that by rejecting the European model relying on government support, the commercial system in the United States "avoided the pitfalls of political, religious, and social conflicts in the use of speech over the radio which no Government could solve." According to Hoover, "[T]he decision that we should not imitate some of our foreign colleagues with governmentally controlled broadcasting supported by a tax upon the listener has secured for us a far greater variety of programs and excellence in service free of cost to the listener." Although Hoover acknowledged the increasing importance of advertising, he stressed that it was at best a necessary evil. The secretary hoped that broadcasters would hold to a distinction between "intrusive" advertising and "unobtrusive publicity."[96]

Hoover reiterated his core principle that broadcasters must demonstrate that they serve the public interest to justify access to the public airwaves. Crucially, for the first time, he clearly indicated a general standard for evaluating service in the public interest. Above all, a broadcaster should be "compelled to prove that there is something more than naked commercial selfishness in his purpose."[97] This criterion clearly favored stations operated by universities and other nonprofit educational institutions. By 1925, these stations were becoming more active politically. An alliance between the radio stations at land-grant universities, represented by the Association of Land-Grant Colleges and Universities, and supporters of radio at the USDA successfully lobbied the Fourth Radio Conference for special recognition. A resolution submitted by the USDA and the land-grant colleges that was adopted by the Fourth Radio Conference stated that the Department of Commerce should give "full recognition" to the needs of radio programs serving farm families, especially those broadcast from state agricultural colleges, and "that adequate, definite, and specific provision should be made for these services within the broadcast band of frequencies."[98]

Hoover's support for interconnection and high power helped lay a foundation for the rise of networks. But the development of network broadcasting depended on further negotiations among the different companies that had helped establish cross-licensing agreements central to the activities of RCA. The original agreements among the major companies were developed before the rise of broadcasting. Since they did not deal with radio broadcasting, the original agreements were ambiguous about the role of the "telephone group," which included AT&T and its manufacturing subsidiary Western Electric, and the "radio group," composed of RCA, Westinghouse, and General Electric. Most important, AT&T claimed that it held the exclusive rights for transmitting toll or advertiser-sponsored programs and for the use of long-lines for interconnection of broadcast stations.[99]

After two years of negotiations with the other companies beginning in 1923, AT&T decided against continuing its involvement with broadcasting. Key officials at AT&T believed the company should specialize exclusively in telephone service to avoid providing ammunition to critics warning of the company's growing influence in all aspects of communications. AT&T agreed to allow RCA to construct a network of broadcast stations; in exchange, RCA would use AT&T's wire system for interconnection.[100] This arrangement proved to be highly lucrative for the telephone company. During the first year of network operations, NBC agreed to pay AT&T eight hundred thousand dollars for connecting fifteen stations.[101] The agreement with AT&T also played a crucial role in determining the technical dimensions of the network system in the United States. Instead of considering alternative technical means of interconnection, notably short-wave relay and transcription technology, NBC relied exclusively on the use of telephone wires.[102]

As part of its decision to withdraw from broadcasting, AT&T agreed to sell to RCA its flagship station in New York, WEAF, for one million dollars.[103] The sale of WEAF underscored the degree to which broadcasting had become commercialized by the mid-1920s. Despite the official government policy refusing to allow the spectrum to be treated as a private-property resource, the sale of WEAF and other stations demonstrated the establishment of de facto property rights in the spectrum. The Department of Commerce allowed stations being bought and sold to include the transfer of the broadcast license. A staff member informed a Senate committee of the department's policy that "the license ran to the apparatus, and if there is no good reason to the contrary, we will recognize that sale and license the new owner of the apparatus."[104] The sale price of stations thus included not only the value of the physical equipment but also the effective value of the government-sanctioned frequency assignment. Of the one million dollars paid to AT&T for the purchase of WEAF, only two hundred thousand was for the physical apparatus; eight hundred thousand dollars covered the value of a license for the full-time use of an exclusive channel in the spectrum.[105]

In a final deal, in January 1926, RCA agreed to cooperate with the other radio companies in establishing the new network. The National Broadcasting

Company (NBC), incorporated officially in September, was jointly owned by RCA (50 percent ownership), GE (30 percent), and Westinghouse (20 percent). The network distributed two types of programs to affiliated stations using AT&T cables: sponsored programs supported by advertising, and "sustaining" programs not funded through commercial sponsorship but produced by the network on its own. NBC sold sustaining programs to affiliates and paid them to rebroadcast sponsored programs.[106]

This development of network broadcasting provided an added incentive for Hoover to work with members of Congress to gain support for legislation giving his department general authority to regulate radio. Even without new legislation, Hoover hoped that he would be able to convert the support he received at the Fourth Radio Conference into meaningful regulatory actions to clear up interference. But not all broadcasters supported Hoover's efforts. Most important, Eugene McDonald, the owner of the Chicago station WJAZ and the president of the National Association of Broadcasters, refused to acknowledge Hoover's authority to assign frequencies and power levels to broadcasters. He intentionally ignored Hoover's order to stop using a frequency reserved for a station in Canada. Hoover's department took legal action against McDonald, accusing his stations of violating the 1912 Radio Act. But in April 1926, Judge James H. Wilkerson of the U.S. District Court of Northern Illinois dealt Hoover a devastating blow by arguing that the 1912 law did not give Hoover authority to deny licenses to stations or to assign frequencies and hours of operation. Responding to Hoover's request for legal advice and guidance to clarify the relationship between the new judicial opinion and the earlier ruling in the Intercity Radio Company case, the attorney general confirmed Wilkerson's judgment, stripping the secretary of commerce of much of his presumed authority over the regulation of broadcasting, including the authority to assign power levels to stations.[107]

Hoover used this ruling as an opportunity to press Congress to pass new legislation. In July, he warned that "the radio situation is in a chaotic stage." Lacking legal authority, he did not threaten to take action against stations not following government guidelines. The Department of Commerce accepted all applications for new licenses; the total number of stations grew to 620 by the end of 1926. The department also informed new applicants that "in view of the recent decision of the Attorney General the Department does not consider it has authority to assign wavelengths. Therefore, each station is at liberty to use any wavelengths they may desire." Complaints from listeners and stations struggling with interference spurred Congress to act.[108]

A legal decision late in 1926 also served as an incentive for Congress to finally pass legislation. The *Chicago Tribune* station WGN took legal action

against a station in a Chicago suburb, WGES, for using a frequency channel very close to WGN's. The owners of WGN complained that its station's
listeners might accidentally tune into WGES when searching for a favorite
channel. Judge Francis Wilson ruled in favor of WGN based on the principle
that "priority of time creates a superiority in right." He reasoned that WGN
should have priority of access to its channel because it had spent years developing an audience for programs broadcast on that particular frequency. This
was a unique legal interpretation that might have led to the establishment of
property rights in the ether if Congress had not acted. As we have seen, at
least at the level of official policy, Hoover and most other officials involved
in communication policy during this period officially opposed treating the
radio spectrum as a private-property resource.[109]

The 1927 Radio Act

Congress finally passed new legislation replacing the 1912 Radio Act in February 1927. The new act, signed by President Calvin Coolidge that same month,
represented a compromise between two points of view in Congress. Representative Wallace H. White of Maine cooperated with Hoover to champion
the major proposal in the House of Representatives, giving the secretary of
commerce general authority to oversee the regulation of radio. Key members
of the Senate—especially Clarence Dill of Washington, the sponsor of the
main Senate bill—preferred giving authority to an independent radio commission composed of apolitical experts representing different regions of the
country. The Radio Act of 1927 represented a compromise between these two
positions. It established an independent radio commission but also stipulated
that, without further congressional action, most authority would revert back
to the Department of Commerce after one year.

Congress authorized the Federal Radio Commission (FRC) to assign
frequencies, power levels, transmitter locations, and hours of operation to
broadcast stations as well as to make regulations "to prevent interference
between stations." Section 4 directed the commission to regulate the technical
quality of station equipment and authorized the commission to formulate
special regulations "applicable to radio stations engaged in chain broadcasting." But significantly the act did not go into detail about regulating this new
development. To limit political interference, no more than three of the five
commissioners appointed by the president with the advice and consent of the
Senate could belong to the same party. Each commissioner had to represent
one of the five geographic zones delineated in the act, with no more than one
commissioner chosen for each zone. The final act included weakened versions

of the antimonopoly provisions included in the original Senate bill. The FRC could deny or revoke licenses of stations owned by companies or individuals that had been convicted of violating the antitrust laws. But Congress allowed for judicial review of FRC decisions. Finally, Section 6 of the new act reiterated the right given in the 1912 law to the president to take control of all radio transmitters during time of war or national emergency.[110]

The Radio Act of 1927 affirmed the view developed by Hoover that radio channels should be considered a public resource for broadcast stations to use as a privilege. The act included language adapted from public-utility legislation directing the commission to make decisions about broadcasters' licenses based on "public interest, convenience, or necessity."[111] Although Congress did not define the "public-interest" standard to allow for flexibility to meet changing conditions, earlier versions of the radio bills in Congress during 1926 indicated that members of Congress favored specific criteria supporting educational and nonprofit broadcasters. Early versions of the White and Dill bills during the spring of 1926 incorporated the resolution of the Fourth Radio Conference encouraging government regulators to make adequate provision for agricultural radio programs broadcast especially by the educational stations operated by land-grant colleges. An early version of the Dill bill included a provision stating that "in said distribution the commission shall give due regard to the requests of educational institutions for opportunities to broadcast educational programs in each state and community."[112] Similarly, language was added to the bill submitted by Representative White during the spring of 1926 providing that each state in the country should have reserved for its use "one wave length." Although the bill did not specifically designate "to whom in each state this privilege should be granted," the representatives of land-grant colleges operating radio stations hoped that after the bill with this provision became law, they would "be in a position to assert the claim that this wave length be assigned to the land-grant college institution in each state."[113]

The final bills passed by the House and Senate in 1926 contained identical language stressing the right of each state "to have allocated to it, or to some person, firm, company, or corporation within it, the use of a wave length for at least one broadcasting station located or to be located in such State." Supporters of land-grant stations believed that the intent of this provision was to "give to each State one frequency or wave length which it could use *as a right* for radio broadcasting." They continued to hope that once this provision became law, stations operated by state institutions could argue that this guarantee of state rights gave them a special, protected status, especially relative to commercial radio stations.[114] But despite agreement by the House and the Senate, the conference committee that determined the final legislation, which included White and Dill, decided to eliminate this state-rights provision. White had opposed including this language in the original House bill. The head of a university station later recalled a heated discussion in which White "insisted that the college stations should have all the rights before the law that other stations have, but no more rights, and he opposed putting them in any group with special privileges."[115] Dill was more sympathetic with the needs of stations operated by institutions of higher education, but he agreed to eliminate the provision guaranteeing state rights during the conference between House and Senate negotiators because he did not think it was realistic for all states to expect to have their own channels, especially if they interpreted the provision as guaranteeing an exclusive right.[116] There simply did not seem to be enough channels available in the broadcast spectrum. Members of the conference committee also believed that a mandate to support educational stations committed to noncommercial public service was implicit in the criteria given to the commission to evaluate stations based on "public interest, convenience, or necessity."[117] And they believed that there was sufficient support for regional, state-financed stations in Section 9 of the act, which stipulated that "the licensing authority shall make such a distribution of licenses, bands of frequency of wave lengths, periods of time for operation, and of power among the different States and communities as to give fair, efficient, and equitable radio service to each of the same."[118]

Supporters of educational broadcasting at land-grant schools hesitated to become directly involved in lobbying Congress because they feared "without question, should our designs in this respect be known, there would be heavy opposition."[119] Immediately before passage of the final legislation, college representatives asked the director of the USDA to intervene by pressuring the conference committee to reinsert language specifically guaranteeing channels to educational institutions, but the director told them it was too late. He determined that "further pressing of [the] question" was not warranted because this "might delay final passage of [the] Bill."[120] Thus, the Radio Act of 1927 did not explicitly instruct the FRC to give preferential treatment to educational stations; however, commissioners looking for guidance from Congress about how they should interpret the public-interest standard written into the law could have found support for favoring educational broadcasters in the congressional debate leading to the final legislation as well as in the tradition established by Hoover of publicly opposing stations committed to a narrow practice of commercial self-interest.

In support of the tradition against censorship established by Hoover, Congress stressed that "nothing in this Act shall be understood or construed to give the licensing authority the power of censorship." But as was the case with

Hoover's Department of Commerce, how to put this position into practice was unclear. The same section of the radio act (Section 29) upholding "the right of free speech" also directed the radio commission to ensure that "no person within the jurisdiction of the United States shall utter any obscene, indecent, or profane language by means of radio communication." Section 19 supported Hoover's policy that commercial programs supported by sponsors needed to include language identifying that fact. Section 18 directed stations choosing to broadcast political messages by candidates for public office to give equal opportunities to all competing candidates. And in general, Congress gave commissioners wide authority to make decisions about the quality of stations based on the extent to which they believed the holders of licenses were broadcasting material in the public interest. Contemporary observers pointed out that this legal right to give preferential treatment to stations that seemed to be better serving the public interest—as opposed to private interests—could be interpreted as a type of censorship.[121]

* * *

The 1927 law was the culmination of Hoover's efforts to obtain congressional authorization during the 1920s for his regulatory policies and practices. The law did not obviously challenge the emerging dominant system of broadcasting, which used mass entertainment as a dominant service increasingly supported by advertising revenue and a network structure interconnecting stations centered on urban markets. Although the 1927 law generally supported minimal regulation, commissioners interested in taking an activist role could justify more robust practices because crucial aspects of the law were ambiguous and open to interpretation, in particular the policy of evaluating the worth of stations based on the standard of "public interest, convenience, or necessity."

This ambiguity was rooted in Hoover's own ambivalence about the relationship between the federal government and the private radio industry. Hoover generally supported industrial self-regulation based on associationalist principles limiting the role of the federal government to helping industry groups work harmoniously. He believed that the best results for broadcasting would occur through a combination of industrial self-interest, public pressure on the part of listeners, and a sense of social responsibility on the part of businessmen. But despite having played a crucial role in the rise of the commercial system of broadcasting, Hoover did not approve of many aspects of that system. He made strong statements against the use of advertising and commercial exploitation in broadcasting, especially the use of direct selling tactics. He emphasized that the broadcasting of entertainment should not overshadow radio's great promise for providing educational, informational, and public-affairs programming. He did not want to see monopoly forces grow to dominate local control and local character. And above all, he emphasized that narrow private interests should never become the dominant force in radio broadcasting. When the members of the FRC evaluated how to apply the 1927 Radio Act to bring order to radio broadcasting, they might have chosen to try to follow this side of Hoover's vision for radio broadcasting, drawing on the less than clear-cut language of the act to apply wide-ranging policies to all aspects of the industry. They could have decided to restructure the industry in a way that would benefit stations owned by institutions of higher education committed to public-interest broadcasting. But as we will see, although the commission did try to dramatically restructure the industry, the reforms did not favor the growth and development of noncommercial public-service radio stations.

4. The Federal Radio Commission and the Decline of Noncommercial Educational Stations, 1927–34

In February 1932, William Gregson, the program director of WUOA at the University of Arkansas, claimed that the FRC was responsible for a recent decision by the university to sell the station to a commercial company. He argued that although the "Commission may still boast that it has never cut an educational station off the air," that fact only tells part of the story. The commission's decisions had the same result, according to Gregson: "It merely cuts off our head, our arms, and our legs, and then allows us to die a natural death."[1] Gregson's experience with the commission was not unusual. A number of other stations were also unhappy with decisions made by the FRC. The organization played a decisive role, during the late 1920s and early 1930s, in the establishment of the dominant system of network-controlled, commercial broadcasting in the United States and in the decline of noncommercial stations operated by state universities. A detailed analysis is necessary to understand this crucial link.

The Establishment of the Commission and Its Initial Work

Although Congress gave the FRC clear legal authority to regulate radio broadcasting, it was weakened by a number of problems during its first year of existence. The Senate refused to support two of the first five men nominated by Hoover to the commission. Two commissioners, John Dillon and William Bullard, died in office during the fall of 1927. A third commissioner, Henry

Bellows—a scholar who taught at the University of Minnesota, helped edit magazines and newspapers, and managed the Minneapolis radio station WCCO—resigned in October. The president chose Ira Robinson to replace Bullard, Eugene O. Sykes to replace Dillon, and Sam Pickard to replace Bellows. Robinson served as the Chief Justice for the West Virginia Supreme Court and ran unsuccessfully as the Republican candidate for governor. Sykes was a Mississippi Democrat who also served on his state's Supreme Court. Pickard directed the radio service program of the United States Department of Agriculture following his early work with educational radio at Kansas State Agricultural College. The two other commissioners who served beginning in 1927 were Orestes H. Caldwell and Harold A. Lafount. Lafount earned a degree in civil engineering from Utah State Agricultural College and managed the Pacific Land and Water Company for a number of years before his appointment to the FRC. As the only commissioner with advanced training in electrical engineering, Caldwell played an especially important role on the FRC.[2] For over fifteen years before joining the commission, he worked for the publisher McGraw-Hill, where he helped establish and edit a number of publications in electronics and radio, including *Radio Retailing, Electronics,* and *Electrical Merchandising.* Members of the Senate, concerned that Caldwell was not sufficiently critical of the growing dominance of RCA, delayed his appointment to the FRC for over a year. The final confirmation vote saw thirty-six senators voting to support Caldwell and thirty-five voting against.[3]

The commission's personnel problems were exacerbated by Congress's failure to approve a budget for the agency. Bellows complained that "we were absolutely without funds to employ any technical assistance whatsoever. . . . The result was that most of us went back to our own offices at night and got out our mail on our own typewriters because we did not have enough stenographers to take care of the mail."[4] Lacking technical experts and funds to conduct field investigations of radio reception, the commission had to rely on staff in the Bureau of Standards, the Navy Department, and other departments of the federal government.[5]

The FRC held an initial series of meetings from March 29 to April 1, 1927, to consider how to improve radio broadcasting. The meetings mainly focused on obtaining engineering advice about technical information necessary to improve reception and reduce interference. The commission also sent out a questionnaire asking stations how their operations served the public interest. Based on information gathered at these hearings, the commission announced a new assignment system for stations to go into effect on June 1. Commissioner Bellows claimed that "practically all stations were given new assignments." The commission authorized new licenses for sixty-day periods to

A meeting of engineers and radio-station operators (standing) with members of the radio commission (sitting at table) to discuss station assignments in 1928. FRC members from left to right: Carl H. Butman, secretary; Judge Eugene O. Sykes, commissioner; Judge Ira E. Robinson, chairman; O. H. Caldwell, commissioner; Sam Pickard, commissioner; and Harold A. Lafount, commissioner. Courtesy of the Library of Congress.

give the allocation an opportunity to "be tested by actual practice." Trial and error was more important than engineering analysis, because of the complicated and unpredictable factors creating interference. According to Bellows, "[O]nly actual experience, and not engineering theory, can be the guide."[6]

Most of the commissioners who formulated the June plan believed that the commission ideally should eliminate over one hundred stations. Commissioner Caldwell argued that "perhaps 100 stations, perhaps 150 stations, the record will show are not operating in the public interest; . . . they are simply, in a strict radio sense, just operating as a driver who drives down Pennsylvania Avenue on the wrong side of the street and is a menace to traffic."[7] But commissioners were not convinced that they had the legal authority to eliminate stations from the airwaves. Bellows questioned whether "under the law as it now stands we can refuse any station a license absolutely if it was licensed under the old law."[8] The commission also feared antagonizing broadcasters and their lawyers. Sykes, who was trained as a lawyer, claimed that if they had tried to eliminate stations, the work would have become bogged down in numerous lawsuits and temporary injunctions.[9] The June reassignment not only shifted frequencies and changed power levels of stations to eliminate long-distance interference and clear frequencies reserved for Canadian stations but also relocated high-power stations away from city centers "in order to prevent interference to the listening public."[10]

Individual Commissioners and Broadcast Policy

In its first attempt to solve the major problems of radio broadcasting, the commission followed Hoover's example and struggled with a crucial tension. They tried to treat radio regulation as primarily a technical problem to be solved through engineering analysis while, at the same time, often taking into account the fundamental social, economic, and political aspects of broadcasting. Although the initial hearings mainly emphasized the need to treat radio as a technical problem, during congressional testimony, commissioners acknowledged that decisions about individual stations also dealt with such qualitative issues as the character of programming. Bellows reported that the June reallocation was based not only on the "physical efficiency of the station" but "most important[ly]" on "the type and character and variety of the program service" provided by the station, as shown in the sworn statement accompanying its application as well as "in the mass of comments" about the station expressed in letters and newspaper reports and in "general expressions of public opinion."[11]

Especially important for this discussion was Bellows's emphasis on the value of general-interest stations "rendering the widest variety of service, stations which gave educational service, religious service, local music, music from distant points, sports—in other words, which served a widely varied audience." According to Bellows, the commission found that these stations "had the most general commendation and the fewest complaints." Bellows emphasized that this did not mean that the commission did not value educational stations and other nonprofit stations serving a more specialized audience. He specifically pointed out to members of Congress that the commission also appreciated "educational stations, university and college stations," and "other stations which rendered admirable service in a more limited field" to a "limited group, a group that wanted that particular type of service."[12]

However, in the fall of 1927, when Bellows addressed the National Association of Broadcasters, the major professional association dominated by commercial broadcasters, he criticized educational broadcasters for not adapting
lectures or talks to the new medium. Bellows told about his own experiences
with "programs arranged by the universities in which the idea was to have
some competent professor come over and talk for an hour without a break."
"After the first ten minutes or so," he argued, the audience "began dropping
off as we knew by the mail." According to Bellows, "[T]he best broadcasting
of educational programs today is done by commercial or general stations
which put on programs sponsored by universities or colleges, with the talks
given by university or college men but always under the direction, control,
censorship if you will of the radio station."[13] This statement should not be surprising, given the fact that Bellows managed the commercial station WCCO
in Minneapolis before joining the FRC.

Bellows believed that the commission did not need to dictate programming choices to stations. He argued that pressure from the commission to
broadcast public-service and educational programs would be sufficient. By
the fall of 1927, the commission's beneficial influence already seemed clear
to Bellows: "There has been a marked improvement in broadcast programs
and I think a good deal of reason for that is that broadcasting stations have
realized that they have got to come up before the Commission" and answer
the question, "What are you doing to justify your existence?"[14]

Commissioner Caldwell shared Bellows's interest in giving preferential
treatment to stations broadcasting "programs of broad interest," but he also
singled out as especially valuable programs "of usefulness from the standpoint
of educational value and of news interest." Caldwell favored ensuring that
radio supported "the cause of humanity and the things that are essential to
the welfare of the people and the extension of knowledge."[15] Despite such
statements praising educational programming, Caldwell believed that commercial stations supported by advertising would produce the best results for
the country. Although he acknowledged that some listeners found commercials annoying, he argued that "the point has not yet been reached where the
annoyance is at all comparable to the great improvement in the programs
that has resulted through the financing of these programs by advertising."
According to Caldwell, the use of advertising had allowed stations to "secure
the very best talent in the United States and to make a market for such talent and bring it into every home."[16] Caldwell also did not believe that the
recent "increasing tendency toward direct references to merchandise and to
products" was a completely negative trend. Unlike Hoover and most other
observers who condemned the use of direct advertising, Caldwell believed

"that in certain parts of the country and to certain audiences direct advertising furnishes a very real service."[17]

Caldwell played down the negative aspects of advertising by deemphasizing the distinction between commercial advertising and publicity and by arguing that all broadcasters were motivated by publicity: "It is . . . my belief [that] nearly every station that is operated, is operated to gain good will or to create publicity." He thought it would be difficult to "draw a line anywhere between, on the one hand, those stations doing educational and good will work and, on the other hand, those stations doing direct advertising." Since he did not believe that this distinction was important, Caldwell claimed that educational stations operated by nonprofit institutions would need to compete directly with commercial stations for valuable assignments.[18]

Despite having worked as an extension editor in charge of educational radio at the pioneer station KSAC at Kansas State Agricultural College, Pickard became a convert to the dominant model of commercial broadcasting. As an FRC commissioner, he argued that the average broadcaster could not do without the support of advertisers to put on quality public-service programs: "[I]t is too expensive a proposition for him." As in the case of Caldwell, Pickard did not think the commission should give preferential treatment to noncommercial broadcasters. If a station can better serve the public with commercially sponsored public-service programs, then "he is entitled to a better place." When pressed by a member of Congress about how the commission should decide between two applicants for the same frequency, one supported by advertisers and one operated by a state agency, Pickard agreed with the member of Congress that "if the State station were equipped to render a valuable service" it "would have a right and preference over the individual on the question of public interest." However, Pickard's idea of "valuable service" was commercial in nature. As with the other commissioners, he believed that the best stations served the largest number of listeners and provided a general format featuring entertainment.[19]

Pickard's support for commercial radio developed mainly after he left Kansas State to become the first director of the radio service of the USDA. Instead of agreeing to mainly support the publicly funded college stations, the USDA chose to follow the tradition it had already established (along with some of the states) for supplying market radio service: to use all available facilities, including commercial stations, while refusing to participate in sponsored programs. Pickard spent the first three months after his appointment on a ten-thousand-mile automobile trip in the eastern half of the country visiting farmers and commercial and noncommercial radio stations. This experience reinforced his growing belief that "competition on the dials now makes it necessary" for agricultural programs to adopt some of the entertainment-based formats used by commercial stations.[20] Pickard's background as a stunt pilot and his outgoing personality left him more open than his boss at Kansas State, Harry Umberger, to the entertainment possibilities of radio.[21]

As the head of the USDA radio service, Pickard sided with the commercial broadcasters who wanted to adopt radio techniques involving showmanship and entertainment. He instructed writers to come up with programs using a "popular style" based especially on dialogues or stories and to eliminate difficult words and scientific terms.[22] He told stations presenting programs that "every fact must be dramatized to the fullest extent."[23] Programs developed during the first year that the service used manuscripts sent to commercial stations, 1926–27, included *A Weekly Letter to Dad,* in which a son in college writes home to his father to tell about the latest scientific advances in agriculture; *Autobiographies of Infamous Bugs and Rodents,* an unintentionally campy program that featured animals as narrators telling about their effects on agriculture; and the *United States Radio Farm School,* which used announcers at the various stations as "schoolmasters" conducting radio classes and giving imaginary inspection tours.[24] Thus, partly because of Pickard's influence, the USDA believed that state and federal agricultural agencies should cooperate with commercial facilities rather than follow the example of some of the land-grant stations and fight against the commercial interests or attempt to create an alternative noncommercial network structure.[25]

In their support of commercial broadcasting, the FRC commissioners emphasized a concept Douglas Craig has called the ideal of "listener sovereignty."[26] They argued that listeners should determine program choice. Since commercial stations seemed to give listeners what they wanted to hear, they appeared to provide a superior service. This argument complemented the emphasis on the importance of technical issues for radio regulation. Commissioners stressed both ideas to support their preference for not considering fundamental changes to the economic and political structure of the industry. In January 1928, Pickard testified at a Senate hearing that the commission primarily tried to "take the listener's point of view" and tried "to do the thing that would be in the public interest for the listener." He emphasized that the commission was interested in keeping track of listeners' concerns rather than investigating the ownership structure of broadcasting stations, the development of network control, or the distribution of patent rights.[27]

The commission used the emphasis on listener control to justify decisions favoring commercial stations delivering a mass audience for advertisers. Caldwell stressed that "the commission has acted wholly, in selecting its channels, on evidence brought to it by the listeners of their interest in the

station." Stations given "so-called preferred channels" were the "most popular stations" and the stations with the financial means to purchase the "best
equipment."[28]

A second issue stressed by the commission dealt with the problem of
censorship. Caldwell justified nonintervention by the FRC in the growing
dominance of commercial broadcasting by appealing to the need to avoid
censorship, including the censoring of advertisements. "It would be most
unwise to censor in any way the programs," Caldwell warned. Instead, he
advocated that program control should be the responsibility of listeners and
station managers. According to Caldwell, decisions about all forms of programming should "be left in the hands of the stations to determine whether it
is of public interest, and the people would manifest that by whether they want
to listen or not, and they can always tune it out if they do not want to listen
to it."[29] Bellows similarly stressed that listeners should take responsibility for
programming choices and commission policy. "It is for you" as listeners, he
argued, "to say whether it shall degenerate into a mere plaything or develop
into one of the greatest forces in the molding of our entire civilization." The
commission could "do only what you tell us you want done."[30]

But sometimes commissioners acknowledged that the issues of listener
sovereignty and censorship were inherently complex. Pickard claimed that
broadcasters were able to respond to listener demands as expressed through
mail sent to stations. He argued that if they received, for example, one hundred letters every day "protesting against an educational talk and giving
reasons, they will cut that down, maybe, from 1 hour to 30 minutes."[31] But
when pressed by Couzens to evaluate whether most stations make decisions
based on rigorous statistical analysis, Pickard acknowledged that efforts to
measure listeners' interests "is guesswork, just like advertising."[32]

Despite emphasizing the issue of noncensorship as a key justification for
FRC policy, a number of commissioners acknowledged the complexities of
trying to avoid censorship. In response to a question from Senator Burton
Wheeler, Democrat from Montana, asking whether "you do maintain something of a censorship when you say that you will stop these junk programs
or you will put a station on a different wave length," Pickard answered "Yes,
the public service, convenience, and necessity clause operates as a censorship in a way."[33] Similarly, Caldwell testified that "while the radio law gives
us no control over censorship, yet so long as there is an excess of demand for
wave lengths over the available supply of wave lengths, in the final analysis
the commission is clothed with a form of censorship."[34] Sykes emphasized
that although the commission does not tell stations "what they can or can

not broadcast," the legal directive to consider what is in the public interest meant that inevitably commissioners "are bound to take into consideration the character of programs that are being broadcast by a station."[35]

FRC Decisions: 1927

The June 1927 reallocation did not meet the commission's expectations. Although listeners in major metropolitan areas appreciated the reduction of interference between powerful nearby stations, in general listeners reported that conditions were "far from satisfactory." According to the FRC, "[C]omplaints which deluged the commission immediately made it apparent that changes would have to be effected." Heterodyne interference resulting from stations operating on the same channel even though separated by hundreds or thousands of miles ruined reception across the entire country, especially in rural areas.[36]

The commission made extensive changes to frequency assignments during the remainder of 1927 and the beginning of 1928. It held over fifty hearings to consider requests from broadcasters for better assignments. The commission reported that its decisions were guided "by the test of public interest, convenience, or necessity." Although it did not attempt to provide the public with a precise definition of this standard, the commission did specifically require stations "to make complete showings of their past record of service" and "their program resources."[37]

Beginning during the fall of 1927, the FRC also attempted to make large-scale changes based on studies of conditions in each of the zones. The commissioners submitted reports based on visits to their respective zones between November 1927 and February 1928. Commissioner Lafount interviewed 769 individuals (including 141 listeners) representing 102 radio stations during a 8,206–mile trip in the fifth zone. The commission believed that the changes it made in this zone were particularly effective. It reported "a vast improvement in radio reception" in that zone.[38]

The commission also attempted to clear heterodyne interference from an especially troublesome band of frequencies, between 600 and 1000 kHz. During November and December 1927, it ordered stations operating on channels in this band to take necessary steps to eliminate their contribution to the problem. Broadcasters had the option of sharing time with other stations, reducing power, improving the quality of the transmission frequency, or finding another channel to use.[39] The commission's effect on the broadcasting industry during 1927 was especially apparent in the increase in the number of stations dividing time. When the FRC was first established, according to the commission secretary, "very few, if any" of the 733 total stations operating in the country divided time. By the end of January 1928, the number of stations dividing time had increased to 264.[40]

The various attempts by the commission to reduce interference by reassigning stations during this period caused major difficulties for educational stations already struggling to survive in the face of competition from commercial stations. For example, the University of Wisconsin station WHA had to deal with a number of changes to its frequency assignment at the same time as it had to fight off efforts by the commercial station KYW in Chicago to deny the educational station exclusive hours to broadcast. The problems with KYW began in January 1927, soon after it joined the NBC network. Prior to this arrangement, KYW had agreed to allow WHA to broadcast three evenings during the week. But the network broadcast one of the programs KYW felt obligated to use during the time set aside for WHA. As a result, the Chicago station demanded all evenings during the week and refused to compromise with the university.[41]

Although initially greeted favorably by the university, the FRC's frequency reassignments only served to complicate WHA's problems. The initial reassignment in May ordered WHA to divide time with the state-owned station in Stevens Point, WLBL. William Lighty, who was in charge of programming at WHA, wrote a colleague in another state that "we in Wisconsin are well pleased with our assignment. We divide time with another state station operated in the center of the state by the Department of Markets, and this division of time can be very satisfactorily adjusted." But this view soon changed. The new channel, 940 kHz, became congested when the commission assigned other stations to it. Lighty complained that the channel was now the "worst crowded assignment that could be made." The commission then agreed in November to shift WHA and WLBL—along with another small commercial station in Wisconsin—to a new channel, 900 kHz. This arrangement was satisfactory, but the commission then decided to assign ten other stations to 900 kHz, including some of the most powerful stations in the country. Lighty recalled that "the resulting interference was so bad that our station could not be heard consistently twenty-five miles from Madison and within this radius there was always a powerful heterodyne." The commission denied repeated requests from WHA for a better assignment during November and December 1927. This action should not be surprising, given the fact that key commissioners seemed to favor general-service commercial stations broadcasting full-time; WHA, by contrast, was only asking for a frequency assignment to broadcast from 7:30 to 9:00 during two evenings per week.[42]

FRC policies during 1927 also caused problems for stations operated by educational institutions in Minnesota. As a result of a frequency shift ordered by the commission in June, the campus station at the University of Minnesota could no longer provide interference-free service to a large area. Carleton College in Northfield, Minnesota, had a similar experience with its station KFMX. After the commission ordered the station to change frequencies in June 1927, the college complained that it now only "covered a very restricted area of approximately 35 miles radius." Since the college had established the station to serve listeners well beyond this distance, campus officials concluded that KFMX was now "practically useless."[43]

The Davis Amendment

The FRC was vigorously attacked during congressional hearings in January and February 1928. Key members of Congress were especially upset by the commission's apparent unwillingness to protect educational stations and the listening public in general from the growing dominance of network commercial radio. Because Congress continued to refuse to give the commission a permanent mandate (it only received its first appropriation in March 1928), the FRC had to take into account the views of powerful members of Congress, especially Senator Clarence C. Dill, Democrat from Washington, and Representative Ewin L. Davis, Democrat from Tennessee, who played pivotal roles in the passage of the 1927 Radio Act.

Dill's main complaint was that the commission had failed to take into account the clear message from Congress to consider unregulated network control by powerful stations supported by corporations as a clear danger. He quizzed Caldwell about why the commission seemed to ignore the legislative provision giving it authority to make "special regulations, applicable to radio stations engaged in chain broadcasting." Dill believed that "the way the commission has treated it is to favor chain stations beyond expression."[44] He did not object to chain broadcasting in principle but insisted that he only wanted "chain broadcasting controlled." Dill thought that the commission should consider the effect of stations joining networks as well as the possibility of giving independent stations—rather than stations connected to the chains—the use of clear channels.[45] Twenty-three of the first twenty-five clear channels were assigned to radio stations affiliated with NBC.[46]

Caldwell's testimony during hearings in the House of Representatives early in 1928 seemed to confirm Dill's complaints about the commission's inattention to the regulation of chain broadcasting. Caldwell told Dill that he "did not know anything about the relations" between the network and station affiliates. He claimed that Congress had "expressly given the commission no authority . . . to prevent a station from going out and buying two hours a day on a chain, if it desires."[47] Commissioner Sykes also stressed that the commission did not take into account whether stations had network connections; they were evaluated "as independent units." He contradicted Dill by arguing that if Congress thought "anything further should be done with reference to regulating chain programs, . . . it is a matter that will be for this branch of government [Congress] and not for the commission."[48]

Caldwell and other commissioners seemed to side with the expansion of networks and the use of high-power stations. Caldwell believed it was "a public necessity" and a democratic imperative "to encourage the use of high power, in order to lay down a strong signal which can be received by the low-priced receiving sets, thus bringing the program to the greatest number of listeners satisfactorily and particularly those equipped with inexpensive apparatus."[49] He also praised "the larger stations" for having "maintained their frequency most admirably" and for having "been the best in the maintenance of radio's rules of the road."[50] According to Caldwell, to adequately serve the extensive rural areas of the country, these larger stations needed to have their own clear channels. But under harsh questioning from members of Congress, he did acknowledge that the thirty-five channels the commission attempted to clear might be too many.[51]

Members of Congress who attacked the FRC were particularly concerned about the fate of local stations. They criticized Caldwell and the other commissioners for failing to heed the provision in the 1927 Radio Act authorizing them to classify stations based on different factors, potentially including the service area of stations and the type of service offered. A rigorous classification scheme taking into account local stations, noncommercial stations, and educational stations as well as large commercial broadcasters, would have led the commission to recognize the need for all types of stations.[52]

Representative Davis's questioning of commissioners during House committee hearings early in 1928 focused especially on the fate of educational and noncommercial stations providing local and regional service. Davis told commissioners about a letter he had recently received from the Association of College and University Broadcasting Stations "complaining very earnestly that they had not been accorded proper treatment" by the commission. He pointed out that members of Congress debating the 1927 Radio Act and officials at Hoover's Fourth Radio Conference had emphasized that regulators should give favorable consideration to educational stations broadcasting "agricultural and home-economics information." Despite this "unanimous expression of sentiment," Davis complained, "nothing has been done along that line."[53]

Davis also linked his criticism of commission policy towards educational stations to a cultural critique of the developing commercial system of broadcasting. He accused the commission of giving "nearly all of the valuable wave lengths" to stations specializing in popular entertainment—especially jazz music—at the expense of stations specializing in educational, public affairs, and traditional music programs. Echoing a "cultural uplift" view of broadcasting promoted by John Reith, the director of the British Broadcasting Corporation (BBC) in England, he thought that the government had a responsibility "with respect to broadcasting to undertake to cultivate a taste for things worth while, rather than yield to so large an extent to the desire on the part of youth for jazz music and things of that sort." Davis criticized the justification by commercial broadcasters—which Commissioner Pickard defended—that they were simply giving listeners what they wanted. He pointed out that broadcasters did not always sufficiently take into account the diversity of the audience; they seemed to mainly cater to young listeners. "I think they have given entirely too much recognition to that portion of our population which wants that character of programs," according to Davis, "and have overlooked the fact that more mature people and more serious-minded people, who perhaps are not as prone to give expression to their views . . . do care for things that are more worth while."[54]

Without giving any specific information, Pickard claimed that the commission had made every effort to support educational stations: "[A]ll college stations that have come to us with problems have had the most sympathetic support of the commission." But Pickard's testimony underscored his lack of understanding of the needs and desires of educational radio stations. Despite much evidence to the contrary, he claimed that "most colleges stress the daytime operation. They feel they have less competition from other stations and less interference and that more effective work can be done in the daytime." But Davis expressed a view closer to the realities of agricultural broadcasting at land-grant colleges when he asked rhetorically, "Is it not a fact that the reason they have taken the daytime is because that is all they could get?"[55]

Davis's support for educational stations operated by state colleges was connected to his wider concern that the commission was not following the guidelines of Section 9 of the 1927 Radio Act, directing it to provide a "fair, efficient, and equitable service" to each of the states and the different regions in the country. Some of the commissioners played down the importance of following a strict interpretation of the provision by pointing out that it did not come from the full Senate or House bills but was added by the conference committee. Davis was upset because commissioners interpreted the provision as directing them to provide an equitable service to listeners in the different geographical zones, even if the service in one zone came from powerful stations broadcasting from another region.[56]

As a Democrat from Tennessee, Davis was a staunch supporter of southern interests in Congress. His call for an equitable distribution of radio facilities was largely driven by his concern that network control of broadcasting based in New York City was dominating all sections of the country, especially the South. He proposed new legislation explicitly directing the FRC to allocate station licenses equitably among the different states and the five zones.

As Craig has pointed out, Davis's contention that the FRC favored New York City and treated the populations in the West and the South as second-class citizens needs to be understood in context. During 1927, the only section of the country that had more than its share of stations was the fourth zone, representing the states in the upper Midwest. The first zone, which included New York City and the rest of the Northeast, did have a disproportionately large share of the country's total station wattage. But the distribution of the most powerful stations again favored the fourth zone. Thus, Davis was correct that regions outside of the South—although not necessarily the Northeast—had more of the powerful radio stations. But the South was not disadvantaged in all categories; it ranked second in access to radio receivers. And the advantage of having powerful transmitters was not entirely clear. An increase in power did not universally correlate with greater coverage. A station's coverage depended on a number of complex considerations not readily dealt with by legislation, including time of day, the season of the year, changing propagation conditions, and interaction with signals from other stations.[57]

Key senators, in particular Clarence Dill, supported Davis's amendment to the bill authorizing the commission for another year. The amendment passed Congress largely based on the support of southerners and westerners. Members of Congress from the Northeast mainly opposed the amendment; the voting of midwesterners was equally divided. The Davis Amendment became law when President Coolidge signed the extension bill for the FRC on March 28, 1928. The amendment directed the commission to completely rethink the allocation of stations in the radio spectrum to ensure an equitable distribution. The FRC had to provide listeners with equality of service in terms of reception and transmission. Specifically, Congress ordered the commission to provide each zone an equal number of stations and frequency assignments as well as equivalent periods of time of operation and power levels. The commission also needed to make a similar "fair and equal allocation" to each state within each zone, based on population.[58]

General Order 32 and the Public-Interest Standard

The reallocation the FRC developed in response to the Davis Amendment was known as General Order 40. The plan was announced on August 30 and went into effect on November 11. Three years after its implementation, Commissioner Lafount praised the plan for providing "the structure or very foundation upon which broadcasting has been built, and upon which the success or failure of every branch of the radio industry must depend."[59] But before developing the final version of General Order 40, the commission issued General Order 32 on May 25, 1928, which ordered 164 stations of questionable value based on "reports of supervisors and other records of information" to justify their existence. The main focus of General Order 32 was the disproportionate number of stations located in the upper Midwest (the fourth zone). Ninety-one of the 164 stations were located in this region. After hearings in July to assess the value of the 164 stations, the commission ordered a number of major changes, which ultimately resulted in the elimination of sixty-two stations.[60]

General Order 32 was especially important because it prompted the FRC to discuss for the first time the meaning of "public interest, convenience, or necessity." In response to repeated requests from stations affected by the order for a "precise definition," the commission stressed that it did not have a legal obligation to give "a precise definition of such a phrase which will foresee all eventualities." As with cases of other general phrases in legislative acts, such as "unfair methods of competition," the commission believed that the Supreme Court would ultimately have to pass judgment about the commission's implementation of the public-interest standard. But the commission did believe it was "possible to state a few general principles which have demonstrated themselves in the course of the experience of the commission." It emphasized that its paramount commitment was to the interest of the "listening public" rather than the "individual broadcaster or the advertiser." Reducing interference to improve service was especially important. The commission stressed that "the test—'public interest, convenience, or necessity'—becomes a matter of a comparative and not an absolute standard when applied to broadcasting stations." It signaled that stations would need to compete for channels in the limited band of frequencies available in the broadcast band. And the commission argued that the Davis Amendment should "be viewed as a partial limitation upon the power of the commission in applying" the public-interest standard.[61]

The August 23 statement listed a number of more specific principles that would continue to guide the commission in determining whether a station deserved a license. Most of these principles reflected earlier policies articulated by regulators at the Department of Commerce before the establishment of the FRC. For example, the commission echoed an earlier prejudice against the use of phonograph records. It argued that "in view of the paucity of channels . . . the limited facilities for broadcasting should not be shared with stations which give the sort of service which is readily available to the public in another form." The commission believed that a station relying mainly on phonograph records "is not giving the public anything which it can not readily have without such a station." The August 23 statement also stressed that stations needed to follow a "regular schedule made known to the public." Further, the commission argued that it could consider the "character" of licensees, their "financial responsibility" and "past record," in determining which stations are "more or less likely to fulfill the trust imposed by the license." Finally, one of the most important principles listed by the commission involved the maintenance of high technical standards, specifically stations needed to use transmitters able to stay on assigned frequencies.[62] This principle reflected one of the first regulations issued by the commission, General Order 7, which fixed the maximum allowed deviation from a station's assigned frequency.[63]

Although some of the commissioners publicly expressed support for radio advertising, including the use of "direct advertising," the statement released with General Order 32 was notably critical. This may have primarily reflected the influence of Commissioner Robinson, who served as acting chair during 1928. The statement acknowledged that most stations relied on advertising for economic support but also stressed that "such benefit as is derived by advertisers must be incidental and entirely secondary to the interest of the public." The statement took a strong stand against direct advertising, including the "quoting of merchandise prices." Because this form of advertising was "usually offensive to the listening public," the commission signaled that a station adopting the practice could potentially lose its license. The statement also emphasized that the commission's negative view of advertising was a primary motivation for its stand against the use of phonograph records: "The commission can not close its eyes to the fact that the real purpose of the use of phonograph records in most communities is to provide a cheaper method of advertising for advertisers who are thereby saved the expense of providing an original program."[64]

Notably absent from the August 23 statement was mention of giving higher priority to general-service broadcasters as opposed to special-interest stations. The fact that the statement did not mention the issue probably indicates that the commission as a whole still could not agree on a policy. The issue was especially important for stations operated by universities and colleges after the implementation of General Order 40, when the commission did adopt a policy favoring stations with a general format. Educational stations were hurt by the commission's tendency to place them in the same category as religious broadcasters and other special-interest "propaganda" stations. The failure of the August 23 statement to discuss the issue of censorship probably indicates that the commission realized that it was indirectly practicing a form of censorship when it used information about the past operational record of stations to decide about the renewal of licenses. As we have seen, some of the commissioners admitted this point during congressional testimony.

Licensing decisions in connection mainly with General Order 32 help illustrate some of the major principles articulated in the August 23 statement, including the regulation of phonograph records, restrictions on excessive advertising, and the commission's willingness to use the past record of a station to decide about license renewal. For example, after investigating the performance of WCRW, operated by a Chicago resident named Clinton R. White, the commission ordered a reduction in power from five hundred to one hundred watts because the station used phonograph records during 75 percent of time on the air and because it existed "chiefly for the purpose of deriving an income from the sale of advertising," especially direct advertising, including the "quoting of prices."[65] The commission refused to renew the license of the Rhode Island station WCOT based on an evaluation that the owner mainly used the station for direct advertising and for his own personal interests (instead of for the interests of his listeners), including to promote his candidacy for mayor of Providence and to conduct personal attacks against his enemies.[66] Similarly, in September, Louis Caldwell recommended that the commission take action to collect evidence against KTNT and its owner, Norman Baker, for using "defamatory language over the air" and for "using a type of loud speaker outside his place of business by means of which he enforces upon large numbers of the citizens of Muscatine, Iowa, material which is designed to bring them to his place of business" and which is "only in the pecuniary interest of the licensee." Caldwell advised the commission to collect evidence of "objectionable features so that a case may be brought against the licensee to revoke his license."[67]

A decision on August 22 demonstrated that the commission did not automatically take action against special-interest nonprofit stations promoting political views. After evaluating the record of WEVD, owned by the Debs Memorial Fund and committed to promoting socialism, the commission decided to grant a license renewal. The ruling pointed out that "undoubtedly, some of the doctrines broadcast over the station would not meet the approval of individual members of the commission." Nevertheless, "this consideration . . . had nothing to do with the commissioners' original action . . . of requiring [the station] to make a showing as to the service being given the public." The commission found that public complaints were not justified; it concluded that "the station has pursued a very satisfactory policy."[68]

Although the August 23 commission statement did not specifically discuss the traditional educational justification for radio broadcasting emphasized especially by Hoover, individual decisions by the commission did take into account this issue when discussing the public-interest value of stations in connection with the implementation of General Order 32. For example, the commission implied that WCOT would have received a positive evaluation if it had been able to demonstrate the "educational or aesthetic value" of its programming. The commission implied that one of the best ways to judge the public-service value of radio broadcasting was in terms of its educational value.[69] This was also the case for WCRW. In deciding about the Chicago station, the commission contrasted the station's practice of serving only the pecuniary interests of advertisers with the broadcast ideal of providing "educational and community civic service."[70]

General Order 40

General Order 32 was not formulated to explicitly take into account the Davis Amendment; General Order 40 was. Although they did not approve of Congress interfering in their work, key commissioners, especially Orestes H. Caldwell, viewed the Davis Amendment as a "golden opportunity" for the commission to legally rid the country of less desirable stations.[71] According to Caldwell, the commissioners "from the very first" believed that they needed to eliminate approximately three hundred broadcasters, a number that corresponded to "the total of those who came on the air during the breakdown of the law of 1926."[72] Caldwell favored closing down stations directly; if this was not possible, he viewed the call for a complete reallocation of radio broadcasting as an opportunity to carry out an early commission proposal from November 1927 to "relegate those stations which seem to be of little or no value to frequencies on which they can make little trouble."[73]

Most of the commissioners did not oppose Caldwell's call for a complete and immediate reallocation of all stations. Caldwell, not surprisingly, played the most important role in helping to formulate General Order 40. Commissioners Caldwell, Pickard, and Lafount served on a special allocation committee that consulted with experts during the spring and early summer of 1928 before formulating General Order 40. In 1931, Lafount argued that Orestes Caldwell is "wholly responsible for the present system of broadcasting in this country."[74]

The commission started planning for a major reallocation soon after passage of the Davis Amendment. During the period before August 1928, when the commission finally received funding for its own engineering division, members of the major professional association for electrical engineers in the United States, the Institute of Radio Engineers (IRE), provided the FRC with technical advice. After a series of meetings during March and April, the engineers recommended a new allocation plan consistent with their interpretation of the best way to implement the different aspects of the Davis Amendment.[75]

The engineers' plan was similar to recommendations the IRE had given Secretary of Commerce Herbert Hoover during the mid-1920s. Radio engineers concluded that the only way to minimize the problem of heterodyne interference resulting from two stations trying to use the same frequency—even when far apart—was to set aside a large number of clear-channel frequencies for the exclusive use of high-power stations serving rural as well as urban areas. An ideal allocation would also have a second class of channel-sharing, low-power stations serving a local audience. And to take into account the large number of stations already operating, the engineers recommended a third class of medium-power stations serving moderate-sized regions. Specifically, the engineers' plan proposed setting aside fifty of the ninety channels available in the United States for the exclusive use of clear-channel stations, thirty-six channels for moderate-power stations, and four channels for low-power local stations. Ten different clear channels would be assigned for each of the five zones. Eighteen of the moderate-power channels would be designated for each zone. Altogether, ninety regional stations would be set aside for the country along with one hundred local stations.[76]

The National Association of Broadcasters and other industry representatives proposed an alternative plan allowing most of the country's nearly seven hundred stations to continue to operate. Unlike the engineer's plan, the industry plan did not recommend true clear-channel stations. It was also largely rejected by the commission. The major difference between the final plan adopted by the FRC and the engineers' proposal was that the FRC decided to only authorize forty, instead of fifty, exclusive channels (eight in each zone). Also, the FRC did not accept the engineers' recommendation to eliminate several hundred stations. Instead, General Order 40 forced many small stations to use the same channel.[77]

The final plan was a compromise developed to accommodate divisions within the commission. Ira Robinson was the only commissioner to vote against the plan; he also refused to participate in its implementation. Robinson favored a more gradual implementation of reforms and specifically opposed the authorization of a large number of high-power, clear-channel stations.[78] Although Pickard played an important role on the reallocation committee and did not vote against General Order 40, he favored less disruptive measures to prevent "great hardship" to his region, Zone 4, centered on Chicago. Pickard feared that Zone 4 would "alone . . . bear the brunt of this proposed action."[79] Since Pickard's zone had a disproportionate share of broadcast facilities, it would likely be most adversely affected by the Davis Amendment.

We have already seen that the commissioners who played an especially important role in the development and implementation of General Order 40—Caldwell, Lafount, and Pickard—expressed views in support of the emerging system of commercial broadcasting using high-power stations and network control. It is also important to point out that all three commissioners had close ties to large commercial broadcasters. When he left the FRC in the early 1930s, Lafount spent twenty years as an executive with commercial broadcasters. After Pickard left the commission in 1929, he took a position as vice president at CBS. One of the strongest supporters of Caldwell's nomination to the commission was Merlin Aylesworth, the president of NBC.[80]

The other key player in the formulation and especially the implementation of General Order 40 was Louis Caldwell (no relation to Commissioner Orestes H. Caldwell). Caldwell was appointed general counsel to the FRC in June 1928. Prior to this date, the commission did not have a legal division. The Department of Justice lent the services of Bethuel M. Webster Jr., special assistant to the attorney general, to help the commission with hearings and court proceedings.[81]

As with most of the commissioners he advised, Louis Caldwell had close connections to commercial broadcasters. Specifically, before accepting the position at the FRC, Caldwell worked for the *Chicago Tribune* station WGN. He also headed the Standing Committee on Communications of the American Bar Association. Although Louis Caldwell did not oppose high-power stations, he was not predisposed to support policies that would lead to the expansion of network control. He was more interested in promoting allocation decisions that would benefit large independent stations like WGN. Caldwell thus favored gradual reforms; like the National Association of Broadcasters and Commissioner Robinson, he opposed radical measures that would automatically eliminate many independent and small stations.

On August 17, 1928, Louis Caldwell sent a memorandum to the commission complaining that General Order 40 would be too disruptive, especially hurting small, local stations by forcing them to compete for the same frequencies or to purchase new equipment to broadcast on the new channels. And he complained that the commission did not appreciate the difficult negotiations stations sharing channels had to face: "Many stations are so radically reduced in power, or limited in time, as practically to be ruined." In an especially perceptive observation, he pointed out that "there is little difference between this method of killing off stations and out-and-out elimination." Along different lines, Louis Caldwell also complained that the allocation would give stations connected to networks favorable treatment in comparison to large independent stations in the Midwest (like WGN). Instead of a radical reallocation, Caldwell favored trying to improve the existing situation by reexamining the results of General Order 32, which he helped first to develop and then to justify to broadcasters. The general counsel argued that instead of ordering stations off the air completely, the commission should seek to cut the amount of power all stations used. According to Caldwell, "[S]uch a course of action will avoid public criticism to the effect that General Order No. 32 was a fiasco and resulted in nothing."[82]

The official implementation of General Order 40 on November 11 marked a new era for the commission, dominated by the majority faction favoring relatively radical policies. Commissioner Robinson and to a lesser degree general counsel Louis Caldwell were largely marginalized. As a staff member employed by the commissioners, Caldwell did not have the option of following Robinson's example by refusing to participate in the implementation of General Order 40. He mainly worked to find ways to ensure that decisions based on the new plan would stand up to legal challenge.

Engineers and Technocratic Legitimation

Most of the commissioners who served on the original commission wanted to eliminate many stations from the broadcast spectrum. Uncertainty about the legal grounds for refusing licenses was one of the main reasons the commission at first primarily worked to find ways to improve existing arrangements. The legal justification for taking extreme measures was enabled by two events: the adoption by Congress of the Davis Amendment and the involvement of engineers who not only played a crucial role in formulating General Order 40 but also in providing a powerful rationale for members of the commission interested in circumscribing issues such as censorship, monopoly control, and the political implications of the public-interest standard.

John Dellinger, the chief radio engineer of the commission who had participated in Hoover's radio conferences as the head of the radio section of the Bureau of Standards, contended that General Order 40 was the "closest approach to the ideal set-up which can be made at this time."[83] He boasted that the plan was in "essential accord with the recommendation of radio engineers."[84] The engineers emphasized that their plan was superior because it was driven by technical considerations, especially the need to reduce heterodyne interference. An emphasis on high-power stations and exclusive or clear channels were the two most important provisions of General Order 40. The engineers who developed the plan contended that the allocation was demanded by rigid engineering principles. High-power stations were part of the "inevitable process of evolution in radio communication" and a "symbol of the progress of the science."[85]

Other members of the commission supported this view, stressing the preeminent role of engineers and technical evaluation. The assistant general counsel for the FRC, Paul M. Segal, argued that because "radio is essentially a scientific, not a legal enterprise . . . the radio engineering profession must supply the impetus, the principles, and the leadership" for the development of broadcast policy.[86] Commissioner Caldwell similarly emphasized that the work of the FRC was primarily based on "sound engineering principles" and "conditions imposed by . . . stubborn scientific facts."[87]

The engineering argument that the commission should mainly treat the allocation of broadcast frequencies as a technical problem gave Louis Caldwell and the commission's legal division a powerful weapon against critics of General Order 40. Caldwell contended that opponents of a national assignment system based on the use of high-power and clear-channel stations did not understand the "principles of engineering" that demanded these arrangements as the only scientifically valid solution.[88] Commission press releases specifically stressed that the legitimacy of General Order 40 was based on the neutrality of technical experts. One announcement pointed out that the commission used "the services of some of the outstanding radio engineers of the country," including consulting engineers "known to be independent of connections which might in any way prejudice their views."[89]

Electrical engineers not only played a crucial role in developing the overall framework for General Order 40 but also in deciding individual station assignments. For example, in November 1928, commission engineers evaluated the request of the radio station operated by Ohio State University, WEAO, to divide on an equal basis the time period between 7:00 PM and midnight with the Cincinnati station WKRC, operated by the Kodel Electrical and Manufacturing Company. After evaluating the case for both stations, the electrical engineers concluded that the university should be able to "put on all the material it can adequately furnish" between the hours of 7:00 and 8:00

PM. Rather than making judgments based on commonly understood engineering or technical considerations, the engineers decided mainly based on the judgment that WEAO "has never been very active and has always divided time."[90] In January 1929, an engineer on the commission evaluated a petition signed by five hundred citizens of Los Angeles requesting that the FRC prohibit a local station, KTM, from broadcasting between 1:00 and 4:00 AM in the winter because they liked to use this ideal time period for long-distance listening. The engineer gave a favorable evaluation of the petition because KTM only broadcast phonograph records during these hours and because the station had deviated from its frequency on more than one occasion. He also decided that the petition had "enough weight for the Commission to take action without waiting to hear the station's side in the matter."[91]

This last evaluation, in particular, underscores the complex factors engineers considered when making decisions. Their decisions took into account issues involving interpretations of administrative law and the public-interest standard in addition to narrowly defined engineering principles and practices. The issue of whether to take into account the connection of stations to chains provides another example along these lines. Despite public assertions during 1928 that the commission did not consider the chain connection of stations, an examination of evaluations by engineers reveals a different situation. The commission engineers who evaluated the request from WEAO to divide time equally with WKRC, for example, made sure that the decision about assigning time during the evening did not adversely affect the chain operation of WKRC.[92] Similarly, in a decision in late September 1928, Dellinger and other engineers on the commission decided to approve a power increase for WMBS so that it could join the CBS network. Dellinger wrote Commissioner Robinson that he "understood that this station . . . will not be taken on the chain with their present assignment."[93]

A confidential document by Dellinger in August 1928 also reveals that the engineers who helped develop General Order 40 included provisions allowing for the future elimination of stations. Dellinger acknowledged that although the plan allowed all stations to continue to operate, it was "so drawn that the number of stations can be reduced at some future time." Further, another statement confirmed Louis Caldwell's suspicions that the commission was attempting to kill off stations by restricting power levels and forcing frequent assignment changes. Dellinger acknowledged that "of course, excessive time divisions, and a few drastic reductions of power, may actually lead to closing down of some stations." He also emphasized that General Order 40 would "stimulate competition between existing stations." Although Dellinger did not explicitly discuss what this competition would involve, he meant something very close to the policy adopted by the commission following the introduction of General Order 40. Stations were encouraged to petition the FRC for a new assignment; other stations affected would then have to send legal representatives to Washington, D.C., to defend their interests. Educational and noncommercial stations were especially hurt by this policy; they could not compete with commercial stations able to hire the best lawyers in Washington.[94]

Although the commission relied heavily on the advice of engineers for individual decisions about station assignments, archival records also reveal that commissioners were often involved in individual decisions. Especially during the early years of the FRC, each commissioner made recommendations to the full commission about station assignments in his own specific zone. The full commission then agreed to the individual recommendation based on the one commissioner's advice. For example, the minutes of the commission for February 13, 1928, recorded that "a number of changes in broadcast assignments and power, recommended by Mr. Lafount, was approved by the individual Commissioners." And on March 27, the minutes recorded that "on the recommendation of Judge Sykes the power of WBT at Charlotte, North Carolina, was increased from 750 watts to 1,000 watts, effective April 1."[95] Despite publicly justifying decisions based on engineering factors or through the use of the neutral language of engineering evaluation, archival records indicate that commissioners—following the example of the engineers—took into account a number of different factors, including the political lobbying of members of Congress. In April 1928, for example, Commissioner Pickard warned Commissioner Robinson against taking any action that would adversely affect the station WSBT, because it was "a 'Sacred Cow' of Senator Jim Watson's."[96]

This state of affairs, in which the commission made decisions based on a number of complex factors but then justified actions based on the neutral language of engineering evaluation, became unstable early in January 1929 when three stations—WLS, WENR, and WCBD—challenged the commission in the D.C. Court of Appeals. As the chief legal counsel, Louis Caldwell had to construct a legal defense that took into account the commission's true motivations. On January 10, Caldwell sent a letter to all the commissioners informing them of "the necessity of preparing a statement of facts and grounds upon which the Commission rests its decisions." The wording of the letter, which stated that "the following reasons for the decisions occur to me," clearly indicates that the commission was not doing a good job keeping accurate records and preparing for a legal defense of its decisions. Instead of simply referring to the commission record for each case, the general counsel had to develop justifications after the fact.[97]

The man who replaced Louis Caldwell as chief legal counsel during the summer of 1929, Bethuel M. Webster, was more vocal in his criticism of the commission. He complained in a December 1929 letter to Commissioner Sykes that the FRC had not been maintaining an acceptable record-keeping system and had been deciding cases based on engineering "facts or considerations" that "had not been introduced publicly" and had not been "made subject to cross-examination at the time of the hearing." "In a number of cases," according to Webster, "the Engineering Division's recommendations include conclusions and decisions from data before it which the Commission itself is bound, under the Act, to reach on its own account, without the assistance of its technical advisors." Webster informed Commissioner Sykes that "the law is perfectly clear that the Commission cannot, under any circumstances, delegate its authority to the Engineering Division."[98]

"Propaganda" Stations and the Public-Interest Standard

Louis Caldwell's defense, in January 1929, of the commission's decisions with respect to the three stations that appealed to the Court of Appeals demonstrates some of the basic principles driving the decision-making process, which had been at least partially obscured by the neutral language of engineering evaluation. Especially important among the reasons given by Caldwell for the commission's actions is one of the basic principles left out of the August 23 analysis of the public-interest standard—the prejudice against "propaganda" stations. In the case of WCBD, Caldwell emphasized that the commission ruled against the station because it did not give general service to the public but was mainly devoted to a "comparatively narrow purpose . . . namely, the furtherance of the interests of a particular religious creed." In a statement meant to codify the reasons for the commission's actions, Louis Caldwell argued that "if the question were entirely new, the Commission would be disposed to deny licenses to organizations for any such limited field of propaganda on the ground that it is impossible to provide stations for all their competitors." "The ideal system," according to the legal counsel, "is to have a station devoted to general public service, a part of which is religious and in which there is no discrimination for or against any particular creed."[99]

The commission more clearly articulated the prejudice against "propaganda" stations as a central principle during the remainder of 1929 as it responded to other legal appeals. The FRC argued that stations committed to a specific program format would effectively discriminate against listeners not interested in the subject. The commission stressed that it would give preferential treatment to "general public-interest stations" providing a "well-rounded program" that included "entertainment, consisting of music of both classical and lighter grades, religion, education and instruction, important public events, discussions of public questions, weather, market reports, and news, and matters of interest to all members of the family." Provided they were of "sufficient importance to the listening public," a free market of ideas and the principle of listener sovereignty would assure that "particular doctrines, creeds, and beliefs" would find a place on general-interest stations. Although the commission contended that it used the term "propaganda station" for "the sake of convenience and not in a derogatory sense," the effect on educational broadcasters was clear. Stations operated by educational institutions were lumped together with religious stations operated by extremists, who were the commission's real target.[100]

Unlike the commission's August 23 commentary on the public-interest standard, the commission's official justifications for its decisions during 1929 accepted advertising uncritically as an economic necessity. The commission tried to distinguish advertising from other forms of propaganda serving private interests; unlike propaganda, which the commission believed was often difficult to recognize, advertising would be obvious to the average listener. But this distinction between advertising and propaganda was also a matter of expediency. The commission in fact recognized advertising as a form of propaganda; it argued that "advertising must be accepted for the present as the sole means of support for broadcasting." Without advertising, "broadcasting would not exist."[101]

In response to legal challenges during 1929, the commission also developed a clearer policy regarding the issue of censorship. The general counsel, Bethuel Webster, echoed the earlier concerns of some of the commissioners who questioned whether it was possible to avoid censorship. "If the word 'censorship' is more broadly construed," according to Webster, "every action of the Commission with reference to broadcasting programs would involve a violation of the [1927 Radio] Act. . . . The right of freedom of speech and freedom from censorship are not absolute and unqualified." The general counsel argued that it was "permissible, without interfering with the right of free speech, to compare the programs of broadcasting stations in order to determine which are rendering the best service."[102] Robinson was the only commissioner who consistently expressed concern that the commission might not be dealing adequately with the section of the Radio Act forbidding censorship.[103] The commission's loose interpretation of the right of free speech with respect to radio was a crucial decision that legitimated its policy against "propaganda" or special-interest stations.

The importance of this evaluation of the censorship issue was also underscored by the critical comments of the former general counsel, Louis

Caldwell. In a reexamination of the work of the commission in 1935, Caldwell accused the commission of overstepping its legal authority by circumscribing freedom of speech. He did not think that a clear legal distinction could be maintained between freedom of the press for newspapers and freedom of expression for radio. According to Caldwell, the FRC used its legal right to interpret the public-interest standard as a "hostile inquisition" stifling controversy and open dialogue.[104]

Federal courts that evaluated challenges to commission authority overwhelmingly sided with the FRC. During the life of the radio commission, from 1927 to 1934, the federal courts ruled on forty-one major cases questioning the basic authority of the commission to regulate broadcasting. According to a study by Don R. Le Duc and Thomas A. McCain, "[T]hese judicial decisions were profoundly significant not only in determining the immediate regulatory role of the FRC, but also the scope and shape of future government-broadcaster control."[105] Of the forty-one cases, thirty-six affirmed the powers of the FRC; the five reversals were based on relatively insignificant factual or procedural matters.[106] Thus, on all major issues the courts ruled that the scarcity of frequencies available for broadcasting as well as the general notion of radio exceptionalism required giving broad discretionary authority to the radio commission. Most important, court decisions sanctioned the commission to take into account the content of broadcast programs when evaluating the contribution of stations to "public interest, convenience, or necessity." Specifically, in *General Electric v. FRC* (1929), *KFKB Broadcasting Association, Inc., v. FRC* (1931), and *Trinity Methodist Church, South, v. FRC* (1932), the federal courts ruled that the radio commission had broad authority to take into account a station's past conduct, including such issues as the making of defamatory and untrue statements and the use of a license for narrow private interests. Court decisions emphasized that the commission could take action against "propaganda" stations, including denying the renewal of a license, without infringing on First Amendment rights of free speech. And the courts did not place limits on the FRC's factual efforts to define "public convenience, interest, or necessity" and to force stations to adjust to this evaluation.[107]

Noncommercial Stations and FRC Policy, 1928–34

The FRC's policies and actions after the adoption of General Order 40 played a crucial role in the establishment of the dominant system of commercial broadcasting in the United States. Controversial stations operated by religious groups and labor organizations were especially vulnerable to FRC assignment policies. But stations operated by educational institutions were also hurt by the FRC tendency to view all noncommercial stations as controversial propaganda outlets operating outside of the ideal commercial model that sought to serve a maximum audience by providing general programming. Despite the idealistic views expressed earlier during the 1920s by Hoover and other government officials about the need to give special consideration to educational stations, insulating them from commercial pressures, the commission refused to distinguish between commercial and noncommercial stations. The commission continued to give less desirable assignments to educational stations and to require the sharing of time.

Two other policies that became especially important after the implementation of General Order 40 also hurt the status of stations operated by institutions of higher education. The first was the decision to allow stations requesting the use of a channel to force affected stations to participate in hearings in Washington. University stations with limited resources had to hire expensive lawyers to defend their use of the spectrum. The second policy forced all stations to conform to high technical standards, mainly to prevent interference. The FRC required all stations, including impoverished educational stations, to purchase new equipment.

The case of the University of Wisconsin station WHA illustrates the difficulties educational stations faced as a result of the commission's actions. Initially, WHA looked forward to receiving a favorable assignment in connection with General Order 40. Difficulties partly caused by previous decisions by the FRC had led the station to take the drastic decision to completely close down during the summer. After the commission announced in September 1928 the proposed frequency assignment for WHA in connection with General Order 40, the official at the university who supervised the operation of WHA, Earle Terry, commented that "the change assures us of a very good wave length." But within a week after this comment was published, three additional stations petitioned the commission for the use of this wavelength. Following its new policy of calling all parties affected by petitions to attend legal proceedings in Washington, the FRC scheduled a hearing for early November. Instead of sending someone to represent the station, the university submitted a long legal brief explaining why the university deserved special consideration. Perhaps not surprisingly, given this lack of representation at the hearing, the commission ruled in favor of the stations also requesting the channel assigned to WHA (570 kHz).[108]

WHA did not resume broadcasting after the summer break until the completion of negotiations on November 19 with the other stations assigned to 570 kHz. The resulting agreement allowed WHA to broadcast from 7:00

to 8:00 PM on Monday, Wednesday, and Friday and every day from noon to 12:45 PM. But almost immediately, WIBO in Chicago began to encroach on the evening time slot set aside for the university. By early January 1929, interference caused by the powerful transmissions of WIBO forced WHA to shift the evening programming to the noon broadcast. But apparently not satisfied with forcing WHA from the evening period, WIBO also began to encroach on the noon broadcast. Terry complained to the radio commission that officials at WIBO insisted that "all of the daytime hours belonged to them and refused to negotiate with us on any basis." They informed Terry that "all of their daytime from 9:00 AM to 1:00 PM is contracted with advertisers and that if they voluntarily give up any of this time, it will be a breach of their contracts with advertisers." The commission refused to become involved in the dispute. After requiring the stations to share a frequency, it did not feel it had any responsibility to oversee negotiations. By refusing to take action to protect the rights of an educational station, it provided de facto support for WIBO's argument that its commercial contracts trumped other considerations, including the public-service role of educational broadcasting and WIBO's violation of time-sharing agreements.[109]

Instead of finding a way to encourage WIBO and the other stations to set aside good time slots for WHA, the commission permitted the university to experiment temporarily with a new frequency, 940 kHz, but only for daytime broadcasting. After it became clear that transmissions on this channel were acceptable, Terry formally applied to the commission in April 1929 for permanent use of the new frequency. For the first time in a number of years, listeners reported satisfactory reception over a wide area. But the station had to abandon its claim of having a right to broadcast during the evening, despite continuing to believe that "the people we wish most to reach are listening at night."[110]

WILL at the University of Illinois also did not have a good experience with assignment decisions by the FRC. The station at first looked forward to the frequency assignment it would receive in connection with General Order 40. The dean believed that the assignment would free the station of "practically all the troublesome interference which made it impossible for the U. of I. programs to be heard at any considerable distance."[111] But according to the station director, after this initial assignment, the commission moved WILL to "two or three other frequencies in the course of eight or ten days."[112] The station finally ended up on 890 kHz, but could only use five hundred watts during the day and 250 watts at night to avoid interference with Canadian stations using the same frequency. Interference caused by powerful stations in Chicago broadcasting on nearby frequencies further reduced the limited coverage of the station. In October 1929, the station director complained that listeners as close as twenty-three miles to the south could not hear the station during the evening.[113] Bad experiences trying to obtain a better assignment led the station director to give up. He informed the president of the university in March 1931 that he had decided against formally applying to the commission for a different frequency and power assignment "because it seemed fool-hardy to make any such move when the possibility of having our request granted seemed so remote," and the costs could be considerable. He pointed out that they would need to pay "suitable legal talent in Washington" approximately one hundred dollars per day. They would also need to defray the expense of witnesses. Altogether, he estimated that a hearing with the commission could cost from two thousand to twenty-five hundred dollars.[114]

Another example of an educational station particularly hurt by assignment decisions of the FRC was the South Dakota State College station KFDY, located in Brookings. The commission ordered the station to shift frequencies a number of times during the late 1920s and early 1930s. University officials reported that "in general each [assignment] was less satisfactory than the preceding one." The university also complained that the commission forced KFDY to share time with commercial stations who "were given the preference in selection of time." For example, after ordering the university station to share a frequency with KMA in Shenandoah, Iowa, operated by the Earl May Nursery Company, the radio commission instructed the South Dakota station "to take what time the . . . station did not use." According to the official in charge of KFDY, "[A] vigorous protest on this order finally led to a compromise." But because of interference with other stations resulting partly from the assignment decisions of the FRC, KFDY could not provide good service to listeners in the state. The station was kept going "mainly in the hope that at some future time more favorable treatment of college stations could be secured."[115]

The other major educational station in South Dakota, KUSD at the University of South Dakota in Vermillion, had similar experiences with the radio commission. In 1930, the station director, B. B. Brackett, complained of a "very bad" assignment. He thought that the radio commission "did not have much idea" about what they were assigning. In Brackett's opinion, KUSD was a victim of the commission's overreliance on trial and error.[116]

But unlike KFDY, KUSD did not report problems sharing frequencies with other stations. Brackett believed that the station was "quite fortunate" with respect to the issue of time division. He did not think it possible to find individuals "more considerate and more friendly" than the people in charge of the two stations on KUSD's frequency—the University of Illinois station

WILL and KFNF, a station in Shenandoah, Iowa, operated by the Henry Field Seed and Nursery Company. The three stations reached an agreement giving WILL and KUSD half of the time each day and KFNF the other half. Brackett reported that KUSD had "never been refused time for special and unusual programs, no matter how badly it cut into the time ordinarily used by our associates." He believed that this arrangement, in which two university stations and a commercial station divided time, was ideal, "if those in charge of the commercial station are reasonable towards and considerate of the educational stations."[117]

Commission rules forcing stations to adopt rigorous technical standards caused major problems for nearly all educational stations, especially during the Depression, when state budgets faced drastic cuts. General Order 116 was a case in point. To meet the June 1932 deadline for compliance with this requirement that all stations maintain a transmission frequency within fifty cycles of its assignment, KOAC at Oregon State determined that it would need to spend thirty-nine hundred dollars for new equipment.[118] Bucknell University, a small private school in central Pennsylvania with limited financial resources, spent over three thousand dollars during 1931 to upgrade its transmitter to be in compliance with FRC rules.[119] In 1931, the University of Vermont station WCAX decided to give up its license rather than spend the necessary six to ten thousand dollars for new equipment. Since it admitted that it used "antiquated" apparatus and only broadcast one evening per week for an hour, the Vermont station was a good example of a marginal station the commission hoped to close down.[120]

The hardships resulting from FRC technical requirements were especially clear in the case of WPSC at Penn State University. Although General Order 40 reassigned WPSC to a new frequency, 1230 kHz, this decision did not represent the most important problem for the station. WPSC's main difficulties resulted from lack of additional funding for new improvements to conform to new regulations. The regular budget of the university only authorized a small expenditure for the operation of the station. The adoption in late October 1930 of a rule requiring improved transmission standards, General Order 97, came at a particularly "disadvantageous time" for WPSC. A member of a committee established to help obtain support for the station warned that there was "no opportunity to secure funds from the legislature with which to reconstruct the transmitter to accord with General Order No. 97 by June 1932, the date set by the Commission." When informed that it would cost between fifteen and twenty thousand dollars to purchase a new transmitter capable of maintaining the engineering standards demanded by the rule, the Executive Committee of the Board of Trustees of the university also declined to provide the necessary funds. Financial retrenchment was the order of the day. On June 21, 1932, the president of the university sent the FRC a telegram protesting "this demand upon [a] public educational institution at [a] time when public funds are seriously curtailed," but he also informed the commission that "in compliance with your telegram we have ceased our broadcast."[121]

Officials at Penn State rejected a suggestion that the station should adopt alternative arrangements cheaper than buying a new transmitter. The president did not think this was advisable mainly because of the likelihood of additional regulations requiring further modifications.[122] Other educational stations satisfied the various technical regulations partly by constructing their own equipment. KUSD, for example, reported in 1933 that it "never had a real appropriation for broadcast equipment." According to Brackett, they "built parts and assembled . . . transmitters piece by piece, paying only a little at a time from odds of general equipment and maintenance funds." Brackett was willing to accept difficult conditions because of the hope that the FRC would adopt policies more supportive of noncommercial stations sometime in the future. The shortage of channels available in the broadcast spectrum meant that once a university abandoned its license, it would likely never be able to regain access to radio broadcasting. According to Brackett, "[I]f we did not hope to get something better in the future, it would not pay for us to continue on the air."[123] He reported in May 1933 that "the idea of continuing the broadcasts" over KUSD was "thoroughly sold" to the president of the university, despite a 40 percent cut in the university budget. According to the station director, the president understood "fully that if we give up now there is practically no chance for us to get back on the air later."[124]

University Policies, Commercialism, and the Decline of University Stations

Although the policies of the radio commission go far to explain the difficult conditions faced by many radio stations at universities during the late 1920s and early 1930s, lack of administrative support also played a crucial role. For example, WHA's problems during the second half of the 1920s partly resulted from lack of support from the president of the university, Glenn Frank. Professor Terry reportedly felt "greatly discouraged" after conferences with Frank to discuss the station. On one occasion, he indicated to a colleague that "he wanted to discontinue the project because of this lack of support." Terry was particularly upset with Frank's decision not to allow him to travel to Washington in the fall of 1928 to defend the station against WIBO's petition to use the same frequency. During the crucial three-year period before the Depression, when the university was relatively well off financially and many commercial stations were investing hundreds of thousands of dollars annually, WHA's yearly operating budget was approximately forty-five hundred dollars.[125]

WHA survived and managed to expand during the 1930s for a number of reasons. Most important, station officials developed a close working relationship not only with many departments at the university but also with many state agencies. For example, in the fall of 1929, the Wisconsin Conservation Commission began a series of broadcasts dealing with wildlife in the state and the relevant rules and regulations for the use of public resources. Other agencies affiliated with the state that established regular programs over WHA included the Department of Public Instruction, the Board of Health, the Highway Commission, the Tax Commission, and the State Historical Society. This cooperation helped convince President Frank of the overall value of radio broadcasting at the university. He argued that "WHA is more than a university activity. It is a broadly conceived state function which touches and serves other agencies of the state." The annual appropriation for the station increased to over nine thousand dollars by the 1930–31 academic year.[126]

Despite the Depression, support for WHA continued during the next few years, again mainly because of increased ties to the state. Elected officials were more willing to support the station, especially after 1932, when a new studio was set up in the state capitol. Programs broadcast from the capitol included the inauguration of the governor and other state officials, the opening session of the legislature, a series of talks by legislators discussing their work, and a weekly program by the Women's Legislative Council. By the early 1930s, after an interlinked network was established between WHA and WLBL—the station further north in Wisconsin operated by the State Department of Agriculture and Markets—90 percent of the population of the state could tune into these and other programs.[127] At least two state agencies that used WHA, the State Highway Commission and the State Board of Health, contributed funds directly to the station during early 1932. Based on the recommendation of Governor La Follette, who also valued WHA's public-service role, the State Emergency Board allocated nearly thirteen thousand dollars to the station in July. The new governor elected later that year instructed the Emergency Board to appropriate the same amount for the 1933–34 fiscal year.[128] By 1933, public documents described WHA as a state-owned and -financed institution, supervised by a state radio committee "consisting of representatives of the various state agencies and colleges of the state university."[129]

The close connection to the state government also helps explain why the Oregon State University station KOAC not only survived during the late

1920s and early 1930s but also began to flourish. The station faced severe financial problems in 1931, especially after the radio commission adopted a new rule requiring stations such as KOAC that held a full-time operating license to broadcast at least twelve hours every day. When the radio commission refused to grant KOAC an exemption from this rule, the State Board of Higher Education authorized the station to examine the possibility of commercialization. But it also requested an analysis of the station's value. In the spring of 1932, the KOAC staff responded by asking the audience to send letters to the station with their evaluations. In a two-day period, nearly three thousand listeners mailed in responses. Only six people thought the station should be discontinued; the rest believed that it deserved continued support. The president of Oregon State University, William Jasper Kerr, presented all the listeners' letters to the next meeting of the Board of Higher Education. His dramatic presentation confirming the value of the station to the state convinced the board to maintain the noncommercial status by funding an operating budget for the following year of thirty-six hundred dollars.

State legislators were also convinced to transform KOAC into a station serving all state agencies, not just the state university in Corvallis. The major event that paved the way for KOAC to become the "State Station" was its transfer to the newly created Oregon State System of Higher Education in 1932. KOAC was no longer expected to only serve Oregon State University; now it also needed to support the public-service activities of the other state colleges and universities, especially the University of Oregon in Eugene. Although full integration with the other campuses and state agencies did not occur until after 1939, this initial decision to recognize the "all-state" status of KOAC was crucial for ensuring continued funding as a nonprofit institution.[130]

Kerr's support again underscores the important role of university administrations in the development of radio stations at universities. Another university president that played an important role in the establishment of a station at his campus, Herman James at the University of South Dakota, explicitly articulated a view of broadcasting that was opposed to the emerging dominant commercial model. James rejected the commercial argument that broadcasters needed to make programming decisions to maximize their audience: "[T]he question of how many people listen in is not involved in the question of the value of the program, for a worthless program listened to by one hundred million people would be improperly taking wave lengths from a useful educational program or series of programs listened to by a few thousand people." James called for the establishment of an alternative view of broadcasting modeled on public education: "It is no more an argument against educational programs to say that few people listen to them, . . . than it would be to say that because only one million students are in colleges and universities out of a potential ten million therefore colleges and universities should be discontinued." He believed that educators should refuse to admit that the "relatively insignificant number of people" who listen to programs produced by university radio stations "is any test of the time or wave lengths that should be assigned to education."[131]

President Farrell at Kansas State University was similarly convinced of the importance of educational radio. Significantly, he had at first been skeptical. Farrell initially opposed spending twenty thousand dollars to establish his university's station because he "doubted whether educational material could be effectively broadcast throughout a long series of years." The station's accomplishments, however, changed his mind. "At virtually every place I visit," Farrell wrote to the president of another university in 1928, "and frequently at places in adjoining states, I am assured of the value of our station by farmers, farmers' wives, and townspeople who voluntarily express appreciation." Based on the record of KSAC, he "was inclined to think that there is an excellent future for educational broadcasting so long as it is carried on by unbiased, disinterested agencies similar to the land grant colleges, and so long as it is kept definitely upon a high plane."[132] Farrell argued that the station was "one of the best investments we have made" because it "greatly increased" the number of people in touch with the university and maximized the ability of the university "to disseminate a very large quantity of information on agriculture, the industries, the home, and on general topics."[133]

KSAC's close connection with agricultural extension at the university underscores another important theme that helps explain why some schools were more successful than others with radio. Extension services tended to be the strongest supporters of radio stations at land-grant universities because they recognized their potential value for communicating the results of university research directly to isolated farmers. The station at Iowa State University, WOI, also flourished during the late 1920s and most of the 1930s because of the close connection to agricultural extension. In 1927–28, agricultural extension accounted for over six thousand dollars of the total annual budget of about fourteen thousand dollars. By 1939–40, agricultural extension was providing the station nearly twenty thousand dollars out of a total annual budget of approximately twenty-six thousand dollars.[134]

Stations at state universities that did not support agricultural research and did not develop close connections to state governments managed to survive often by successfully involving the entire campus in broadcasting. WSUI at the State University of Iowa installed a system of lead-sheathed cables across the entire campus linking the radio station with all the major buildings.

Engineer L. L. Lewis standing near the WOI transmitter and senior operator John
Miller, seated at control panel, Iowa State College of Agriculture, 1939. Courtesy of
the University Archives, Iowa State University Library.

By 1931, the station was capable of broadcasting any university event from
anywhere on campus. During that same year, over twenty departments at
the university participated in WSUI radio programs.[135]

Although some stations at universities unable to adjust to FRC rules because of budget cuts during the Depression simply folded, some decided to
sell or lease to commercial interests. Noncommercial station owners were
under constant pressure to adapt to the emerging dominant model. In 1932,
T. M. Beaird, the director of the radio station at the University of Oklahoma,
complained about how "commercial interests" were "gaining headway every
day" partly by enticing noncommercial station owners with generous offers.
"Is it not true," Beaird asked, "that some of our own men are beginning to sell
the foundation stones upon which the structure of educational broadcasting is
established by 'binkering' with commercial interests when they have lovely and
rosy pictures painted by these interests trying to entice them to 'sell time.'"[136]

Stations in states with strong traditions of supporting the noncommercial status of public universities, especially in the Midwest, were in the best position to resist commercial pressures.[137] Iowa State Agricultural College had a number of offers during the late 1920s to accept advertising over WOI; however, the State Board of Education in Iowa repeatedly reaffirmed the policy that a public institution receiving state and federal funds should not accept commercial advertising.[138]

State governments in the southern United States generally were more willing to allow radio stations at state universities to adopt commercial practices. For example, there is no evidence that anyone in Arkansas raised objections to the decision by KUOA at the University of Arkansas to accept advertising after the state eliminated funding in 1931. But the decision to commercialize also did not help the station gain a useable frequency. The program director complained in February 1932 that "the Federal Radio Commission has come along and has taken away all of the hours that are worth anything and has left us with hours that are absolutely no good either for commercial programs or for educational programs."[139] Facing nearly impossible conditions, the university first leased the station to a hotel in May 1932 and then sold it to a private broadcasting company. University officials were particularly upset because after they sold the station, the radio commission decided to assign KUOA to full daytime operations on a desirable frequency.[140]

The State of Alabama also did not oppose the decision to allow WAPI, originally connected to Alabama Polytechnic Institute (Auburn University), to commercialize. The station moved from Auburn to Birmingham late in 1928 to become a cooperative venture among the major Alabama state universities. The station had always placed a strong emphasis on broadcasting entertainment in addition to programs developed by the extension service at Auburn. As early as 1928, the station director in Auburn inquired about gaining an affiliation with the NBC network so it could broadcast professional-quality entertainment. NBC officials rejected the application, arguing that "there weren't enough people in southeast Alabama to make expensive line rental practical."[141] But after the station was moved to the larger market in the middle of the state, the network accepted WAPI's offer of affiliation.[142]

In April 1930, in response to increasingly severe restrictions on public funding during the Depression, WAPI also agreed to accept local commercial advertising.[143] No evidence exists indicating that state or university officials raised questions about the propriety of a public institution relying on commercial advertising. When the issue of local advertising was first proposed to the Board of Control of the station in 1929, the only concern addressed was the effect on program standards. The station director argued that "local commercial programs can be broadcast without lowering the standard of the station." He reassured board members that standards "would be raised because no concern can afford to pay $200 an hour for time . . . without getting the very best talent available."[144]

* * *

The above examples demonstrate the importance of local support for the growth and development of radio stations at state universities. Support from faculty and especially university administrations was in many cases crucial for station survival. WHA at the University of Wisconsin and KOAC at Oregon State provided an important new model for university broadcasting based not only on academic traditions of extension education but also on state traditions of public service. Although the impact of local structural forces in the development of university stations can not be underestimated, decisions by the FRC were, in a general sense, more significant. Support from university administrations and state governments might have been more forthcoming, even during the Depression, if federal regulators had taken actions to protect and nurture educational stations.

The FRC played a crucial role in the establishment of the system of network-controlled, commercial broadcasting in the United States. Although many observers during the early and mid-1920s disapproved of the use of advertising by radio stations, key members of the commission accepted advertising as the only practical method for funding radio broadcasting. The commission did continue on occasion to speak out against the excessive use of direct advertising, but other issues became more important in the effort to reduce interference between stations through the construction of a rational frequency-assignment system. Especially important was the decision to give preferential treatment to stations serving a general audience. "Propaganda" stations that seemed to serve specialized audiences were singled out for harsh treatment. In practice, this meant that the commission gave preferential treatment to high-power commercial stations and stations connected to one of the two commercial networks, NBC and CBS. Stations operated by institutions of higher education were grouped with religious broadcasters and other special-interest "propaganda" stations. The best frequency assignments went to "general purpose" commercial broadcasters. The commission gave university stations serving local regions poorer frequency assignments. The neutral language of technical evaluation and the involvement of engineers helped give legitimacy to decisions that involved complex social, political, and economic issues. The commission's decision to allow stations to compete for the use of frequencies was also particularly difficult for university stations and other local broadcasters that did not have the financial resources to support the legal costs required to defend the use of frequencies in hearings in Washington, D.C.

The radio commission could have pointed to earlier traditions to justify giving university stations and other noncommercial broadcasters preferential treatment. Supporters pointed to the clear evidence from Hoover's radio conferences and the debates in Congress leading up to the passage of the 1927 Radio Act of a consensus view that favored the work of pioneer noncommercial broadcasters. Commissioners could have interpreted the criteria of "public interest, convenience, and necessity" in a way that would favor the work of noncommercial university stations. They chose not to follow this path, and the courts generally supported the commission's policies; however, the earlier traditions were not forgotten. At the same time as the FRC was helping to consolidate network-controlled commercial broadcasting, counterforces were beginning to gather momentum.

5. Education and the Fight to Reform Radio Broadcasting, 1930–36

In 1932, Walter Woehlke, a journalist concerned about developments in radio broadcasting, wrote that his "contacts with the general public" had led him to conclude that "dissatisfaction with the present broadcasting system is well nigh universal." Based on personal experiences, he believed that "out of one hundred persons you will not find more than five who are satisfied; of the other 95 percent, more than one-half are ready to support any kind of movement for a drastic change."[1] This statement undoubtedly exaggerated public opinion; however, it does indicate that during the same period as the FRC was supporting the consolidation of commercial, network broadcasting, a substantial number of listeners were not happy with the trend. We do not have reliable empirical data to evaluate public opinion during this period, but as Robert McChesney has pointed out, "[I]t does appear . . . that, at the very least, the response to commercial broadcasting in these years was far more negative than it would be thereafter." Congress and the FRC received numerous letters from members of the public protesting the excesses of commercial advertising. *Business Week* reported in 1932 that broadcasting was "threatened with a revolt of listeners. . . . Newspaper radio editors report more and more letters of protest against irritating sales ballyhoo."[2] Even FRC commissioners warned the industry that if it did not clean up its act, the public would begin to call for drastic reform, including the "demand that the government take over the radio and operate it, as England does, as a government monopoly."[3]

These complaints about advertising reflected new developments in commercial broadcasting. Advertising became more pervasive in the late 1920s and early 1930s as commercial stations, feeling the economic bight of the Depression, relaxed earlier self-imposed restrictions. The average number of commercial hours per week on CBS and NBC increased from fourteen in 1927 to thirty-five in 1930. The amount of money spent by advertisers on radio similarly rose from 3.8 million dollars in 1927 to 26.8 million dollars in 1930.[4] Direct, more intrusive advertisements, which increasingly mentioned prices, became more pervasive.[5] Advertising agencies also increasingly began to play a more important role in the production of specific programs.[6]

Worries about the monopoly power of RCA and NBC also threatened to turn public opinion against the commercial radio industry. A number of attempts were made during the 1920s to convince Congress and the Federal Trade Commission to take strong action against the "radio trust." Although these attempts were unsuccessful, they did play a role in the decision of the Hoover administration, in 1930, to investigate RCA for violations of antitrust legislation.[7]

Public opposition to the policies of the FRC was stimulated especially by the actions of one of its members, Commissioner Ira E. Robinson. Robinson opposed the system of reallocation known as General Order 40 when it was formulated in 1928. He made high-profile public statements arguing that the reallocation unfairly supported the large commercial stations and networks at the expense of small stations, especially the pioneer stations operated by institutions of higher education. He called himself "an advocate of educational broadcasting."[8] Because he was an important public figure and because he actively added his voice to public calls for change, Robinson's support for the cause of educational broadcasting played an important role in stimulating a climate for reform during the late 1920s.

Despite the many critical voices beginning to call for change during the 1920s, attempts to create a unified movement did not occur until the end of the decade. Before this time, groups and individuals upset with the state of broadcasting in the country mainly focused on their own individual concerns. The best organized group opposed to commercialization and the policies of the FRC was the Association of College and University Broadcasting Stations (ACUBS). Although the stations connected with this group initially modeled educational broadcasting on formal classroom instruction, they became interested in a broader understanding of educational broadcasting involving a generalized commitment to the promotion of noncommercial public-interest content. Education was viewed not only as formal instruction but also informal socialization or "development and adjustment."[9]

Reformers were concerned about the impact of radio on the public. They worried that broadcasting was becoming one of the most important factors

WHO SAYS THEY NEVER COME BACK?

The reaction against the excesses of advertising that motivated broadcast reformers during the early 1930s is depicted in this 1931 cartoon. Radio advertisers are compared to old-time snake-oil salesmen. *Washington Post,* April 17, 1931.

shaping children and adults. Its influence appeared to threaten to neutralize the role of traditional institutions, including the school, the home, religious organizations, civic groups, and political institutions. Since radio programs were shaped by the dominant force of advertising, reformers focused especially on the possible dangers of commercialization and monopoly control by commercial forces.

Organizing the Reform Effort: The Wilbur Committee and the Payne Fund

The federal government played a crucial role in organizing various groups and individuals interested in reforming radio in the spring of 1929. Ray Ly-man Wilbur, President Hoover's secretary of the interior who was also in charge of federal education policy, took a personal interest in educational radio broadcasting by formally calling for a special meeting of radio experts to discuss the problem. Wilbur was familiar with the difficulties faced by institutions of higher education trying to maintain radio stations. He came to Washington after serving as the president of Stanford University, which had to discontinue its radio station because of insufficient funds.[10]

Wilbur's views about radio became clear during meetings of a group called the Advisory Committee on Education by Radio (commonly referred to as the "Wilbur Committee"). He emphasized that broadcasting held great potential for adult education and formal education for children in schools. He also believed that radio had great potential because of its ability to bring state and local government officials "into immediate contact with the schoolroom." But more importantly, Wilbur praised radio's potential to uplift audiences by stimulating interest in continuing education. He wanted to use radio to "get at that great mass of people who are more or less dulled to the things that are going on around them." The radio might "get into that domain somewhat and get the natural curiosity of everybody aroused to new things."[11] The commissioner of education under Wilbur, another Californian named William John Cooper, shared an interest in using radio to support education. As the commissioner of education for California before he came to Washington, he used his department to support the development of a special series of radio programs for schools, the *Standard School Broadcast,* transmitted over the Pacific Coast network of NBC and sponsored by the Standard Oil Company of California.[12]

The main organization that lobbied Wilbur to establish a formal committee in the spring of 1929 was the National Education Association (NEA). The NEA, in turn, acted in response to pressure from a private philanthropic foundation, the Payne Fund, an organization based in Cleveland that would play a major role in efforts to reform radio during the 1930s. Frances Payne Bolton formally established the fund in 1927 to support efforts to build up civil society through education and social reform. Bolton inherited money from her grandfather, who made a fortune through investment with Standard Oil. Unlike other major foundations that were established with large initial endowments, such as the Carnegie Corporation and the Rockefeller Foundation, for specific projects the Payne Fund relied on direct donations from Frances Payne Bolton and two other members of her family, her sister, Elizabeth Blossom, and her brother, William Bingham II. The Payne Fund primarily saw its role as providing seed money for worthwhile projects that, once launched, would be able to obtain further support from other sources, including other philanthropies. The fund lacked an endowment because Bolton established a temporary organization.[13]

The Bolton family was committed to the reform or progressive activities of the Republican party. Frances Payne Bolton's grandfather, Henry B. Payne, represented Ohio in the U.S. Senate. Her husband served as a Republican member of the House of Representatives from Cleveland until his death in 1939. After Frances Bolton was elected to replace her husband, she served in his seat for the next twenty-nine years. Because of the political activities of the family, Frances and her siblings tried to keep work with the fund from public view. Individuals and organizations receiving money donated by Bolton and her sister and brother were told that it came from anonymous benefactors.[14]

Initially, the Payne Fund's radio activities focused on the use of radio for schools. Armstrong Perry, a freelance journalist who had served as an executive with the Boy Scouts of America, would play a central role in the radio work of the foundation. His interest in using radio for education was long-standing. In 1922 he testified for the Boy Scouts at the First National Radio Conference, advocating the establishment of a series of government-sponsored radio stations. His earliest work supported by the Payne Fund was a study for the NEA examining the potential use of radio in the schoolroom. Perry's major conclusion was to favor the creation of a national school of the air. The initial work he conducted during 1928 and 1929 focused on this objective.[15]

The school broadcasts on the West Coast sponsored by the Standard Oil Company underscored an important tension structuring events analyzed in this chapter. Although all reformers interested in supporting a public-service or educational ideal for radio broadcasting criticized the growing tendency for radio in the United States to rely on advertising and entertainment programs, they disagreed about the proper relationship between educational institutions and the commercial networks. Initially, officials with the Payne Fund and the Wilbur Committee were willing to at least consider working with the commercial networks and advertising companies. Perry believed Cooper's earlier involvement with the Standard Oil Company provided an important precedent justifying his decision to consider obtaining assistance from "commercial sources" for his investigation in the field of radio education.[16] But this decision was not adopted lightly. Perry told an educator in Ohio, in August 1929, that he "felt the same reluctance about seeking help from the industry that educators do."[17] Despite agreeing to investigate commercial funding sources, he took a strong stand in favor of adopting policies that would prevent commercial forces from influencing educational content. Perry's 1928 survey for the NEA concluded that radio-education programs broadcast over commercial networks had to be "prepared by educators" and "unhampered by the necessity of carrying propaganda for any commercial" organization.[18]

The Wilbur Committee initially tried to include a range of views about the relationship between education and radio broadcasting. A fact-finding sub-committee established to survey research on radio education and to propose specific actions included commercial network executives as well as educators like Perry. Perry wrote a separate report based on his own independent investigation of radio activities across the country.[19]

Levering Tyson and the Carnegie Corporation

Initially independent of the Wilbur Committee and the Payne Fund, the Carnegie Corporation also began to take an interest in the use of radio broadcasting for education, especially adult education. This interest dated from 1926, when the philanthropic foundation established by Andrew Carnegie organized the American Association for Adult Education and included radio broadcasting as one area for further investigation. The corporation received advice about radio and adult education from a faculty member at Columbia University in charge of the Home Study Department, Levering Tyson. Tyson became one of the key participants in the efforts beginning in the late 1920s to reform radio broadcasting. To understand the significance of this involvement, it is important to first discuss his early experiences with radio at Columbia University.

Tyson became fascinated with radio and recognized its possibilities for university extension after hearing the early broadcasts by KDKA, including the 1920 election returns. Tyson later recalled that he "hot-footed it to Pittsburgh, because the job I held at Columbia was of a character which indicated the potential usefulness to the University of a mechanism that would enable an educator to get the ear of a large and widely dispersed audience." He could not, at first, convince the Columbia faculty to participate in experiments with the new technology.[20] This changed when some of the early radio stations serving New York City invited faculty to participate in broadcasts. But Tyson and other educators at the university were hesitant to agree to these early experiments. According to Tyson, the "industry was conducting its activities in such an extremely superficial way from the educational point of view that we did not want to lend our name to anything done at that time."[21] The university adopted a new policy in 1923, when an invitation came from AT&T's new station, WEAF.[22] Tyson convinced the university to treat this offer differently because AT&T was willing to give educators control over experiments with educational programming.[23] Tyson also likely treated the company differently because of the influence of one of his "very good friends" on campus, Michael Pupin, a professor of electrical engineering at the university who had worked with AT&T for many years and supported Tyson's efforts to experiment with the use of radio for university extension.[24]

Tyson initially judged the experiment with WEAF a success. The university first broadcast three fifteen-minute talks on English literature followed by a regular course on the poetry of Robert Browning. According to Tyson, "[T]he course was well received, commented upon very widely all across the country, and neither the broadcasting company nor ourselves needed any further demonstration." During the next two years, the university successfully broadcast a number of other courses covering academic subjects.[25] In 1925 Tyson argued that "without doubt there is a considerable and constantly increasing group of people who are now willing to listen to lectures by radio on topics of serious educational interest." He believed that evenings were the most important time for broadcasting university programs. But Tyson also recognized in 1925 that "the relatively small public now ready to listen-in are so greatly outnumbered by the so-called radio fans that the broadcasting stations must continue to cater to the demands of the very heavy majority."[26]

By the mid-1920s, major broadcasters were under increasing pressure to find sources of support; they were no longer willing to experiment with programs that did not appeal to large audiences. Broadcasting became a commercial business selling listeners to advertisers, especially after the establishment in 1926 of the National Broadcasting Company by RCA. WEAF was purchased from AT&T to serve as a central hub for the new commercial network. Unlike AT&T, which was willing to allow Tyson to experiment with university programs (even as the company pioneered radio advertising), NBC was more interested in maximizing an audience to sell to advertisers during the potentially lucrative evening hours. The network thus took away the evening hours it had been offering the university. Within a year the university abandoned broadcasting.[27]

Columbia's experience with commercial stations was a familiar pattern repeated across the country. While other educators became embittered and blamed the loss of access to the airwaves on unregulated commercial forces, Tyson's response was notably different. He accepted the decision by NBC as simply a good business practice: "This was extremely valuable time and the audience attracted to educational programs were small compared to those who already were listening to the elaborate (even for that time) entertainment the commercial programs provided."[28] But Tyson remained intensely interested in the public-service possibilities of radio broadcasting, especially the relationship between radio and education. At some point during the late 1920s, he became convinced that educators interested in using radio to serve the public needed to create new forms of programming adapted to the practices of commercial networks. Tyson argued that educators needed to develop "a technique of presentation that will admit of an educational program being listened to."[29]

Despite this position, it is important to point out that Tyson initially agreed with other educators involved in broadcasting, who argued that the government needed to protect stations committed to educational broadcasting. In 1925, he called on the federal government to "assign a separate wavelength for broadcasting of educational subjects by all stations."[30] By 1930 he had abandoned this position. His new view required not only cooperation with commercial stations but also an active search for new sources of funding for innovative radio programs. Tyson sought to reform broadcasting, arguing that the country needed to decide "whether broadcasting is to be a powerful social instrumentality or merely a device for amassing commercial profit."[31] But Tyson decided that the system needed to be reformed from within, with the assistance of major philanthropic foundations such as the Carnegie Corporation, which had "sufficient authority to force" the commercial networks "into the educational field."[32]

Personal ties between Tyson and individuals connected with the Carnegie Corporation, especially the president, Frederick P. Keppel, explain why the foundation asked Tyson to serve as an advisor on radio and adult education. Keppel had been the dean at Columbia when Tyson was a student. Tyson, who referred to the Carnegie president as "Dean" in correspondence, initially advised Keppel to wait until after Congress passed the 1927 Radio Act before deciding about how to integrate radio into the activities of the American Association for Adult Education. The foundation formally secured Tyson's services in 1928. Keppel arranged to have Columbia give Tyson a leave of absence to conduct preliminary research funded not only by the Carnegie Corporation but also by an individual grant directly from the philanthropist John D. Rockefeller Jr.[33]

Tyson's views about the importance of working with commercial broadcasters partly reflected the influence of Keppel and other officials with the Carnegie Foundation. The organization specifically directed the American Association for Adult Education to work with commercial broadcasters.[34] Members of the foundation sought to reform the free enterprise system rather than to replace it with radical alternatives. Henry Suzzalo, the president of a related Carnegie-funded organization, the Carnegie Foundation for the Advancement of Teaching, wrote Keppel in 1931 that he wanted "to see radio under private operation succeed in this country" through support of high-quality public-service programs, "because such a success would remove one of the chief arguments for public ownership of the radio system now being urged by the radical politicians."[35] Although the committee organized by Secretary of the Interior Wilbur in the spring of 1929 did not initially include Tyson or officials from the Carnegie Corporation, an early meeting did decide to "ascertain what plans" the Carnegie people have "in mind for surveying part of the field in an effort to establish cooperative relations."[36] The Wilbur Committee not only kept track of the activities of Tyson's work with the Carnegie Corporation to avoid duplication but also accepted Carnegie funds to keep the committee operating.[37]

Armstrong Perry and the National Committee for Educational Radio

Despite the involvement of different groups in the work of the Wilbur Committee, the meetings and investigations conducted during 1929 and 1930 did not lead to a unified position. Two opposing camps holding divergent understandings of the relationship between education and commercial broadcasting developed and became polarized. One camp was led especially by Perry and became identified with the Payne Fund. Individuals connected with this group established the National Committee on Education by Radio (NCER). Using grants from the Payne Fund, the NCER focused especially on supporting independent noncommercial radio stations, especially those located at colleges and universities. The other camp was led by Tyson and became closely identified with the Carnegie Corporation. Grants from this organization helped Tyson establish a rival group, the National Advisory Council for Radio in Education (NACRE). Unlike the NCER, Tyson's organization sought to cooperate with the commercial networks by producing educational or public-service programming acceptable to broadcasters and educators.

During the spring of 1929, Tyson initially believed that his education group, rather than Perry's, would play the most important role in the Office of Education's effort to reform broadcasting. The fact-finding subcommittee appointed by Cooper included the presidents of the two networks, William S. Paley of CBS and Merlin H. Aylesworth of NBC. Perry decided to conduct his own research and submit a separate report partly because Cooper failed to appoint educators in charge of university and college radio stations.[38]

But largely because of Perry's efforts during the next twelve months, the educational reformers funded by the Payne Fund gained the support of the Office of Education. Equally important was the change Perry underwent while conducting research for the fact-finding committee during the second half of 1929. While visiting land-grant schools in the Midwest he learned,

apparently for the first time, about the unique problems of university stations trying to use radio to extend the educational benefits of institutions of
higher education.[39] Educators told Perry about the need to set aside separate
wavelengths for noncommercial stations to prevent their demise. He was
shocked to learn about recent decisions by the FRC, especially the requirement that stations needed to be prepared to defend licenses at expensive
hearings in Washington. College officials also convinced Perry that commercial broadcasters could not be trusted to maintain support for high-quality
public-service programs. Perry's visits thus resulted in an alliance with the
university broadcasters. He successfully managed to convince the Payne
Fund and the Office of Education that the most pressing need was not to
work with commercial broadcasters, which seemed a doomed strategy, but
to work to support the preservation and growth of noncommercial university
stations. He was convinced that educators had to have control over radio to
maintain standards. This would only be possible if stations were controlled
by educators and committed to noncommercial goals.[40]

Cooper appointed Perry to head a new radio section of the Office of Education in April 1930. The Payne Fund lent the services of Perry on a part-time
basis to the Office of Education when it became clear that the office would not
receive funds from Congress until later in the year.[41] Perry used his position
to convince Cooper to support reforms more radical than those advocated
by Tyson and the Carnegie Corporation. He convinced Cooper to call a new
conference of educators in October 1930 to discuss the radio situation. Unlike
the conferences supporting the Wilbur Committee, the new conference was
not interested in discussing how to work with commercial broadcasters.[42] As
the conference secretary, Perry decided whom to invite. He made sure that
educators representing university and college radio stations upset with the
status quo dominated the meeting.[43] Prior to the meeting, Cooper directed
Perry to meet with members of the ACUBS to secure the "active leadership
of that group."[44]

The October conference authorized by Cooper passed two major resolu-
tions. The first called for the passage of legislation in Congress setting aside
15 percent of broadcast channels for educational and nonprofit organizations.
The second resolution called on Cooper to establish a new committee composed of educational organizations that would work to "protect and promote"
educational radio.[45] Following the meeting, Cooper organized the NCER,
appointing Joy Elmer Morgan, editor of the *Journal of the National Education
Association,* as the chairman. In January 1931, the Payne Fund accepted the
committee's request for a five-year, two-hundred-thousand-dollar grant.[46]

The NCER represented nine educational groups, including the NEA and the ACUBS as well as the Jesuit Education Association, the National Catholic Education Association, and the National Council of State Superintendents.[47] Support from the ACUBS was especially important because the members of that organization could potentially mobilize support in Congress. Perry and the NCER sought to argue in favor of establishing "rights of states and education in radio." Since many of the radio stations at institutions of higher education were pioneer stations, they could make an especially strong case for special treatment based on "established vested rights in the air."[48]

Perry had received assurances from the Payne Fund before the October meeting that funding would be available for the new organization. Prior to the meeting, Perry agreed that the NCER should include "go-getters, fighters, people who were sore out of their own experiences."[49] Importantly, the members of the fund had agreed that Perry could use the new organization to spearhead a political lobbying campaign seeking to convince Congress to set aside frequencies for noncommercial and educational stations.[50] "The acquiring by Congressional act of the reservation of any number of channels for education or other non-commercial purposes," Perry informed the Payne Fund in July 1930, "will be a direct blow against the monopolistic intentions and efforts of commercial broadcasters and other vast industrial combinations."[51]

Lobbying Congress for Broadcast Reform

The ACUBS had been actively lobbying Congress to adopt a policy in favor of special frequencies for educational stations during the 1920s.[52] Perry likely first heard about the idea from members of this organization. The effort was given new life early in 1929 by the only radio station in the country owned and operated by a labor union, the Chicago station WCFL. The Chicago Federation of Labor established the noncommercial station in 1926 not only to serve members of the union but also to educate all citizens about the needs of labor. Like the stations operated by universities, WCFL was hurt by the decisions of the FRC. The station owners decided to mobilize labor organizations to lobby Congress to conduct an investigation of the commission after failing to receive permission to use a fifty-thousand-watt clear channel.[53]

The labor activists supporting WCFL convinced a Republican member of the Senate from Illinois, Otis Glenn, to propose a bill reserving separate clear channels for the use of the Departments of Labor, Agriculture, and the Interior (specifically the Office of Education). The departments could then allow nonprofit groups representing the interests of labor, agriculture, and education to use the clear channels with their own high-power stations.[54] Perry first found out about this proposal in April 1930 when he visited Congress as part of his work with the Office of Education. The resolution did not receive widespread support in Congress partly because the organizations representing the interests of labor, agriculture, and education were not working together to create a united front. One major problem was that the USDA did not support the proposal, largely, as Perry pointed out, because "of fear of alienating commercial stations, which are carrying loads of agricultural programs." The labor interests also had not mobilized the support of educational organizations. Perry complained to a staff member at the Payne Fund on April 15 that because "education has not raised its voice . . . nobody [knew] what was wanted. The educators themselves don't know."[55]

Although Bolton, representing the Payne Fund, supported the lobbying campaign planned by Perry and the NCER, a staff member at the fund did express concern that the group not challenge commercial interests directly. Specifically, the secretary of the Payne Fund, Ella Phillips Crandall, advised Perry against attacking the commercial networks' monopoly control. She told Perry not to "enter into combat with the powerful radio chains and accept the inevitable implications of rash stupidity at best and open opposition at worst to the commercial interests."[56]

Crandall represented Bolton's interests. Bolton played a direct role in the work of the fund, serving as president after 1931 when the first president, H. M. Clymer, had to resign because of deteriorating health. Bolton also took a direct interest in the organizations receiving support from the fund, including the NCER. Perry met with Crandall regularly to keep her informed about the fund's activities. He also met with Bolton directly, including at her home in Cleveland. Bolton recommended specific activities for the NCER.[57] Perry, in turn, made sure that Bolton knew of major decisions involving the work of the committee. Bolton told one of the leaders of the NCER that the Payne Fund "was not like other groups. . . . We are keenly interested in every possible angle of the activities which we sponsor and we like to be known for our ideas as well as our money."[58]

But Bolton and the staff at the Payne Fund were also concerned that these contacts not become common knowledge. Besides worrying about jeopardizing her husband's political career, Bolton was aware that the professional educational groups belonging to the NCER "would peculiarly resent what they might consider interference from the Fund." Perry and Crandall decided that any move on the part of the Payne Fund to influence the NCER should "necessarily be carried out with great delicacy."[59]

The NACRE versus the NCER

During the same period when Perry and the Payne Fund were organizing the NCER, Levering Tyson was working to establish the NACRE.[60] Tyson initially did not realize that Secretary of Education Cooper had appointed Perry to head the radio office. He wrote in July 1930 that he "didn't give very much thought to his [Perry's] presence in the picture until I met him in Washington [in February] and found that Dr. Cooper had appointed him radio education specialist."[61] Tyson recalled that "during the latter part of the spring I was struck by the fact that he seemed obsessed with the idea that the one way to solve the problems of educational broadcasting is to get some wave length definitely assigned to education."[62] During the October conference in Chicago, Tyson failed in an attempt to have the NACRE designated as the main organization to oversee the reform of radio. The conference also voted to require Cooper to act without consulting Tyson and his group.[63]

After the October conference, when he realized Cooper was supporting Perry and the "15 percent crowd," Tyson became deeply embittered.[64] He complained that Perry and the other educators "thumbed their noses at the Council."[65] He also felt that Cooper had stabbed him in the back. Nearly two years after the October 1930 Chicago conference, Tyson was still furious with Cooper, Wilbur, Perry, and supporters of the NCER. He refused to "compromise with that bunch," blaming them "for the feeling which has grown . . . that we [the members of the NACRE] are a smoke screen blown up by industry to aid monopolistic tendencies."[66]

This dispute also reflected fundamental social and geographical differences between the two groups. The NCER represented local, midwestern reform traditions. The Payne Fund was based in Ohio, and the ACUBS was dominated by midwestern universities. The NACRE and the Carnegie Institution, along with the two commercial networks, were based in New York City. The cultural and social dimensions of this distinction is clear in a 1927 letter to a New York resident from the head of the radio station at Nebraska Wesleyan University, J. C. Jensen. "In common with a number of other gentlemen from the great metropolis," he complained, "you seem to have the idea that everything worthwhile in music and education and morals centers in New York."[67] The two groups also represented different traditions of adult or extension education. Tyson argued that at Columbia they had pursued this form of education "from an entirely different angle" from that of universities in the Midwest.[68] The division between the two groups also included an important political dimension. When Henry Suzzallo, the Carnegie president, expressed his views about wanting to see privately supported broadcasting succeed in the United States, he specifically singled out the people he believed were the main opponents—"RADICAL politicians in congress who come from the middle west."[69]

The NCER, *Ventura Free Press,* and Congressional Lobbying

While Tyson and his organization focused on finding ways to get educators and commercial broadcasters to cooperate in developing new radio programs, the NCER and the Payne Fund focused on two main activities: lobbying Congress for new legislation and providing direct assistance to noncommercial stations. An analysis of the lobbying activities of the reformers is important for understanding not only the complex nature of debates about the nature of broadcasting in the United States but also the reasons this side of the reform movement largely failed.

Armstrong Perry, Joy Elmer Morgan, and the secretary and research director of the NCER, Tracy Tyler, spearheaded the lobbying campaign in Congress. They also tried to influence public opinion through numerous articles and speeches. Importantly, all three held personal views more radical than the official policy of the committee they represented. Partly because Bolton at the Payne Fund wanted to avoid counterproductive confrontations involving direct attacks on the commercial radio industry, the initial lobbying campaign did not call for drastic reform of the system. During 1930 and 1931, the three men lobbied members of Congress to adopt separate frequencies. But all three privately believed that the country would be better served by a publicly funded, noncommercial system modeled on the BBC. Perry developed a close working relationship with officials at the BBC during a three-month research trip to Europe in 1931 to study foreign radio-broadcasting systems.[70]

Although they did not publicly advocate radical views in favor of government control, all three, especially Morgan, did employ radical political language. Morgan argued in extreme end-time terms that the world was at a crucial point in its history. According to Morgan, radio broadcasting would determine whether the world followed the path of "chaos or a world-order of civilization. . . . Whether it shall be one or the other will depend largely upon whether broadcasting be used as a tool of education or as an instrument of selfish greed."[71] Perry believed that he was fighting against evil forces attempting to control all of radio. He was convinced that RCA and NBC dominated "the situation by means of pressure and force."[72] This view led him to link decisions by the FRC to conspiracies involving industry and government officials. The fact that a number of FRC officials took high-paying jobs with the commercial industry after making decisions favoring commercial network broadcasters provided strong support for this view. But suspicions of conspiratorial connections led him further. In January 1931, he wrote a colleague involved in the reform movement about his suspicion of a connection between the apparent fact that "several" FRC officials were Mormons and the fact that "none of them has favored the educational stations."[73]

The Payne Fund also supported a complementary lobbying effort by a business entrepreneur, H. O. Davis, who had managed several film companies, served as editor of the *Ladies Home Journal,* and worked with the Hearst newspaper chain. Davis used his position as a member of the board of directors of the Payne Fund to get support for a separate lobbying campaign in Washington. The fund awarded a fifty-thousand-dollar grant to Davis from 1931 to 1933. A small California newspaper he had recently purchased, the *Ventura Free Press,* served as a base of operations for the campaign. The Payne Fund provided the services of one of its staff members, S. Howard Evans, to spearhead the lobbying effort in Congress. Evans, like Bolton, was a progressive Republican. He also shared Perry and Morgan's admiration for the BBC as well as their missionary zeal. In a revealing remark, he concluded a memorandum with the statement that his work was akin to someone "advocating Christianity in a world that is decidedly pagan."[74]

The two groups supported by the Payne Fund actively lobbied Congress to seek support for the reform of radio during the early 1930s. Although they came close on several occasions to achieving success in Congress, the passage of the Communications Act of 1934, by giving definite legal authority to the system of commercial, network radio, essentially ended the reformers' efforts in Congress. Congress passed the act to consolidate federal regulation of all forms of communications. The act established the Federal Communications Commission (FCC) to oversee wireless and wired communications. But significantly, the language authorizing the FCC to regulate broadcasting mainly came from the 1927 Radio Act. Although one legacy of the reform movement was that it "delayed" the consolidation of the industry for five years, it also helped to preserve a minimal level of support for noncommercial public-service broadcasting. Further, as Robert McChesney has argued, the debates during this period represented "the sole instance in which fundamental questions of ownership, support, and control of the media could be broached in legitimate public discourse in the United States."[75]

Reform Failures

An analysis of the strategies reformers and their opponents used helps us understand the reasons the reformers were not successful. Especially important was the inability of the reformers supported by the Payne Fund to work with other groups with more experience and more support in Congress. Although the labor officials working with WCFL did not succeed in pushing through new legislation, in 1930, setting aside frequencies for labor, agriculture, and education, they came close. Otis Glenn succeeded in having the amendment attached to a separate bill being considered on the floor of the Senate. Lobbying by labor helped him bypass the committee structure. Although the bill passed unanimously in the House and Senate, committee leaders dropped the crucial amendment in the conference committee held to reconcile the two bills.[76]

NCER officials did not make an attempt to actively cooperate with labor. Given the near success of labor leaders in 1930, the two groups might have been able to achieve limited reform. Independent from the work of the labor activists, the NCER convinced Senator Simeon Fess, Republican from Ohio, to introduce, in January 1931, a separate measure in Congress calling for the reservation of 15 percent of radio channels for the use of educational institutions. At the same time that Perry and Morgan were lobbying unsuccessfully for the Fess Bill, in January 1932, supporters of WCFL convinced members of both houses of Congress to introduce separate legislation establishing a clear channel for organized labor. Although the NCER agreed to issue public statements in support of this new legislation, the group did not offer to provide strong political support.[77]

Officials with the NCER did not work with WCFL for a number of reasons. Questions about the ethical standards of Chicago labor unions seems to have been one important factor. At least one person connected with Davis's *Ventura Free Press* campaign advised against working with the labor activists in Chicago because of their reputation for graft and corruption.[78] An elitist tendency of the educators belonging to the NCER also played a role. WCFL primarily served the working classes with programming that tended to be more populist than that of some of the educational stations. Probably most important, the educational stations belonging to the NCER had learned from their dealings with the FRC the importance of drawing a sharp distinction between their stations and those of labor unions and religious organizations. The FRC tended to lump educational stations together with "propaganda" stations operated by these special-interest, nonprofit groups. To avoid harsh treatment by the commission, educational broadcasters needed to distance themselves from stations like WCFL.

A lack of cooperation between the two groups funded by the Payne Fund also hurt the lobbying campaign of the broadcast reformers. Bolton had agreed to fund Davis partly because she did not like the fixed-percentage proposal of the Fess Bill. Officials at the Payne Fund were also critical of the work of Perry, Morgan, and Tyler with the NCER. In March 1932, Crandall complained that they had not made any effort to "understand the entire political situation in Congress" or to collaborate "with the established committees of the two houses of Congress under whose auspices radio legislation is necessarily formulated."[79]

While the NCER was trying to win support in Congress for the Fess Bill, the *Ventura Free Press* pursued a more general objective. With the support of Bolton at the Payne Fund, Davis and Evans tried to convince members of Congress to support a resolution calling for an independent investigation of radio broadcasting in the country. They believed that this more limited objective would serve as an important first step towards the goal of specific reform legislation.[80] Their model was Canada, which established an independent committee to reevaluate national broadcast policy. In 1932, the government decided to implement major changes, notably by establishing the noncommercial, government-funded Canadian Broadcasting Company, which was modeled on the BBC.[81] Thus, instead of working together on a common objective, the two groups supported by the Payne Fund pursued different lobbying goals during 1931. They did not work together until the following year when Perry and Morgan agreed to stop pursuing the Fess Bill.

Clarence Dill and Broadcast Reform

Although the lack of unity among broadcast reformers helps explain the failures of the movement, the hostility of key leaders in Congress was also a crucial factor. A major problem for the reformers was that leaders of committees with oversight of communications policy could block legislation before all members of Congress had a chance to cast direct votes. Although these leaders were mildly sympathetic with elements of the reform agenda, they generally opposed fundamental changes to broadcasting in the United States.

The most important legislator involved in communications policy in the House of Representatives was Ewin L. Davis, Democrat from Tennessee. As the head of the House Merchant Marine, Radio, and Fisheries Committee, Davis had coauthored the Radio Act of 1927. He spoke out publicly against unpopular broadcast practices, especially involving the concentration of economic power, but he generally did not support major restructuring. Perry pointed out that "every word of the anti-monopoly provision in the 1927 Radio Act, including capital letters, commas, and periods, was carefully etched by hand by none other than our own friend Ewin L. Davis."[82] The most important senators involved in broadcast policy were Clarence C. Dill, Democrat from Washington, and Wallace White, Republican from Maine.

Dill was the leader of the Senate Committee on Interstate Commerce. Dill and White had helped author the 1927 Radio Act. Most observers in government and industry viewed Dill as the most influential member of Congress with respect to broadcast policy.[83]

Dill's interaction with the reform movement was complex. During the late 1920s, he was one of the strongest critics of the monopoly power of RCA, threatening to introduce new legislation to break up the company. By the early 1930s, his views had moderated considerably. Although Dill continued to make highly critical remarks stressing the need to curb monopolistic forces and the commercialization of broadcasting, he also gave a number of speeches praising the superiority of the commercial system. In 1931, he privately told the reformers that he sympathized with their cause, but also emphasized that he was "not prepared to go all the way with" them.[84] By 1932, this view seems to have hardened. He grew increasingly frustrated with the reformers' missionary zeal, comparing them to "churches." During a speech in April, he referred to members of the NCER as "people who are looking for something to reform and [who] seize upon anything they can find in advertising which they claim is objectionable to the morals of the people."[85] The reformers were puzzled by the transformation. Perry complained to a colleague in November that while Dill "was on the right side once, those who know the situation best are inclined to shake their heads and dismiss the subject with the declaration that every man has his price. Just what Dill's price was nobody knows."[86]

Dill played a major role stifling the reform movement.[87] Even when advocates seemed to have the support of most members of Congress, Dill managed to kill substantive reform proposals. Although his motivations were undoubtedly complex, clumsy actions by the broadcast reformers likely played a role in the hardening of his position. When it became clear, beginning in 1932, that Dill would use his powerful position as committee chair to block reform legislation, Davis and Evans with the *Ventura Free Press* decided to look for ways to hurt him politically in his home state. They concluded that "in order to get anywhere we have to blow [the] hell out of Dill." Evans informed newspapers in Washington State about Dill's apparent hypocrisy. But he also went further by attempting to uncover evidence of corrupt practices to "discredit" Dill. They discontinued these activities when it became clear that they would not be successful, but not before Dill seems to have discovered their plans. The ill-advised tactic helped turn Dill against the broadcast reform movement.[88]

Senator Dill, not surprisingly, played a central role in the passage of the 1934 Communications Act. The most important person in the House of Representatives was Sam Rayburn, a Democrat from Texas who took charge of the House Merchant Marine, Radio, and Fisheries Committee after Ewin Davis's unexpected defeat in the 1932 election. Both men wanted to avoid a situation where reformers would use the opportunity provided by discussion of new legislation to promote their agenda. To keep this from happening they included language requiring the proposed new regulatory agency, the FCC, to conduct a study on the need for major reform in radio broadcasting.[89] Dill told the reform lobbyists with the NCER and the *Ventura Free Press* that they did not need to testify about broadcast problems during the congressional debate about the new legislation. Not wanting to alienate Dill further, officials with the groups agreed to his request. By April, it appeared likely the proposed legislation would pass Congress after Dill and Rayburn managed to get industry support.[90]

However, a new source of opposition entered the picture unexpectedly on March 15, during the final day of debate on the bill in hearings before Dill's Senate Committee for Interstate Commerce. Father John B. Harney, the superior general of a Roman Catholic order known as the Missionary Society of St. Paul the Apostle (also called the Paulist Fathers), submitted a proposal requiring Congress to set aside 25 percent of the channels in the radio spectrum for nonprofit stations like the New York station he had helped establish, WLWL. Harney took this action after the FRC ruled against his station in February.[91]

The Senate committee voted to reject Harney's amendment. In an effort to placate Harney, Dill added language requiring the proposed FCC to evaluate the proposal in its overall review of broadcast policy. But this did not satisfy Harney. Incensed with his treatment by the Senate, he decided to use Catholic groups across the country to support a full-scale lobbying campaign. Congress, the FRC, and the White House received thousands of telegrams and letters supporting Harney's proposal. The Senate received petitions from over sixty thousand citizens. Harney also distributed twenty thousand copies of a pamphlet he wrote, "Education and Religion vs. Commercial Radio." Harney's campaign emphasized the moral issue of saving a religious station providing wholesome programming appropriate for children. Commercial stations, by contrast, tended to offer entertainment programs of questionable moral character. This remarkable grassroots movement had a dramatic effect on members of Congress. Two members of Dill's committee, Robert Wagner, Democrat from New York, and Henry Hatfield, Republican from West Virginia, were now willing to sponsor the proposal, which became known as the Wagner-Hatfield Amendment.[92]

By the end of April, the amendment appeared to have a good chance of winning congressional support. Harney succeeded in convincing the labor activists connected with WCFL to join the lobbying campaign. He also received strong support from a recently appointed FRC commissioner, James Hanley, who sympathized with the plight of nonprofit stations after witnessing their treatment by the commission. But importantly, the leaders of the NCER did not actively lobby for the Wagner-Hatfield Amendment. This again demonstrates a major problem with the reform movement supported by the Payne Fund. The most influential groups could not come together in support of a common lobbying strategy. The NCER did not join with labor and the Paulists after Dill assured the educators that they would not be successful. He convinced NCER officials to wait until the FCC was established and then let the new agency evaluate the proposal.[93]

This lack of unity contributed to the defeat of the Wagner-Hatfield Amendment in the Senate by a vote of forty-two to twenty-three. President Franklin D. Roosevelt also did not support the reform effort. Roosevelt needed the support of commercial broadcasters to counteract the active opposition of newspaper owners to his New Deal agenda. Following passage of the Communications Act of 1934, the new communications commission decided in January that Harney's proposal was not necessary. The creation of the FCC thus led to a final consolidation of the network commercial system.[94]

The Radio Industry and Congressional Lobbying

The failings of the leaders of the reform movement only partially explain the downfall of reform efforts in Congress. The radio reformers were also outmaneuvered by a commercial industry dominated by an alliance of the two networks and the major trade association, the National Association of Broadcasters. Broadcast industry officials were extremely effective lobbyists. Tyler argued that the radio lobby was "one of the most powerful here in Washington."[95] Unlike the reformers, the radio lobby functioned as a unified force. Although fiercely competitive businessmen, the leaders of NBC and CBS cooperated in the development of a shared strategy to fight off proponents of structural change. Former FRC officials hired by the networks were especially effective in the development of lobbying strategies. One of the most important was Henry A. Bellows, a former commissioner employed by CBS as a lobbyist during the early 1930s. Moreover, major communication executives, such as David Sarnoff at RCA and Owen D. Young at GE, had direct access to members of Congress and the president.[96]

Control of access to the airwaves gave the commercial broadcasters a form of political power as well. Members of Congress and the president needed access to radio stations not only for political campaigning but also to com-

A listener to WBIG in Greensboro, North Carolina, vividly portrayed the virtues of the American System of radio broadcasting in this 1936 cartoon. *Broadcasting,* March 1, 1936, p. 18.

municate government policy to the public.[97] The networks were especially generous in providing airtime to government officials. They also used their control of access to the airwaves to splinter and weaken the reform movement. Perry described this as a "policy of tying up influential groups by gifts of time on the air." As we have seen, one potential ally that could have provided political support for the reformers, the USDA, effectively backed the status quo because of the generous amount of airtime it received from the networks. Perry was astounded when the head of the department "frankly and courageously admitted" to him in a private conversation that his refusal to support the reformers was "due to the favors received from the commercial stations."[98]

This network strategy helps explain the lack of unity among educators as well. Particularly damaging was the defection, in 1932, of a recent president of the NEA, Francis Hale. The leaders of the NCER were incensed when Hale accepted a generous offer from NBC, in early January, to cooperate with Tyson's rival organization in the presentation of a series of broadcasts on education policy. Hale explained to Tyson that she accepted the offer because it would allow her to reach a large national audience: "I feel very much elated over this chance to reach millions of people where only hundreds might have been reached otherwise."[99] According to staff at the NCER, soon after accepting the offer from NBC, her position on broadcast policy also changed. They believed that she had effectively allowed "herself to be bought off by NBC." Before she had accepted NBC's offer of airtime, her "attitude had been one of entire agreement with the Committee's purposes and plans." Within two months of accepting the offer, they complained, "she was actually under the domination of NBC officials and avowedly arguing from their point of view."[100]

The networks were not all-powerful, however. On a handful of occasions, as we have seen, the reformers almost managed to convince Congress to pass new legislation. On these occasions, the networks used one of their most effective strategies: they compromised on limited reforms to split the reform movement and defeat calls for radical change. The best example occurred in May 1932. NBC decided to cut a deal when it realized the extent of congressional support for a labor-sponsored bill setting aside a radio channel for the labor movement. Labor leaders believed that a separate channel was necessary to protect WCFL from network encroachment. "Even the National Association of Broadcasters," according to Perry, "had conceded that the Bill was practically sure of passage."[101] The deal NBC made was to allow WCFL to increase its power from 1,500 to 5,000 watts and to give it full-time use of the channel it shared with the NBC station KJR in Seattle. In return, organized labor agreed to stop lobbying Congress for fundamental broadcast reform. The reform activities in Congress were thus seriously damaged when the FRC accepted the arrangement. Although officials with the NCER had not been actively cooperating with labor, they still felt betrayed by the arrangement, which took place behind closed doors.[102]

Stabilizing College Stations

Unlike the lobbying activities of the NCER that did not achieve the organization's major objective of fundamentally changing the broadcast industry, the organization's Service Bureau and related divisions were more successful in their limited objectives. They helped support, stabilize, and coordinate the remaining noncommercial stations operated by universities.

The founders of the NCER were initially interested in establishing a national network linking the noncommercial college and university stations.[103] They recognized that many of these stations were not thriving in part because of a lack of coordination. Most college and university stations were operating in isolation during the 1920s. Although twenty-two stations belonged to the ACUBS in 1930, its budget was only one hundred dollars. When a British expert connected with the BBC made a tour of educational stations in the United States in 1930, he found that there was "no coordination of their work, and they hardly get to know about one another's experiments, valuable though these may be in individual cases."[104] An American broadcast official who conducted a similar study confirmed this view. "One of the most interesting things to me," he reported, "was how little each one knew about the other. In case after case what another university was doing was only hear-say, and many times the wish was expressed to visit some of the other stations."[105]

Although the NCER decided against creating a national noncommercial network, the organization did try to coordinate the work of college and university stations.[106] One of the most important forms of coordination established by the NCER was to organize useful research projects and ensure that the results were distributed to university stations. Tyler headed the Research Division and was in charge of publishing a weekly bulletin, *Education by Radio,* which helped disseminate and coordinate the work of educational stations. Tyler also organized an informal broadcast network for college and university stations that facilitated the sharing and distribution of radio scripts and transcribed programs. The bureau was willing to circulate recorded programs free of charge, but it could not pay the cost of program production.[107]

The Service Bureau helped educational stations deal with the policies of the FRC and fight off attacks from commercial operators. Perry became the director of the Service Bureau in 1931 after leaving the Office of Education. During the four-month period from June through September 1931, he discovered that of 440 applications from stations requesting new privileges, ninety involved frequencies occupied by educational stations. In these and other cases during the early 1930s, the Service Bureau informed educational stations of the "proposed encroachments" and offered expert assistance.[108] In 1932, the organization hired a legal expert in Washington, D.C., Horace L. Lohnes, to give legal advice to stations and to represent them at FRC hearings in Washington.[109] The NCER provided legal and engineering advice as well as representation at FRC hearings free of charge.[110]

The Service Bureau also sent general advice about dealing with the FRC to all universities with radio stations. Particularly valuable was a list of "Essential Don'ts for Broadcasting Stations." A former commissioner of the FRC constructed the list of thirty-five problems and mistakes to avoid. For example, "Don't operate your transmitter except when a licensed operator is on watch."[111] Privately, the Service Bureau advised stations that political support was important as well. In 1931, it told KFDY at South Dakota State College of Agriculture that it should convince the governor, attorney general, senators, and other politicians to lobby the FRC. Apparently thanks to the advice of the Service Bureau, the FRC renewed the station's license and allowed it to install a new transmitter.[112]

Tyler visited colleges and universities to provide advice directly and to learn about local problems. Many of these visits occurred during extended cross-country trips. On a visit to Nebraska Wesleyan University in 1933 he met with the radio committee for the university's station WCAJ as well as with the members of the board of trustees and the university lawyer.[113] When the Oregon State station KOAC had to scramble to find new sources of funding to satisfy new FRC requirements during the early 1930s, staff with the Service Bureau visited the state and helped find new funding through cooperation with other state institutions.[114]

Although it is difficult to argue that the Service Bureau's support directly changed FRC decisions, the organization's role was nevertheless very important. Not having to worry about spending money on representation at FRC hearings was a great help for universities with limited funds during the Depression. The director of WEAO at Ohio State University argued that the support of the NCER was crucial in convincing the FRC to allow the station an increase of power to one thousand watts. He told Tyler that he doubted "if it would have been possible to secure this increase in power had it not been for the assistance and counsel of the Committee."[115] Other examples of the Service Bureau making a difference with the FRC included the assistance it provided WEAO and KFKU in 1933 and 1934, respectively, in the successful effort to convince the commission to authorize power increases. It also played a crucial role, in 1933, in the commission's decision to allow WSUI at the University of Iowa to expand the number of hours daily it operated.[116]

* * *

The work of the Service Bureau demonstrates that the broadcast reform movement of the early 1930s was not a complete failure. Most important, the NCER helped stabilize the approximately thirty university and college stations that survived the Depression and the hostile decisions of the FRC. But additionally, the movement opened up a debate for the first time about such crucial issues as the impact of advertising-based commercial broadcasting on democratic values and institutions. It also had an important impact on the practices of the commercial networks. To avoid congressional scrutiny, the networks resisted extreme forms of commercialization, partly by protecting public-service or educational programs from the demands of advertisers. As late as 1937, an NBC executive warned a colleague that they needed to protect these kinds of programs because they were "far from out of the woods with Congress and with the radicals who would gladly rend us limb from limb and throw our parts to institutions which would destroy us."[117]

The major flaw was the lack of unity and coherence among the different groups involved in reform activities. This lack of organizational coherence was matched by a lack of conceptual coherence. Reformers looking for alternatives to the commercial system in the United States could not agree about the character of a viable alternative. This was an especially important problem because reformers were interested in convincing Congress to set aside channels specifically for stations forming an alternative structure. While the NCER emphasized that the alternative system should be completely noncommercial, other reformers, including the two groups with the most experience and influence in Washington—Catholics and labor activists—believed that the alternative system only needed to be committed to "nonprofit" goals. The Paulist station WLW, in particular, was interested in using a limited amount of advertising. Harney did not believe advertising was inherently evil. As long as a station only used it to take care of the basic operational costs of the station, he believed it should be allowed.[118] The NCER found this position unacceptable.

It is important to point out that the NCER reformers traditionally preferred the term "educational" rather than "noncommercial" to describe their activities. But increasingly, the word "educational" acquired a broader meaning, encompassing more than formal instruction. By the mid- and late 1930s, we begin to see the use of the terms "public broadcasting" or "public-service broadcasting" to describe this new entity. In 1935, the NCER reported that it "now views broadcasting in the broader light of public welfare rather than in that part of such a program which is included in the work of a school station."[119] This new understanding led the group to propose for the first time the establishment of a public-broadcasting service paralleling and supplementing the commercial system.[120] Although the collapse of the reform movement in the mid-1930s forced the organization to drop the idea almost immediately, the proposal served as an important precedent for later developments. These new terms helped give the reform movement a broader meaning; it also pointed to a solution to the problem of funding. "Public" tended to indicate that a preferred alternative system would depend on sources of public funding, including especially state governments.

During this same period, Tyson also preferred the term "public radio" rather than "educational radio." In 1933 he told the president of the University of Chicago, Robert Hutchins, that he was "fighting the battle for public broadcasting."[121] He also made a distinction between the "public-service elements" of broadcasting and the "strictly entertainment" phases.[122]

NBC successfully pressured Bolton and the Payne Fund to cut off support for the more radical actions of the NCER. In September 1935, NBC officials warned her in a private meeting that her husband's political activities would be jeopardized if she continued to fund a group hostile to the commercial system. Recognizing her weakened position, she told the NCER that future funding would depend on a commitment to cooperating with commercial stations and networks. Perry, Morgan, and Tyler were forced out. The new president of the NCER praised the commercial system for "making exceptionally fine broadcasts to . . . American listeners."[123]

Ironically, at the same time that the Payne Fund and the NCER were winding down their activities and adjusting to the legislative mandate given to the commercial system in 1934 and 1935, Tyson and his organization, the NACRE, were moving in the opposite direction. Tyson became increasingly frustrated with the practices of the commercial networks, especially their tendency to not follow through on promises to give the NACRE specific blocks of airtime for educational or public-affairs programs. Tyson complained to NBC in 1932, for example, when it sold airtime to a commercial company after originally promising it to his organization: "[P]erhaps you can understand the feeling of individuals such as the members of the Council after all the efforts that have been expended" to develop "good educational programs when the time so dramatically promised earlier is sold to Eno's Fruit Salts."[124] His relationship with CBS deteriorated to the point where he was accused by the network of being "a communist or having communistic leanings."[125] Not surprisingly, he quit the NACRE in 1937, complaining about "the futility of arriving at a working combination under the American system between broadcasters and educators." According to Tyson, it was "hopeless."[126] Thus, while the NCER decided that they had no alternative but to try to work with the networks, Tyson, the founder of the NACRE, decided that cooperation was impossible. According to Tyson, education and commercial broadcasting were simply incompatible. This is an important theme that provides a central frame of reference for analyzing broadcasting during the 1930s and beyond.

6. Broadcast Practices and the Stabilization of Noncommercial Stations during the 1930s and 1940s

The approximately thirty noncommercial stations operated by universities that managed to survive the decisions of the FRC faced overwhelming economic problems during the Great Depression in the 1930s. Red Barber, an announcer at the University of Florida station WRUF who went on to become a well-known sports announcer in Cincinnati and New York, recalled that at one time during the early 1930s economic shortfalls forced the state to pay all university employees in "script." According to Barber, to help staff survive during this period, the agricultural-experiment station at the university "gave us milk . . . they gave us bunches of greens, they gave us sweet potatoes."[1]

The economic downturn hit KUSD at the University of South Dakota especially hard. A severe drought during this period deepened the impact of the economic downturn in this part of the country. South Dakota was particularly sensitive to the drought because of agricultural practices involving intensive cultivation more appropriate for the eastern United States rather than the drier regions of the Great Plains. Per capita income in the state dropped from $417 in 1929 to $188 in 1932.[2] The legislature cut the appropriation for the university in 1932 by a staggering 40 percent. Although the president of the university wanted the radio station to continue, support from the Board of Regents of Education was less certain. B. B. Brackett, the staff member in charge of the station, worried that the regents were politicians dependent on the support of the Farmers Union, a group that would "be willing to ruin all our public schools" to "save the individual tax-payer 50 cents." Despite the "depressing, stultifying, and reactionary conditions," Brackett managed to fight off efforts to eliminate the station.[3] But the station did not grow significantly during the 1930s. In 1941 it was still only broadcasting at five hundred watts. A number of other university stations had installed five-thousand-watt transmitters by this date.[4]

Ironically, however, despite these two examples, most state university stations thrived during the 1930s. How do we explain this? How did stations manage to gain support for expansion? More generally, what kind of programming did they broadcast during the 1930s and 1940s? How did this compare to the 1920s, when university stations played an important role creating a local public culture?

Surviving the Depression

Until the early 1930s, WILL at the University of Illinois had difficulty attracting listeners partly because it did not have sufficient power to compete with commercial stations in Chicago. This changed dramatically in 1936. The director reported during the following year that the station had "made more progress in the last twelve months than during any like period in its fifteen years of broadcasting." It doubled the station's coverage area by investing nearly thirty thousand dollars in physical improvements. At the same time, it increased the number of hours on the air by 75 percent.[5]

Similarly, the budget for WOI at Iowa State grew from $14,640 in the 1927–28 academic year to $26,346 in 1940–41.[6] The 1940–41 budget included the salaries of eight station employees. The number of hours WOI broadcast more than doubled between 1930 and 1939.[7] WOI was fortunate in having a better channel lower in the broadcast frequency band (640 kHz). A lower frequency required less power to transmit a signal over a given distance compared to a channel higher in the radio band (for example 1500 kHz). According to the station director, WOI had "an extraordinarily favorable place on the air."[8] KOAC at Oregon State also had a favorable frequency assignment at 550 kHz.

Of the dozens of stations that operated during the 1920s, KOAC was one of the most successful. It continued to flourish during most of the 1930s. The number of hours per week the station broadcast increased from thirty during the 1930–31 academic year to over seventy in early 1933.[9] By this date, the station employed ten full-time staff and a number of part-time employees. This contrasted with the earliest days of broadcasting at the university, when, according to station director Kadderly, he personally "planned all the programs and did most of the announcing."[10] The station continued to expand during the late 1930s and early 1940s. In 1941, it received permission from the FCC to install a five-thousand-watt transmitter. The station was also particularly well positioned to compete with other stations. It did not have to share its frequency with other broadcasters, and it was one of three university stations in the country at that time not limited to daytime broadcasting. The other two stations were WSUI at the University of Iowa, which received an unlimited-time license from the FCC in 1935, and the Purdue University station WBAA, which received a similar license in 1941.[11]

Although in the early 1930s only a few university stations were operating five-thousand-watt transmitters, by 1942, ten stations were broadcasting at this power level. High power produced a stronger signal over a larger area. Of the approximately fifteen major state university radio stations limited to daytime operations in the late 1930s and early 1940s, most did not have to share the use of frequencies with other stations. This was another major change from the late 1920s and early 1930s.[12]

WHA at the University of Wisconsin made an especially dramatic improvement in the 1930s. The number of hours per week it broadcast increased during the first three years of the decade from less than ten hours to fifty-four hours. The station power went from 750 watts in 1932 to 2,500 watts in 1934 and then increased again two years later to five thousand watts. At this point, no other radio station in the state of Wisconsin broadcast at a higher power level.[13] The station also received superior facilities for its new equipment in 1934. The refurbished building, called Radio Hall, included three offices, a large visitors' lounge, and three separate studios located around a central control room. One studio was large enough for a seventy-piece band. In 1937, work was completed on a new wing that included a drama studio, another control room, a workshop, an observation room, and four more offices.[14]

The visitors' lounge was particularly unique because of its design scheme, described as "Indian *motif moderne.*" The design underscored the local character of the station and its radio programs. An instructor in the art department designed the modernistic furniture made by local cabinet-makers using native Wisconsin oak. The lampshades were shaped like Indian "tom-toms." A sandstone frieze on the walls of the room reproduced Indian petroglyphs from cave walls in Wisconsin. The prehistoric carvings represented animals native to the state. The rugs on the floor as well as the cushions on the couches and chairs were made by Native Americans.[15] According to the new director, Harold McCarty, the reception area combined "the oldest evidences of communication in the state [the cave petroglyphs] . . . with the most modern means of communication."[16] The visitors' lounge was especially important because the station encouraged listeners to "look behind the scenes and see what is happening."[17] WHA staff promoted the pioneer work of the station.

They called it the "oldest educational radio broadcasting station in the United States." A mural on the north wall of the reception lounge, completed in 1943, emphasized this pioneer role. The mural portrayed the early history and development of radio broadcasting at the university. It depicted the crucial early leaders, including William Lighty and Earle Terry.[18] Because Radio Hall was originally used as a heating plant, underground tunnels connected the building to the rest of the campus. The old steam tunnels were ideal for the construction of the cable network linking the studios at Radio Hall to other buildings on campus.[19]

Reasons for State Support

How did radio stations operated by state universities receive support from state governments during the 1930s in spite of the severe financial depression? Efforts by broadcast reformers connected with the NCER played an important role. They actively lobbied state governments and provided staff at university stations with assistance in organizing and mobilizing support. The ACUBS also became more active during the 1930s. The group reorganized in 1934 under a new name, the National Association for Educational Broadcasters (NAEB). The association provided station directors and other staff at university and college radio stations a strong sense of community. Correspondence between members during the 1930s underscores how they viewed their organization and their profession as a distinct "brotherhood," given identity by their common fight against commercial forces. When Josef Wright, the director of WILL, wrote a letter to other station directors in 1934, he addressed it to "the Similarly Hardworking Brothers in that Great Paternity of Radio."[20] John Dunn, a staff member at the University of Oklahoma station WNAD, similarly used the term "brother" when referring to other members of the NAEB.[21]

Some of the leaders of the NAEB entered radio during the previous decade. Members of the older generation included Carl Menzer at the University of Iowa (WSUI), Wallace Kadderly at Oregon State (KOAC), and W. I. Griffith at Iowa State (WOI). Two especially important members of the new generation were Harold McCarty and Harold Engel at the University of Wisconsin. McCarty became program director in 1931; Engel was appointed assistant director during the following year. McCarty's background was more diverse than the members of the previous generation. He began his education as an engineering student but spent years in a variety of other activities, including working as a vaudeville performer, touring the Pacific as a member of a dance band, teaching the violin, and gaining practical experience in business.

Harold B. McCarty in the WHA studio, 1931. Courtesy of the
University of Wisconsin–Madison Archives.

After working at WHA for three years, McCarty benefitted from a special
Rockefeller Foundation fellowship that allowed him to travel to Great Britain
to study the practices of the BBC.[22] A number of women also participated in
the "brotherhood," at least on the edges as directors of women's programs at
university stations. For example, Zelta Feike Rodenwold, a home economics
expert with a master's degree from Iowa State, became the director of women's
programs at Oregon State in 1935.[23]

Universities and colleges successfully persuaded cash-strapped state governments to fund radio stations during the 1930s by convincing them that their work was particularly important during the Depression. When staff at the University of Wisconsin filed an application for a power increase, they argued that their radio activities had provided "educational opportunities to compensate for retrenchments in school, home, farm, and personal budgets."[24] The use of state-funded university stations to broadcast to schools was especially useful because it provided a cost-effective way to compensate for budget cuts affecting local schools, especially in rural areas. State-funded stations could be used to "save traveling expenses and to carry on, at least partially, the services of field workers and extension teachers who are withdrawn."[25] In 1934, the Ohio Emergency School Administration, a Depression-era agency, specifically set aside funds for an Emergency Radio Junior College. It sought to give the many unemployed citizens in the state who were unable to attend college an opportunity to listen in on college courses over the air. Although listeners could not receive college credit, they could take proficiency examinations upon completing the radio courses and use the results to facilitate entry to universities.[26] Radio stations at land-grant colleges also played an important role educating farmers about New Deal–era agricultural programs. WOI, for example, broadcast detailed information about the Agricultural Adjustment Act of 1933 and the 1936 farm-adjustment program.[27]

University stations also managed to gain support from state governments by demonstrating their usefulness to elected officials, department administrators, and statewide organizations. WHA at the University of Wisconsin and KOAC at Oregon State pioneered the state-supported public-service model. Staff at WHA stressed that the station was "especially anxious to arrange for programs by persons outside the city of Madison to emphasize the fact that this is a state station and that its benefits and influences should be state-wide."[28] The overall justification for the "Wisconsin plan for state radio service" stressed that the state is a "relationship between the people and their public servants," that this relationship "must constantly be cultivated and strengthened," and that this can be accomplished "only through close communication" using radio broadcasting, the most powerful form of modern communication.[29]

Faced with a serious budget crisis in the early 1930s, KOAC also decided to make itself available to state government agencies and other state universities. The station promoted programming that clearly served the entire state. For example, in 1932, the station broadcast a series on the poets of Oregon produced by a well-known poet in Portland.[30] Beginning in 1940, the station also produced a series in cooperation with the State Highway Commission "designed to acquaint residents of Oregon, and visitors too, with recreational opportunities within the state." The program specifically used residents from hundreds of communities across the state.[31] The station reported in September 1941 that nearly three hundred citizens traveled to the radio studio to participate in the broadcasts.[32]

Officials in Iowa considered linking the two major radio stations at Iowa State and the University of Iowa, creating a single statewide network. Instead, each station mainly tried to carve out a particular niche. They decided that neither station "could adequately serve its specialized audiences if the merger occurred." Most important, Iowa State emphasized agriculture and home economics; the University of Iowa did not. In 1937, the two stations did establish an educational network to jointly broadcast eighteen hours of programming per month to the entire state. Civic and community organizations across the state used most of this airtime.[33] Like the University of Wisconsin, the university stations in Iowa decided to cooperate partly as a way to ensure state funding. The director at WSUI, Carl Menzer, confided to Harold McCarty at WHA that the "idea of rebroadcasting programs from WSUI and WOI is really a sort of under-cover way of going about a selling campaign." According to Menzer, "If we can cover the state (which is not now done) with programs we know the people want, we figure that maybe the thing will get so well known that it will come to the attention of the legislature. In other words, it seems that the crying need is a lot of publicity."[34]

Significantly, the federal government provided crucial material support for noncommercial university stations during the 1930s. Federal support was the dream of some of the key broadcast reformers analyzed in chapter 5. Although President Roosevelt did not support the reformers' efforts to fundamentally restructure the industry, his New Deal programs did provide substantial funds to hire station personnel and construct new facilities. For example, in 1938, the Works Project Administration (WPA) funded 45 percent of the cost of a new four-hundred-foot antenna for WOI at Iowa State.[35] Even more significant, during the following year, two more federal grants covered 45 percent of the cost of a new transmitter ($29,767) and new facilities ($149,816) for the station. The new facility for WOI, termed a "miniature Radio City," included some of the latest equipment found at major commercial stations, including the most up-to-date soundproofing material for studio walls and floors and a recording studio with triple glass windows for sound insulation.[36] The WPA also helped fund the construction of WHA's Radio Hall facilities and a new one-hundred-thousand-dollar state-of-the-art facility at Michigan State in 1940.[37] Three separate WPA projects were in operation at the Ohio State station WOSU during 1937.[38] Another New Deal program, the National

Youth Administration, supported the employment of students at a number of university radio stations. In 1937, for example, all but one of the twelve staff members working for WNAD at the University of Oklahoma were "drawn from the National Youth Administration rolls."[39]

Although state and federal support played an important role in the development of radio stations at state universities, commercial opposition continued to hinder growth. We see this especially in the way the networks sought to limit the use of transcription technology. By the 1930s, educational stations recognized the advantages of collaboration. Most important, they decided to look for ways to share programming. The stations did not have the resources to create a network using telephone cables. Transcribed or recorded programs provided a much cheaper potential alternative. By the 1930s, new recordings were available that operated at 33 ⅓ rpm, instead of 78 rpm. The slower speed also meant that longer programs could be recorded and played back over the air.[40]

As early as 1930, university stations sought to develop a "wax chain" to take advantage of this new technology.[41] Radio stations could use their own recording units to record programs appropriate for their stations and then circulate them to the other stations. The University of Iowa was one of the first stations to use a recording unit to make transcriptions of programs. Carl Menzer reported that even after replaying individual recordings as many as two hundred times, the quality remained excellent.[42] Perry with the NCER stimulated renewed interest in 1935 to form a "chain of broadcasting stations for educational and other purposes."[43] Most university stations were familiar with recording technology by this time because they had tried out Menzer's unit. Wright at the University of Illinois reported that "so far as I've been able to determine, the idea of an exchange of recordings is 'Swell'"; however, he also complained that a lack of funds was stifling development.[44]

But funding was not the only problem stifling the use of transcription technology. Federal policy that discouraged the use of electrical recordings was also an important factor. The FCC continued to require stations to announce before and after each program that they were broadcasting an electrical recording. Analysts recognized that especially for small stations unaffiliated with networks and with limited resources to pay for talent, electrical recordings were "a godsend." Importantly, however, they also recognized that the networks were "sincerely and wholeheartedly opposed to electrical transcriptions."[45]

The networks, especially NBC, viewed transcriptions as a fundamental threat. Before the mid-1930s, NBC did not allow its own stations to use electrical transcriptions. It also successfully lobbied federal regulators to maintain the official policy that effectively discouraged stations from using transcriptions. But by the mid-1930s, both networks were involved in the electrical transcription business. NBC established a separate department in 1935 for the manufacture and sale or lease of recorded programs "to advertisers and their agencies, and directly to radio stations for broadcast purposes."[46] NBC president M. H. Aylesworth supported this decision, but only after company officials assured him that they would lobby FCC commissioners to strengthen the rules requiring a strict announcement when stations used records or electrical transcriptions. Vice president Frank Russell assured Aylesworth that a number of key commissioners had promised him privately that they did not plan to change the regulations.[47]

When an independent transcription company tried to convince the FCC to relax the rules involving the announcement of transcriptions and records in June 1935, Aylesworth pressured his staff to oppose the move. "If radio is to become a self-winding phonograph it certainly is the end of network broadcasting," he argued. "Network broadcasting of live talent would be badly damaged with a resulting loss of revenue to NBC and Columbia." Aylesworth was willing to support the Transcription Department, but only if the network structure was given first priority and the commission rules were kept "as strict as possible."[48] With the FCC rules discouraging the use of transcription technology and the two networks partially controlling the technology, university stations found it difficult to take advantage of electronic transcriptions to link stations across the country.

Objectives of Noncommercial Stations

What were the objectives of noncommercial educational radio stations during the 1930s and early 1940s? The practice of using radio stations to publicize universities became less prominent during this period. Stations deemphasized this objective in response to the policies articulated by the FRC. Nevertheless, publicity continued to serve as a rationale for the operation of university and college radio stations. As late as 1941, the annual report for WSUI at the University of Iowa included "promotion" as one of the purposes for the radio station.[49] The comptroller of the University of Minnesota, who was concerned about the "business side in educational administration" rather than the purely educational, wrote that he "did not shun the publicity feature" and did not "undervalue its importance," but he did "believe that an extension of its instructional and informational service is the more important."[50]

The head of the radio station at the University of Illinois, Josef Wright, was particularly sensitive about not overemphasizing the publicity role for his station. Unlike other university and college stations, WILL was operated by the "public information" or publicity office of the university. Wright wrote in 1933 that his station was "not used as a publicity medium, but rather . . . solely to take educational material and good entertainment matter to those within our listening area." Nevertheless, he also believed that one objective of the station should be to relay to the public how "a large portion of our income goes into research work" and how this work "pays a handsome dividend each year on the money invested" by the state.[51]

An objective that became more important during the 1930s was the use of stations for training students in broadcasting. KOAC at Oregon State, for example, reported in the late 1930s that the station functioned as "a training school for more than one hundred college students."[52] At least two stations, KUSD at the University of South Dakota and KWSC at the State College of Washington, became largely student-operated, although faculty retained overall control.[53] This new objective was especially important for stations that were underfunded during the Depression. Using stations as laboratories for students helped university officials justify the expense. In 1943, the head of KUSD told a state politician that the station was worthwhile because it served as "an excellent laboratory" for students, giving "them training that would be helpful in the ever-increasing field of radio."[54]

Stations during the 1930s continued to emphasize that their primary commitment was to education and information. But they also developed a deeper justification based on observations about the role of electronic communications in modern society. Specifically, they emphasize that, "whether we like it or not," most of the country was being educated by radio "in one way or another." McCarty at WHA emphasized that the citizens using radio in his state "accept information, they acquire tastes, they form desires which either lift or lower their general level of intelligence and appreciation." He argued that although the State of Wisconsin did "not desire to control that level at any particular height," it was "definitely obligated somehow to elevate that level." The state and the state university thus had an obligation, he believed, to use radio to lift "the level of understanding and appreciation of our people, of helping to create an enlightened citizenry."[55] Radio seemed an ideal means to educate citizens, which was essential for a healthy democracy. This theme became more important during the 1930s as a justification for public-service or educational broadcasting.

Radio stations operated by institutions of higher education differed from the average commercial station not only because of their commitment to the education and uplift of citizens but also because of their commitment to noncommercial values. The noncommercial element became increasingly central to the unique identity of university and college stations. Instead of using the term "educational broadcasting," they increasingly used the term "public-service" broadcasting. "Public service" referred especially to the tradition of state government service to citizens. WSUI argued that its primary purpose was "to give to the people of the state of Iowa a public service program not available through other channels."[56] Rather than work toward maximizing audience size, university stations sought to serve specialized audiences with quality programming. Staff at KOAC acknowledged that "our programs are not of much interest to the great mass of listeners."[57] Unlike commercial stations that had to satisfy the demands of advertisers, KOAC did not believe that it had a mission to serve everyone. The director of WOI at Iowa State agreed. According to Griffith, the station "should attempt to be of service to that part of the public that [could] make best use of its program material."[58]

Staff at WHA at the University of Wisconsin went further than others in articulating a unique vision for the station. This was the case partly because the staff developed the idea of the station serving as a "state service agency," committed to the public interest rather than the interests of commercial operators. Engel stressed that they had "no quarrel with commercial stations. We are in separate fields. They operate with profit as a basic motive. We operate as a state service agency. We tend to our own business and pray they will do likewise."[59] He viewed WHA programming as "unique in character."[60] The distinction between education or the public interest and commercial considerations was absolute. According to McCarty, "[T]here can be no compromise with commercialism. There must be a definite divorce between education and advertising."[61] Writing in 1936, Engel was more explicit about the importance of select, quality programming. WHA should not, he argued, always have to worry about "appealing to the great mass of listeners." According to Engel, "several" of the programs broadcast by the Wisconsin station "appeal to only a small selected group" of listeners. "Why shouldn't there be what you might call a quality program as opposed to a mass program?" Engel argued. "I see no reason why we need to interest *all* the listeners *all* of the time. I think it's much more essential to keenly interest different groups of listeners part of the time."[62]

WHA and other stations operated by institutions of higher education stressed three other issues that helped distinguish their stations from the majority of commercial broadcasters. First, unlike commercial stations tied to the restrictive demands of advertisers, noncommercial educational broadcasters argued that they were free to try out new and innovative techniques and program styles. According to Engel, they were "free to experiment in the true public service phases of broadcasting."[63] Second, university stations emphasized that they served the needs of local and regional communities. Most commercial stations, by contrast, were dominated by the decisions of network executives based in New York City. When WHA applied for a construction permit from the FRC in 1933, the university emphasized that "the programs broadcast are planned for Wisconsin audiences and deal with problems peculiar to this station."[64] Especially unique examples of local programming included an *Indians for Indians Hour* broadcast by the University of Oklahoma station WNAD and a humor program broadcast by the Iowa State station WOI that featured a made-up Swedish character called Ole Bjorkness.[65] Finally, university and college stations emphasized that their service was superior because it was driven by an academic commitment to disinterested expertise. WHA stressed that its programming was "highly reliable, coming directly from the state's noncommercial service agencies."[66] Commercial stations, by contrast, were more likely to provide advice based on the interests of the advertisers paying for programming.

Performers broadcasting an *Indians for Indians Hour* program on the University of Oklahoma station WNAD, 1943. Courtesy of the Western History Collections, University of Oklahoma Libraries.

At least two university stations during the 1930s questioned whether edu-cational stations should broadcast entertainment programs. WEAO at Ohio State argued that "entertainment even of an intellectual kind can better be given by trained entertainers."[67] Wright at WILL similarly warned against try-ing to compete with commercial stations by broadcasting programs featuring professional entertainment because "the comparison of what we might put on inexpensively with what the others are doing would be more harmful than good."[68] Most stations, however, did broadcast programs meant to entertain as well as to educate.

A desire to uplift audiences continued to guide some decisions about pro-gramming, especially those about music selections. Staff at WOI argued that the station only broadcast programs that were "wholesome and give to our programs a distinctive Iowa State College atmosphere."[69] In 1936, KUSD at the University of South Dakota pointed out that its broadcasts of "fine and substantial music" were meant to aid "in elevating the preference of the listen-ers above much of the music given on most of the commercial broadcasts."[70] During the 1920s, WHA, under the leadership of William Lighty, had been eclectic in its musical selections. This situation seems to have changed by the 1930s. In 1935, the station officially announced that it broadcast "very little popular music." The decision was part of the station's overall effort to differ-entiate itself from commercial stations. According to WHA, it did not need to broadcast popular music because there was "plenty of desirable material which does not fall in the category of that being done by commercial stations."[71]

An analysis focusing on the desire by university stations to uplift audi-ences only helps us understand one aspect of a complex picture. The uplift theme focuses exclusively on the type of music broadcast. In some cases, the quality of the presentation, based on academic standards of technical fidelity, was the most important factor. The main concern of the School of Music at Oregon State, for example, was not whether KOAC was playing jazz, classi-cal, or "hillbilly" music. The main concern was that the station used inferior circuits to transmit programming from a studio at the University of Oregon campus in Eugene to the station headquarters at Corvallis. Because the sta-tion used "speech-only" circuits, "all overtones and many of the basic tones of instrument music" were lost. A professor at the School of Music stressed how "disheartening" it was for "many members of the music school to have the quality of their musical programs distorted by poor quality transmission."[72]

Some stations in the 1930s also began to view music and other forms of entertainment as a way to attract listeners. WOI increased the amount of music from 25 percent of the schedule in 1927 to 50 percent in 1938. Musical selections at the Iowa State station included not only classical and jazz but also other forms of popular music such as old-time fiddle music and folk

Red Barber, a radio announcer on the University of Florida station WRUF, standing at the microphone with string band, ca. 1930s. Photo UF000298281, courtesy of the Special Collections, University of Florida Archives.

music by a Scandinavian American "Viking Accordion Band."[73] W. I. Griffith, the WOI program director, argued in 1934 that the station needed "more program material of an entertainment nature to fill in between speeches to add interest and variety to the program and in this manner maintain an audience of listeners for the educational material."[74] In 1937, WILL broadcast "popular music" for thirty-five or forty minutes early in the day because, according to the director, "[I]t would be absolutely impossible to hold the average listener with heavy programs throughout the day." Wright believed that it was necessary to have a variety of musical selections "to sugar-coat the educational-informational type of program so that listeners will not run away." But he also admitted that this issue was a "perplexing problem."[75]

Broadcast Techniques and Commercial Values

In tension with the desire of many stations to emphasize their unique character by contrasting their role with that of commercial stations was a tendency to also adopt some of the broadcasting techniques used by commercial stations. By the 1930s, most broadcasters recognized that radio represented a new communication medium inherently different from older forms of communication. In 1936, for example, a University of Iowa administrator wrote that "there seems to be substantial evidence to the effect that radio, if it is to be successful, must develop its own techniques. It is not just the 'putting on the air' of something that existed for other purposes or other audiences."[76] But commercial broadcasters believed that they had the best understanding of radio technique. They not only argued that commercial broadcasting was the best system for the country but also that their new broadcasting techniques best took advantage of the intrinsic demands of the new technology.

Given this context, broadcasters, not surprisingly, felt pressured to adopt the new techniques developed by the dominant commercial stations. For example, the head of agricultural programs for the GE-owned station WGY in Schenectady, New York, encouraged the staff at the University of Illinois station WILL to adopt guidelines for the presentation of radio talks that he helped develop at his commercial station. The guidelines encouraged WILL to accept the argument that radio was inherently a commercial medium meant to entertain. According to this view, all stations, including ones operated by institutions of higher education, needed to accept the reality that radio was all about selling: "Every radio speaker has something to sell. He is selling himself, an idea, a bulletin, or a service. When you broadcast, you should use a selling technique." And because radio was seen as "primarily a source of entertainment," a person speaking over the radio "in addition to being a salesman, must be a showman."[77] The guidelines listed specific recommendations, including advice to use humor, human-interest stories, and dramatic values: "[H]umor may be anecdotes, cleverly turned phrases, or strong colloquial speech." John Baker, the extension radio specialist of the USDA, gave similar advice to the Kansas State station KSAC in 1939. According to Baker, "[S]howmanship is needed in educational radio broadcasts the same as in the commercial field. There has been a decided lack of showmanship in educational radio programs."[78]

Because the large commercial stations and networks had some of the best equipment, it made sense to assume that they also might have developed some of the best techniques. Given this context, it is understandable that KSAC and WILL took seriously the advice they received from commercial operators. In 1937, when the head of the agricultural extension department at the University of Illinois received suggestions from the person in charge of educational programs at another commercial station, he distributed them to other staff in the department. The recommendations encouraged broadcasters to use "wordage better suited for the eye than the ear," sound effects "where appropriate," and, in general, more dramatic action, suspense, and conflict.[79]

A number of university stations not only considered adopting techniques developed for commercial radio, but evidence indicates the direct influence of these techniques and perspectives on general considerations involving programming. An official with KSAC argued in 1931 that they should not "be content to sit back and lack an appreciation of the advertising side of radio." "We too," he pointed out, "are advertising. We are advertising our educational wares. We are advertising those wares for the express purpose of offering assistance to the listener."[80] Similarly, a representative for WSUI told the FRC during the same year, "We realize that the techniques and principles of successful broadcasting which have succeeded in the commercial world must be observed in the field of educational broadcasting."[81] At least one university station, WNAD at the University of Oklahoma, adopted the use of contests, a program form peculiar to the commercial environment.[82]

This example opens up the issue of whether there are techniques or uses of radio intrinsic to the medium. What is distinctive about radio as a form of mediated communication? Some differences between radio broadcasting and simple face-to-face communication seem relatively clear, especially in the use of radio for education. Whereas regular classroom instruction takes place in a structured and disciplined setting, most forms of educational radio broadcasting take place in the context of unstructured domestic settings. One tip for radio speakers used by KUSD reflected this difference. It told potential radio speakers that they should "visualize yourself as a guest, speaking to a family in its living room and observe the rules of conduct and courtesy which properly apply."[83] Related to this issue of the audience setting was the obvious difference that radio broadcasting only involved a person's voice. In a classroom setting, by contrast, the entire body of the lecturer is involved. An observer pointed out that "on the platform, the voice, the disarming smiles, and the gestures intermingle their effect on the listener; but the microphone separates them in a pitiless way."[84]

Commercial radio operators argued that the technology intrinsically demanded techniques of showmanship and commercial popularization. But this belief assumed that the goal of all radio stations was to maximize audience size. As we have seen, many university and college stations decided that they wanted to offer an alternative to commercial stations courting mass audiences. They were more interested in serving specialized groups; quality was more important than quantity. University radio stations also argued that they could draw on distinctive noncommercial, public-service traditions using techniques involving showmanship or popularization. For example, WILL emphasized that one of the best techniques it used with its farm programs was to personalize or humanize the topic by reporting "how some particular farmer or homemaker or a group of them are following a certain improved and recommended practice and profiting from it." Commercial stations also emphasized this issue of personalizing presentations through the use of anecdotes or human-interest stories. But WILL did not simply adopt a practice developed by commercial operators; as one staff member pointed out, this practice was "nothing more than an adaptation of the demonstration method of teaching" developed by experts at nonprofit institutions of higher education working in support of agricultural extension.[85]

Commercial stations argued that they were serving listeners by giving them what they wanted. They criticized university stations for giving the public what professors at universities thought they should have. This view ignored the fact that commercial operators' first priority was to serve advertisers. It also assumed that university stations did not care about their audiences. But especially by the 1930s, university stations did try to take into account, in a somewhat systematic way, the views of listeners.

By the 1930s, a number of techniques were available to evaluate audiences. These included letters to stations, solicited or unsolicited; questionnaires sent by mail; telephone surveys; personal interviews; informal observations, such as reports from county extension agents; and recording devices attached to radios. During the 1920s and the early 1930s university and college radio stations mainly relied on feedback they received from letters sent to stations from listeners. As early as the mid-1920s, land-grant stations working with agricultural extension departments and the USDA conducted surveys of farm families to help measure the effectiveness of agricultural broadcasts. Based on these studies and additional ones during the 1930s, most experts agreed that the use of radio as an "extension method" was "superior to many of the older and more established extension methods." But they believed that it was most effective when used in conjunction with other practices involving direct contact with extension agents. They also determined that it was "particularly superior as a means of transmitting timely information" to farm families, most notably the transmission of market reports and weather forecasts.[86]

Although some stations conducted general audience surveys during the 1930s, universities were not able to commit funds during the Depression to large-scale, systematic surveys. Private philanthropic foundations were willing to provide grant support for surveys. The Princeton Radio Project, funded by the Rockefeller Foundation in 1938, included a survey of rural Iowa radio listeners. An analysis of the 5,771 families surveyed concluded that the Iowa State station WOI ranked fourth among stations listened to most frequently in the daytime. The study reported that WOI listeners were wealthier, better educated, older, and more conservative than the average Iowa radio listener. Further, the statistics verified that WOI's audience included a large number of Iowa State alumni and listeners specifically interested in campus activities.[87]

Aline Watson Hazard, host of the *Homemakers' Hour* on the University of Wisconsin station WHA, using a shortwave transmitter to broadcast from a rural location, ca. 1939. Courtesy of the University of Wisconsin–Madison Archives.

Although the lead researcher, Alberta Curtis, recommended that the station continue to focus on "leadership in ideas rather than in the kind of success desired by commercial stations," she also provided advice about specific changes the station might adopt to expand the audience.[88] Importantly, the station decided to accept her recommendations for the *Homemaker's Half Hour* program. Curtis called for "greater variety of information on homemaking." To "compete with the pervasive soap operas," she also suggested making the program more entertaining. The station decided to hire a new women's programming director, Eleanor Wilkins, a member of the university's foods and nutrition department. The station's 1939 annual report pointed out that as the radio personality "Martha Duncan," she took full advantage of her "journalist's nose for news, an actresses's flair for the dramatic, and a business woman's way of doing things." The station reported that the recommendation to hire her played a key role in "revitalizing the *Homemakers' Half Hour.*"[89]

A comparison of the Princeton survey with another survey of rural Iowa radio listening conducted locally by WOI during that same year underscores the difficulties involved in using this method. The second survey focused especially on the number of Iowa farm families that listened to the station. Whereas the Princeton Radio Study mainly assumed that all radio stations desired to maximize audience size, the local survey took into account that many university stations were more interested in serving specialized audiences. The local survey found that 75 percent of Iowans who used market reports from radio stations listened to WOI. This fact justified the station's commitment to broadcasting agricultural information. The station broadcast market reports six times every day except Sunday; each report lasted approximately twenty minutes. Altogether during the 1930s, market reports took up nearly 20 percent of the daily broadcast schedule. One analyst has pointed out that this commitment "gave WOI a great advantage with farmers, even though it cost listenership among the 'general radio audience.'"[90]

Other university stations came to the same conclusions about the difficulties of using surveys. Not only did they tend to assume that all stations sought to maximize audience size rather than serve specialized audiences, they also failed to take into account qualitative issues. Letters sent to stations, although not a good source of systematic knowledge about the size of audiences, did provide one of the best ways for broadcasters to obtain qualitative information about listeners' interest in programs. Stations believed that the best letters were unsolicited.[91] But even letters submitted in response to station requests are valuable for revealing qualitative information about the likes and dislikes of listeners. The letters in general also reveal listeners' views about the distinctive aspects of university stations they especially appreciated.

A number of letters indicate that these stations appealed to listeners who did not view a sharp separation between education and entertainment because they received a great deal of pleasure from the informational and educational programming. Bessie Meyer of Dundee, Oregon, wrote the Oregon State station KOAC in 1933 to compliment it for having "such a fund of information at your disposal." "I'm getting so much pleasure out of this," she wrote, "I'll have to be careful not to let it interfere with my 'home work.'"[92] Another listener in Oregon wrote that her husband "enjoys and is helped by the news and farm hour both noon and at night. There is much of interest in every educational program."[93]

The uplift theme that helped shape some of the programming at stations operated by universities also appealed to regular listeners who did not like the popular music and sensational programs broadcast by commercial stations. "I wish to tell you," C. H. Jones wrote KOAC, "that I enjoy your programs over the radio very much, as they are sensible and educational, not having any of that trashy stuff, that is given so much over other radios." Another KOAC listener, Will Mooney of Portland, complimented the station for broadcasting such "an agreeable contrast . . . to the nauseating jazz and puerile stuff" broadcast by commercial stations that "pounds our ear drums, when in a moment of relaxation from work and worry." This listener concluded that "there is still hope for the country with its rising generation, if the same grown-ups will insist on the radio feeding us on more milk and honey and less garbage and slop."[94] Parents appreciated the "wholesome" programming broadcast by KOAC in contrast to "so many so-called children's programs" that "upset" children because they were so "sensational."[95] A WHA listener in Madison, Wisconsin, told the station that she used to feel that "radios were the 'invention of the Devil,'" but after listening to the station's farm program and the *College of the Air* program, she has "been completely won over" to the view that radio can support uplifting values.[96]

Other listeners appreciated the local nature of programming offered by university and college radio stations as well as other unique features that only institutions of higher education could provide. One listener in Beloit, Wisconsin, wrote WHA that he especially appreciated their local weather forecasts. According to the Beloit listener, the big commercial stations "seem to think that weather is of no importance, when, in fact, it means everything."[97] Continuing a trend that began in the 1920s, many listeners especially appreciated broadcasts of sporting events from university stations. When a KOAC listener wrote to thank the station for broadcasting the school's basketball games, she explained that she was "unable to attend such gatherings in the evening, and the rest of the family did not have the necessary money."[98]

A unique KOAC program meant to "entertain as well as to instruct" led to a particularly compelling and unique letter of appreciation from one listener in Oregon. The *Philosopher of the Crossroads* was an "informal and chatty" discussion program presented by a local author, Anthony Euwer. Topics discussed included "history, travel, literature, philosophy (of the homely kind), archaeology, and science." Euwer largely based the program on his personal experiences and on his extensive knowledge of literary figures and other personalities.[99] In her letter to the "Philosopher," the Oregon listener told about two major tragedies in her life, the accidental death of her twenty-year-old son and a more recent tragedy involving a second son who could not find employment in the midst of the Depression, despite having completed a master's degree from Harvard and having almost finished a Ph.D. from another major school in the East. She told how the family had "worked hard, saved much, sacrificed much that he might acquire this training." It was a "bitter blow," she wrote. "[A]t times I've felt my brain giving under the strain." But the KOAC program was a great comfort. "Your quiet little talks,

Mr. Philosopher, have helped me more than I can tell you." They were "a great comfort to anguished, bewildered souls."[100] This example not only shows how stations were experimenting with new programs that attempted to develop an informal style but also underscores how listeners responded well to this type of program. They formed emotional bonds with local characters over stations operated by state universities. Commercial stations, especially ones tied to networks, were less likely to broadcast programs such as this.

The general trend during the 1930s was for stations operated by institutions of higher education to create a separate, loosely connected, state-supported broadcasting system presenting programs not offered by commercial stations. Nevertheless, commercial values and showmanship techniques developed by commercial stations did influence the operation of some stations. The degree of influence mainly depended on the impact of key leaders. WOI and KOAC best illustrate this theme. During the late 1930s and early 1940s, important members of the staff at both institutions favored broadcasting programs that could compete with programs on commercial stations.

Andy Woolfries, the beloved announcer and assistant program manager at WOI, favored not only broadcasting alternative programming but also actively trying to compete with commercial stations for a general audience. Unlike other broadcasters who viewed themselves as educators first and broadcasters second, Woolfries argued in 1936 that he considered himself "a radio man who has been connected with an educational broadcasting station for more than fifteen years." Woolfries believed that "both educational and commercial stations face the common fundamental problem of attracting and holding the greatest possible audience." It is perhaps not surprising that Woolfries held this view; he was a popular announcer who managed to receive a relatively generous salary during the Depression and who had turned down even more generous offers from commercial stations because of his commitment to the station and the community.[101]

Woolfries compared "the radio situation" in any region to the "midway of a carnival." He argued that radio stations were in competition just as the tents of different carnival shows were "fighting for customers—cleverly, bitterly, unceasingly"—using "every device known to showmanship." In vivid terms, he described how the tent of an educational station compared unfavorably to the tent of a fifty-kilowatt commercial station. The fifty-kilowatt tent is a "thing of beauty" where "no expense has been spared," flaunting "such familiar names as Heifetz, Pons, Roosevelt, Stokowski, Guest, Benny, Vallee, Bowes, Dragonette, and a host of others equally well known." By contrast, the tent housing the educational "show" was "poorly situated, small, dingy, displaying a time-worn sign announcing an educational lecture at 10:15 A.M."

Although it may be "dignified and conservative," it is not "well calculated to attract a large, general audience."[102]

Woolfries called for the popularization of educational programs, even if this meant treating the educational content as secondary to the goal of attracting and holding an audience. He favored the adoption of new techniques to spice up talks and other presentations, including the use of a dialogue format or the dramatization of programs.[103] Instead of broadcasting programs modeled on formal classroom education, Woolfries believed that the station should focus on developing general broadcasting projects such as programs with an objective of "lifting listeners' appreciation levels." He held up his *Music Shop* as an example of the type of program he thought university stations should broadcast. Although the program was educational, he argued that it "has proved capable of meeting commercial competition." This judgment was based partly on the many letters from listeners and by the fact that a nearby network station offered a fifty-dollar reward for any station employee who could suggest a program able to compete with WOI's *Music Shop*. To humanize and popularize the music, Woolfries added biographical details of composers' lives. For example, when he played Beethoven's *Turkish March,* he told the audience that the composer enjoyed pouring cold water on his hands while he was working. For operatic excerpts, he made sure to describe the setting and story.[104]

Because Woolfries was only the assistant director, his desire to compete directly with commercial stations was never fully realized during the 1930s. However, by 1943 the official policy statement for WOI did change. It emphasized that the station needed to present "program matter to its audience in such a manner and of such a kind, and in such a way, that the largest possible continuous listening audience may be available." Although the official statement emphasized that the station should not "indulge in cheap appeals or condescensions," it also stressed that the average person needed to be kept in mind. The station was expected to present programs "not for the intelligent alone, but the great middle class."[105]

A change also occurred at KOAC during the early 1940s when Allen Miller became the new program director.[106] Miller had been in charge of the radio office at the University of Chicago. Rather than build its own station, the university decided to broadcast programs over commercial stations. Although he was committed to ideals of noncommercial educational broadcasting, his experience with commercial stations and networks left him more open than the average university station manager to commercial techniques and the general orientation of the commercial system. Miller announced at the April 1943 meeting of the Advisory Council on Radio Policy that he planned to "embark on a general program of popularization of KOAC broadcasts in both music and speech." Since the council agreed to use this phrase instead of a radically different passage from the previous minutes of the December meeting calling for "more use of ballet and semi-classical music in program planning," Miller's impact clearly led to a new direction in the work of the station, at least until he left two years later.[107]

Programming Innovations during the 1930s

Although much of the programming on university stations during the 1930s continued traditions developed in the previous decade, three especially important innovations partially developed earlier became much more significant. The first was the practice of broadcasting special educational programs to schools. Commercial stations, especially the national networks, also transmitted "schools of the air"; however, university and college radio stations viewed this as properly their domain.

Supporters argued that school broadcasts could bring the best teachers, as well as major national events and national political figures, to every school in the country: "The voice of the President of the United States speaks directly to the people. The most perfect of ballroom or symphonic music, stories, lectures, dramas—all are ready to enrich and delight the hearers."[108] The call for using radio in schools was part of the progressive education movement that sought to adjust students to modern industrial society. Advocates claimed that educators needed to keep up with the times. They thought it was inappropriate to give students the equivalent of a horse-and-buggy education in an age of gasoline-powered automobiles.[109] The new technique, they argued, would enrich the curriculum, stimulate the imagination, expand horizons, and provide teachers with relief from "the strain of continual direction of class work."[110]

Some educators, however, did not support the new approach to teaching. A number of teachers opposed the use of radio in schools because they feared the new technology would threaten their jobs.[111] Others believed that mechanical and scientific aids "have usually been forced upon the pedagogic world by the commercial interests involved and that rarely has the educator group taken the lead."[112] More generally, some educators criticized the new innovation for threatening to introduce "more mass education and standardized thinking."[113]

Educators first experimented with broadcasting to schools during the early 1920s. The deputy superintendent for Oakland city schools organized one of the earliest experiments over a commercial station in 1924.[114] The formation of the national networks NBC and CBS by the late 1920s meant that schools across the country could simultaneously receive the same broadcasts. The most significant early network effort was a music-appreciation program presented over NBC beginning in 1928 by the director of the New York Symphony Orchestra, Walter Damrosch. CBS also organized an *American School of the Air* program during this period. Another early program, broadcast only on NBC stations on the West Coast, was the *Standard School Music Appreciation Hour,* sponsored by the Standard Oil Company of California.[115]

The Damrosch program was particularly important in stimulating interest in school radio programs. In 1934, over seventy NBC affiliates broadcast the program; the network claimed that six million school children listened to it in classrooms across the country. In 1933, NBC distributed more than seventeen thousand instructor's manuals and 105,000 student notebooks published specifically in support of the program.[116] A number of local stations across the country, including stations operated by institutions of higher education, also produced their own "schools of the air" and various other school programs during the 1930s. Stations operated by land-grant institutions were particularly interested in serving rural schools. Organizers argued that "the smallest, poorest, and most isolated rural school can now hear speakers who are authorities in their respective fields."[117] The Wisconsin station WHA broadcast a wide assortment of school programs for different subjects, including nature study, music, civics, geography, and current events. Operators of university stations believed that their programs were superior to the offerings of commercial stations because they were free from commercial influence and because they were organized and operated by professional educators who had an intimate knowledge of local conditions.

A number of states invested relatively large amounts of money in the installation of radio receivers in schools during the 1930s. New school buildings were designed to take advantage of schools of the air and other school programs. New schools either had radio receivers wired directly into buildings (usually a central receiver connected to a public address system) or they had buildings constructed with specific outlets for radios. In 1936, the Office of Education reported the use of 11,501 receiving sets in schools across the country; in addition, 824 schools were using receivers connected to centralized sound systems.[118]

Ironically, one of the poorest states in the country, Alabama, went further than many states in planning for the use of radio in schools. The project was driven during the late 1920s by the enthusiasm of Governor Bibb Graves, who became enamored with the idea of using a state-supported system to transmit market information directly to farmers and to broadcast educational programs to every school in the state. Plans for two new schools in Montgom-

Students listening to a special school broadcast, Madison, Wisconsin, October 1931. Photo Whi-18402, courtesy of the Wisconsin Historical Society.

ery, the segregated African American school and the main city high school, specified equipment and wiring for radio.[119] State officials chose a system to avoid commercial influence. According to Armstrong Perry, "the receivers were selected on performance under controlled conditions rather than from sales talks."[120] This was an important issue because radio manufacturers were helping to drive the interest in this form of broadcasting as a way to sell receivers to a new market. Although about one hundred schools in the state installed receivers, the Depression largely derailed Graves's grand vision.[121]

Commercial and noncommercial stations broadcast schools of the air. In most cases the commercial programs remained unsponsored, but educators argued that important differences remained. Commercial operators would inevitably feel pressured to emphasize the size of the audience rather than the quality of programs. A more specific difference became clear in the case of the *Ohio School of the Air.* Although educators connected with the State Department of Education controlled the program, they used a major commercial station in Cincinnati, the Crosley Radio Corporation station WLW. The organizers of the school of the air were generally pleased with WLW, especially since the company never tried to use its name with the program.[122] One major problem did stand out, however: the program had to follow the copyright agreement imposed on the station by the ASCAP. To avoid a copyright-infringement suit, they knew they could not use some material, including "the works of Guest, Field, and Riley." The major problem was what they did not know. They had to check "every quotation of poetry and prose" to see if it was in the public domain; if it was not, they had to check to see if they had the permission of the copyright owner. The main driving force behind the *Ohio School of the Air,* Ben H. Darrow, complained to the secretary of the NCER about the need to spend an "interminable" amount of time on telegrams and telephone calls to deal with the copyright issue. According to Darrow, "[T]his strikes at the very roots of success of educational broadcasting."[123] The NCER secretary told him that the copyright situation was different for educational stations. The ASCAP gave these noncommercial stations a "general release, saying that so long as they do not perform for money they may use protections free of charge." He believed that because noncommercial stations operated by universities were nonprofit, the legal concern of financial damage could never be an issue.[124]

University stations also emphasized that their school programs were superior to the offerings of commercial stations because of their local character. Critics pointed out that commercial-network school programs did not take into account local conditions in different regions of the country. The organizers of school programs broadcast by university stations, by contrast, often worked closely with teachers in the region. Despite limited funds in the mid-1930s, the staff at KOAC toured schools across a large part of western Oregon to discover reactions to the station's *School of the Air* program and to "correlate as best we could in a short time our schedule with theirs."[125] One of the major conclusions of these visits was not to emphasize programs of the "master/teacher type"; instead, the station designed programs to assist scheduled activities of teachers in the classroom.[126]

Staff working with WHA at the University of Wisconsin made extended visits to classrooms in the state and conducted detailed investigations of students' responses. They found that some programs were more effective than others in capturing the attention of students. For example, instructors reported that *Young Aviators* was the most popular of all programs for older students. However, they believed that the program was "more pure entertainment than it might be and the carry over into the class is not great." In general, investigators reported that the impact of programs depended heavily on the initiative of the individual teacher: "[T]hese uses vary from 'just listening' to making the program an integral part of the curriculum and using it as a 'jumping off place' for a whole week of activities." They found that teachers were especially anxious for prepared material that would give them more guidance about how to integrate programs into the curriculum.[127]

A second especially notable broadcasting practice used by university stations was group listening. Although first developed during the 1920s from practices employed by agricultural extension services, it became more important during the 1930s, especially at the Iowa State station WOI and the Oregon State station KOAC. Listener groups mostly served women. Through these "clubs," women not only participated in imagined communities over the air but also in real communities in homes and community centers. The main listening clubs organized by WOI were the Homemakers' Radio Clubs and the Radio Child Study Clubs. The homemaker clubs met in homes to discuss homemaking, family life, child care, and related issues introduced on the *Homemakers' Half Hour.* Some of the clubs also participated in an art-appreciation program. They discussed works of art based on reproductions sent to them by the university. The station sent out hundreds of copies of prints to club listeners during the 1930s.[128] The homemaker radio clubs organized by KOAC dealt with similar "family life problems." During the 1933–34 season, the station enrolled fifty-three clubs, made up of 596 women. Club members usually met at 2:30 PM, in time to tune in to the 3:00 PM program. During the first ten or fifteen minutes, the program would answer questions sent in by club members. After listening to the program, the group would discuss questions from the outline supplied by the station. At the end of the meeting, the secretary of each radio club sent the station a report indicating the number of members present, the general reaction to the broadcast, and questions the group wanted to have addressed in a future broadcast. Although staff at the university were interested in stimulating a free discussion of different ideas, they also viewed the radio clubs as a way to promote "the intelligent adoption of recommended practices."[129]

While many broadcast practices developed by universities were also adopted by commercial stations, group listening was different. It was largely unique to noncommercial stations operated by state universities because the networks, especially NBC, actively opposed the practice. A number of European broadcasters also adopted the practice, apparently independently of noncommercial stations in the United States. Despite the extensive use of group listening by the BBC and other broadcasters in western Europe, NBC characterized the practice as mainly a communist invention imported from the Soviet Union to spread government propaganda. Network executives emphasized that the natural, all-American place for radio was in the home. "The American institution of home life has driven our people back to their 'fire-sides' . . . to listen to radio," according to one executive. "This is natural and the discussion of radio programs within the family is still the best variety of honest criticism we will ever receive."[130]

At least one university station seemed to partly accept NBC's argument about the natural location for listening. The radio advisory committee at the University of Illinois decided against organizing listener groups, arguing that this practice contradicted the main advantage claimed for radio—"that it brings information, education, and entertainment into the home and to the fireside." The committee believed that listener groups were "best adapted to conditions where there are few or no radio sets in the homes." Since most farm families in Illinois had radios by the 1930s, it did not seem necessary to ask farmers to travel to meetings where they would get material they could just as easily receive at home over the radio.[131]

Public-affairs or related programming discussing controversial political and social issues was a third form that became more important beginning in the 1930s. Most university stations inherited from the 1920s a policy of avoiding controversial programming. Since most radio stations at institutions of higher education received public funding, they were sensitive about avoiding actions that might alienate significant sections of the public. The Purdue station WBAA, for example, announced in its 1932 annual report that staff had "decided that controversial subjects such as politics, religion, and commercial advertising be kept off the programs broadcast by the University."[132] WSUI at the University of Iowa also declined to broadcast political speeches or programs dealing with "any subjects which are of such a controversial nature that listeners might object."[133]

WOI seemed to be particularly sensitive to public criticism, especially when the criticism involved the moral character of the station. When a Jesuit priest wrote WOI, in 1941, to complain about a passage of a book read over the air that included a description of a naked native girl, the person in charge of the program wrote back promising that he would warn "all our radio readers again to be careful to omit any allusion which could possibly give offense to any of our listeners."[134] The priest was particularly upset because he had invited students to listen with him to the program and because the reader recommended the book, "promising that all who did would feel that they made a real journey." "Yes," the priest responded sarcastically, "I imagine that any young man or boy listening in would feel that meeting naked native girls racing towards them would be a real journey in their young lives."[135]

The station's extreme concern about avoiding this type of criticism was partly a reaction to the visit, in 1933, of the popular Protestant evangelist Aimee Semple McPherson. During her stay in Iowa, she pointedly railed against state universities, characterizing them as "dens of iniquity." As a direct response to McPherson's attack, WOI added a fifteen-minute *Matin Period* near the beginning of each day's broadcast. The program began with a religious recording and the reading of a psalm, followed by a five-minute inspirational talk by a clergyman or a member of the faculty, before ending with a recording of a hymn or a religious anthem. Griffith, the station director, admitted that he added the program to help establish "in the minds of the public that a state institution is not necessarily a Godless institution."[136]

Although most university stations did not broadcast programs dealing with controversial political issues during the 1930s, a change occurred towards the end of the decade. The increased interest in world events immediately preceding the Second World War led a number of stations to introduce new types of public-affairs programs. Hitler's example drove home the lesson that radio was "not simply an instrument of peace and persuasion" but also could be used "as an instrument of coercion, a weapon of war."[137] By not broadcasting open-ended and free discussions of controversial issues, university staff realized that they could be accused of practicing a form of censorship common to totalitarian regimes. Directors of radio stations responded by stressing the importance of broadcasting for keeping citizens of democracies intelligent and informed. "The achievement of this goal," they argued in 1939, "is America's most certain safeguard against political and economic demagogery and dictatorship."[138]

The staff at the Oregon State station KOAC first tried to convince the State Board of Higher Education to change its policy against discussion of controversial issues during the late 1930s. The program manager complained in 1938 that this policy "has caused me and our radio staff more concern than any other single administrative problem." The manager pointed out that "controversial questions are almost invariably vital questions of special public interest." The staff had been forced on a number of occasions to deny discussions of important issues. For example, the station had to deny a talk sponsored by the American Association of University Women because "while this talk contained only one or two specific statements which might have been definitely pointed to as objectionable, the entire tenor of the talk was what those of a different opinion might consider to be pacifistic." Since the people denied the right to use the station could argue that the station was practicing censorship, the manager feared that this policy was doing more harm than good. Because of the policy, the station always asked to see a copy of talks before they were broadcast. "Freedom of speech," according to the station manager, "is one of the fundamental principles of our Constitutions," and "any suspicions of censorship is objectionable to the American public."[139] Despite the complaints of station staff, the Board of Higher Education maintained the policy into the 1940s. As late as 1946, the station cited this directive when it declined to broadcast a program dealing with a controversial political issue.[140]

The University of Illinois station WILL also tried to critically address its policy against controversial programs around the same time as the Oregon station. In 1939, the Board of Trustees adopted a new policy statement that attempted to more fully define this issue. The university decided that three subject areas were clearly too controversial to be discussed over the air: "partisan political issues," "sectarian religious questions," and "questions involving equality or relationship of races." The station could broadcast academic discussions involving different views within established disciplines because they were based on "careful scientific research" or standards of academic professionalism.[141] During this same period, the station introduced public-affairs programs in which small groups of faculty (or students under faculty supervision) debated and discussed important public issues.[142] A similar pattern occurred at Iowa State during the late 1930s. WOI introduced a public-affairs program called *Let's Talk It Over,* which allowed for an open, extemporaneous discussion.[143]

Unlike the other university stations during the 1930s that sought to remain nonpartisan by avoiding discussions of controversial political and social issues, the University of Wisconsin station WHA decided early in the decade to deal with the problem directly by offering a "comprehensive program of political education." Partly because of the state's progressive political traditions, officials at the station were more open to creating a schedule based "on the premise that the success of a democracy depends upon an informed and enlightened citizenry."[144] The person who replaced Lighty as the station's program director, H. L. Ewbank, a professor in the speech department, played an especially important role developing public-affairs programming. Ewbank organized the first program to deal with controversial issues in March 1931. The program discussed a variety of viewpoints on timely political, social, and economic problems.[145]

The next step in the station's effort to introduce political education occurred in 1932. University staff proposed to offer free airtime to political candidates running for office during the upcoming state election later that year. Everyone, including the different political candidates, accepted the offer. WHA and the other state-supported station, WLBL, offered the candidates a total of two half-hour periods each weekday during the four weeks preceding the election in November. Each candidate would receive the same amount of time. They drew lots to determine the schedule. Station officials agreed not to censor the broadcasts. Representatives of the parties with candidates on the ballot signed the agreement: the Democratic party, Prohibition party, Republican party, Socialist party, Independent Socialist-Labor party, and the Independent Communist party. "So successful was the 1932 experiment," according to the assistant director Harold Engel, "that it was continued in virtually the same basis" with the other elections during the 1930s.[146] Engel believed his station provided an example for other state-supported stations for recreating "in this machine age the sort of unhampered and intimate and sustained discussion of public issues that marked the New England town meeting and the Lincoln-Douglas debates."[147]

The Dilemma of Support without Strings

A major dilemma for state-supported radio stations was how to conduct political education but remain independent of state control. This problem was especially important for WHA and WLBL, because the stations managed to maintain support during the 1930s partly by serving state interests. The staff members at WHA recognized this danger and tried to develop policies to minimize the risk of political interference. The director of the station, Harold McCarty, warned that the station should not "get too closely tied up with the state government but keep as much as possible of academic freedom."[148] Official station policy stressed that "while the distinction is sometimes difficult to make," differences should be maintained between "'education' as opposed to 'propaganda,' or 'news' and 'information' as opposed to 'promotion.'"[149]

One of the difficulties staff at WHA needed to deal with was the fact that they did not decide to provide equal time to all political parties for purely altruistic reasons. In 1932 a staff member at WHA admitted that the decision to allow different political candidates to "fill the air with a lot of political malarkey preparatory to the coming primary" was partly a "subtle move to get some politicians back of our plans for a hook-up with WLBL."[150] Nevertheless, the station was proud of its record of providing equal time to all political parties, including the strongest opponents of elected officials. Politicians praised the station for "the impartial manner in which time is distributed among the various candidates," for the "lack of censorship exercised . . . over the speakers," and for giving "equal consideration" to "those favoring and those opposing the administration."[151]

Although not always recognized at the time because of the dominance of the commercial system, the problem of support without strings was also an issue for commercial stations. Proponents of state-supported public-service broadcasting argued that advertisers could influence or effectively censor programs just as easily as the state. To gain a deeper understanding of this threat of control by advertisers and the government, the next chapter will analyze an important educational program broadcast over commercial stations, the *University of Chicago Round Table*. But first it is important to analyze this tension in the context of universities trying to combine commercial and educational objectives. Noncommercial stations operated by institutions of higher education increasingly emphasized during the 1930s that the incompatibility between educational or public-service objectives and commercial values demanded the establishment of a separate system providing an alternative to the dominant system of network-controlled commercial broadcasting. Failed attempts to combine commercial and educational objectives during this period provided strong support for this argument.

The tensions resulting from a university station trying to combine commercial and educational objectives were particularly clear in the case of the University of Florida station WRUF, which officially began broadcasting in October 1928. The station at first assumed a dual role. State government officials and Florida business leaders who promoted the establishment of WRUF were mainly interested in using the station to promote state commerce and to attract residents from northern states. They called the station the "Voice of Florida." But instead of establishing it as an independent entity serving the entire state, the legislature turned the station over to the University of Florida to manage. The university tried to combine the traditional educational function of radio stations at state universities with the objective of providing high-quality entertainment representing the best of Florida.[152]

In general, university officials were not overly enthusiastic about having the station. The acting president informed a correspondent in June 1928 that "some of us have felt that it is not exactly the function of the University to operate this station, but we have it, and we are determined to put forth our best efforts" for its "success."[153] Bert C. Riley, the director of the General Extension Division who managed the station, at first tried to block its establishment until the legislature promised to set aside sufficient funds for programming and personnel. Although in the end the state generously set aside one hundred thousand dollars for a powerful five-thousand-watt station that would be "excelled by none in every mechanical detail," Riley argued that little was left over for programming and continuing operations. He especially worried about additional funding, since the station was "out of the beaten path" and did not have the quality of "local talent found in the larger universities." Riley complained to a colleague that people expected him to have "a Ringling Brothers circus top with people expecting great things . . . and now it will be impossible to do more than give them a dog and pony show."[154]

The university station was not only expected to provide professional-quality entertainment programming modeled on the commercial networks but also to use advertising. This latter position became clear immediately before WRUF began regular transmissions, when the state attorney general ruled that the Board of Control of the university was ultimately responsible for the management of the station and that the board could allow commercial advertising following the "usual customs and practices incident to the operation of radio stations generally."[155]

Severe financial problems during the 1930s forced the station to increasingly rely on advertising. In 1933, after the governor and the State Budget Commission recommended that the university investigate leasing the station to a private company, the Board of Control directed WRUF to accept advertising but also provided general guidelines.[156] The board told the station that it could only accept unsolicited advertising. The new station director, Garland Powell, also decided that to avoid competition with print media the station should require advertisers using WRUF to advertise in newspapers as well.[157]

But these restrictions did not address a more fundamental tension involving the conflict between commercial interests and publicly supported agricultural extension. Officials in charge of research at the agricultural-experiment station objected in November 1932 to WRUF's use of Morton Salt Company advertising that promoted the product's value for curing meat. Officials in charge of research at the station pointed out that the company's claims contradicted the official recommendations of state and federal agencies against using "smoked salt" for the preservation of meat. Researchers only recommended refrigeration or true smoking. The assistant director of the research station complained that since "farmers do not distinguish between the University, the Experiment Station, and WRUF," the practice placed the division in "a peculiar position when the gospel goes out in relation to Morton's salt and our workers then have to say that they do not approve of it."[158]

Garland Powell defended the use of Morton's advertisements by arguing that the Board of Control only instructed him to accept unsolicited advertising. The board did not give him specific rules for rejecting advertising based on content: "They more or less left it in my hands to decide upon the merits of the article advertised." The policy Powell developed was to only accept advertisements from "reputable firms and reputable advertising agencies." He decided that since "the Morton Salt Company maintains laboratories, and a research division with recognized authorities at its head," their claim had to be accepted as "just as good as any other method." Powell's response underscores the problematic status of the radio station, which was trying to function as a commercial station presenting entertainment to a large audience and an educational station grounded in the work of university extension. Especially in the context of the severe financial constraints of the Depression, Powell resisted giving priority status to research conducted by other parts of the university.[159] Significantly, when the university appointed Powell in 1930, it gave him more independence from the General Extension Division, which had been responsible for managing the station.[160]

For officials at the experiment station, the issue of developing a consistent policy for all parts of the university was paramount. The director wrote Powell that the question involved was not one of "responsibility, honesty of purpose, or integrity of the Morton Salt Company," nor was it "one that is concerned with . . . how carefully they have investigated the value of their own product." Rather, for the agricultural-experiment station director, the question was "one of policy on the part of WRUF and the extent to which this policy is in conflict with that of the University of Florida Agricultural Experiment Station."[161] Whether or not the station decided to stop broadcasting the advertisement is not clear; however, it appears that Powell refused to develop a policy for accepting advertising consistent with the work of the extension service since a similar problem occurred less than two years later. In January 1934, the extension director complained about a proposal Powell seemed to support authorizing the American Agricultural Chemical Company to sponsor the noontime *Florida Farm Hour* program, which the extension service funded at a rate of approximately five thousand dollars per year. The director considered commercial sponsorship of the extension service program as "unethical" because it would "amount in Essence" to the extension division "contributing at least $5,000 a year . . . to the material used in the advertising program of the American Agricultural Chemical Company."[162]

The experience of WWL, operated by Loyola University, a private Jesuit university in New Orleans, illustrates not only the tension between public service and commercialism but more specifically the difficulties involved in trying to continue the educational function of broadcasting after a university station completely commercialized. Loyola first experimented with broadcasting as early as 1922. By 1929, it had a full-time, clear-channel station using a five-thousand-watt transmitter. By this date, the university was completing the transition to commercial status. The station director, a priest named W. A. Burk, recalled in January 1933 how, about three years earlier, they believed the station should remain "strictly non-commercial" and devoted almost exclusively to education. But "gradually," according to Burk, they began to recognize that "preparing an educational program extending to twelve and a half hours per day was an impossible task." The station "constituted a fearful drain upon the university's resources." The university decided to accept advertising to pay for "worthwhile talent" necessary for building up an audience. Burke justified the decision to become a commercial operator because it would give the station a larger audience that would then be available for educational programs. According to Burk, "[W]hen we did put on educational programs we would have somebody to listen to them!"[163]

Burk argued that the decision to commercialize had played a crucial role in the university's success in fending off attacks from other stations for the use of its clear channel: "[E]ach time we have come off with flying colors and been declared invulnerable by the commission itself." If the station had remained "solely or exclusively religious or educational," he was convinced that it would have "long since" lost its superior assignment. But despite Burk's assertion that commercialization had improved the educational mission of the station, by 1933 educational programming amounted only to about fifteen minutes per day. And despite the station's nearly complete adoption of commercial programming, the station was still operating at a loss. The effect of commercialization on the traditional function of a university station is especially evident in the length Burk went to justify the university's ownership of such a commercial station. In a letter to the program director of WHA, Burk argued that "it might be truly said that all of our entertaining and even commercial features are educational in character, since we allow nothing that is low or vulgar or of bad taste to go out from our station."[164] The only way a university could justify operating a station that had made the transition to commercial operations was to expand the definition of education well beyond traditional institutional understandings of the term.

The tension between education and commercialism took on different dimensions for universities that did not establish or maintain their own stations but accepted the offers of commercial stations to give educators complete access to the airwaves. The promises of commercial stations did not conform to the realities. For example, in 1934, the University of California at Berkeley complained about having to shift "the most popular program we have ever tried," a program called *The University Explorer*. Until the end of September, three of the most important stations in California—KFI in Los Angeles, KFSD in San Diego, and KPO in San Francisco—broadcast the program at 9 PM on Sundays. For the first program in October, the university agreed grudgingly to shift the broadcast time to 9:30 PM because of a conflict with a Jack Benny program sponsored by General Foods and a less memorable program sponsored by a "cut-rate dentist" named Dr. Painless Parker. But the university protested when, without warning, another NBC station in Los Angeles, KECA, broadcast the program instead of KFI. And a week later NBC decided to shift the time again. University officials were not sure of the reason for this second shift but believed it was "squeezed out through the sale of time . . . to a patent medicine, Crazy Water Crystals, and to RealSilk Hosiery Mills." The network offered to broadcast the program during other times considered reasonably desirable, but because it could not give "some assurance" that there would be no more shifts for at least "a few weeks," the university decided to discontinue the program temporarily. After contacting officials with the other major network, CBS, the university decided to accept an offer of "a choice of several desirable hours and a chain of from 8 to 13 stations." The Columbia network promised to "do their best to preserve the continuity" of the university's programs, but officials at the school were skeptical about being able to "keep these times." Harold Ellis, the manager of the University News Service, informed a correspondent that the university was not upset with NBC executives. The problem was with "the system under which they are operating," which forced them always to give preference "to cash customers."[165]

* * *

The 1930s represented a transitional period in the early history of noncommercial broadcasting in the United States. At the same time as the network-oriented commercial system was becoming dominant during the early years of the decade and a number of marginal noncommercial stations gave up their licenses, a loosely organized alternative system gained stability. Despite the hardships of the Depression, a number of key radio stations operated by state universities managed to obtain increased state support and, for the first time, federal patronage. Although the New Deal came too late to change the policies of the FRC during the beginning of the decade, New Deal programs provided significant grants to university stations during the late 1930s. This served as an important precedent for developments during the 1960s, when the federal government provided substantial funds for educational broadcasting, especially for television stations but also for radio.

The Wisconsin station WHA and the Oregon station KOAC provided important models for noncommercial broadcasting. Both stations linked the use of radio for extension education to traditions of state-supported public service. These and other stations drew on earlier innovations to develop new forms of programming, including broadcasts to public schools and programs developed in conjunction with the technique of group listening. These program forms were especially important because they built on authentic local relationships by engaging with local audiences and local institutions. While commercial stations became increasingly tied to national networks that were mainly interested in selling audiences to national advertisers, noncommercial university stations remained tied to local and regional communities.

Important innovations also occurred during the 1930s with the development of public-affairs programming. Progressive political traditions unique to Wisconsin led WHA to play a particularly important role along these lines. During the 1920s and the first half of the 1930s, many university stations avoided discussions of controversial subjects. This restriction prevented the full development of public-affairs programming until the late 1930s, when a number of stations critically reexamined this policy. Stations increasingly emphasized the important role of broadcasting in the maintenance of a healthy democracy. Supporters argued that only noncommercial stations committed to serving the public rather than the interests of advertisers could present a full range of views, including controversial minority positions. While commercial stations treated listeners as consumers, noncommercial state university stations increasingly treated listeners as citizens. WHA led the way in using radio to promote political education and in opening the airwaves to different points of view. The rise of totalitarianism in Europe during the late 1930s underscored the power of radio for political control through the use of propaganda. Discussion-forum programs introduced during this period by stations operated by universities reflected a new view of the political importance of broadcasting.

Most stations during the 1930s increasingly emphasized that they were providing the public with programming not offered by commercial stations. Stations such as WHA and KOAC were especially important in pushing for a distinct role for noncommercial university stations. The BBC provided an important model for a number of officials connected with stations at state universities during the 1930s. They wanted to create a separate system of noncommercial public broadcasting that would focus on the quality of different forms of programming rather than the number of people listening. Officials argued that they needed to draw a sharp separation between their work and the activities of commercial broadcasters. Freedom from commercial considerations meant, among other things, the freedom to experiment with new innovations in radio programming. As the noncommercial justification became more important, stations increasingly used the term "public-service" or "public" broadcasting instead of "educational broadcasting."

Despite the new emphasis on the unique nature of noncommercial broadcasting, a number of stations during this period were ambivalent about this separatist goal. The academic and noncommercial commitment of university stations was consistent with a focus on serving select audiences; extension traditions and state traditions of public service were consistent with a desire to maximize audiences. The desire to serve large sections of the public led some staff to emphasize the need to adapt techniques developed by commercial stations. We see this especially with WOI and KOAC during the early 1940s, when key personnel pushed the stations to adopt showmanship techniques to serve the great middle classes with a broad range of programming rather than primarily use stations to "educate the educated." But efforts by university stations to popularize material did not simply reflect the influence of techniques developed by commercial stations. Radio stations at universities drew on home-grown techniques of extension education to serve broad audiences.

Increased ties to the state meant that university stations needed to worry about the problem of state government control. Unlike the BBC and public broadcasters in other countries that were established as independent institutions, public-service stations operated by universities were not insulated in the same way from government influence. However, by the late 1930s, many university stations moved away from earlier concerns about not broadcasting controversial programs to avoid jeopardizing public funding. The problem of support without strings was more important for educational programs over commercial stations. University stations pointed to numerous examples of the incompatibility between commercial values and educational or public-service objectives. They believed this fundamental incompatibility demanded the construction of a separate noncommercial system grounded in institutions of higher education.

7. Network Practices, Government Oversight, and Public-Service Ideals

The University of Chicago Round Table

Every Sunday from the early 1930s to the mid-1950s, NBC presented over its nationwide network of stations a unique program, the *University of Chicago Round Table*, produced by one of the best research universities in the country. Contrasting the intelligent discussion on the *Round Table* with the commercial offerings over radio, mainly meant to entertain, promoters stressed that "there are no black-faced comedians, no crooning tenors, no whispering baritones gracing the faculties of the University of Chicago." Neither did this "eminent institution of higher learning" have "any commodity to advertise nor any political ax to grind." Officials in charge of the program acknowledged that the public "deserves to be entertained" but also believed that citizens deserve "to hear lively news and authoritative interpretation of contemporary affairs."[1]

A study of the *University of Chicago Round Table* is especially important because it exemplified a type of program that became increasingly central to public-interest broadcasting, as practiced on noncommercial and commercial radio stations. The *Round Table* was not only one of the earliest, longest-running, and popular public-affairs radio programs, but unlike similar programs broadcast by commercial stations, it was organized and produced by university educators. A study of the *Round Table* provides a unique opportunity to explore crucial tensions central to the organization of noncommercial and commercial broadcasting in the United States. Educators saw this as an opportunity to use the new powerful electronic medium to establish an ideal public sphere for political conversation and dialogue based on sound scholarship. But they faced significant obstacles as commercial and governmental pressures sought to restrict access and influence programming in the context of some of the major political and social issues confronting the United States during the 1930s and 1940s: isolationism, wartime civil rights, and the collapse of the attraction to communism.

The University of Chicago and Early Radio

Like other educational institutions during the early years of radio broadcasting, the University of Chicago sought to use radio to extend its educational mission to citizens not formally enrolled as students. As we have seen, before the acceptance of advertising as the primary means of financing broadcasting, the owners of most stations were motivated by the institutional goodwill or publicity they expected to receive from their broadcasts. Given this context, it should not be surprising that the University of Chicago was not only motivated by the educational possibilities of radio but also by its potential publicity value. In 1924, the director of publicity for the university convinced the administration to initiate a regular schedule of programs broadcast from the campus over the radio station WMAQ, operated by the *Chicago Daily News*. The administration hoped that alumni the university was interested in convincing to contribute to a development campaign would appreciate the effort by the university to serve the community using radio.[2]

The first president of the school, William Rainey Harper, had been especially interested in adult education and in ensuring that the university served the Chicago community. Harper established University Extension as one of five original core divisions. Through correspondence courses and extension lectures, Harper and his successors sought to disseminate the benefits of the university widely.[3] Radio seemed ideal for "promoting this wider contact with the great social groups around the University." One lecture or talk could reach thousands of citizens "who might otherwise feel very remote from the world and work of the University."[4]

At first, the university primarily experimented with broadcasting lectures over the air.[5] In April 1926, WMAQ agreed to pay half the cost of installation and the entire rental costs of a telephone line to a lecture hall on campus from which radio courses would be broadcast.[6] The director of programming at WMAQ, Judith Waller, was especially instrumental in establishing this cooperative relationship.

Staff in charge of extension work at the university resisted incorporating radio courses into the home-study program. A radio committee organized by the administration decided that offering university credit for radio courses "would be an unfortunate step from every point of view."[7] But this decision against awarding credit did not mean that the university was against broadcasting regular university classes. Beginning in 1927, the university broadcast sections of survey courses that would appeal to wide audiences.[8] At the same time, the university also experimented with less formal radio broadcasts. Especially important was an early effort to broadcast commentary on current events or public affairs.[9] Members of the university community interested in participating in radio included Thomas Vernor Smith, a Texas-born philosopher and political scientist who was elected to the U.S. House of Representatives in 1938; Allen Miller, one of Smith's students at Chicago who became the first head of the radio office at the university; and Percy Boynton, a member of the English department who was in charge of organizing one of the first classroom broadcasts.[10]

WMAQ was willing to give the University of Chicago its choice of time for broadcasting in the mid-1920s; by 1930 the station forced the university to use less desirable hours.[11] Faced with these realities, the director of the radio office, Allen Miller, believed that if the university wanted to continue to use local radio stations and possibly present programs over the commercial networks (NBC and CBS), it needed to "make our educational broadcasts interesting to the average audience." But this did not mean that the university had to adopt practices developed by commercial stations. Rather, he believed that it could still offer educational courses, but they would need to avoid specialization. And he argued that the "primary aim" of the university's radio programs should be "to stimulate interest in further education."[12]

Miller continued to encourage broadcasts of classroom courses after 1930. But he also helped develop new programs not based on formal classroom teaching, including *The Professor at the Breakfast Table*, which listened in as a professor and his wife discussed over breakfast general issues learned from books. Altogether, in February 1931, the university was broadcasting sixteen programs for a total of eleven hours per week.[13]

Round Table Origins

Of all the new programs developed during this period, the *University of Chicago Round Table* was the most important. The idea for the program originated with T. V. Smith, who went on to become a regular participant on the program for nearly a decade. Smith had suggested to a discussion group meeting in the faculty club dining room that "it was a pity our discussions couldn't burn up the airwaves."[14] Unlike other groups that were limited to specialized discussions for specific departments, Smith's group was open to faculty from different departments interested in any topic. Smith claimed that "lacking a specialty, I was a sort of specialist-of-things-in-general." Miller discussed Smith's suggestion and convinced a wealthy businessman, Clarence Sills, to donate five thousand dollars to the university for the program. The university mainly used the money to cover the cost of the broadcast lines between the university and the radio station.[15] The program's name came from the shape of the tables used for discussion at the faculty club. In reality, the table specially made for the radio program was triangular.[16]

The *University of Chicago Round Table* first went on the air in February 1931. The weekly Sunday program brought together faculty for an informal, extemporaneous discussion of contemporary social, economic, and political issues. Fundamental concepts about the social responsibility of higher education underpinned the program. Miller and Smith wanted to take advantage of the traditional role of universities "in recording, maintaining, and interpreting the events of society" based on a commitment to truth and enlightenment.[17] The *Round Table* was committed to the idea that universities were "the best symbol our society affords of integrity, of social responsibility, and of knowledge."[18]

The *Round Table* format was also based on a commitment to the traditional political view that the health of a democracy depended on an educated and informed citizenry. Miller and Smith recognized the important role of radio broadcasting in this mission of keeping citizens informed and educated. Rather than lecture to listeners, the program provided a full discussion of issues by participants holding different points of view. The informal conversational style helped give listeners the sense that they were participating in the program. Questions listeners might have would likely be injected into the free-flowing discussion by one of the participants.

The university found that three participants were an ideal combination for the *Round Table*. They provided a balanced means of getting across a range of views and of demonstrating that issues were not "all black or all white."[19] The program prided itself on avoiding extreme positions and not playing up controversy in a sensational manner. During the 1930s, the *Round Table* developed a group of fifteen to twenty faculty members to participate in the program. The "inner core" of faculty who most frequently appeared included—in addition to T. V. Smith and Percy Boynton—Harry D. Gideonse in the economics department; William H. Spencer, the dean of the School of Business; and Harold Lasswell, a professor of political science and an expert on communications and propaganda. As it developed a national audience, the *Round Table* also increasingly included political and business leaders outside the university as participants.[20]

Officials at the university stressed the unique contribution of the *Round Table* to broadcasting in the United States. They claimed that it was the first program on the air that did not use scripts. More important, they emphasized that it was not a "current events or commentator program" but the first and most important program broadcast by commercial stations in which university professors recognized their responsibility as interpreters of modern life.[21] Miller hoped that the *Round Table* would show "that intelligent people who hold differences of opinion can engage in friendly discussion and, through it, can come to a closer understanding of the basic point at issue."[22]

The university contrasted their program with other public-affairs discussion or forum programs partially patterned after the *Round Table* but using debate techniques and a studio audience that was often encouraged to ask questions, including most importantly NBC's *Town Meeting of the Air* and CBS's *People's Platform*. Academic staff committed to educational broadcasting criticized such programs for using showmanship techniques and "playing up emotionalism and exploiting mob psychology."[23] The *Town Meeting of the Air* prominently featured audience laughter and applause and sometimes polled the audience before and after a debate.[24] Unlike the other forum programs, the *Round Table* tried to consistently use faculty who could relate narrow issues to broad political, economic, or social themes informed by social-scientific and humanistic analysis. During a discussion in 1938 titled "Problem of Propaganda in the United States," University of Chicago faculty members presented a historical analysis of different meanings of propaganda, beginning with the Holy Roman church. They quoted a number of authorities with differing points of view, including Henry David Thoreau and Supreme Court Justice Oliver Wendell Holmes Jr., and then used this broad context to discuss narrower and timelier questions such as whether citizenship should be taught in schools.[25]

The early development of the *Round Table* coincided with the inauguration of a new president of the university in 1929, Robert M. Hutchins. The thirty-year-old president valued the radio office's efforts to provide adult education, but he also recognized that the fiscal realities of the Depression meant that many activities of the university would need to be severely cut back. His administration encouraged the radio office to find outside sources of support.[26] The radio office faced severe budget problems during the early 1930s, especially with the expiration of the Sills gift.[27] Hutchins placed a new emphasis on the publicity value of radio. To enhance the national reputation of the university, he favored programs "that can be developed with sufficient interest to win chain [network] support, and yet with sufficient dignity to be representative of the University of Chicago."[28]

Hutchins encouraged the radio office to convince WMAQ's network, NBC, to broadcast the *Round Table*. Judith Waller informed a meeting of the university radio committee in February 1932 that there were "two attitudes at NBC towards educational radio." The program director at the network, John Royal, was hostile. Waller described Royal as a "one-time actor who has no respect for educational features and who, in fact, seems lacking in appreciation of anything cultural."[29] Royal led the faction at NBC that advocated a broad definition of education—"all experience of whatever type."[30] He praised the popular NBC show *Amos 'n' Andy,* which featured white actors performing "blackface" routines using racial stereotypes, for its educational value. "When *Amos 'n' Andy* first went on," according to Royal, "they taught a lot of people to use the tooth-brush. I don't suppose this would come under the heading of education, but it really was, and is."[31] A faction at the network supporting a stricter definition of educational radio based on academic standards was led by the first vice president, John Elwood.[32] Although Waller feared that this faction represented a minority, Elwood's influence prevailed in favor of the University of Chicago. In 1933, the network agreed to accept the *Round Table* as a "network sustaining feature," defined as a program not sponsored by advertisers.[33]

William Benton and the Round Table

Commercial pressures forced local stations to drop a number of the University of Chicago programs during the early and mid-1930s. Partly to help find new sources of support for the radio office, President Hutchins appointed William Benton to the post of vice president in 1937. Benton and Hutchins were friends from their undergraduate years at Yale University. Benton had gone into the advertising business after college and had acquired a great deal of wealth after establishing his own firm, Benton and Bowles. But he made a dramatic break from the advertising business in the mid-1930s, deciding instead to commit his life to public service—in the tradition of many members of his family who were educators and religious leaders. Hutchins was especially interested in having Benton come to Chicago to conduct a consumer survey to determine ways to improve the public image of the university. Benton's real interest, however, was in overseeing the university's involvement in radio. Hutchins gave him the authority he wanted; after studying the activities of the radio office, Benton decided to focus the university's resources on improving the *Round Table* program.[34]

By 1937, the *Round Table* had already gained a national reputation for innovative programming using thirty-seven NBC-affiliated stations. Benton hoped to get philanthropic support to allow the *Round Table* to develop nationally.[35] He thought that the audience in 1937, probably between 750,000 and a million listeners weekly, could "with improved production techniques, with publicity, and with a good period of time, be perhaps trebled or quadrupled."[36]

University of Chicago Round Table radio program (1942 broadcast); from left to right: Harold D. Lasswell (professor of political science, University of Chicago), Byron Price (U.S. censorship director), and William B. Benton (vice president, University of Chicago). Courtesy of the Special Collections Research Center, University of Chicago Library.

Benton felt particularly qualified to oversee the operation of the university's radio office because his advertising firm had become a leader in producing entertainment-based radio programs during the mid-1930s. Benton and his business partner Chet Bowles pioneered a number of innovations, including the first use of live audiences and the cueing of audiences with cards telling them to "applaud" or "laugh." Instead of following the traditional practice of only relying on announcers to give commercial messages during breaks in programs, they created a new program, the *Maxwell House Show Boat,* that indirectly inserted the commercial product into the program. During the show, actors reproduced all the sounds normally made when drinking coffee, including sipping, smacking lips together, and clinking cups. Sales of Maxwell House coffee increased 85 percent within a year after the show went on the air.[37]

Benton warned that "if the great universities do not develop radio broadcasting in the cause of education, it will, perhaps, be permanently left in the hands of manufacturers of face powder, coffee, and soap"; however, he continued to generally equate "good broadcasting" practices with the commercial system built on "radio publicity" and showmanship.[38] Benton specifically criticized the *Round Table* for not incorporating professional techniques developed for commercial programs. A study conducted by his former business partner supported this evaluation. Bowles believed that the voices of participants were too monotonous and the "arguments were far more academic than they needed to be." He wanted the discussion to be "taken out of the textbook atmosphere and brought down to simple examples of common, everyday people and how the problems under discussion affect them." Further, Bowles suggested ways to treat the audience as consumers: for example, have them "vote on which presentation they feel is more convincing and . . . announce the result of this vote each week."[39]

Miller resisted Benton's efforts to introduce to the *Round Table* values learned from his years working with commercial radio. Benton's aggressive efforts—he believed that the "best defense is an attack"—led to a major break with Miller. An executive at NBC wrote that Benton had "supreme contempt" for Miller.[40] Miller thought that the idea of having listeners vote went against the desire to avoid presenting "current economic, political, and social situations as all black or all white." He also believed that audiences did not necessarily want highly polished voices; they responded well to "authoritative voices and informality."[41] Miller worried that any effort to introduce techniques that faculty might consider undignified would jeopardize the "task of selling radio to all of the people in the university." "With so many of them," according to Miller, "I believe that we are close to success, but this success would be turned to defeat should anything approaching the ballyhoo of commercial radio creep into our broadcasts." He opposed Benton's desire to increase the size of the audience if this meant sacrificing quality and losing the key group of listeners who appreciated academic standards.[42]

Benton also alienated executives at NBC. They resented his efforts to assert control over programming, especially his attempt to get a better time for the *Round Table*. Sunday morning at 11:30 Central time conflicted with church services across much of the country.[43] Benton's motivations were undoubtedly complex; he was interested not only in creating better programs serving the public interest—based on his own understanding of professional radio— but also in promoting the University of Chicago. Judith Waller's opinion of

Benton was less charitable. She thought he was primarily committed to using radio to raise money and conduct public relations for the university.[44] John Royal advised his superior at NBC that "sometimes we should stand firm against such personalities who try to run our business."[45]

Despite his criticisms of Miller, Benton never put into practice Bowles's extreme recommendations, such as having the audience vote for winners and losers. He did try to experiment with minor changes to the format, including the use of a moderator and more elaborate outlines. But Benton did not change the "fundamental formula of the Round Table—point for point discussion among qualified authorities."[46] Despite generally refusing to make the program less academic, he still succeeded in expanding the national audience. The number of network-affiliated stations broadcasting the program increased from thirty-seven in May 1937 to sixty-eight stations in July 1939.[47] Nine additional stations were added after the university hired a station relations and promotion director, who corresponded with and visited over a dozen station managers.[48] In May 1940, the university estimated that the Round Table had an audience of between four and five million.[49]

The Sloan Foundation and Political Bias

Benton also succeeded in obtaining support from a private foundation. Beginning in 1938, the University of Chicago received a major grant from the Sloan Foundation, a philanthropic institution established in 1934 by the automobile executive Alfred P. Sloan. During the next seven years, the foundation awarded over three hundred thousand dollars to the university for radio programming. Support from the Sloan Foundation allowed the Round Table to hire for the first time a production director and a research director and to bring in nationally known participants from outside the university. The university also took the program around the country and eventually overseas, using a specially constructed portable "Round Table" with removable legs (again actually a triangular table). Finally, the university used the grant to help pay the cost of publishing and mailing transcripts of programs and suggestions for supplementary readings.[50] During the ten-year period ending in 1948, the Round Table sent out three million of these publications (at a charge of ten cents each).[51]

Although the Sloan Foundation initially wanted to see the Round Table "modernized" by changing the format to appeal to a larger audience, Benton successfully resisted these suggestions, arguing partly that "we might be in for a cat and dog fight all along the line, starting right out with Allen Miller."[52] But the university did adopt a specific request from the Sloan Foundation.

The foundation was interested in the "dissemination of economic knowledge." In response, the university sought to make "the economic content of each show as significant as possible."[53]

The *Round Table* gained a reputation for being a politically left-leaning program. According to Benton, David Sarnoff, the president of NBC's parent company, RCA, related how "his friends occasionally criticized him for the *Round Table,* implying that the program was a bit radical."[54] Hutchins had appointed Benton as vice president with the expectation that he would help to counter the public perception that the University of Chicago taught radical views. In 1937, Benton was advised by his assistant at the university, John Howe, to give talks to business groups emphasizing that "there are no Communists on the faculty of the University of Chicago" and that the majority of the faculty voted for the Republican candidate in the 1936 presidential election.[55]

The Sloan Foundation did not seem to have a major problem with the perceived bias of the *Round Table* until a broadcast on April 22, 1945, featuring a discussion with Friedrich Hayek about his book *The Road to Serfdom.* The Sloan Foundation felt that Hayek had not been dealt with fairly; it threatened to withdraw support unless the university made changes to the direction and organization of the *Round Table.*

Hayek, an Austrian-born economics professor at the London School of Economics, was the best-known critic of a centrally planned economy. His popular book published by the University of Chicago Press claimed that government limitations on free markets led to totalitarianism. Hayek appeared on the *Round Table* with Charles E. Merriam, a political science professor who served on the National Resources Planning Board under Franklin D. Roosevelt, and Maynard C. Krueger, a faculty member at the university who had been a Socialist candidate for vice president of the United States.

Following the broadcast, Alfred P. Sloan personally wrote the university complaining that the other two participants had dealt harshly with Hayek. Sloan threatened to cut off future support for the radio office unless the university worked to take into account his criticisms.[56] The executive director of the Sloan Foundation made a personal trip from New York to specifically point out three systematic problems with the *Round Table* when it dealt with economic issues: (1) it always had "two 'leftists' teamed up with only one 'conservative'"; (2) the "conservative" always had "far less time" to present his views than the "leftists"; and (3) the summaries made by the last speaker on the program (usually a "leftist," according to the foundation) did not fairly treat the other two participants.[57]

In the fall of 1945, a "special committee of paid outside experts" appointed by the foundation studied the program and generally supported the critical views of Sloan and the foundation's Board of Trustees. Revealingly, not all members of the board wanted the *Round Table* to take a balanced or neutral approach. Some actually thought that the program "should be 'rightist' in content and effect." But the executive director of the foundation succeeded in convincing all members that the *Round Table* should strive for neutrality when presenting economic issues. Towards this end, the foundation presented the university with three general recommendations. First, it requested that the *Round Table* always have a neutral moderator who would ask questions and summarize arguments fairly. The foundation preferred having only two main participants, "one at each end of the philosophic spectrum"; however, when more than two views on an issue existed it would accept more participants as long as the program included a moderator. Second, the foundation asked that when a participant summarized views, that person should first write up the summaries and get the approval of the other participants. Finally, the foundation wanted to play a role in decisions about hiring executive secretaries, program directors, and research assistants for the *Round Table*. The Board of Trustees did not want to assert control but did want to have the opportunity to give advice.[58]

The directors in charge of the *Round Table* defended the Hayek-Merriam-Krueger program. They pointed out that the *Round Table* was not meant to present a debate between polarized positions. Rather, they emphasized the unique academic nature of the program and the fundamental idea "that university professors have a distinctive contribution to make to the discussion of public policy—in terms of competence, knowledge, and disinterested concern for the general welfare." John Howe, an administrator at the university who assisted Benton in overseeing the radio office, argued that Krueger and Merriam represented two additional points of view rather than a single view opposed to Hayek. According to Howe, Merriam "probably had more experience with government planning, including federal planning under every administration since that of President Taft, than any academic man in the country." But he was not a socialist; at one time he had been a Republican candidate for mayor of Chicago. Krueger, however, was a socialist; but Howe argued that Krueger's views represented a "new kind of socialism which is apprehensive of the consequences of central planning of the economy." Krueger thought that socialism should be developed at the local instead of the national level.[59]

The radio office's relationship with the Sloan Foundation remained uncertain during 1946, but by the spring of 1947 the foundation was satisfied with the university's efforts to take into account its criticisms.[60] Most important, the radio office experimented with innovations suggested by Sloan for the

Round Table, including the use of moderators and more extensive use of "roving reporters" who would "give voice to the 'man in the street.'"[61]

NBC and Censorship

Executives at NBC also complained about the Hayek program during the summer of 1945. Frank Mullen, an NBC vice president, asked Judith Waller when she was "going to throw the Round Table off the network." The Hayek broadcast only confirmed his view that "the Chicago faculty were a bunch of radicals." After finding out from Waller about Mullen's comments, Howe warned Benton that they "were probably faced with a continuous low-pressure campaign" against the *Round Table* by NBC executives.[62]

The criticisms from the network were potentially more serious because enemies at NBC had been trying to gain control over the series and impose commercial standards since the late 1930s. Educational or public-affairs programs like the *Round Table* were always in tension with the dominant profit motives of commercial stations. The *Round Table* was particularly vulnerable because the network did not require local stations to take the "sustaining" series. Although the network paid its affiliates if they broadcast the program, many stations could make twice as much if they sold the time locally.[63] The commercial pressures on radio stations during the Depression not only led to undesirable shifting of stations and cancellation of programs but also efforts to try to influence the content of broadcasts. As an institution of higher education committed to ideals of academic freedom and independence, the University of Chicago resisted efforts to censor programs, but as long as the institution had to rely on commercial outlets for access to the airwaves this tension was unavoidable.

At least as early as June 1931, Hutchins warned broadcasters that the university would not accept any efforts to control the content of programs. He reported that as of that date, "no such instance has ever occurred."[64] But in 1934 Hutchins did admit that "on a few occasions . . . very diplomatic efforts to control the speakers have been made." For example, at least one faculty member agreed to change a section of a manuscript he had submitted for broadcast over NBC in response to objections from certain network officials.[65]

By 1939, commercial pressures at NBC led an executive who increasingly sought to assert control over public-interest programs, William Preston, to warn the university that the network was "going to ask for more authority over all educational programs."[66] *Round Table* programs on controversial topics that might offend large groups of listeners were especially vulnerable. In an extreme case, in 1940, when Benton relayed a suggestion about presenting a

Round Table titled "Is There a God?" Sherman Dryer at the university radio office and Judith Waller at the network were stunned. Waller wrote Dryer that the network would "under no circumstances consider accepting the idea!!"[67] Dryer agreed categorically. "A topic like this on a Sunday *Round Table* would hurt our prestige for weeks," he told Benton. "The very title would offend listeners. . . . Neither NBC nor the University can afford to admit that there isn't [a God]." The response to the proposal also underscored the fact that the organizers of the *Round Table* stayed away from cultural, philosophic, or religious topics. Dryer wrote Benton that the "Round Table is a program primarily concerned with social, political, and economic subjects—*practical* subjects; I do not think you can afford to deal in metaphysics after ten years on the air."[68]

Controversial political or social issues of national importance favored for discussion by Dryer and other members of the university community could also be vetoed by network officials concerned about offending listeners. One of the most controversial political issues that corporate officials preferred to ignore was the issue of civil rights for African Americans. The *Round Table* initially scheduled a program entitled "Is the Negro Oppressed?" for May 12, 1939, featuring a guest appearance by the secretary of the National Association for the Advancement of Colored People (NAACP). But Judith Waller at NBC worried that the program would offend southern whites. She wrote Preston that the subject was "so controversial in the South that it appears particularly essential that we have well balanced discussions if it is to be accepted in the area." She favored having a southern white appear along with the NAACP secretary to present a "balanced" view.[69]

The university did not broadcast the "Negro Round Table" program as planned; officially it was indefinitely rescheduled. The *Round Table* instead broadcast an "urgent" program about a major coal strike that unexpectedly came up. But Sherman Dryer, the program director at the university, worried that most listeners would assume that the university had cancelled the "Oppressed Negro" program because of pressure from the network. Dryer wrote Benton that "of course we cancelled the Negro program in order to put on the broadcast of the coal strike—you know it and John Royal knows it, but does the public know it?" He believed that they needed to reschedule the program "purely from a public relations angle." Dryer warned that already some of the faculty suspected the program had been cancelled because of "external influences."[70]

Benton took the issue up directly with Niles Trammell, the Georgia-born executive vice president of NBC. The university, according to Benton, had received "quite a few letters," especially from Communist papers and left-wing individuals, asking when the university was going to reschedule the "Oppressed Negro Program." He related that both Dryer and T. V. Smith—an influential force on the *Round Table* and a Texas native—favored broadcasting the program. Benton presented a proposal from Dryer to take into account the fears of Waller. Instead of calling the program "Is the Negro Oppressed?" Dryer suggested the less controversial title "Today's American Negro." And he was willing to assent to Waller's recommendation that the program include a "southerner."[71]

John Royal helped convince Trammell to cancel the program. Royal believed any "ethnic program" would be "difficult and dangerous to be discussed by the Round Table," including programs dealing with "Today's American Jew" or "Today's American Catholic." But he believed that a program about African Americans would be especially dangerous, particularly because of pressure from leftists: "Anyone who knows what's going on in this country realizes that the Communists are making a very strong play to arouse the Negroes in America." Royal in particular did not trust Dryer. He warned Trammell that Dryer held "radical or at least 'broad minded' tendencies, and we of the National Broadcasting Company do not intend to let this energetic young man maneuver us into some embarrassing positions." Royal rejected Dryer's suggestion that they include a southerner, remarking that "you as a Southerner, know more than anyone else that you cannot *discuss* the nigger question."[72]

Royal recommended that "if the *Chicago Round Table* anticipates further subjects of this sort, I think we should cancel the *Round Table,* because the danger is not worth it." "Our country," Royal argued, "is too sensitive at the moment to discuss any racial, color, or religious problem."[73] Trammell agreed with Royal's position against broadcasting the proposed program. After making this position clear to Benton, he wrote to Royal, "I don't think you will hear from this matter again."[74] Although Dryer's attempt to broadcast a program dealing with African Americans was halted, he did manage to convince the network to accept a program on "the Jews." After the program was broadcast in January 1940, Dryer wrote Benton that it "was one of our most successful. We received 500 letters on it Monday, and 1,400 letters on it Tuesday."[75]

World War II, Federal Policy, and the Round Table

In principle, the university opposed all forms of censorship, not only attempts by commercial stations and networks to control programs but also efforts by the federal government to dictate content. Hutchins was a strident defender of academic freedom. Especially beginning in the mid-1930s, he success-fully fended off attacks from conservative trustees and state investigating committees concerned about faculty teaching and research policy, including possible "Communist influences." But as we have seen, individual members of the radio office did not consistently resist efforts by outsiders to control university radio programs. Although they generally did not allow federal officials to dictate radio-program policy at the university, the extreme event of the Second World War was an exception. When the country entered the war in December 1941, the radio office sought to place its resources in the service of the war effort.[76]

During the period leading up to the attack on Pearl Harbor, Benton and Hutchins were sympathetic to isolationists who did not want the United States to become embroiled in another European war. Benton, in particular, was closely linked to the anti-interventionist America-First Committee, especially through his former business partner Chet Bowles. Benton and Hutchins wor-ried that the country's involvement in the war might result in a repeat of the attack on civil liberties that occurred immediately after World War I. They favored strengthening democratic institutions at home to provide a symbol for the world and an alternative to military action against totalitarianism overseas.[77]

Benton was particularly concerned that the university maintain high stan-dards of neutrality and objectivity, especially by not using the *Round Table* to stir up passions. In February 1940, he wrote Dryer that he "shuddered" at the implications of a proposed program tentatively titled "When America Goes to War." The phrase gave him "the willies." He preferred a program on "If America Goes to War," discussing "what a war might do to our social and economic structure . . . portraying what a helluva mess the country will be in if we go to war."[78] Despite his initial preference for adopting commercial techniques on the *Round Table,* Benton's experience with the intervention debate over radio gave him a much better appreciation of the central role of sober university professors on the series. His assistant, John Howe, wrote Benton, "I'd be willing to sacrifice showmanship, and dramatic values, in favor of a cool—even dull—discussion."[79]

Benton was especially concerned about many programs over commercial networks that were indirectly promoting interventionist views favored by the administration of President Franklin D. Roosevelt. The pro-interventionist bias of commercial radio mainly reflected the networks' desire to cooperate with the Roosevelt administration to put an end to aggressive investigations not only aimed at regulating network practices but also at convicting radio broadcasters of violating antitrust laws. Additionally, the networks hoped that if the country did enter the European war and the administration was pleased with their cooperation during the prewar debates over intervention, the president would be less likely to want to assume control over radio broadcasting (as happened during the First World War and was authorized by the 1934 Communications Act).[80]

In response to a specific *Round Table* program on May 21, 1940, Benton warned that the series could "come as close to being a Big Bertha as anything in radio today, and we must guide ourselves to make sure we don't corrupt it into poison gas."[81] He was upset with a vigorous attack on isolationists by one of the participants. Benton complained that the commentator "seemed to me to be a propagandist for an idea, distorting the program, and taking it far from the main stream and the main opportunity." He warned that the program had a responsibility to promote dispassionate objectivity, since "the public doesn't know what to think. . . . Emotions are beginning to run high, and these subjects are going to become more and more difficult to handle with any kind of objectivity." Benton warned that "it won't be long before anyone who attempts objectivity may be accused of being a traitor."[82]

Sherman Dryer also shared Benton's concern about providing a balanced discussion free of sensational drama.[83] But Dryer did not share the strong anti-interventionist views of Hutchins, Benton, and Howe. He believed that most faculty on campus and most listeners to the *Round Table* shared his lack of sympathy for isolationists. In response to Benton's remarks about the treatment of isolationists on the May 21, 1940, program, Dryer wrote that he did not think there were "too many these days."[84] He also reminded Benton that the radio office could not interfere with the content of broadcasts.[85]

However, immediately after the United States entered the war, Dryer no longer emphasized this fundamental commitment against censorship. He stressed that "it is naturally the intention and desire of the University of Chicago to make all of its facilities, not only the *Round Table,* available to the service of the government." Dryer institutionalized "emergency" policies that had been formulated six months earlier when the radio office believed that war was "a real possibility."[86]

Operating under "emergency status" meant that "if ever certain government policies seem inconsistent with the University's policies, the University will not permit their discussion on the Round Table." Dryer stressed that his office would work towards selecting participants "of unquestioned loyalty and patriotism to discuss and occasionally criticize, not major . . . goals on which the country should be united, but methods used to arrive at goals." The university avoided broadcasting programs dealing with specific controversial topics such as whether there should be a "negotiated peace" or whether the

United States should "cooperate with Red Russia." The radio office also gave *Round Table* participants specific instructions telling them "what not to say or do on the air in light of the nation's wartime status."[87]

Despite these efforts to cooperate with the federal government during the war, Dryer privately told Benton immediately after Pearl Harbor that he did not think the changes would cause radical adjustments. He was assured by various government officials that the university would not have to worry about censorship as long as the *Round Table* did not go out of its way to criticize government policy.[88] Besides producing its own programs in support of the war effort, the federal government made suggestions to producers of regular programs about incorporating relevant war themes into their scripts.[89] But the various agencies in charge of coordinating war information did not make an unusually large number of requests to the University of Chicago for changes to the *Round Table*. In January 1943, Dryer reported that "since Pearl Harbor, not more than half a dozen suggestions have been made by government agencies." He accepted the suggestions "in three or four instances, since they were good suggestions by any standard." The university radio committee believed that "these government suggestions were not unreasonable, and that there are fewer of them than might be expected."[90]

Despite this lack of direct control by the government, most *Round Table* programs did deal with topics related to the war. During the period from the attack on Pearl Harbor in December 1941 through early February 1943, only nine of fifty-nine programs were not related specifically to the war. Dryer admitted that he scheduled forty programs "with the recognition on our part that they would serve to clarify issues" declared important by the Office of War Information. In recognition of its importance to the war effort, the *Round Table* was classified by the federal government as one of a select number of network programs valued for its wartime contribution.[91]

Dryer and Benton continued to criticize programs on the commercial networks that sensationalized war information, especially those produced by various agencies of the federal government. In March 1942, Dryer complained to Benton about a new series produced by the Radio Division of the propaganda-oriented Office of Facts and Figures titled *This Is War!* For thirteen weeks beginning on Valentine's Day 1942, individual programs used drama and emotional appeal to convince listeners to support the war effort. One program declared that "the enemy is Murder International, Murder Unlimited; quick murder on the spot or slow murder in the concentration camp. . . . The enemy is a liar also. A gigantic and deliberate and willful liar." By broadcasting the *This Is War!* series, Dryer believed the government was forcing a "hysterical dramatic propaganda series down the throats of all of the four networks, and is going all-out to hystericize the American people every Saturday night."[92]

In contrast to this flagrant use of propaganda, Dryer and other university officials sought to present sober programs on the *Round Table* that avoided emotionalism. John Howe argued that the "central problem" of radio in wartime was whether "radio's job is primarily to inflame our people emotionally, or whether it is primarily to keep them informed, and to give them a clear, honest, serious set of convictions on what we're fighting for."[93] Before the war, Dryer instructed the "roving reporter" used experimentally on the *Round Table* to "be rather flip and smart"; however, during the war he specifically directed him to "be a pretty sober and accurate reporter of other people's opinions, and not to work too hard to be a radio personality in his own right."[94]

One of the issues that some federal officials encouraged radio broadcasters to address during the war was the topic of race. In May 1942, Dryer saw an opportunity to renew his attempt to organize a "Negro Round Table" when Archibald MacLeish, the former Librarian of Congress appointed to oversee the Office of Facts and Figures, warned the radio industry that discontent among African Americans could prove a major threat to national security.[95] He encouraged broadcasters to present programs combating Japanese propaganda about a "white man's war" by publicizing the role of African Americans in "our fighting forces and factories." Picking up on this theme, Dryer argued that the university had "a patriotic obligation" to discuss the issue of race. The attack on Pearl Harbor, he claimed, changed everything: "The Negro problem today is not, as it was before December 7, a Southern problem. It is now a nationwide problem which the government has officially recognized." But this first attempt during the war to broadcast a program on the *Round Table* about African Americans was again vetoed by Trammell at NBC.[96]

By 1943, an outbreak of racial unrest in a number of cities made it more difficult for NBC to put off broadcasting a *Round Table* program about African Americans.[97] Although NBC continued to resist, it did allow a program in April that mainly discussed African American civil rights, but only after Benton convinced Dryer to use the general title "Minorities."[98] The program did not in fact include any "minorities." Two white University of Chicago faculty members and a southern, white newspaper editor represented different points of view.[99] According to Dryer, the mail received in response to the program had been "extraordinarily heavy—some 500 letters a day." He claimed that "only an infinitesimal percentage of the letters have been critical; overwhelmingly they vote approval and enthusiasm."[100]

Dryer was more successful with a *Round Table* program in July. This time, network executives were willing to allow a direct discussion of race relations;

they mainly fought to prevent the participation of an African American, in fear of alienating southern whites. NBC executives and administrators at the University of Chicago stressed that choosing participants based on their race would violate a *Round Table* policy of not using participants "as representatives or spokesman" for any group.[101] When discussing communism, for example, the radio office declined an offer from the Communist party to send representatives to participate on the *Round Table*.[102] But the university was never completely consistent in carrying out this policy. Although university officials argued that they only chose participants based on "their scholarly competence and objectivity," the *Round Table* had included many government officials who functioned as partisan advocates. Nevertheless, the university did attempt to remain consistent and work around NBC's objections by making sure that African American participants were eminently well-qualified as scholars.[103] For the July 1943 program titled "Race Tensions," the organizers chose E. Franklin Frazier, chair of the Department of Sociology at Howard University.

During the planning for the July 1943 program, Judith Waller was the main person at the network who resisted Dryer's efforts.[104] Waller was mainly concerned about the reaction of southern whites. She confided to administrators at the university that she was "losing sleep" worrying about their reaction. She felt that "regardless of the 'scholarly competence and objectivity' of a Negro participant," the public would regard that person as a "spokesman or representative" for African Americans and that in general "the race situation was sufficiently explosive so that it would be better to postpone a discussion until 'things cooled off.'" Waller initially approved the panel, "with her fingers crossed," but then changed her mind and threatened to cancel the program unless it also included a southern white.[105] Dryer at first objected "on the ground that four participants are unwieldy" and "that the three participants already lined up for the broadcast were men of integrity and competency." Waller acknowledged that his reasons "were good" but stressed that he needed to take into account the fact that "the South was 'irrational.'" Dryer finally came up with a compromise acceptable to Waller: they included the southerner she suggested, the University of North Carolina sociologist Howard Odum. Instead of including him as a discussion participant, however, they only used him to briefly introduce the program.[106] After the broadcast, Dryer reported that "on the whole, our mail on this program, which was rather heavy," expressed approval. But he was disgusted with a number of critical letters from the South, "almost all" of which "criticized the negro because 'he is a menace to white women.'"[107]

Postwar Period

During the late 1940s and early 1950s, the record of the *Round Table* was mixed. On the one hand, the number of stations broadcasting the series peaked in the early 1950s, with ninety-eight NBC affiliates and twenty non-commercial educational stations carrying the weekly program. Listener surveys indicated that the *Round Table* was among the top ten most popular radio programs in the country. Listeners heard intelligent discussion by academic participants and distinguished world leaders, including John F. Kennedy, Jawaharlal Nehru, and Adlai Stevenson. Stations in England and Canada rebroadcast individual programs. More than twenty-one thousand listeners subscribed to the transcripts, and the *Round Table* won a number of awards for broadcast excellence.[108]

University of Chicago Round Table radio program (January 25, 1948, broadcast), program titled "Higher Education for All"; from left to right: T. R. McConnell, Louis Wirth, Earl J. McGrath. Courtesy of the Special Collections Research Center, University of Chicago Library.

But on the other hand, NBC and the Sloan Foundation continued to give the *Round Table* only lukewarm support. Writing in 1949, the new director of the radio office, George Probst, believed that the Sloan trustees were "simply indifferent to the program." According to Probst, the trustees "have the simple reaction that they have supported the RT [*Round Table*] long enough."[109] Although there is no direct evidence for other reasons the Sloan Foundation lost interest in supporting radio at the University of Chicago, the foundation may have also not approved of some of the programs broadcast during the late 1940s that dealt with issues of world peace. Early in 1950, Probst refused to broadcast a series of programs dealing with military defense proposed by the Department of Defense.[110]

As we have seen, NBC officials in New York had been trying to gain control over the *Round Table* since at least the late 1930s. Such executives as John Royal, who believed that radio was primarily an entertainment medium, continued to criticize the series for relying on professors and for not being willing to add "vitality and pep."[111] In 1949, Sterling Fischer, the director of public-service and educational programs at NBC, revealed that he was under pressure from other executives to drop the use of "University of Chicago" in the title, because they did not like the "free advertising" the university was receiving.[112]

One of the main reasons the network avoided trying to interfere with the *Round Table* before the war was its fear of the FCC. New Deal commissioners appointed by President Roosevelt pressured commercial stations to support public-affairs programs such as the *University of Chicago Round Table*. By contrast, a number of commissioners serving immediately after the war were generally less interested in actively trying to influence program policy.[113] Harold Lasswell argued that the networks had gotten "cocky" when the federal government did not take direct control during the war despite threats by the Roosevelt administration prior to Pearl Harbor. According to Lasswell, when the FCC did not take "any effective steps to make the public service broadcast respected," the networks tried "to sell their sustainers to sponsors" and to "cut their 'public service' to the bone."[114]

The networks also were generally less interested in supporting radio after the war because they preferred to invest more resources in the development of television. NBC and CBS had introduced the public to television immediately before the war; but the new broadcast medium was effectively delayed until the end of hostilities.[115] Probably because radio was a low priority for NBC during the late 1940s and early 1950s, there was a high turnover for executives in charge of program policy for the *Round Table* and other programs. Probst complained in 1950 about having to acquaint for the fourth time a new programming executive at NBC with the virtues of the *Round Table* and the reasons the network should continue to carry it.[116] Given this declining support for radio, especially public-service radio, NBC decided to end the *University of Chicago Round Table* radio series with the last broadcast on June 12, 1955.[117]

* * *

The *University of Chicago Round Table* represented one of the most important efforts by a major research university to use the new medium of radio broadcasting to extend the benefits of the university to all citizens. The organizers of the program were committed to the idea that academic experts should play a central role in the formation of public opinion. The *Round Table* sought to demonstrate to the public the benefits of a rational conversation among dispassionate academics committed to the pursuit of truth and the advancement of knowledge. The program combined a Progressive-era commitment to academic expertise with a belief in the value of education for a democracy.

One of the greatest fears of the *Round Table* organizers was that radio broadcasting would end up in the hands of propagandists who would use the new medium to manipulate citizens. Events in Europe during the 1930s seemed to confirm their worst fears, as totalitarian governments—especially in Germany and the Soviet Union—used radio to consolidate and maintain political control. Because of these concerns, *Round Table* conversations specifically avoided using propagandistic techniques of emotional drama and sensationalism. The program was committed to cool, detached, rational dialogue. University organizers rejected a format used by other public-affairs programs that involved the studio audience in adversarial "black-and-white" debates. They believed that such techniques relied on the emotional manipulation of mob psychology.

The *Round Table* faced a fundamental tension in attempting to use a commercial medium to extend the benefits of the university to the general public. The university's commitment to academic values of freedom of speech and enlightened discourse inherently conflicted with the interests of commercial stations committed to making a profit by maximizing the number of listeners to sell to advertisers. Even with sustaining programs, access to airwaves was always mediated by the ultimate commercial goals of radio networks. The *Round Table* had to deal with pressure to treat listeners as consumers rather than citizens and to expand the number of listeners by adopting radio techniques based on traditions of showmanship. The organizers of the program finessed this latter tension by succeeding in increasing the size of the audience by publicizing the program rather than by drastically changing the program format.

But in other ways, the university did adapt to the demands of professional commercial broadcasting. For instance, the *Round Table* increasingly relied on scripted formats. And in a number of individual cases the university gave in to network demands that the *Round Table* not broadcast controversial programs, notably discussions involving the experiences of African Americans.

The role of the federal government was more complex. On the one hand, the network's support for the *Round Table* was generally dependent on pressure from federal regulators anxious to see radio supporting public-service programming. On the other hand, during World War II, the *Round Table* cooperated with government censors by agreeing to follow rules constraining wartime programming. But during the war the university maintained its commitment to sober, dispassionate discourse. The *Round Table* staff consistently avoided extreme forms of propaganda relying on emotional drama. Perhaps most important, the wartime experience played a crucial role opening up the public sphere for the discussion on the *Round Table* of the controversial issue of civil rights for African Americans.

A detailed analysis of the *Round Table* is especially important because it exemplified a type of program that was becoming central to noncommercial broadcasting. The essential tensions dealt with by the program also help deepen our understanding of the complex relationships among funding sources, program formats, and academic values. The increasingly important role of public-affairs programming to noncommercial radio would become especially clear during the postwar period, when the involvement of the federal government helped open up a new era in the history of noncommercial broadcasting in the United States.

Epilogue

Noncommercial educational radio stations expanded significantly in numbers during the 1940s and 1950s. But the new stations did not operate on the AM band; they broadcast on a newly opened band of frequencies set aside by the FCC for frequency modulation (FM). In 1940 the FCC reserved five out of forty channels for the exclusive use of noncommercial stations. The NAEB and the U.S. Office of Education succeeded in convincing the FCC to expand the number of reserved noncommercial channels to twenty when it moved FM stations to the band of frequencies from 88 to 92 MHz. After years of failed attempts, educators finally succeeded in gaining exclusive frequencies for noncommercial stations committed to public-service broadcasting.[1]

Quantitatively, the FCC's decision to reserve channels for noncommercial stations led to a "renaissance" in educational broadcasting as the number of new educational FM stations increased to nearly three hundred in September 1966.[2] But most of these stations were poorly financed, and their signals were weak because they transmitted at low power levels. Forty-five percent of educational FM stations broadcast at ten watts, covering only a few miles.[3] FM stations in general also had difficulty attracting audiences because federal regulators did not require manufacturers to produce receivers capable of receiving broadcasts in both AM and FM bands. Broadcasters and manufacturers were more interested in committing limited resources to the development of television. For these reasons most educational FM stations, like FM in general, remained marginalized during the 1950s and 1960s.[4]

Most noncommercial FM stations were licensed to colleges and universities.[5] A number of the older AM stations at universities switched to the FM band; others added an FM station and broadcast the same programming.

Some of the FM stations, especially the ones linked to the older AM stations, followed the extension tradition pioneered by land-grant schools and broadcast a broad range of public-service programming. But most educational FM stations did not try to serve a broad audience; instead they served specific groups with programs commercial stations would not broadcast. Especially important was the broadcasting of classical music. This became the major justification for a number of FM stations operated by colleges and universities. The practice became easier to justify as commercial stations increasingly specialized in the programming of popular music.[6]

A major goal of supporters of noncommercial educational radio since at least the 1930s was station interconnection, ideally on a national level. They viewed this as essential for their survival. The NCER made important, but limited, efforts during the 1930s to establish a program-exchange network. More significant work was accomplished during the 1950s, with the establishment of a "bicycle network," in which tapes from member stations as well as from the BBC and the CBC were mailed to stations one after another. Grants from the Kellogg Foundation provided crucial support for the maintenance of this tape network, which helped create a sense of social solidarity among stations.[7] However, the technical quality of the network and programming was not consistently high. The tapes sometimes arrived at stations in shreds. True high-quality interconnection would need to wait for the development of a live network structure.[8]

Another private granting agency, the Rockefeller Foundation, sponsored two important seminars dealing with the future of educational or noncommercial broadcasting in 1949 and 1950. These meetings at the Allerton House Conference Center at the University of Illinois were especially significant because, for the first time during the postwar period, educators, scholars, and public officials discussed the common purposes and goals for a nationwide noncommercial broadcasting service. Significantly, the seminars emphasized the crucial role of educational radio for supporting democratic traditions and institutions.[9]

The most important foundation supporting educational broadcasting during the 1950s and 1960s was the Ford Foundation. Support provided by a subsidiary granting agency established by the Ford Foundation in 1951, the Fund for Adult Education (FAE), played a particularly important role in the postwar history of educational broadcasting. Although the FAE ostensibly supported all forms of educational broadcasting, it was primarily interested in television. For example, radio only received limited support from the major institution the FAE helped establish in 1952 to raise the quality of programming, the Educational Television and Radio Center (ETRC).[10]

Beginning in the early 1950s, the FAE worked successfully to convince the FCC to set aside specific channels for educational television; it encouraged educational institutions and community organizations to establish television stations; and it provided grants-in-aid to institutions to help construct stations. Altogether between 1953 and 1961, the fund gave nearly four million dollars to thirty-three educational television stations to help purchase equipment. A substantial number of the new television stations were operated by universities; however, community organizations established a number of them in major metropolitan regions. In addition to a grant of one million dollars to establish the ETRC, the FAE gave an additional three million dollars for the development of new programming during the mid-1950s. Altogether during the 1950s and early 1960s, the Ford Foundation gave over eighty million dollars to help establish noncommercial educational television.[11]

Interest in television also grew to dominate the work of the NAEB. A reorganization in 1963 that placed radio and television within separate divisions effectively institutionalized radio's secondary status. Lobbying by the NAEB convinced the federal government in 1962 to provide substantial funds for educational broadcasting. But the Educational Television Facilities Act of 1962 did not authorize funds for radio. The legislation provided thirty-two million dollars for the construction of new educational television stations and for the purchase of additional equipment for existing television stations. In connection with these decisions, the Ford Foundation decided to eliminate radio from the Educational Television and Radio Center. The foundation replaced the center with a new organization, the National Educational Television (NET) network. By the early 1960s, the NAEB, private foundations, and the federal government had all "come under the post–World War II spell of television."[12]

Cold-war concerns that led the federal government to adopt policies to compete with the Soviet Union in science, technology, and education help explain the enthusiasm for educational television during the late 1950s and early 1960s. The psychological shock caused by the Soviets when they succeeded in orbiting the first artificial satellite, *Sputnik I,* in October 1957 led Congress to pass new legislation increasing support in these fields. Title VII of the National Defense Education Act of 1958 appropriated millions of dollars for research and experimentation in the use of electronic media for education. Although this legislation was mainly concerned with the use of media for formal instruction, it also stimulated interest in the general use of electronic media, especially television, for adult education.[13]

The major legislation that ushered in a new period in the history of noncommercial broadcasting in the United States was the Public Broadcasting

Act of 1967. Signed into law by President Johnson in November, it represented an important transition from educational broadcasting as practiced
by university stations to a new federally defined understanding of public
broadcasting. But to understand this transition to a new conception of educational or public broadcasting, we need to understand the crucial role of
community stations and community leaders in major metropolitan regions,
especially Boston and New York City. These community stations, rather than
the older land-grant stations, played a key role in the passage of the 1967
legislation.[14]

WGBH in Boston played the most important role in the transition to a new
form of noncommercial broadcasting. Wealthy civic leaders, especially Ralph
Lowell, a member of the Lowell family in Boston, worked with faculty at Harvard and the Massachusetts Institute of Technology to establish WGBH-FM
and WGBH-TV during the 1950s. Rather than viewing these institutions as
extensions of state systems of public education, the civic leaders in Boston
modeled the organization of noncommercial broadcasting on museums or
other cultural institutions supported by private philanthropy. Jack Mitchell,
a participant in the establishment of public broadcasting, argues that WGBH
and other community stations "represented something of a noblesse oblige:
the responsibility of the educated, the prosperous, and the privileged to look
after the less-fortunate majority."[15]

Ralph Lowell and other civic leaders involved in the establishment of
WGBH were closely tied to major private foundations interested in education
and civic improvement, including the Ford Foundation and Carnegie Corporation as well as to the eastern liberal political establishment represented
by the Kennedy and Johnson administrations. President Johnson supported
the use of federal funds for a national system of noncommercial educational
television because of its potential role in his administration's Great Society
programs. Sensing the interest of the Johnson administration in educational
television, Ralph Lowell and other civic leaders involved with WGBH proposed in 1965 the formation of a national commission to investigate federal
involvement in the formation of a national system of educational television.
Johnson expressed support for the establishment of such a commission. The
advocates convinced the Carnegie Corporation to fund the venture with a
grant of five hundred thousand dollars. The aim of the Carnegie Commission on Educational Television was to "conduct a broadly conceived study of
noncommercial television" focusing "principally, although not exclusively,
on community-owned channels and their services to the general public."[16]
James R. Killian Jr., the president of the Massachusetts Institute of Technology, chaired the commission.

The January 1967 report of the Carnegie Commission, which provided a blueprint for the Public Broadcasting Act of 1967, reflected the goals of a Johnsonian Great Society. The report assumed a broad definition of education. It used the phrase "public television" to distinguish the new endeavor from older practices based on narrower understandings of education, especially practices related to instructional broadcasting. The commission's call for a system of public broadcasting was partly based on traditions pioneered by the BBC. John Reith, the dominant first director, established an organization with a broad mandate to educate, inform, and entertain. Although the commission based its report on a study of all systems of noncommercial broadcasting around the world, it emphasized that it was proposing "an indigenous American system arising out of our own traditions and responsive to our own needs."[17] An important indigenous tradition was the one pioneered by state university radio stations, especially at land-grant schools. These schools generally assumed a broad understanding of education; they included a broad range of programming meant to inform, instruct, improve, enlighten, uplift, and entertain.

Consistent with its expansive understanding of education, the Carnegie Commission argued that all programming could be considered educational. Television, it believed, "replenishes our store of information, stimulates our perceptions, challenges our standards, and affects our judgment." "In the sum of what it presents," according to the commission, television "is as profoundly educative as life itself is educative, and perhaps all the more so because there is no formal syllabus to which we can refer so that we may see what we have learned."[18] Partly because it held to this expansive understanding of education, the commission argued that the noncommercial aspect of public broadcasting was the element that would make it particularly distinctive. Unlike commercial television, which served a homogenized mass audience, public television would provide programming for groups not served by commercial stations. By doing so, it would potentially expose the entire public to a diverse range of views and perspectives. "Through a civilized exchange of ideas . . . Americans will know themselves, their communities, and their world in richer ways." Like the BBC, public television would provide diversity and excellence by broadcasting the best examples of a wide range of programming.[19]

Significantly, the Carnegie Commission's report only focused on television. Noncommercial educational radio came close to being left out of plans for public broadcasting in the United States. Advocates of federal support for public broadcasting apparently worried that radio's weakness would hinder planning for the development of public television.[20] The two media were also represented by two increasingly polarized groups. State university radio stations in the Midwest championed noncommercial educational radio. Community stations in major cities, especially WGBH in Boston, led the television faction. Jack Mitchell has detailed how educational radio forces "organized a guerilla operation to slip the words 'and radio' into the public television act recommended by the Carnegie Commission."[21] Employees of the University of Michigan FM station WUOM played a key role in this process. The station manager, Ed Burrows, used his position of leadership within the NAEB to get radio included in the 1967 legislation. He relied especially on two former WUOM staff members, Jerrold Sandler and Dean Costen. Sandler, the executive secretary of the radio division of the NAEB, actively lobbied members of Congress. As the deputy undersecretary for the Department of Health, Education, and Welfare, Costen was in charge of drafting all education legislation. He added the words "and radio" to the legislation written in response to the recommendations of the Carnegie Television Committee. When the television advocates tried to undo Costen's work, Burrows, Sandler, and other members of the radio division of the NAEB successfully lobbied Congress to include radio in the final legislation.[22]

While television advocates were holding meetings leading to the Carnegie Commission report, advocates of educational radio at the NAEB conducted separate meetings that led to another major report on educational radio, *The Hidden Medium: Educational Radio*. Herman Land, a consultant hired by the radio division of the NAEB, published the report in April 1967, the same month that the Senate Commerce Committee began hearings on the proposed public-broadcasting legislation. The report helped convince members of Congress to use the inclusive phrase "public broadcasting" in the titles of the bills before the House and the Senate.[23]

The *Hidden Medium* underscored the weak state of educational radio in the country and the potential benefits that would result from increased support and development, especially on a national level. The report provided the first systematic survey of the actual state of educational radio across the country. It was based on results from a twenty-five-page questionnaire sent to 320 educational radio stations as well as qualitative data from fifty field interviews and a number of regional meetings.[24] Land found that educational radio stations were "underfinanced, underequipped, underpromoted, and under-researched." Despite these handicaps, educational radio, according to the report, still "manages not only to survive and fill its traditional cultural role, but to move forward, innovate, experiment."[25]

Significantly, the *Hidden Medium* echoed the Carnegie Commission Report on Public Television by emphasizing noncommercial radio's potential to serve Johnson's goals for a Great Society. "In addition to serving the needs of those already well endowed," the report argued, educational radio "must respond to the developing needs of the total society. . . . It is beginning to bestir itself on behalf of the special groups . . . such as the disadvantaged, the elderly, the minorities, etc., for whom it appears uniquely equipped to fill the media vacuum that generally prevails."[26] The report implicitly recognized that to obtain federal support, educational radio needed to move away from the primary objective of many FM stations, providing classical music to specialized audiences. Instead, the Land Report effectively reaffirmed and extended the traditional goals of land-grant stations. Most important, Land emphasized the importance of in-depth public-affairs programming, a format that had become increasingly central to radio stations at state universities.

The report implicitly called for an updated version of a programming philosophy pioneered especially by William Lighty and other staff members at the Wisconsin station WHA. Lighty helped develop a public-service role for the station that favored broadcasting a diverse range of programming to enhance the knowledge base of listeners. Rather than simply uplift in a coercive manner, WHA sought to engage the interests and diverse views of listeners. The Land Report echoed the Carnegie Commission's study by stressing that radio would need to address not only the concerns of rural minorities but also minority groups in large urban centers. Noncommercial educational radio would need to address "problems of poverty and minority groups" as well as offer programming "for the socially disadvantaged like the aged and the blind."[27]

Although the report called for a national system, it also wanted educational radio to promote local issues. The Land Report affirmed the progressive tradition of public-affairs programming pioneered especially by WHA. The Wisconsin station was one of the first to emphasize the importance of noncommercial public-affairs programming for the maintenance of an educated citizenry and a healthy democracy, a justification that became especially important for noncommercial university stations after the mid-1930s and a justification that was particularly consistent with the Johnsonian vision of the important role of mass media in a Great Society.

The Public Broadcasting Act of 1967 implemented the Carnegie Commission's recommendation to establish a nonprofit, nongovernmental agency in charge of disbursing federal funds for public broadcasting. The commission favored a national system of public funding rather than the system of state or local funding used previously by educational radio stations. The Corporation for Public Broadcasting (CPB) provided funding to the two networks subsequently established, National Public Radio (NPR) and the Public Broadcasting System (PBS). The law restricted the CPB from owning or operating stations or networks as well as from producing or distributing programs. Congress did not implement all the recommendations of the Carnegie Commission. Most important, it did not accept the recommendation that federal funds disbursed by the CPB come from a manufacturer's excise tax on receivers (specifically television sets). Funding had to come from annual appropriations.[28]

The Public Broadcasting Act, the Carnegie Commission Report, and the Land Report only gave general guidelines for establishing radio and television public broadcasting systems. The specific character of the two networks and their relationship to the CPB needed to be invented. The first major recommendation came from Hartford Gunn, the president of WGBH in Boston and the individual chosen to become president of PBS soon after the television network was established late in 1969. Samuel Holt, another Boston resident connected with Harvard University's Extension Service who helped design an educational broadcasting course over WGBH-TV, wrote the second major proposal, which was based on a study he conducted that year with funding from the CPB and the Ford Foundation.[29] The two proposals partly represented the division between university stations and community stations such as WGBH. Gunn represented the outlook of television-oriented community stations. He recommended the establishment of a public radio system led by a half-dozen community radio stations in major urban regions. Gunn gave state university stations in the Midwest a secondary role in his proposed network. Although Holt also had an affiliation with WGBH, he was more open to the involvement of university stations in the operation of the national public radio network he proposed.[30]

Gunn and Holt emphasized that the proposed public radio network should specialize in public-affairs and news programming. They thought that noncommercial public radio would allow for academically rigorous, in-depth analysis. Both proposals did not closely adhere to the Johnsonian vision of a Great Society; they did not stress the importance of serving minorities and the disadvantaged. They also did not advocate serving a mass audience with a diverse range of programming. Both men believed that public radio would need to compete with commercial stations for audience share by adopting the commercial practice of narrowcasting. The narrow audience served by both proposed systems would be composed of listeners especially interested in a particular format focused on news and public affairs. As we have seen, this format had become more important with educational stations at state universities beginning especially during the late 1930s. The *University of Chicago Round Table* also provided an important model demonstrating how noncommercial public-affairs programs could appeal to a specific, relatively large segment of the population. Gunn's proposal called for programming centered on "tightly formatted, in-depth national and international news and public affairs, with the emphasis on analysis, commentary, criticism, and good talk." Both proposals envisioned a system that would appeal mainly to an educated audience. This was a demographic traditionally important to many university stations. The continuity between educational radio and public radio is thus clear. But unlike land-grant stations, in particular, which also tried to serve other segments of the population with a diverse schedule of programming aimed at different audiences, the proposed public radio system would remain primarily focused on the target audience of educated and relatively affluent citizens.[31]

Holt's proposal was more influential than Gunn's, mainly because Gunn left out the politically influential midwestern land-grant radio stations. Holt proposed the establishment of a new organization in Washington, D.C., composed of noncommercial educational and community stations, which would elect the board of directors for the new institution. The CPB accepted Holt's recommendation; the result was NPR. Unlike PBS, which could not produce its own television programming, NPR had a mandate to provide new programs for the public radio network.[32]

Holt's argument in favor of narrowcasting played an important role in the development of NPR. This did not mean that Johnsonian Great Society values were completely rejected. Key individuals involved in the establishment of NPR shared the vision expressed by the Carnegie Commission and the *Hidden Medium* about serving all Americans, especially minorities and the disadvantaged. The most important individual was William Siemering. Siemering's background reflected the multiple influences feeding into the development of public broadcasting. Most important was the fact that he grew up in a home located next to the transmission towers of the University of Wisconsin station WHA. Midwestern traditions of adult education were a key influence on his early development. Both parents worked as actors with Chautauqua tent shows that toured the Midwest during the early twentieth century. The Chautauqua shows brought music, drama, lectures, and inspirational talks to small towns and rural communities. Siemering viewed these shows as an important influence inspiring the development of educational radio. As a student at the University of Wisconsin, he worked for WHA, serving as an on-air announcer and a member of the technical staff. In 1962, Siemering accepted a position offered by a former Wisconsin faculty member who became an administrator at the State University of New York (SUNY) at Buffalo to establish a new radio station at the university modeled on WHA.[33]

Following the pattern established by other new educational stations, the SUNY-Buffalo station WBFO specialized in playing classical music. Siemering, however, also included programming that adapted progressive traditions of community service developed at the University of Wisconsin to the new problems of the 1960s, especially race relations and the Vietnam War. While WHA focused especially on serving rural households, WBFO sought to ensure service to economically disadvantaged urban minorities. To give African Americans an opportunity to communicate their problems to the larger community, Siemering established a studio in the poor section of the city. He also opened up the station to a variety of opinions on the Vietnam War. His major innovation was to not primarily rely on educators, public officials, and leaders of civil-society groups to present and debate different points of view. Siemering used radio to create a public forum for discussion of controversial issues by broadcasting the unfiltered views of average citizens. A new program he introduced, *This Is Radio,* sought to introduce authenticity into public debates presented over the radio by allowing for the unstructured development of major public issues during a four-hour time period.[34]

Siemering became the first program director of NPR when it was established in 1970. A number of the first staff members shared his vision for a populist system responsive to the concerns of all Americans, especially minorities. The first network program, *All Things Considered,* reflected Siemering's innovative views about public-affairs programming. The program emphasized diversity, authenticity, the voices of average citizens, and innovative aesthetics.[35]

But from the beginning, NPR faced an essential tension in its operations. A number of early leaders of the new network were not convinced that public radio should move away from the traditional academic focus on excellence and quality. They believed that expert opinion and structured presentation were more important than cutting-edge experimentation and a diversity of voices. This tension was partly inherited from educational radio as practiced by broadcast stations at state universities. University stations often had conflicting objectives: in some cases, to mainly serve all citizens with useful, educational programming and, in other cases, to mainly seek to "educate the educated."[36]

By the 1970s, as the network became established and the number of listeners grew, it had to deal with a new tension: whether to become part of the establishment or remain outside the dominant power structure. Specifically, NPR faced the dilemma of whether to compete with the commercial networks, effectively becoming a fourth network, or to provide a less centralized, alternative system, more responsive to member stations across the country.

Equally important was the problem of how the network could depend on government funding and remain independent from government control. NPR did not gain the amount of independence exercised by the BBC. The U.S. network was dependent on annual congressional appropriations rather than funds derived from an established license fee on receivers. It also faced the threat of political interference from the CPB board of directors appointed by the president.[37]

Beginning especially during the 1980s, political pressure forced public broadcasting to increasingly rely on corporate contributions. In 1984, the FCC ruled that corporate underwriters supporting public broadcasting could include not only the name of the company but also their products and services. In practice, this meant that the distinction between underwriting and advertising became increasingly blurred. Public broadcasting also increasingly used audience analysis and related marketing techniques originally developed for commercial radio to collect data to use to gain the support of underwriters.[38] Despite this erosion in the noncommercial character of public broadcasting, the new system did realize important goals of the reform activists of the 1930s, including national coverage and federal involvement. The new system was the product of a new era in the history of broadcasting in the United States, but early patterns provided a crucial context for the new developments.

Abbreviations for Archival Collections

AgrExp/FL

Agricultural Experiment Station Campus and State Correspondence, 1921–47, University of Florida Archives, Gainesville.

AgrSub/IL

Agricultural, Consumer, and Environmental Sciences, Dean's Office, Subject Files (1895–1994, 2006), Series 8/1/2, University of Illinois Archives, Urbana.

Auburn Archives

Special Collections and Archives, Ralph B. Draughon Library, Auburn University, Auburn, Alabama.

Avery Corr

Office of the Chancellor, Samuel Avery Correspondence, Record Group 2/9/3, University Archives and Special Collections, Love Library, University of Nebraska at Lincoln.

Boye Papers

John A. Boye Papers, University Archives and Special Collections, Love Library, University of Nebraska at Lincoln.

Carnegie Files

Carnegie Corporation Grant Files, Series 1, Columbia University Rare Book and Manuscript Library, Columbia University Libraries, New York.

Chase Papers

Papers of President Harry Chase, Series 2/7/1, University of Illinois Archives, Urbana.

CoopExt/Auburn

Records of the Alabama Cooperative Extension Service, Record Group 71, Special Collections and Archives, Ralph B. Draughon Library, Auburn, Alabama.

CoopExt/KSU

Cooperative Extension Historical Files, U91.7, University Archives and Manuscripts, Hale Library, Kansas State University, Manhattan.

Dellinger Records

General Records, J. Howard Dellinger, Records of National Institute of Standards and Technology, Record Group 167, National Archives and Record Center, College Park, Maryland.

DeptJrnlsm/IL

Records of Department of Journalism and Communications, Series 13/6/803, University of Illinois Archives, Urbana.

Dock/FCC

Docket files, Records of the Federal Communications Commission, Record Group 173, National Archives and Record Center, College Park, Maryland.

Engel Papers

Harold A. Engel Papers, Wisconsin Historical Society Library Archives, Madison.

ExDir/FCC

General Correspondence, 1927–46, Office of the Executive Director, Records of the Federal Communications Commission, Record Group 173, National Archives and Record Center, College Park, Maryland.

ExtensionSubject/Neb

University of Extension/Division of Continuing Studies, subject files, series 24/1/5, University Archives and Special Collections, Love Library, University of Nebraska at Lincoln.

GenCorr/Commerce

General Correspondence, General Records of the Department of Commerce, Record Group 40, National Archives and Record Center, College Park, Maryland.

GenFiles/Chicago

General Archival Files, Special Collections Research Center, University of Chicago Archives.

Goddard Papers

Ralph Willis Goddard Papers, College of Engineering Collection, Rio Grande Historical Collections, New Mexico State University, Las Cruces.

Gordon Papers

Edgar B. Gordon Papers, Wisconsin Historical Society Library Archives, Madison.

Hanson Papers

Malcolm P. Hanson Papers, Wisconsin Historical Society Library Archives, Madison.

Hoover/Iowa

Herbert Hoover Presidential Library, West Branch, Iowa.

ISU Archives

University Archives and Special Collections, Parks Library, Iowa State University, Ames.

Jansky Papers

Cyril Moreau Jansky Papers, Wisconsin Historical Society Library Archives, Madison.

KOAC Records

KOAC Records (1923–65), Record Group 15, Oregon State University Archives, Corvallis.

KSU Archives

University Archives and Manuscripts, Hale Library, Kansas State University, Manhattan.

Lighty Papers

William H. Lighty Papers, Wisconsin Historical Society Library Archives, Madison.

McCarty Papers

Harold B. McCarty Papers, Wisconsin Historical Society Library Archives, Madison.

Miller Papers

Allen Miller Papers, Wisconsin Historical Society Library Archives, Madison.

Min/FRC

Minutes of the Federal Radio Commission, Office of the Secretary, Records of the Federal Communications Commission, Record Group 173, National Archives and Record Center, College Park, Maryland.

MSU Archives

Michigan State University Archives, East Lansing.

NACRE Records

Records of the National Advisory Council on Radio in Education, New York Public Library.

NAEB Papers

National Association of Educational Broadcasters Papers, Wisconsin Historical Society Library Archives, Madison.

NBC Records

Records of the National Broadcasting Company, Wisconsin Historical Society Library Archives, Madison.

OffEdu

Records of the Office of Education, Record Group 12, National Archives and Record Center, College Park, Maryland.

OSU Archives

Ohio State University Archives, Columbus.

Payne Fund Records

Payne Fund Inc. Records (1924–72), Western Reserve Historical Society Library, Cleveland, Ohio.

PresPapers/Chicago

Presidents' Papers, Special Collections Research Center, University of Chicago Archives.

Pres/Oregon

President's Office Records, Record Group 13, Oregon State University Archives, Corvallis.

Pub/IL

Public Information Director's Office, Public Information Subject File (1919–96), Series 39/1/1, University of Illinois Archives, Urbana.

RD/FCC

General Records, 1910–34, Radio Division, Records of the Federal Communications Commission, Record Group 173, National Archives and Record Center, College Park, Maryland.

SDPB Papers

South Dakota Public Broadcasting Papers, University Archives and Special Collections, I. D. Weeks Library, University of South Dakota, Vermillion.

Slagle Papers

Robert L. Slagle Papers, University Archives and Special Collections, I. D. Weeks Library, University of South Dakota, Vermillion.

SoundDiv/LC

Recorded Sound Division, Library of Congress, Washington, D.C.

Tigert Papers

Papers of John James Tigert, Office of the President, Subseries P7a, Group Correspondence 1928–47, University of Florida Archives, Gainesville.

UofIowa Archives

Special Collections and University Archives, Main Library, University of Iowa, Iowa City.

USD Archives

University Archives and Special Collections, I. D. Weeks Library, University of South Dakota, Vermillion.

USDA

Records of the United States Department of Agriculture, Record Group 16, National Archives and Record Center, College Park, Maryland.

VicePres/Chicago

Office of the Vice President Records, Special Collections Research Center, University of Chicago.

Weeks Papers

Papers of I. D. Weeks, University Archives and Special Collections, I. D. Weeks Library, University of South Dakota, Vermillion.

WHA Corresp.

University Extension, Educational Communications, WHA Radio and Television General Correspondence (1915–29), Series 41/6/2/5, Steenbock Library, University of Wisconsin Archives, Madison.

WHA Subject Records

University Extension, Educational Communications, WHA Radio and Television Subject (1920–47), Series 41/6/2/5, Steenbock Library, University of Wisconsin Archives, Madison.

Willard Papers

President Arthur Willard Papers, Series 2/9/1, University of Illinois Archives, Urbana.

WOI/Griffith Records

WOI AM-FM Records—W. I. Griffith Director, University Archives and Special Collections, Parks Library, Iowa State University, Ames.

WOI Radio and TV Records

University Archives and Special Collections, Parks Library, Iowa State University, Ames.

WOI Records

Unprocessed WOI Records, University Archives and Special Collections, Parks Library, Iowa State University, Ames.

WOSU Records

Records of WOSU and WOSU-FM, Record Group 8/d-4/1, Ohio State University Archives, Columbus.

WSUI Collection

WSUI Collection, Special Collections and University Archives, Main Library, University of Iowa, Iowa City.

Notes

Prologue

1. Ann M. Velia, *KOB, Goddard's Magic Mast: Fifty Years of Pioneer Broadcasting* (Las Cruces: New Mexico State University Press, 1972), 134–35.

2. Ibid., 134–35, 154–67.

3. Table No. 3, "Report on Radio Broadcasting Stations for Year 1922," file 1675, box 137, RD/FCC.

4. Erik Barnouw, *A Tower in Babel: A History of Broadcasting in the United States,* vol. 1 (New York: Oxford University Press, 1966), 209.

5. Lizabeth Cohen, *Making a New Deal: Industrial Workers in Chicago, 1919–1939* (New York: Cambridge University Press, 1990), 142.

6. Michele Hilmes, *Radio Voices: American Broadcasting, 1922–1952* (Minneapolis: University of Minnesota Press, 1997), xvi. Despite the limited primary sources available, some studies of early independent stations do exist. For analyses of independent stations operated by private businesses and serving local regions during the 1920s, see especially Cohen, *Making a New Deal,* 132–43; Derek Vaillant, *Sounds of Reform: Progressivism and Music in Chicago, 1873–1935* (Chapel Hill: University of North Carolina Press, 2002), 234–69; Clifford J. Doerksen, "'Serving the Masses, Not the Classes': Station WHN, Pioneer of Commercial Broadcasting of the 1920s," *Journal of Radio Studies* 6 (February 1999): 81–100; J. Steven Smethers and Lee Jolliffe, "Homemaking Programs: The Recipe for Reaching Women Listeners on the Midwest's Local Radio," *Journalism History* 24 (Winter 1998–99): 138–47; J. Steven Smethers and Lee B. Jolliffe, "Singing and Selling Seeds: The Live Music Era on Rural Midwestern Radio Stations," *Journalism History* 26 (Summer 2000): 61–70; J. F. Evans, *Prairie Farmer and WLS* (Urbana: University of Illinois Press, 1969); Robert Birkby, *KMA Radio: The First Sixty Years* (Shenandoah, Iowa: May Broadcasting Co., 1985); Reynold M. Wik, "Radio in the 1920s: A Social Force in South Dakota," *South Dakota History* 11 (Spring 1981): 93–110; Lori Rohlk, "'Sisters of the Skillet': Radio Homemakers in Shenandoah, Iowa, 1920–1960" (M.A. thesis, University

of Nebraska at Lincoln, 1997); Barnouw, *Tower in Babel*, 75–188; George H. Douglas, *The Early Days of Radio Broadcasting* (Jefferson, N.C.: McFarland, 1987); Clifford J. Doerksen, *American Babel: Rogue Radio Broadcasters of the Jazz Age* (Philadelphia: University of Pennsylvania Press, 2005). Also see the articles in *Journal of Radio Studies* 8.2 (Spring 2001) on the beginnings of farm and rural radio, especially Steve Craig, "'The Farmer's Friend': Radio Comes to Rural America, 1920–1927," 330–46; and Stephen D. Perry, "Securing Programming on Live Local Radio: WDZ Reaches Rural Illinois, 1929–1939," 347–71. On the early history of local stations operated by nonprofit organizations, see especially Nathan Godfried, *WCFL: Chicago's Voice of Labor, 1926–1978* (Urbana: University of Illinois Press, 1997), 1–105; Tona J. Hangen, *Redeeming the Dial: Radio, Religion, and Popular Culture in America* (Chapel Hill: University of North Carolina Press, 2002), 57–79; and Susan Smulyan, *Selling Radio: The Commercialization of American Broadcasting, 1920–1934* (Washington, D.C.: Smithsonian Institution Press, 1994), 66–67.

7. Robert W. McChesney, *Telecommunications, Mass Media, and Democracy: The Battle for the Control of U.S. Broadcasting, 1928–1935* (New York: Oxford University Press, 1993), 254. For a general overview, based on published sources, of radio stations established by institutions of higher education, see J. Wayne Rinks, "Higher Education in Radio, 1922–1934," *Journal of Radio Studies* 9 (December 2002): 303–16. Also see S. E. Frost Jr., *Education's Own Stations: The History of Broadcast Licenses Issued to Educational Institutions* (Chicago: University of Chicago Press, 1937). Frost's book does not cite the primary sources he apparently used. For this reason, I have generally avoided using the work. Instead, I have relied on primary sources for my analysis of the practices of university radio stations, especially those from archives across the country.

8. For the number of land-grant stations in 1924, see "Agriculture Has Big Interest in Radio," *Official Record: United States Department of Agriculture*, vol. 3 (October 22, 1924): 1, 5. For the 1930 figure, see "Memorandum for the Chairman, Executive Committee, American Association of Land Grant Colleges and Universities," December 5, 1930, folder "Radio, 1924–1953," box 112, AgrSub/IL.

9. Rinks, "Higher Education in Radio," 304.

10. For the early history of broadcasting, see especially Susan J. Douglas, *Inventing American Broadcasting, 1899–1922* (Baltimore: Johns Hopkins University Press, 1987); Hugh G. J. Aitken, *Syntony and Spark: The Origins of Radio* (New York: Wiley, 1976); Hugh G. J. Aitken, *The Continuous Wave: Technology and American Radio, 1900–1932* (Princeton, N.J.: Princeton University Press, 1985); Christopher H. Sterling and John Michael Kittross, *Stay Tuned: A History of American Broadcasting*, 3d ed. (London: Lawrence Erlbaum Associates, 2002), 5–51; Barnouw, *Tower in Babel*, 7–74; Smulyan, *Selling Radio*. Also see recent books on the history of broadcasting in the United States during the 1930s and 1940s: Jason Loviglio, *Radio's Intimate Public: Network Broadcasting and Mass-Mediated Democracy* (Minneapolis: University of Minnesota Press, 2005); Kathy Newman, *Radio Active: Advertising and Consumer Activism, 1935–1947* (Berkeley: University of California Press, 2004); Elizabeth Fones-Wolf, *Waves of Opposition: Labor and the Struggle for Democratic Radio* (Urbana: University of Illinois Press, 2006). This study is informed especially by recent work in the history of technology that emphasizes the complex interaction between technological development and social change, in particular the social construction of technology. Recent studies in the history of broadcasting that

follow this approach include Douglas, *Inventing American Broadcasting*; Ronald R. Kline, *Consumers in the Country: Technology and Social Change in Rural America* (Baltimore: Johns Hopkins University Press, 2000), 113–27; Hugh R. Slotten, *Radio and Television Regulation: Broadcast Technology in the United States, 1920–1960* (Baltimore: Johns Hopkins University Press, 2000); and Wiebe E. Bijker, Thomas Hughes, and Trevor Pinch, eds., *The Social Construction of Technological Systems* (Cambridge: Massachusetts Institute of Technology Press, 1987).

11. This analysis is mainly based on the rhetorical statements of reformers, rather than on the actual practice of stations. See, for example, Douglas, *Inventing American Broadcasting*, 309–14 (quotation on 313); Hilmes, *Radio Voices*, 17; Smulyan, *Selling Radio*, 95–97; and J. Fred MacDonald, *Don't Touch That Dial: Radio Programming in American Life from 1920 to 1960* (Chicago: Nelson-Hall, 1979), 10. For the beginnings of a more nuanced view of educational radio, see especially Derek Vaillant, "'Your Voice Came in Last Night . . . but I Thought It Sounded a Little Scarred': Rural Radio Listening and 'Talking Back' during the Progressive Era in Wisconsin, 1920–1932," in *Radio Reader: Essays in the Cultural History of Radio*, ed. Michele Hilmes and Jason Loviglio (New York: Routledge, 2002), 63–88. Although Ronald Kline also primarily emphasizes the uplift theme in his analysis of agricultural broadcasting, his recent book on the introduction of new technologies on farms provides an exemplary model for analyses taking into account the interaction between producers and consumers of modern technologies in the creation of individual, contested modernities. See Kline, *Consumers in the Country*. On the social and cultural significance of the uplift discourse expressed in newspapers and farm periodicals during the 1920s, see Randall Patnode, "'What These People Need Is Radio': New Technology, the Press, and Otherness in 1920s America," *Technology and Culture* 44 (April 2003): 285–305.

Chapter 1

1. Cyril M. Jansky (untitled report prior to February 1922 radio conference), folder 5, box 7, Jansky Papers.

2. Herbert Hoover, "Opening Remarks," *Proceedings of the Fourth National Radio Conference and Recommendations for Regulation of Radio. . . . Nov. 9–11, 1925* (Washington, D.C.: Government Printing Office, 1926), 5.

3. Aitken, *Continuous Wave*, 28–249.

4. Douglas, *Inventing American Broadcasting*, 3–101; Aitken, *Syntony and Spark*, 179–297.

5. Aitken, *Continuous Wave*, 28–249; Douglas, *Inventing American Broadcasting*, 35, 44, 48–50, 169–70, 244–45.

6. For example, the University of Nebraska reportedly "initiated wireless studies in 1899." See Robert Earl Lee, "A History of Radio Broadcasting at the University of Nebraska" (M.A. thesis, University of Nebraska, 1952), 2. This assertion is based on a 1934 unpublished paper dealing with the history of radio at the university. Also see Frost, *Education's Own Stations*.

7. The public universities listed in *Radio Service Bulletins* of the U.S. Department of Commerce (Bureau of Navigation) issued licenses during this period include the Uni-

versity of Arkansas, the State College of Washington, the University of Virginia, the University of Washington, Cornell University, Montana State College, Iowa State College of Agriculture and Mechanical Arts, Alabama Polytechnic Institute, the State University of Iowa, Ohio University, the University of California, the University of Maine, Pennsylvania State College, the University of Missouri, the University of North Dakota, Ohio State University, Kansas State Agricultural College, North Dakota Agricultural College, the University of Kansas, and the University of Wisconsin. The private schools that received special licenses during this period, listed in the *Radio Service Bulletins,* include Harvard University, Washington University, Nebraska Wesleyan University, the University of Pittsburgh, Beloit College, Carnegie Institute of Technology, Worcester Polytechnic Institute, Union College, Saint Joseph's College, Miami University, and St. Louis University.

8. John Stanley Penn, "The Origin and Development of Radio Broadcasting at the University of Wisconsin" (Ph.D. dissertation, University of Wisconsin–Madison, 1959), 66, 80–81. For a general history of WHA, also see Randall Davidson, *9XM Talking: WHA Radio and the Wisconsin Idea* (Madison: University of Wisconsin Press, 2006).

9. "Weather Forecasts Sent by Wireless," *University of Wisconsin Press Bulletin,* December 13, 1916 [clipping], folder "WHA-Historical," box 49, McCarty Papers.

10. John C. Schmidt, "Radio's Last Pioneer," *Baltimore Sun* [clipping], folder 11, box 1, Engel Papers.

11. Penn, "Origin and Development," 77–81.

12. C. M. Jansky Jr. to J. M. Mack, November 13, 1958, folder "WHA-Historical," box 49, McCarty Papers.

13. Penn, "Origin and Development," 92–120 (F. W. Nolte quoted on 104).

14. Ibid., 125–37 (L. L. Call quoted on 133).

15. Velia, *KOB,* 6–20, 48–70 (newspaper story quoted on 9).

16. Adrian E. Dalen, "A History of KUSD: The University of South Dakota Radio Station," (M.A. thesis, University of South Dakota, 1949), 1–3, USD Archives. For further evidence of Lawrence's leadership role, see Ernest Orlando Lawrence to H. O. Peterson, n.d. (probably 1921), folder 2, box 1, Boye Papers.

17. "KSAC and 9YV Revisited," *K-Stater,* May 1982 (clipping), KSU Archives.

18. James M. Rosene, "The History of Radio Broadcasting at Auburn University (1912–1961)" (M.A. thesis, Auburn University, 1968), 13–30, Auburn Archives.

19. Marie Perkins Rachut, "History of the State University of Iowa: The Radio Station WSUI" (M.A. thesis, University of Iowa, 1946), 6–12, 18, UofIowa Archives; Carl Menzer, "Fifty Years of Broadcasting at the University of Iowa," folder "Menzer, Carl Vignettes," 1968, box 2, WSUI Collection; "Broadcasting since 1917, Menzer Will Retire in July," February 15, 1968, *Daily Iowan* [clipping], Carl Menzer subject file, UofIowa Archives. The station was first assigned the call letters WHAA in June 1922; after January 1925 it was licensed as WSUI.

20. Clinton B. DeSoto, *Two Hundred Meters and Down: The Story of Amateur Radio* (West Hartford, Conn.: American Radio Relay League, 1936), 16–37; Douglas, *Inventing American Broadcasting,* 187–215; Hilmes, *Radio Voices,* 35–46. For the "imagined community" concept, see Benedict R. O'G. Anderson, *Imagined Communities: Reflections on the Origin and Spread of Nationalism* (London: Verso, 1991). For a general discussion of the history of amateurs or ham operators, see Kristen Haring, *Ham Radio's Technical Culture* (Cambridge: Massachusetts Institute of Technology Press, 2007).

21. DeSoto, *Two Hundred Meters and Down*, 38–50; Douglas, *Inventing American Broadcasting*, 206, 233–39, 293–96.

22. Amateurs made numerous requests for technical assistance from the operators of the University of Nebraska radio station, for example. See 9YY operator to Westinghouse Electrical and Manufacturing Company, December 8, 1921, folder 1, box 2, Boye Papers.

23. The story about the first station at the University of Nebraska is told in F. C. Holtz to Ferris Norris, July 26, 1933, folder 1, box 1, Boye Papers. For the example of the high school student working with the University of Wisconsin, see W. H. Lighty to W. Patrick, February 18, 1925, folder "Correspondence-1925, Feb.," box 21, Lighty Papers.

24. On experimenters at universities using reports from amateurs to conduct their research, see Penn, "Origin and Development," 83.

25. For discussion by an amateur about having a conversation with the professors from these universities at an American Radio Relay League meeting in Chicago, see O.M. to H. O. Peterson, October 31, 1921, folder 2, box 1, Boye Papers.

26. One of Terry's students at the university, R. J. Oetjen, quoted in Penn, "Origin and Development," 74.

27. Velia, *KOB*, 54, 65.

28. Dalen, "History of KUSD," 1–2.

29. Velia, *KOB*, 56.

30. Bureau of Navigation, Department of Commerce, *Radio Service Bulletin* 27 (March 1, 1917): 9.

31. "Hertzian Telegraphy at the Physical Society," *The Electrician* (London) 40 (January 28, 1898): 452–53 (quotation on 453).

32. Douglas, *Inventing American Broadcasting*, 156–57.

33. Ibid., 171–77 (quotation on 176).

34. Barnouw, *Tower in Babel*, 34–35.

35. Gordon Greb and Mike Adams, *Charles Herrold, Inventor of Radio Broadcasting* (London: McFarland, 2003), 6–11, 64–100, 221 (for a published report in 1910 of Herrold's "wireless phone concerts" to amateurs, see 6). Herrold apparently also broadcast news from the local paper to amateurs as early as 1914 or 1915 (99).

36. Douglas, *Inventing American Broadcasting*, 247–48, 293–95.

37. Greb and Adams, *Charles Herrold*, 101–8 (Newby quoted on 105). Amateurs who were not primarily motivated by commercial considerations but mainly interested in promoting their hobby also increasingly experimented with voice and music broadcasting after 1914. See Sterling and Kittross, *Stay Tuned*, 45.

38. "Radio Service Starts New Midway Program," *Official Record: United States Department of Agriculture* 8 (July 4, 1929): 1, 3. On the importance of the Country Life Movement in the early twentieth century as a motivating factor for agriculture officials seeking to bring urban developments and values to rural areas, see Kline, *Consumers in the Country*. On the use of university radio stations for social reform, also see Vaillant, "Your Voice Came in Last Night."

39. Deborah Fitzgerald, *Every Farm a Factory: The Industrial Ideal in American Agriculture* (New Haven, Conn.: Yale University Press, 2003), 17.

40. Quoted in Velia, *KOB*, 63.

41. Penn, "Origin and Development," 140–42.

42. For the early history of radio regulation in the United States, see Slotten, *Radio and*

Television Regulation, 1–20. On the early relationship between amateurs and the federal government, see Douglas, *Inventing American Broadcasting,* 216–39; and Philip T. Rosen, *The Modern Stentors: Radio Broadcasters and the Federal Government, 1920–1934* (Westport, Conn: Greenwood Press, 1980), 20–33. For the quotation, see "Suggestions for the Use of the Daily Market and Weather Radio Broadcasts," February 9, 1922, folder 6, box 1, WHA Subject Records.

43. 1913 report in student newspaper, quoted in Kathleen Ann Moran, "From a Toy to a Tool: The Emergence and Growth of WOI to 1940" (M.S. thesis, Iowa State University, 1981), 7.

44. See "Report of Inter-Departmental Board Appointed by President Roosevelt," *Monthly Weather Review* 51 (January 1923): 8; Report of the Chief of the Weather Bureau in U.S. Department of Agriculture, *Annual Reports of the Department of Agriculture for the Year Ended June 30, 1915* (Washington, D.C.: Government Printing Office, 1915), 66.

45. "A Historical Outline of Radio Station KSAC," n.d., subject file, KSU Archives. This may be correct, but there are no surviving primary documents supporting the claim.

46. Report of the chief of the Weather Bureau in U.S. Department of Agriculture, *Annual Reports of the Department of Agriculture for the Fiscal Year Ended June 30, 1905* (Washington, D.C.: Government Printing Office, 1905), 16.

47. Chief of Division of the Weather Bureau to Eric Miller, October 14, 1915, folder "Weather Broadcasting: Historical," box 93, McCarty Papers. Statistics for other methods of distribution are from the report of the chief of the Weather Bureau in U.S. Department of Agriculture, *Annual Reports of the Department of Agriculture for the Year Ended June 30, 1916* (Washington, D.C.: Government Printing Office, 1916), 55.

48. Report of the Chief of the Weather Bureau in U.S. Department of Agriculture, *Annual Reports of the Department of Agriculture for the Year Ended June 30, 1916* (Washington, D.C.: Government Printing Office, 1916), 55.

49. "250 Amateurs Take Reports in Iowa," *Electrical Experimenter* 6 (September 1918): 548.

50. Eric Miller to the News Editor of the *Milwaukee Journal,* December 4, 1916, folder "Weather Broadcasting: Historical," box 93, McCarty Papers.

51. Eric Miller to chief of the U.S. Weather Bureau, September 30, 1915, folder "Weather Broadcasting: Historical," box 93, McCarty Papers.

52. Eric Miller to the News Editor of the *Milwaukee Journal,* 4 Dec. 1916, folder "Weather Broadcasting: Historical," box 93, McCarty Papers.

53. "Weather Forecasts Sent by Wireless," *University of Wisconsin Press Bulletin,* December 13, 1916 [clipping], folder "WHA-Historical," box 49, McCarty Papers.

54. Eric Miller to the News Editor of the *Milwaukee Journal,* December 16, 1916, folder "Weather Broadcasting: Historical," box 93, McCarty Papers.

55. Rachut, "History of the State University of Iowa," 5.

56. Ibid., 3–4; "Basketball Game Reported by Wireless," *University of Wisconsin Press Bulletin,* January 19, 1916, folder "WHA-Historical," box 49, McCarty Papers. The University of Minnesota broadcast the results of sporting events as early as 1912 using its experimental station 9X1. See Ronald A. Smith, *Play-by-Play: Radio, Television, and Big-Time College Sport* (Baltimore: Johns Hopkins University Press, 2001), 14–15.

57. Malcolm Hanson to his mother, September 27, 1920, folder "Broadcast Data Verification," box 49, McCarty Papers.

58. President Jardine to Herbert Hoover, August 1, 1924, file "9f–School of Air–Radio," President Jardine/Farrell Papers 1924–25, KSU Archives.

59. Ralph Goddard to Tom Charles, December 20, 1922, folder 6, box 110, Goddard Papers.

60. H. O. Peterson to H. L. Owens, August 3, 1921, folder 2, box 1, Boye Papers.

61. Amateurs made numerous requests for technical assistance from the operators of the University of Nebraska radio station, for example. See 9YY operator to Westinghouse Electrical and Manufacturing Company, December 8, 1921, folder 1, box 2, Boye Papers. On experimenters at universities using reports from amateurs to conduct their research, see Penn, "Origin and Development," 83. The story about the first station at the University of Nebraska is told in F. C. Holtz to Ferris Norris, July 26, 1933, folder 1, box 1, Boye Papers. For the example of a high school student working with the University of Wisconsin, see W. H. Lighty to W. Patrick, February 18, 1925, folder "Correspondence-1925, Feb.," box 21, Lighty Papers. On "good advertising" for departments, see H. O. Peterson (operator of radio station 9YY) to H. L. Owens, August 3, 1921, folder 2, box 1, Boye Papers.

62. Operator of station 9YY to Howard S. White, August 1, 1921, folder 2, box 1, Boye Papers.

63. Malcolm Hanson to Herbert L. Whittemore, January 16, 1922, folder "Correspondence, 1918–1922," box 1, Hanson Papers.

64. "Radio Broadcasting at the University of Minnesota," February 10, 1922, folder "Correspondence and Notes Re: UM Radio (1920–28)," box 5, Jansky Papers.

65. On the role of Wheeler and his son, see testimony of J. Clyde Marquis, "Official Report of Proceedings before the Federal Communications Commission: Hearings . . . before the Broadcast Division of the Federal Communications Commission on Section 307(c) of the Communications Act of 1934," November 9, 1934, 13690, box 539, docket 2537, Dock/FCC.

66. "Radio Market News Service," USDA Radio Information Circular No. 1, April 15, 1922, 1–3, box 555, docket 2537, Dock/FCC. For details on use of different government stations, see "Report of the Agricultural Radio Conference," December 4, 1924, 3, folder "Radio Legislation," box 1369, entry 17, USDA; "Farm Radio Making Rapid Growth," March 13, 1926, 1–3, folder "Radio Legislation," box 1369, entry 17, USDA. On the Arlington station and delivery by messenger, see "Nation-wide Radio Market News Service," *Hoard's Dairyman* 64 (December 8, 1922): 607 and 630. On broadcasts of naval stations during 1922, see attachments to W. A. Wheeler to R. W. Goddard, July 7, 1922, folder 7, box 110, Goddard Papers.

67. "Radio Market News Service," USDA Radio Information Circular No. 1, April 15, 1922, 3, box 555, docket 2537, Dock/FCC. Testimony of J. Clyde Marquis, "Official Report of Proceedings before the Federal Communications Commission: Hearings . . . before the Broadcast Division of the Federal Communications Commission on Section 307(c) of the Communications Act of 1934," November 9, 1934, 13689–90, box 539, docket 2537, Dock/FCC. On the use of telephone exchanges and problems with expensive telegrams, see "Agricultural Radio Conference under the Auspices of the United States Department of Agriculture" [transcript of proceedings], December 4, 1924, 16–17, folder "Radio Legislation," box 1369, entry 17, USDA. For an excellent discussion of the use of telephone networks by farmers that provided a model for using radio to broadcast specific programs, see Kline, *Consumers in the Country*, 119.

68. Memorandum from E. N. Meador to USDA Secretary, December 23, 1929, folder "Radio News Svc.," box 1448, entry 17, USDA.

69. See J. W. Stafford, "Radio History of Purdue University," 2, folder "Radio Educational Programs: Purdue University, 1930–32," box 4, Pub/IL. For other universities that trained military personnel, see Frost, *Education's Own Stations*, 21, 73, 219, 222, 246, 275, 322, 433.

70. On the use of coded messages and the crucial role of amateurs, see "Report of the Agricultural Radio Conference," December 4, 1924, 3, folder "Radio Legislation," box 1369, entry 17, USDA; "Farm Radio Making Rapid Growth," March 13, 1926, 2–3, folder "Radio Legislation," box 1369, entry 17, USDA. On 2,500 licensed amateurs, see "Market Reports by Wireless," *Successful Farming*, May 1921, copy in folder "Radio Service Broadcasting History," box 1, USDA.

71. Testimony of J. Clyde Marquis, "Official Report of Proceedings before the Federal Communications Commission: Hearings . . . before the Broadcast Division of the Federal Communications Commission on Section 307(c) of the Communications Act of 1934," November 9, 1934, 13691, 13693, box 539, docket 2537, Dock/FCC.

72. On estimates by county agents, see "Use of Radio by Farmers: Survey of 1925 with Comparisons, 1923–1924, as Reported by County Agricultural Agents," September 1925, 3–4, 6, box 555, docket 2537, Dock/FCC; "Report of Number and Use of Radio Sets on Farms in the United States, April 1, 1927," 3, box 552, docket 2537, Dock/FCC. For the 1930 census estimate of radios owned by farmers, see "Radios Most Popular," *Rural Electrification News* 3 (June 1938): 10. The 1930 census figure is lower than the estimate made by county agents, who probably had a tendency to mainly base their estimates on the practices of wealthier farmers active in extension activities. The county agents estimated that 25 percent of farmers owned radios by April 1927. The 1930 census estimated that over 50 percent of city residents owned radios. For a discussion of urban ownership, see Hilmes, *Radio Voices*, 29.

73. Penn, "Origin and Development," 87, 144–45. On USDA instructions for building crystal sets, see testimony of J. Clyde Marquis, "Official Report of Proceedings before the Federal Communications Commission: Hearings . . . before the Broadcast Division of the Federal Communications Commission on Section 307(c) of the Communications Act of 1934," November 9, 1934, 13692, box 539, docket 2537, Dock/FCC; "How to Make and Operate a Simple Receiving Outfit," *Literary Digest*, June 17, 1922, clipping in folder 5, box 2, WHA Subject Records. On Ohio State University bulletins, see Richard H. Madden, "Radio at the Ohio State University, 1910–1926," n.d., 6, folder "WEAO: 1922–1933," information file, OSU Archives.

74. On New Mexico, see "Instructions for Building a Radio Set and Principles of Radio Communication," Extension Circular 77, November 1923 (quotation on 4), New Mexico College of Agriculture and Mechanic Arts, folder 5, box 3, Goddard Papers. On the offer of partially constructed sets, see R. W. Goddard to J. K. Andrich, March 21, 1923, folder 8, box 110, Goddard Papers.

75. Ralph Goddard to Burt Minor, November 2, 1923, folder 13, box 111, Goddard Papers.

76. On average price of high-quality receivers, see W. M. Jardine, "Report of the Secretary," in U.S. Department of Agriculture, *Yearbook of the Department of Agriculture, 1925* (Washington, D.C.: Government Printing Office, 1925), 47. For Minnesota statistics, see

H. Akers Berry, "WLB-WLB-WLB-Minneapolis Market Report!" *The Farmer* (St. Paul, Minn.), March 4, 1922, 40, copy in folder 5, box 2, WHA Subject Records. Letters quoted in "Use of Radio by Farmers: Survey of 1925 with Comparisons, 1923–1924, as Reported by County Agricultural Agents," September 1925, 13–14, box 555, docket 2537, Dock/FCC. On the price of radios and the estimate that because radios used by farmers during the 1920s were generally battery powered, farmers were only able to listen for less than one hour every day, see Kline, *Consumers in the Country*, 115, 126.

77. "Survey of the Use of Radio by Farmers, 1924, with Comparison to 1923, from Questionnaire Returned to County Agents," folder "Radio, 1924–1953," box 112, AgrSub/ IL, 8, 12.

78. For examples of reports of farmers owning high-priced sets (over four hundred dollars) in rural Oregon, see "Report of the Radio Technical Committee," May 25, 1923, microfilm reel 7, KOAC Records. On results of the survey, see "Study Radio Use by Iowa Farmers," *Official Record: United States Department of Agriculture*, vol. 4, July 22, 1925, 1–2 (quotation on 2). See W. M. Jardine, "Report of the Secretary," in U.S. Department of Agriculture, *Yearbook of the Department of Agriculture, 1925*, 47, for the quotation from the secretary. The letter from Washington County, Indiana, quoted in "Use of Radio by Farmers: Survey of 1925 with Comparisons, 1923–1924, as Reported by County Agricultural Agents," September 1925, 10, box 555, docket 2537, Dock/FCC. The last letter is quoted in G. C. Biggar, "What Farm Folks Are Getting by Radio: A Real Service for Rural America," *Successful Farming*, November 1925, copy in folder "Historical Material-R&TV Service," box 1, entry HRTB, USDA.

79. Fitzgerald, *Every Farm a Factory*, 3, 6.

80. On earlier efforts to coordinate extension work, see Testimony of J. Clyde Marquis, "Official Report of Proceedings before the Federal Communications Commission: Hearings . . . before the Broadcast Division of the Federal Communications Commission on Section 307(c) of the Communications Act of 1934," November 9, 1934, 13694, box 539, docket 2537, Dock/FCC.

81. Penn, "Origin and Development," 84–85, 89. The date refers to the time when the Radio Corporation of America (RCA) was formed by the major electrical and communications companies in the United States.

82. For the important role of engineers in formulating a public-service role for radio, see especially Slotten, *Radio and Television Regulation*. For the Lyon quotation, see Eric R. Lyon to Earle M. Terry, September 12, 1921, folder 4, box 1, WHA Subject Records.

83. For the Jardine quotation, see W. M. Jardine to J. O. Hamilton, April 11, 1922, file "44a-Radio," Papers of President Jardine, KSU Archives. Jardine's fears were partly based on difficulties university stations were having convincing radio manufacturers to sell them transmitters and other apparatus. On experiences at the University of California, see Allyn G. Smith to W. H. Lighty, April 8, 1924, folder "1924, Mar. 21–Apr. 10," box 19, Lighty Papers. The purchased transmitter was transferred to the electrical engineering department for use in research.

84. On the Minnesota station, see W. M. Jardine to J. O. Hamilton, April 11, 1922, file "44a-Radio," Papers of President Jardine, KSU Archives. On the University of Illinois station, see M. S. Ketchum to David Kinley, October 28, 1924, folder "Radio Programs, 1924–37," box 27, AgrSub/IL.

85. For the 1924 figure, see "Agriculture Has Big Interest in Radio," *Official Record:*

United States Department of Agriculture, vol. 3, October 22, 1924, 1, 5. For the 1930 figure, see "Memorandum for the Chairman, Executive Committee, American Association of Land Grant Colleges and Universities," December 5, 1930, folder "Radio, 1924–1953," box 112, AgrSub/IL. For a general discussion of university stations based on published records, also see Rinks, "Higher Education in Radio," 303–16.

86. The call letters used here were the ones common during the 1920s. The earliest stations started out with different designations. WHA, for example, was known as 9XM until January 1922, and WAPI in Alabama was first licensed in 1922 as WMAV ("We Make a Voice").

87. For 1923 range of WOI, see R. K. Bliss to Extension Directors, November 20, 1923, folder "Radio, 1923–30," box 84, AgrSub/IL. For the 1926 range of WOI, see W. I. Griffith, "Annual Report: Radio Activities of Broadcasting Station WOI . . . June 30, 1926," WOI Records. On WEAO, see "Radio Broadcasting Station WEAO," July 15, 1925, folder "WEAO: 1922–1933," information file, OSU Archives.

88. Discussion of leased-wire policy in letter from WAPI to Andrew Hopkins, September 4, 1931, folder "Location–Land Lease Telephone Rental," box 38, McCarty Papers.

89. Moran, "From a Toy to a Tool," 60; "Annual Report: Radio Activity of Broadcasting Station WOI, Fiscal Year Beginning July 1, 1926," folder "Photos for Thesis," WOI Records; W. I. Griffith, "Report on Broadcasting Station WOI, Appendix A: Special Report Past, Present, and Future Program of Broadcasting Station WOI," December 24, 1927, WOI Records.

90. On the use of forms and receptacles, see "Radio Broadcasting by the University of Wisconsin," February 1922, folder "WHA Historical," box 49, McCarty Papers; Boyd Nestelrode to U.S. Weather Bureau, November 30, 1921, folder "Weather Broadcasting: Historical," box 93, McCarty Papers (quotation). On the idea for the use of receptacles at Wisconsin, see Penn, "Origin and Development," 152. For the number of amateurs, see Eric Miller to chief, U.S. Weather Bureau, December 3, 1921, folder "Weather Broadcasting: Historical," box 93, McCarty Papers. On the telephone company in Iowa, see "Broadcast Schedule WOI," vol. 26, November 9, 1927, 7, WOI Records. On the use of radio market reports from a station at St. Louis University by a rural Illinois telephone company, see "Telephone Subscribers Get Radiophone Market Reports," September 21, 1921, unidentified newspaper clipping, folder 5, box 2, WHA Corresp.

91. P. O. Davis, "A Centralized Unit in Educational Broadcasting," in *Education on the Air: First Yearbook of the Institute for Education by Radio* (Columbus: Ohio State University Press, 1930), 61–76. On the origin of the practice in Alabama, see Rosene, "History of Radio Broadcasting," 28. Before 1926, when the station began broadcasting an average of ten hours per week, the station at the Alabama Polytechnic Institute was not successful in reaching a wide audience during the daytime. For the most part, the signal could only be picked up by receivers within the county (36).

92. On the Wisconsin station, see the statement of B. B. Jones (Wisconsin market official) in "Agricultural Radio Conference under the Auspices of the United States Department of Agriculture" [transcript of proceedings], December 4, 1924, 11–13 (quotations on 12–13), folder "Radio Legislation," box 1369, entry 17, USDA. A December 1924 publication by the Wisconsin Department of Markets lists seven broadcast times. See "Market and Market Reports," *State of Wisconsin Department of Markets Bulletin* 5 (December 1, 1924):

1–18, copy in folder 1, box 5, Engel Papers. On the special need for evening broadcasting by the Wisconsin Department of Markets, which the university station could not guarantee because of reduced staff during the summer and increased costs for expanded service, see B. B. Jones to E. M. Terry, July 5, 1922, folder 4, box 1, WHA Subject Records; and E. M. Terry to B. B. Jones, August 11, 1922, folder 4, box 1, WHA Subject Records. The Department of Markets also decided to set up its own station to save money on leased-wire fees by combining its two state offices that were using the leased-wire network. See B. B. Jones to E. M. Terry, October 28, 1922, folder 4, box 1, WHA Subject Records. The stations in Nebraska and Missouri were located in each state's capitol building. For Nebraska, see Samuel Avery to C. W. Bryan, December 13, 1922, folder "Bryan, Charles W.," box 1, Avery Corr. For Missouri, see Statements of Arthur T. Nelson, Missouri State Marketing Commissioner, in "Agricultural Radio Conference under the Auspices of the United States Department of Agriculture" [transcript of proceedings], December 4, 1924, 16–17, folder "Radio Legislation," box 1369, entry 17, USDA.

93. J. Austin Hunter, "Crop and Market Reports by Radio," in "Agricultural Radio Conference under the Auspices of the United States Department of Agriculture" [transcript of proceedings], December 4, 1924, 9–11, folder "Radio Legislation," box 1369, entry 17, USDA. On the market-information network in New England, see Testimony of J. Clyde Marquis, "Official Report of Proceedings before the Federal Communications Commission: Hearings . . . before the Broadcast Division of the Federal Communications Commission on Section 307(c) of the Communications Act of 1934," November 9, 1934, 13697–98, box 539, docket 2537, Dock/FCC. The Pennsylvania State Department of Markets experimented with a consumer-information service using home-economics experts. See C. W. Warburton, "The Educational Use of the Radio," folder "Radio Legislation," box 1369, entry 17, USDA. On a unique market-information network in California, which used a short-wave station operated by the State Department of Agriculture, see S. G. Rubinow to Walter V. Woehlke, July 8, 1931, folder 1073, box 56, Payne Fund Records.

Chapter 2

1. Madden, "Radio at the Ohio State University," (*Columbus Citizen* quoted on 9). This paper refers to primary sources without giving references. The original documents are apparently missing from the archives.

2. Unknown author to J. D. Phillips, August 9, 1926, folder 7, box 2, WHA Subject Records.

3. See the prologue n.11.

4. Cornell University decided against starting a radio station in 1922 for this reason. See H. W. Riley to W. M. Jardine, March 25, 1922, file "44a-Radio," Papers of President Jardine, 1922–23, KSU Archives. For a general overview, based on published sources, of radio stations established by institutions of higher education, see Rinks, "Higher Education in Radio," 303–16.

5. On the number of hours, see "Radio Stations Owned by Educational Institutions," n.d., file 9f–School of Air–Radio, Papers of President Francis Farrell, 1926–27, KSU Archives. For "Science for Service" slogan, see "KOAC Radio Program, 1925–26," microfilm reel 7, KOAC Records. For "seat in front of the microphone" quotation, see Morse Salis-

bury, "Contributions of Radio to Informal Adult Education," in *Education on the Air: First Yearbook of the Institute for Education by Radio* (Columbus: Ohio State University Press, 1930), 149–68 (quotation on 151). For Umberger's testimony, see "Agricultural Radio Conference under the Auspices of the United States Department of Agriculture" [transcript of proceedings], December 4, 1924, 2, folder "Radio Legislation," box 1369, entry 17, USDA.

6. On scripts being read by station announcers, see W. H. Lighty to Malcolm C. Hanson, March 12, 1930, folder "Correspondence-1930, Mar.–Apr.," box 35, Lighty Papers. For the views of the Florida official, see B. C. Riley to W. H. Lighty, April 3, 1923, folder "1923, Jan.–Apr.," Lighty Papers. For the Illinois example, see H. W. Mumford to Josef F. Wright, May 6, 1936, folder "Radio, WILL, 1928–53," box 112, AgrSub/IL. For the action of the president of Ohio State, see "WEAO's Proposed Findings of Fact (to the Federal Radio Commission)," December 23, 1931, folder 1048, box 55, Payne Fund Records. For the "victims" remark, see A. S. Pearse to W. H. Lighty, October 18, 1923, folder "1923, Oct. 16–31," box 17, Lighty Papers.

7. R. W. Goddard to A. M. Harding, January 25, 1929, no folder, box 20, Goddard Papers.

8. For the views of the faculty at KOB, see C. F. Monroe to R. W. Goddard, December 29, 1925, folder 17, box 110, Goddard Papers. On the comments of the director of extension at New Mexico State, see C. F. Monroe to R. W. Goddard, December 29, 1925, folder 17, box 110, Goddard Papers. For the views of the faculty member at Wisconsin, see Cecil Russell to W. H. Lighty, June 1, 1926, folder "Correspondence-1926, June," box 25, Lighty Papers. For the last example, see C. F. Monroe to R. W. Goddard, May 20, 1925, folder 18, box 110, Goddard Papers.

9. See, for example, R. K. Bliss to Extension Directors, November 20, 1923, folder "Radio, 1923–1930," box 84, AgrSub/IL.

10. Richard Basil Ridgway, "A Historical Study of KSAC Radio, Kansas' First Educational Radio Station" (M.A. thesis, Kansas State University, 1972), 56.

11. "Supplemental Broadcasting Schedule to Iowa State College of Agriculture and Mechanic Arts," November 25, 1925, WOI Records.

12. For a schedule of early WHA farm programs, see "How Do You Get Us Now?" n.d., folder 19, box 1, WHA Subject Records. On the origins of the noontime farm program and the morning program for women at WHA, see Penn, "Origin and Development," 143–44, 319. For KOAC, see W. L. Kadderly, "An Outline of Broadcasting Activities: Station KOAC—The Oregon Agricultural College, College Year 1926–1927," microfilm reel 7, KOAC Records. For WOI, see "Broadcasting Schedule WOI," November 9, 1927, folder 8, box 20, Goddard Papers; "Supplemental Broadcasting Schedule to Iowa State College of Agriculture and Mechanic Arts," November 25, 1925, WOI Records. For KSAC, see "History of Extension in Kansas, 1914–1939," file B-21/F-9, CoopExt/KSU. On the origins of the program for women at WEAO, see "WEAO Radio Program," January 1, 1930, folder "WEAO: 1922–1933," information file, OSU Archives. On WEAO broadcasting farm programs throughout the day, see "Radio Broadcasting Station WEAO," July 15, 1925, folder "WEAO: 1922–1933," information file, OSU Archives.

13. "Broadcasting Schedule WOI," November 9, 1927, unmarked box, WOI Records.

14. Madden, "Radio at the Ohio State University."

15. Ridgway, "Historical Study of KSAC Radio," 56–57. For the quotation and for a discussion of WOI's rural school program, see Iowa State University president to C. R. Snyder, February 5, 1925, file "9f–School of Air–Radio," President Jardine/Farrell Papers, 1924–25, KSU Archives.

16. Ridgway, "Historical Study of KSAC Radio," 58.

17. Earle Terry to Willebald Weniger, March 16, 1925, folder 12, box 1, WHA Subject Records.

18. C. W. Warburton, "The Educational Use of Radio," n.d., folder "Radio Legislation," box 1369, entry 17, USDA.

19. Ibid. For Minnesota, see Agricultural Extension Director to C. W. Warburton, January 19, 1926, folder "Radio Legislation," box 1369, entry 17, USDA. Colleges not oriented toward agriculture, including the University of Iowa and the University of Kansas, also experimented with college courses over their own radio stations during this early period. For the University of Iowa, see William G. Raymond to C. W. Warburton, January 18, 1926, folder "Radio Legislation," box 1369, entry 17, USDA. Tufts University and the University of Nebraska presented courses over nearby commercial stations. For Nebraska, see "The University Extension Division–June 30, 1930," folder "History of Extension Division," box 2, ExtensionSubject/Neb.

20. On statistics, see "History of Extension in Kansas, 1914–1939," file B-21/F-9, CoopExt/KSU. On the selection of material in courses, see "Radio Extension Courses: Catalogue," Kansas State Agricultural College, September 1924, 18–20, file "9f–School of Air–Radio," President Jardine/Farrell Papers, 1924–25, KSU Archives.

21. "Agricultural Radio Conference under the Auspices of the United States Department of Agriculture" [transcript of proceedings], December 4, 1924, 5, folder "Radio Legislation," box 1369, entry 17, USDA.

22. Harry Umberger, "The Influence of Radio Instruction upon Farm Practices," in *Education on the Air: Third Yearbook of the Institute for Education by Radio* (Columbus: Ohio State University Press, 1932), 274–90.

23. Von V. Pittman Jr., "Station WSUI and the Early Days of Instructional Radio," *The Palimpsest* 67 (March/April 1986): 42–44.

24. "State University of Iowa Broadcast Correspondence Courses for Credit from 1925 to 1927—Resumed This Plan in Modified Form in 1929," folder "Station WSUI History," box 2, WSUI Collection.

25. Pittman, "Station WSUI," 43–45.

26. "State University of Iowa Broadcast Correspondence Courses for Credit from 1925 to 1927—Resumed This Plan in Modified Form in 1929," folder "Station WSUI History," box 2, WSUI Collection.

27. S. E. Frost quoted in ibid.

28. Julia Grant, "Modernizing Mothers: Home Economics and the Parent Education Movement, 1920–1945," in *Rethinking Home Economics: Women and the History of a Profession,* ed. Sarah Stage and Virginia B. Vincenti (Ithaca, N.Y.: Cornell University Press, 1997), 55–74 (quotation on 63). Also see other articles in this book, especially Carolyn M. Goldstein, "Part of the Package: Home Economists in the Consumer Products Indus-

tries, 1920–1940," 271–96. See also Carolyn M. Goldstein, "From Service to Sales: Home Economics in Light and Power, 1920–1940," *Technology and Culture* 38 (January 1997): 121–35; Kline, *Consumers in the Country,* 1–19, 159, 208–11.

29. "History of Extension in Kansas, 1914–1939," file B-21/F-9, CoopExt/KSU. For the use of this format over WHA, see radio scripts from the late 1920s in folder 19, box 1, WHA Subject Records. For WOI, see "Broadcasting Schedule WOI," November 9, 1927, 12, folder 8, box 20, Goddard Papers. For the experience of the Wisconsin professor, see J. G. Halpin to W. H. Lighty, December 30, 1926, folder "Correspondence–1926, Dec. 11–n.d.," box 26, Lighty Papers.

30. C. F. Monroe to heads of departments, October 21, 1925, folder 15, box 110, Goddard Papers.

31. On the importance of group activity to adult education, see W. H. Lighty, "Adult Education," n.d., folder "Correspondence-1927, Nov.," box 29, Lighty Papers. On the Washington radio club and radio parties in California, see "Boys' and Girls' Farm Radio Clubs," *Hoard's Dairyman* 71 (May 25, 1926): 574. On WOI clubs, see "Broadcast Schedule WOI," vol. 26, November 9, 1927, WOI Records. On the early practice of meeting at the home of an owner of a radio receiver or at a local business with a radio, see Steve Craig, "'The Farmer's Friend': Radio Comes to Rural America, 1920–1927," *Journal of Radio Studies* 8 (Spring 2001): 341; Steve Craig, "'The More They Listen, the More They Buy': Radio and the Modernizing of Rural America, 1930–1939," *Agricultural History* 80 (Winter 2006): 5. On the use of clubs or groups with extension work, see Goldstein, "From Service to Sales," 136; Grant, "Modernizing Mothers," 55–74.

32. Goldstein, "From Service to Sales," 133; Goldstein, "Part of the Package," 275–76.

33. For the phrase "special stunts or tricks," see J. B. Hasselman, "The Contribution of Broadcasting to Agriculture," *Education on the Air: Second Yearbook of the Institute for Education by Radio* (Columbus: Ohio State University Press, 1931), 122–31 (quotation on 128). "Tune in for WLS Tonight," unidentified newspaper clipping, April 12, 1924, folder "WLS, 1924–59," box 112, AgrSub/IL. The program was the first to use the new call letters; the old name for the Chicago station was WES.

34. For the example of KQW, see S. S. Knight to R. A. Oakley, February 28, 1926, box 1220, entry GCOS, USDA. On the case involving smoked salt, see Wilmon Newell to Garland Powell, November 26, 1932, folder "WRUF, 1930–1947," box 3, AgrExp/FL.

35. On publicity as a motivation for universities to operate radio stations, see "Report on Radio Broadcasting Station [WOI], January 1926," unprocessed box, WOI Records.

36. WOI listed publicity as the third purpose of the station, behind market service and education. See W. I. Griffith to Members of the Faculty, 1926, folder "Notices . . .," box 1, subject file, WOI Radio and TV Records. On the WEAO example, see "Radio Broadcasting Station WEAO," July 15, 1925, 6–7, folder "WEAO: 1922–1933," information file, OSU Archives. On KOB, see R. W. Goddard to W. J. Jenkins, January 2, 1924, folder 10, box 111, Goddard Papers. The views of the University of Nebraska station were reported in the *Daily Nebraskan,* quoted in R. McLaran Sawyer, *Centennial History of the University of Nebraska,* vol. 2, *The Modern University, 1920–1969* (Lincoln, Neb.: Centennial Press, 1973), 29. On the KUSD example, see Dalen, "History of KUSD," 18. For the last quotation, see W. I. Griffith, "Annual Report: Radio Activities of Broadcasting Station WOI . . . June 30, '31," 2, WOI Records.

37. William G. Raymond to Oscar Johnson, August 22, 1924, folder "WSUI . . . 1924–1925," box 2, WSUI Collection.

38. "Forthcoming" KOB program, September 30, 1924, folder "Radio, 1924–25," box 113, Goddard Papers; Rosene, "History of Radio Broadcasting," 46.

39. R. W. Goddard to L. J. Reynolds, April 1, 1924, folder "Radio, 1924–25," box 113, Goddard Papers.

40. "Brief History of KUSD Broadcasting Station, Owned and Operated by the University of South Dakota," January 13, 1931, folder 4, box 33, Slagle Papers; for the last quotation, see B. B. Brackett to Josef P. Wright, January 26, 1935, folder 5, box 1, NAEB Papers.

41. W. I. Griffith to Members of the Faculty, November 30, 1929, folder "WOI Policy and Organization," box 1, WOI/Griffith Records.

42. "Report on Radio Broadcasting Station," January 1926, unmarked box, WOI Records.

43. Pittman, "Station WSUI," 38–52 (quotation on 42).

44. C. A. Wright quoted in Madden, "Radio at the Ohio State University," 14.

45. Untitled WILL memorandum beginning, "We have received a petition," n.d., folder "Radio Correspondence, 1925–30," box 3, Pub/IL.

46. Josef F. Wright to Kendall Banning, February 25, 1934, folder "R-Radio, 1922–33," box 3, Pub/IL.

47. Malcolm Hanson to Andrew W. Hopkins, June 17, 1931, folder "WHA-Oral History," box 49, McCarty Papers.

48. Kansas State University president to C. R. Snyder, February 5, 1925, file "9f–School of Air–Radio," President Jardine/Farrell Papers, 1924–25, KSU Archives.

49. Harry Umberger to F. B. Nichols, December 11, 1924, file "9f–School of Air–Radio," President Jardine/Farrell Papers, 1924–25, KSU Archives.

50. W. H. Lighty, "Adult Education," n.d., folder "Correspondence-1927, Nov.," box 29, Lighty Papers.

51. Harold B. McCarty, "Highlights in the History of WHA: A Salute to Several Radio Pioneers," folder "History," box 49, McCarty Papers.

52. For the first quotation, see W. H. Lighty to C. G. Gaum, September 2, 1926, folder "Correspondence-1926, Aug. 21–Sept. 10," box 25, Lighty Papers. On Lighty asking for letters from listeners, see "Radio Announcement," March 14, 1925, folder 20, box 1, WHA Subject Records. On December 1926 evening programming, see "Educational Radio Broadcast Program," n.d., Nov.–Dec. 1926, folder 22, box 1, WHA Subject Records. On records played by WHA, see "Records for First Week in July" (probably 1928), folder 23, box 1, WHA Subject Records. For the last quotation, see W. H. Lighty to B. C. Riley, November 19, 1928, folder "Correspondence-1929, Nov. 16–Dec., n.d.," box 34, Lighty Papers.

53. W. H. Lighty to Earle C. Reeves, May 14, 1925, folder "Correspondence-1925, May," box 22, Lighty Papers; W. H. Lighty to B. C. Riley, November 4, 1924, folder "1924, Nov.," box 20, Lighty Papers. For the "bookish" quotation, see W. H. Lighty to George B. Zehmer, June 11, 1927, folder "Correspondence-1927, June 11–30," box 28, Lighty Papers. For the last quotation, see W. H. Lighty, "Educational Radio Broadcasting," talk presented April 1923, 8, folder "WHA-Historical," box 49, McCarty Papers.

54. For the KOAC example, see W. L. Kadderly, "An Outline of Broadcasting Activities:

Station KOAC—The Oregon Agricultural College, College Year 1926–27," n.d., 4, microfilm reel 7, KOAC Records. Margaret H. Haggart, "Report of Radio Committee, 1927–1928," n.d., WOI Records.

55. C. H. Alsmeyer to E. M. Terry, February 21, 1925, folder 11, box 1, WHA Subject Records.

56. E. M. Terry to C. H. Alsmeyer, February 27, 1925, folder 11, box 1, WHA Subject Records.

57. W. I. Griffith, "Annual Report: Radio Activities of Broadcasting Station WOI . . . June 30, '31," 3, WOI Records.

58. J. J. Ryan et al. to chief operator of station WHA, April 14, 1923, folder 8, box 1, WHA Subject Records.

59. Radio Mike to Radio Station WHA, January 10, 1924, folder 6, box 1, WHA Subject Records.

60. "Station WEAO Now Using New Equipment," March 26, 1926, *Columbus Citizen* [newspaper clipping], folder "Newspaper Clippings: 1922–28," WOSU Records.

61. William G. Raymond to President Jessup, May 12, 1924, folder "WSUI . . . 1924–1925," box 2, WSUI Collection.

62. W. F. Reeve to WHA, January 10, 1927, folder 16, box 1, WHA Subject Records.

63. Walter J. Duborg to WHA, January 11, 1927, folder 15, box 1, WHA Subject Records.

64. Vaillant, "Your Voice Came in Last Night," 78.

65. Edgar B. Gordon, "Radio Pioneering," folder 13, box 1, Gordon Papers. On Lighty's role in convincing Gordon to use live talent in March 1922, see Penn, "Origin and Development," 187.

66. Ole Berge to Edgar B. Gordon, July 5, 1922, folder "1922, June–Oct.," box 16, Lighty Papers.

67. C. M. Jansky to J. M. Mack, November 13, 1958, folder "WHA-Historical," box 49, McCarty Papers.

68. Jansky quoted in John C. Schmidt, "Radio's Last Pioneer: Washington Engineer Began in '16 on Experimental Station in Wisconsin" [newspaper clipping], folder 11, box 1, Engel Papers.

69. Malcolm Hanson to Andrew Hopkins, June 17, 1931, folder "WHA-Oral History," box 49, McCarty Papers.

70. "WKAR AM/FM Michigan State University," MSU information folder "Radio Broadcasting," MSU Archives.

71. Moran, "From a Toy to a Tool," 11.

72. Ellery B. Paine to M. S. Ketchum, March 27, 1925, folder "Radio Correspondence, 1925–30," box 3, Pub/IL.

73. Penn, "Origin and Development," 174–75.

74. Malcolm Hanson to Andrew Hopkins, June 17, 1931, folder "WHA–Oral History," box 49, McCarty Papers.

75. Penn, "Origin and Development," 181–82 (Brown quoted on 182).

76. Earle Terry to J. D. Phillips, March 13, 1925, folder 7, box 2, WHA Subject Records.

77. "Report on Radio Broadcasting Station," January 1926, unmarked box, WOI Records.

78. "Radio Broadcasting Station WEAO," *Ohio State University: University Studies* 2 (July 15, 1925), folder "WEAO: 1922–1933," information file, OSU Archives.

79. Lee, "History of Radio Broadcasting."

80. Goddard to S. Donnell, November 8, 1923, folder 4, box 111, Goddard Papers.

81. Carl Menzer, "Vignettes: Fifty Years of Broadcasting at the University of Iowa," folder "Menzer, Carl Vignettes," box 2, WSUI Collection.

82. Moran, "From a Toy to a Tool," 83.

83. "WKAR AM/FM Michigan State University," n.d., information file, MSU Archives.

84. Dalen, "History of KUSD."

85. "Radio Broadcasting Station WEAO," *Ohio State University: University Studies* 2 (July 15, 1925), folder "WEAO: 1922–1933," information file, OSU Archives.

86. Madden, "Radio at the Ohio State University."

87. Dalen, "History of KUSD," 11.

88. "Radio Needs," n.d., folder 2, box 841, Shaw Papers, Radio, 1932–35, Collection UA2.1.11, MSU Archives.

89. Earle Terry to J. D. Phillips, June 1, 1925, folder 7, box 2, WHA Subject Records.

90. E. W. Murphy to B. F. Miller, November 29, 1927, folder 7, box 2, WHA Subject Records.

91. Earle Terry to E. A. Birge, April 11, 1924, folder 2, box 1, WHA Corresp.

92. "Notes on Development of the College Radio Station, KFDJ," October 9, 1925, microfilm reel 7, KOAC Records.

93. "WKAR AM/FM Michigan State University," information folder: "Radio Broadcasting," MSU Archives.

94. Rosene, "History of Radio Broadcasting," 21.

95. American Society of Composers, Authors, and Publishers to Broadcasting Station WAPI, December 27, 1929, folder "Radio (2)," box 8, CoopExt/Auburn.

96. Madden, "Radio at the Ohio State University."

97. W. H. Lighty to W. Patrick, February 18, 1925, folder "Correspondence-1925, Feb," box 21, Lighty Papers. Earle Terry to Willebald Weniger, March 16, 1925, folder 12, box 1, WHA Subject Records.

98. R. W. Goddard to Lloyd N. Case, October 29, 1923, folder 3, box 111, Goddard Papers.

99. R. W. Goddard to B. C. Riley, May 30, 1928, folder 1, box 110, Goddard Papers.

100. B. B. Brackett to Tracy F. Tyler, September 7, 1934, folder 5, box 1, NAEB Records.

101. B. B. Brackett to Armstrong Perry, January 13, 1933, folder 1096, box 57, Payne Fund Records.

102. Malcolm Hanson to Andrew W. Hopkins, June 17, 1931, folder "WHA–Oral History," box 49, McCarty Papers.

103. Velia, *KOB*, 134–35.

104. V. A. C. Henmon to W. H. Lighty, May 19, 1926, unmarked folder, box 38, McCarty Papers.

105. [?] Baldwin to W. H. Lighty, April 6, 1926, unmarked folder, box 38, McCarty Papers.

106. A. L. Dayton to Station KOB, December 11, 1928, no folder, box 20, Goddard Papers.

107. R. W. Goddard to Edward J. Ryan, October 30, 1928, no folder, box 20, Goddard Papers.

108. C. F. Monroe to R. W. Goddard, December 29, 1925, Goddard Papers.

109. "WKAR AM/FM Michigan State University," n.d., MSU Archives.

110. F. R. Calvert to Charles L. Hill, March 29, 1930, folder "WLBL General Correspondence," box 32, McCarty Papers. For the Polish-American remark, see F. R. Calvert to Charles L. Hill, April 4, 1930, folder "WLBL General Correspondence," box 32, McCarty Papers.

111. William Lighty to B. C. Riley, November 23, 1927, folder "Correspondence–1927, Nov.," box 29, Lighty Papers. William Lighty to B. C. Riley, November 23, 1927, folder "Correspondence–1927, Nov.," box 29, Lighty Papers.

112. Moran, "From a Toy to a Tool," 36, 84 (quotation on 36).

113. Ibid., 86–87.

114. Ibid., 89–90 (quotation on 90).

115. For example, the University of Oklahoma station WNAD introduced a *Radio Book Club* in 1934. See T. M. Beaird to Frank E. Schooley, January 22, 1935, folder "N.A.E.B. Bulletin Material, February 1935," box 2, Pub/IL.

116. Moran, "From a Toy to a Tool," 92–94.

117. W. H. Lighty to Frank L. McVey, March 10, 1925, folder "Correspondence–1925, March," box 21, Lighty Papers.

118. "WHAA" [partial station pamphlet] attached to William G. Raymond to M. S. Ketchum, March 30, 1925, folder "Radio Correspondence, 1925–30," box 3, Pub/IL.

119. Moran, "From a Toy to a Tool," 44–45.

120. Ibid., 34–35.

121. Umberger to Frank McFarland, December 19, 1924, file "9f–School of Air–Radio," President Jardine/Farrell Papers, 1924–25, KSU Archives.

122. R. W. Goddard to the Wireless Press, October 24, 1922, folder 6, box 110, Goddard Papers.

123. R. W. Goddard to National Broadcasting Co., July 25, 1929, no folder, box 20, Goddard Papers. On the role of the Board of Regents, see R. W. Goddard to J. Miller Co., August 14, 1928, no folder, Goddard Papers.

124. W. H. Lighty to Samuel R. Guard, April 27, 1926, folder "Correspondence–1926, Apr.," box 24, Lighty Papers.

125. R. W. Goddard to Sears Roebuck Agricultural Foundation, April 19, 1926, folder 18, box 110, Goddard Papers.

126. W. I. Griffith to members of the faculty, 1926, folder "Notices . . .," box 1, subject file, WOI Records.

127. See, for example, the list of chapel talks for the 1925–26 school year in "Annual Report: Radio Activities of Broadcasting Station WOI, Fiscal Year Beginning July 1, 1925, closing June 30, 1926," 57, WOI Records.

128. Walter Burr, "A Radio Rural Church Service," n.d., file "9f–School of Air–Radio," President Jardine/Farrell Papers, 1924–25, KSU Archives.

129. John A. Stover to Walter Burr, February 6, 1925, file "9f–School of Air–Radio," Papers of President Francis Farrell, 1924–25, KSU Archives.

130. Francis Farrell to Emmet Brown, October 8, 1926, file "9f–School of Air–Radio," Papers of President Francis Farrell, 1926–27, KSU Archives.

131. Douglas E. Williams, "The History of KFJM" (M.A. thesis, University of North Dakota, 1958), 1, 4–5.

132. Ibid., 6–19.

133. H. J. Heim to Ferris W. Norris, July 24, 1933, folder 1, box 1, Boye Papers.

134. Penn, "Origin and Development," 141–42.

135. Partial document (page one missing), first section on page two reads "Radio Broadcasting by the University of Wisconsin," February 1922, folder "WHA Historical," box 49, McCarty Papers.

136. Nimmons quoted in E. L. Burrows, "A 'Super-Powered' Goodwill Ambassador: Establishing WRUF at the University of Florida, 1925–1940," *Florida Historical Quarterly* 79 (Fall 2000): 165.

137. R. W. Goddard to Mr. Blackwell, April 14, 1922, folder 10, box 110, Goddard Papers.

138. R. W. Goddard to W. T. Blackwell, February 16, 1928, folder 10, box 110, Goddard Papers.

139. Carl Menzer, "Vignettes: Fifty Years of Broadcasting at the University of Iowa," folder "Menzer, Carl Vignettes," box 2, WSUI Collection.

140. Madden, "Radio at the Ohio State University."

141. "WOSU Radio History," n.d., 3–4, OSU Archives.

142. Ibid., 3–4, (announcement quoted on 3); "Memos, News Releases: 1926–1940, 1966–1980, 1982," records of the Telecommunications Office, record group 8/d/1, OSU Archives (this document also refers to primary sources no longer available).

143. On the creation of national networks and debates about the use of advertising, see especially Smulyan, *Selling Radio*.

Chapter 3

1. Aitken, *Syntony and Spark*, 233; Douglas, *Inventing American Broadcasting*, 69–70.

2. Douglas, *Inventing American Broadcasting*, 101, 106 (quotation of report changes on 67).

3. Ibid., 119–22.

4. Ibid., 106–19, 124.

5. Aitken, *Continuous Wave*, 253; Douglas, *Inventing American Broadcasting*, 124–26.

6. Rosen, *Modern Stentors*, 20; Douglas, *Inventing American Broadcasting*, 124–25; Linwood S. Howeth, *History of Communications: Electronics in the United States Navy* (Washington, D.C.: Government Printing Office, 1963), 211.

7. Douglas, *Inventing American Broadcasting*, 126–37.

8. Ibid., 140–41.

9. Howeth, *History of Communications*, 118–20.

10. Douglas, *Inventing American Broadcasting*, 216–17.

11. Ibid., 208–10.

12. Marvin R. Bensman, *The Beginning of Broadcast Regulation in the Twentieth Century* (Jefferson, N.C.: McFarland and Co., 2000), 6–7.

13. Ibid., 8.

14. 1912 Wireless Act reprinted in Barnouw, *Tower in Babel*, 291–99.

15. Douglas, *Inventing American Broadcasting*, 235.

16. Aitken, *Continuous Wave,* 250–301; Douglas, *Inventing American Broadcasting,* 269–76.

17. Douglas, *Inventing American Broadcasting,* 247–79.

18. Ibid., 279–84.

19. Ibid., 285–90; Aitken, *Continuous Wave,* 302–479.

20. Douglas, *Inventing American Broadcasting,* 171–77 (Eddy quoted on 175).

21. Ibid., 269–76.

22. Ibid., 280.

23. Barnouw, *Tower in Babel,* 66–70; Douglas, *Inventing American Broadcasting,* 299–300.

24. Bensman, *Beginning of Broadcast Regulation,* 29–30.

25. Table No. 1, "Report on Radio Broadcasting Stations for Year 1922," file 1675, box 137, RD/FCC.

26. Bensman, *Beginning of Broadcast Regulation,* 30.

27. Ibid., 29.

28. Rosen, *Modern Stentors,* 28. On the influence of Hoover's son, see Bensman, *Beginning of Broadcast Regulation,* 31.

29. Rosen, *Modern Stentors,* 26–27, 44–46.

30. Bensman, *Beginning of Broadcast Regulation,* 10.

31. Rosen, *Modern Stentors,* 49–53.

32. On the belief in legal justification for the Department of Commerce, see testimony of Alfred Goldsmith, "Radio Telephony Conference," March 23, 1923, folder 3, box 7, Jansky Papers.

33. Quoted in Bensman, *Beginning of Broadcast Regulation,* 35.

34. Douglas B. Craig, *Fireside Politics: Radio and Political Culture in the United States, 1920–1940* (Baltimore: Johns Hopkins University Press, 2000), 37.

35. "Minutes of Open Meeting of Department of Commerce Conference on Radio Telephony," February 28, 1922, 95, folder 1, box 7, Jansky Papers.

36. Hoover testimony in "Minutes of Open Meeting of Department of Commerce Conference on Radio Telephony," February 27, 1922, 22, folder 1, box 7, Jansky Papers.

37. Craig, *Fireside Politics,* 38–39.

38. "Minutes of Open Meeting of Department of Commerce Conference on Radio Telephony," February 28, 1922, 95, folder 1, box 7, Jansky Papers.

39. Craig, *Fireside Politics,* 19.

40. Hoover, "Opening Remarks," 5.

41. "Statement of the Secretary of Commerce at the Opening of the Radio Conference on February 27, 1922," 1, file 67032/31, box 131, GenCorr/Commerce. On the early use of advertising by radio, see Smulyan, *Selling Radio,* 94–111.

42. Quoted in Barnouw, *Tower in Babel,* 133.

43. "Report on Radio Telephone Conference," 1922, 1, folder 6, box 7, Jansky Papers.

44. Ibid., 2.

45. "Report of Department of Commerce Conference on Radio Telephony," 1922, 9–10, folder "Commerce–Radio Conf. Nat. First, Reports & Resol.," box 496, Hoover/Iowa.

46. Associate Professor of Physics to J. M. Wilkinson, May 3, 1922, folder 5, box 1, WHA Subject Records.

47. "Report of Department of Commerce Conference on Radio Telephony," 1922, 11–12, folder "Commerce–Radio Conf. Nat. First, Reports & Resol.," box 496, Hoover/Iowa.

48. "Statement of the Secretary of Commerce at the Opening of the Radio Conference on February 27, 1922," 2, file 67032/31, box 131, GenCorr/Commerce.

49. Bensman, *Beginning of Broadcast Regulation,* 44–47.

50. Ibid., 69–73.

51. Bensman, *Beginning of Broadcast Regulation,* 70–72 (radio inspector quoted on 70; acting secretary and department radio license quoted on 72).

52. Ibid., 74.

53. Associate Professor of Physics (University of Wisconsin) to J. D. Phillips, May 5, 1923, folder 4, box 1, WHA Subject Records.

54. Quoted in Bensman, *Beginning of Broadcast Regulation,* 74.

55. Ibid., 75.

56. Quoted in ibid., 74.

57. Hilmes, *Radio Voices,* 44–50.

58. Rosen, *Modern Stentors,* 37.

59. See statement by Commissioner Carson, February 1922, against the use of phonograph records by amateurs, in Bensman, *Beginning of Broadcast Regulation,* 41.

60. H. J. Heim to Ferris W. Norris, July 24, 1933, folder 1, box 1, Boye Papers.

61. "Radio Conference—Statement at the Opening," March 20, 1923, folder 3, box 7, Jansky Papers; Bensman, *Beginning of Broadcast Regulation,* 75–79 (Hoover quoted on 75).

62. Rosen, *Modern Stentors,* 58–60.

63. "Radio Conference—Statement at the Opening," March 20, 1923, folder 3, box 7, Jansky Papers.

64. Press Release, Department of Commerce, April 2, 1923, folder 3, box 7, Jansky Papers.

65. "Statement by John V. L. Hogan of Principles to Guide Administration of Present Radio Law," March 20, 1923, folder 3, box 7, Jansky Papers.

66. W. H. Lighty to E. M. Terry, January 25, 1924, folder "1924, Jan. 21–Feb. 10," box 18, Lighty Papers.

67. For use of term "public broadcasting" by Hoover during the second conference, see Department of Commerce Press Release, April 2, 1923, folder 3, box 7, Jansky Papers.

68. Arthur Batcheller to Commissioner of Navigation, January 9, 1923, file 1484, box 127, RD/FCC.

69. Arthur Batcheller to Commissioner of Navigation, January 10, 1922, file 1675, box 137, RD/FCC.

70. John Dillon quoted in Bensman, *Beginning of Broadcast Regulation,* 76.

71. Hooper quoted in ibid., 79–80.

72. Harbord quoted in Rosen, *Modern Stentors,* 46.

73. Craig, *Fireside Politics,* 18–19; Smulyan, *Selling Radio,* 40.

74. Hoover quoted in U.S. Department of Commerce, *Recommendations for Regulation of Radio: Adopted by the Third National Radio Conference . . . October 6–10, 1924* (Washington, D.C.: Government Printing Office, 1925), 3.

75. "Statement by Secretary Hoover at Hearings before the Committee on the Merchant

Marine and Fisheries on H.R. 7357, 'To Regulate Radio Communication, and for Other Purposes,' March 11, 1924," 3, folder "Commerce Papers–Radio; Corres., Press Releases, 1924 Jan–March," box 489, Hoover/Iowa.

76. Hoover to Wallace White, December 4, 1924, quoted in Bensman, *Beginning of Broadcast Regulation,* 116.

77. "Statement by Secretary Hoover at Hearings before the Committee on the Merchant Marine and Fisheries on H.R. 7357, 'To Regulate Radio Communication, and for Other Purposes,' March 11, 1924," 4, folder "Commerce Papers–Radio; Corres., Press Releases, 1924 Jan–March," box 489, Hoover/Iowa. Later in 1924, Hoover did suggest that the industry consider a 2 percent tax on radio-set sales, but he apparently soon realized that this would never be accepted. See McChesney, *Telecommunications, Mass Media, and Democracy,* 16.

78. "Radio Talk by Secretary Hoover, Washington, D.C., March 26, 1924," 9, folder "Commerce Papers–Radio; Corres., Press Releases, 1924 Jan–March," box 489, Hoover/Iowa.

79. Bensman, *Beginning of Broadcast Regulation,* 123–25 (Carson quoted on 124; Inspector Deiler quoted on 125). July 1922 statement quoted in Craig, *Fireside Politics,* 46.

80. Barnouw, *Tower in Babel,* 179–81.

81. Hoover quoted in Bensman, *Beginning of Broadcast Regulation,* 138.

82. Ibid., 133.

83. Rosen, *Modern Stentors,* 79.

84. E. M. Terry to C. W. Horn, March 16, 1925, folder 14, box 1, WHA Subject Records.

85. Wilson Wetherbee to E. M. Terry, October 2, 1925, folder 11, box 1, WHA Subject Records.

86. E. M. Terry to C. W. Horn, October 8, 1925, folder 14, box 1, WHA Subject Records.

87. Ibid.

88. Untitled report by J. D. Philips, March 3, 1925, folder 7, box 2, WHA Subject Records.

89. E. M. Terry to Wilson Wetherbee, October 8, 1925, folder 14, box 1, WHA Subject Records.

90. Penn, "Origin and Development," 276–82 (Lighty quoted on 281–82).

91. "Brief History of KUSD Broadcasting Station, Owned and Operated by the University of South Dakota," January 15, 1931, folder 4, box 33, Slagle Papers.

92. Herbert Hoover, "Radio Problems and Conference Recommendations" [radio address], November 12, 1925, 2, folder "Commerce Papers: Radio—Conferences—National Fourth," box 489, Hoover/Iowa.

93. Rosen, *Modern Stentors,* 79.

94. *Proceedings of the Fourth National Radio Conference and Recommendations for Regulation of Radio . . . November 9–15, 1925,* 7, 13.

95. Ibid., 3.

96. Ibid., 1, 5.

97. Ibid., 7.

98. Ibid., 11.

99. Rosen, *Modern Stentors*, 86.

100. Ibid., 86–91.

101. Barnouw, *Tower in Babel*, 185.

102. Smulyan, *Selling Radio*, 42–64.

103. Craig, *Fireside Politics*, 28.

104. Quoted in Barnouw, *Tower in Babel*, 174.

105. Ibid., 185; Hugh G. J. Aitken, "Allocating the Spectrum: The Origins of Radio Regulation," *Technology and Culture* 35 (October 1994): 709; Slotten, *Radio and Television Regulation*, 42.

106. Rosen, *Modern Stentors*, 90; Craig, *Fireside Politics*, 29.

107. Bensman, *Beginning of Broadcast Regulation*, 156–76.

108. Ibid., 176–81 (Hoover quoted on 178; Department of Commerce quoted on 177).

109. Quoted in Bensman, *Beginning of Broadcast Regulation*, 180.

110. Radio Act of 1927, reprinted in Barnouw, *Tower in Babel*, 300–315.

111. Craig, *Fireside Politics*, 52, 56.

112. Quoted in C. W. Warburton to T. B. Symons, May 5, 1926, folder "Radio Legislation," box 1369, entry 17, USDA.

113. H. Umberger to Paul V. Maris, April 22, 1926, box 1220, entry GCOS, USDA.

114. Untitled document reproducing testimony of the National University Extension Association, n.d., folder 1065, box 56, Payne Fund Records.

115. J. C. Jensen to Armstrong Perry, October 8, 1930, folder 1099, box 57, Payne Fund Records.

116. Dill testimony reproduced from *Congressional Record*, n.d., folder 1065, box 56, Payne Fund Records.

117. McChesney, *Telecommunication, Mass Media, and Democracy*, 33.

118. Radio Act of 1927, reprinted in Barnouw, *Tower in Babel*, 305 (section 9 quotation).

119. H. Umberger to Paul V. Maris, April 22, 1926, box 1220, entry GCOS, USDA.

120. A. F. Woods [USDA director] to C. W. Pugsley, February 8, 1927; and C. W. Pugsley to A. F. Woods, February 7, 1927, box 1295, entry 17F, USDA.

121. Radio Act of 1927, reprinted in Barnouw, *Tower in Babel*, 300–315.

Chapter 4

1. William S. Gregson to B. B. Brackett, February 25, 1932, folder 3, box 1, NAEB Records.

2. McChesney, *Telecommunications, Mass Media, and Democracy*, 22.

3. Gerald V. Flannery, ed., *Commissioners of the FCC, 1927–1994* (New York: University Press of America, 1995); Craig, *Fireside Politics*, 60.

4. Bellows testimony, Senate Committee on Interstate Commerce, *Hearings on the Confirmation of Federal Radio Commissioners*, part 1, 70th Cong., 1st Sess., January 7, 1928, 80.

5. Sykes testimony, House Committee on the Merchant Marine and Fisheries, *Hearings on H.R. 8825*, 70th Cong., 2d Sess., January 27, 1928, 65.

6. Federal Radio Commission, *Annual Report of the Federal Radio Commission to the*

Congress of the United States for the Fiscal Year Ended June 30, 1927 (Washington, D.C.: Government Printing Office, 1927), 4–11 (quotations on 9, 11).

7. Caldwell testimony, House Committee on the Merchant Marine and Fisheries, *Hearings on H.R. 8825,* 70th Cong., 2d Sess., January 31, 1928, 125.

8. H. A. Bellows to A. F. Woods, April 27, 1927, box 1295, entry 17, USDA.

9. Sykes testimony, House Committee on the Merchant Marine and Fisheries, *Hearings on H.R. 8825,* 70th Cong., 2d Sess., January 26, 1928, 3.

10. Ibid., 3.

11. Bellows testimony, Senate Committee on Interstate Commerce, *Hearings on the Confirmation of Federal Radio Commissioners,* part 1, 70th Cong., 1st Sess., January 7, 1928, 83.

12. Ibid., 83–84.

13. Bellows comments, Proceedings, National Association of Broadcasters, Fifth Annual Convention, 1927, 19, file 3601, box 168, RD/FCC.

14. Ibid., 17.

15. Caldwell and Senator Smith testimony, Senate Committee on Interstate Commerce, *Hearings on the Confirmation of Federal Radio Commissioners,* part 2, 70th Cong., 1st Sess., February 3, 1928, 162, 171.

16. Caldwell testimony, House Committee on the Merchant Marine and Fisheries, *Hearings on H.R. 8825,* 70th Cong., 2d Sess., February 1, 1928, 103.

17. Ibid., 135.

18. Ibid.

19. Pickard testimony, House Committee on the Merchant Marine and Fisheries, *Hearings on H.R. 8825,* 70th Cong., 2d Sess., February 8, 1928, 206, 217–18, 223–24.

20. "Broadcasting Stations at Service of Farmers," *Official Record: United States Department of Agriculture,* vol. 5, August 4, 1926, 1–2 (quotation on 2).

21. Although Umberger believed that the station should not broadcast entertainment, in 1925 Pickard favored broadcasting an "inter-society sing" as part of a special first-anniversary program for the station. He wrote the college president, "I realize that cheap comedy and jazz should be taboo but believe that these groups are capable of arranging a high class, ten minute program which would increase the prestige of our station." See Sam Pickard to Francis D. Farrell, November 10, 1925, file "9f–School of Air–Radio," Papers of President Farrell, 1925–1926, KSU Archives.

22. Sam Pickard to radio station WTAM, n.d., box 1220, entry GCOS, USDA.

23. News release, USDA, "Factors to Observe in Preparing Radio Copy," December 4, 1926, folder "Radio Talks, Science," box 70, Record Unit 7091, Smithsonian Institution Archives, Washington, D.C.

24. *Report of the Secretary of Agriculture* (Washington, D.C.: Government Printing Office, 1926), 56.

25. Harry Umberger to C. W. Warburton, April 21, 1926, folder "Radio legislation," box 1369, entry 17, USDA. The secretary of agriculture also did not want to examine the possibility of having the department construct its own stations. He did not think that Congress would allocate the funds, and he feared that "if the Department sought and obtained frequency assignments of its own, it might conceivably be confined to the small number of channels assigned to it," rather than being able to have the "privilege of broadcasting

on virtually every channel" through "the cooperation of existing broadcasting stations." See Arthur W. Hyde to [U.S. Senator] Wesley L. Jones, January 29, 1931, folder "Radio Jan–June," box 1636, entry 17, USDA.

26. Craig, *Fireside Politics*, 75.

27. Pickard testimony, Senate Committee on Interstate Commerce, *Hearings on the Confirmation of Federal Radio Commissioners*, part 1, 70th Cong., 1st Sess., January 6, 1928, 13.

28. Caldwell testimony, House Committee on the Merchant Marine and Fisheries, *Hearings on H.R. 8825*, 70th Cong., 2d Sess., January 31, 1928, 109.

29. Caldwell testimony, House Committee on the Merchant Marine and Fisheries, *Hearings on H.R. 8825*, 70th Cong., 2d Sess., February 1, 1928, 136.

30. Bellows speech, Federal Radio Commission, *Annual Report*, 1927, 7.

31. Pickard testimony, Senate Committee on Interstate Commerce, *Hearings on the Confirmation of Federal Radio Commissioners*, part 1, 70th Cong., 1st Sess., January 6, 1928, 18.

32. Ibid., 18.

33. Wheeler and Pickard testimony, ibid., 19.

34. Caldwell testimony, Senate Committee on Interstate Commerce, *Hearings on the Confirmation of Federal Radio Commissioners*, part 2, 70th Cong., 1st Sess., February 3, 1928, 171.

35. Sykes testimony, House Committee on the Merchant Marine and Fisheries, *Hearings on H.R. 8825*, 70th Cong., 2d Sess., January 30, 1928, 78–79.

36. Federal Radio Commission, *Second Annual Report of the Federal Radio Commission* (Washington, D.C.: Government Printing Office, 1928), 8.

37. Ibid., 8–9.

38. Ibid., 10.

39. Ibid., 9–10.

40. Carl H. Butman to commissioners, January 31, 1928, box 128, file 20-2, entry 100A, ExDir/FCC.

41. Penn, "Origin and Development," 292–94; W. H. Lighty to B. E. McCormick, January 13, 1927, folder "Correspondence–1927, Jan.," box 27, Lighty Papers.

42. Penn, "Origin and Development," 294–97 (Lighty quoted on 294, 296). For the last Lighty quotation, see W. H. Lighty to G. B. Zehmer, May 15, 1928, folder "Correspondence–1928, May," box 31, Lighty Papers.

43. "Statement in Behalf of the University of Minnesota of Minneapolis and St. Paul, Carleton College and . . .," 2–4, folder "Correspondence and Notes Re: UM Radio (1920–28)," box 5, Jansky Papers.

44. House Committee on the Merchant Marine and Fisheries, *Hearings on H.R. 8825*, 70th Cong., 2d Sess., January 31, 1928, 109.

45. Senate Committee on Interstate Commerce, *Hearings on the Confirmation of Federal Radio Commissioners*, part 1, 70th Cong., 1st Sess., February 3, 1928, 186.

46. McChesney, *Telecommunications, Mass Media, and Democracy*, 20.

47. House Committee on the Merchant Marine and Fisheries, *Hearings on H.R. 8825*, 70th Cong., 2d Sess., January 31, 1928, 109.

48. House Committee on the Merchant Marine and Fisheries, *Hearings on H.R. 8825*, 70th Cong., 2d Sess., January 27, 1928, 55.

49. House Committee on the Merchant Marine and Fisheries, *Hearings on H.R. 8825*, 70th Cong., 2d Sess., February 7, 1928, 184.

50. House Committee on the Merchant Marine and Fisheries, *Hearings on H.R. 8825*, 70th Cong., 2d Sess., January 31, 1928, 104.

51. Ibid., 124.

52. Ibid., 107–8.

53. House Committee on the Merchant Marine and Fisheries, *Hearings on H.R. 8825*, 70th Cong., 2d Sess., February 9, 1928, 228.

54. Ibid., 230–31.

55. Ibid., 228–30.

56. House Committee on the Merchant Marine and Fisheries, *Hearings on H.R. 8825*, 70th Cong., 2d Sess., February 1 and 8, 1928, 173–76, 225–26.

57. Craig, *Fireside Politics,* 64–65.

58. Federal Radio Commission, *Second Annual Report,* 11.

59. Lafount quoted in McChesney, *Telecommunications, Mass Media, and Democracy,* 34.

60. Federal Radio Commission, *Second Annual Report,* 16.

61. Ibid., 166–68, 170.

62. Ibid., 168–69.

63. Ibid., 20.

64. Ibid., 168.

65. Ibid., 155–56.

66. Ibid., 152–53.

67. Louis G. Caldwell to Commissioner Pickard, September 18, 1928, file 20-2, box 128, entry 100A, ExDir/FCC.

68. Federal Radio Commission, *Second Annual Report,* 154–55.

69. Ibid., 152–53.

70. Ibid., 155–56.

71. "Caldwell Urges Station Cut as Only Solution," box 36, Dellinger Records.

72. *Congressional Digest,* October 1928, copy in box 36, Dellinger Records.

73. November 29, 1927, Min/FRC.

74. O. H. Caldwell to "Members of the FRC," July 26, 1928, file 20-2, box 128, entry 100A, ExDir/FCC. On the role of Lafount, see Federal Radio Commission, *Second Annual Report,* 17. Lafount quoted in McChesney, *Telecommunications, Mass Media, and Democracy,* 22.

75. Slotten, *Radio and Television Regulation,* 52–53.

76. Ibid., 53.

77. Ibid., 54.

78. Federal Radio Commission, *Second Annual Report,* 17.

79. Sam Pickard to members of the radio commission, August 31, 1928, file 20-2, box 128, entry 100A, ExDir/FCC.

80. McChesney, *Telecommunications, Mass Media, and Democracy,* 21–22.

81. Federal Radio Commission, *Second Annual Report,* 3.

82. Recommendations to Commission attached to Louis G. Caldwell to Federal Radio Commission, August 17, 1928, file 20-2, box 128, entry 100A, ExDir/FCC.

83. John H. Dellinger, "Explanation of Allocation of Aug. 13," August 13, 1928, folder "Allocation," box 37, Dellinger Records.

84. John H. Dellinger, "Analysis of New Broadcast Station Allocation," September 14, 1928, in Federal Radio Commission, *Second Annual Report,* 216.

85. "Material on High-Power Broadcasting for Transmittal to House and Senate Committees on Radio Legislation," January 11, 1926, 4, 29, 30, box 139, file 173NR, ExDir/FCC.

86. Paul M. Segal, "The Radio Engineer and the Law," *Proceedings of the Institute of Radio Engineers* 18 (June 1930): 1040–41.

87. "Statement by O. M. Caldwell" [press release], October 15, 1928; O. M. Caldwell, "What the Re-allocation Is to Accomplish," September 5, 1928, box 36, Dellinger Records.

88. "The Problem of Radio Reallocation," *Congressional Digest* 7 (1928): 271.

89. Ibid., 271.

90. George O. Sutton to Judge Robinson, November 8, 1928, folder "October 1, 1928–March 14, 1929," box 129, file 20-2, Entry 100A, ExDir/FCC.

91. Guy Hill to Lafount, January 14, 1929, box 129, file 20-2, entry 100A, ExDir/FCC.

92. George O. Sutton to Judge Robinson, November 8, 1928, folder "October 1, 1928–March 14, 1929," box 129, file 20-2, Entry 100A, ExDir/FCC.

93. J. Howard Dellinger to Ira Robinson, September 28, 1928, box 128, file 20-2, entry 100A, ExDir/FCC.

94. J. H. Dellinger, "Explanation of Allocation of Aug. 13 (Confidential)," August 13, 1928, folder "Allocation 1928," box 37, Dellinger Records.

95. February 13, 1928, and March 27, 1928, Min/FRC.

96. Sam Pickard to Judge Robinson, April 14, 1928, box 128, file 20-2, entry 100A, ExDir/FCC.

97. Louis Caldwell to Commissioners Sykes, Pickard, Lafount, and Caldwell, January 10, 1929, folder "October 1, 1928–March 14, 1929," file 20-2, box 129, entry 100A, ExDir/FCC.

98. Bethuel M. Webster to Eugene O. Sykes, December 6, 1929, folder "June 1, 1929–Dec. 31, 1929," file 20-2, box 129, entry 100A, ExDir/FCC.

99. Louis Caldwell to Commissioners Sykes, Pickard, Lafount, and Caldwell, January 10, 1929, folder "October 1, 1928–March 14, 1929," file 20-2, box 129, entry 100A, ExDir/FCC.

100. Federal Radio Commission, *Third Annual Report of the Federal Radio Commission* (Washington, D.C.: Government Printing Office, 1929), 34.

101. Ibid., 35.

102. Federal Radio Commission Press Release, September 11, 1929, folder "June 1, 1929–Dec. 31, 1929," file 20-2, entry 100A, ExDir/FCC.

103. On Robinson expressing concern about the implications for censorship of individual decisions see, for example, April 4, 1928, Min/FRC.

104. Quoted in Craig, *Fireside Politics,* 75.

105. Don R. Le Duc and Thomas A. McCain, "The Federal Radio Commission in Court: Origins of Broadcast Regulatory Doctrines," *Journal of Broadcasting* 14 (Fall 1970): 394.

106. Craig, *Fireside Politics,* 75.

107. Le Duc and McCain, "Federal Radio Commission in Court," 403–4.

108. Penn, "Origin and Development," 299–301 (Terry quoted on 299).

109. Ibid., 300–302 (Terry quoted on 302).

110. Ibid., 303–5 (Terry quoted on 304).

111. M. L. Burlison to Farm Advisers, September 18, 1928, folder "Radio, WILL, 1928–53," box 112, AgrSub/IL.

112. Josef F. Wright to Morse Salisbury, March 25, 1930, folder "Radio Correspondence, 1925–30," box 3, Pub/IL.

113. Josef F. Wright to John H. Camlin, October 10, 1929, folder "Radio–Letters and Telegrams to Commission, 1928–31," box 4, Pub/IL.

114. Josef F. Wright to Harry Chase, March 2, 1931, folder "Radio," box 18, Chase Papers.

115. "Station KFDY, South Dakota State College," n.d. [probably early 1930s], folder 1057, box 55, Payne Fund Records.

116. B. B. Brackett to J. C. Jensen, May 13, 1930, folder "KUSD–correspondence/misc., 1927–1928," box 1, SDPB Papers.

117. Ibid.

118. W. Weniger to Paul V. Maris, November 20, 1931, reel 7, KOAC Records.

119. Station WJBU program director to James W. Baldwin, folder 1102, box 57, Payne Fund Records.

120. F. W. Kehoe to J. E. Morgan, March 2, 1931, folder 743, box 38, Payne Fund Records.

121. Frost, *Education's Own Stations*, 320, 324–30 (quotations on 327, 329).

122. Ibid., 328–29.

123. Unknown author [probably B. B. Brackett] to H. B. McCarty, April 21, 1933, folder 1, box 2, NAEB Papers. For the last quotation, see B. B. Brackett to Armstrong Perry, January 13, 1933, folder 1096, box 56, Payne Fund Records.

124. B. B. Brackett to Tracy P. Tyler, May 19, 1933, folder "KUSD–correspondence/ misc., 1927–1928," box 1, SDPB Papers. The University of Illinois also expressed the need to continue support for its station to reserve the use of a channel in the spectrum. See memorandum beginning "the committee believes that because of its importance," April 16, 1931, folder "A-Radio, 1932–34," box 1, Pub/IL.

125. Penn, "Origin and Development," 305–8 (Lighty quoted on 305).

126. Penn, "Origin and Development," 348, 352, 356–57 (Frank quoted on 352).

127. H. B. McCarty to Herman Kehrli, March 4, 1933, folder 14, box 2, WHA Subject Records. For the 90 percent figure, see Kenneth Gapen to Geoffrey Norman, April 25, 1933, folder 15, box 2, WHA Subject Records.

128. Document beginning "Mr. Wright addressed Mr. McCarty of Wisconsin," folder 17, box 2, WHA Subject Records; Penn, "Origin and Development," 348, 352, 356–57 (Frank quoted on 352).

129. "Wisconsin State Broadcasting Station: A Summary of Facts and Figures," 1933, folder 2, box 1, Engel Papers.

130. James M. Morris, *The Remembered Years: A Personal View of the Fifty Years of Broadcasting—Radio and ETV—That We Call KOAC* (Corvallis, Ore.: Continuing Education Publications, 1972), 17–20. For the "all-state" quotation, see "Radio Station KOAC:

A Historical Resume of Its Educational Program Service," May 1933, reel 7, KOAC Records.

131. Herman G. James to T. M. Beaird, September 24, 1934, folder "KUSD–correspondence/misc., 1927–28," box 1, SDPB Papers.

132. F. D. Farrell to A. G. Crane, February 10, 1928, file "9f–School of Air–Radio," President Farrell Papers, 1927–28, KSU Archives.

133. F. D. Farrell to E. D. McGarry, May 11, 1928, file "9f–School of Air–Radio," President Farrell Papers, 1927–28, KSU Archives.

134. Moran, "From a Toy to a Tool," 27–28, 31–33.

135. Rachut, "History of the State University of Iowa," 31, 62.

136. T. M. Beaird to B. B. Brackett, January 21, 1932, folder 3, box 1, NAEB Papers.

137. For example, the state government in Iowa consistently supported WOI's rejection of a number of proposals to use advertising. See Moran, "From a Toy to a Tool," 30.

138. Ibid., 30–31.

139. William S. Gregson to B. B. Brackett, folder 3, box 1, NAEB Records.

140. Frost, *Education's Own Stations,* 24.

141. Rosene, "History of Radio Broadcasting," 50–64 (Davis quoted on 53).

142. G. N. McClelland to L. N. Duncan, March 11, 1929, folder "Radio (2)," box 8, CoopExt/Auburn.

143. "History: WAPI-TV and Radio," n.d., vertical file, Auburn Archives.

144. Director, WAPI, to Board of Control of Station WAPI, March 20, 1929, folder "Radio (2)," box 8, CoopExt/Auburn.

Chapter 5

1. Quoted in McChesney, *Telecommunications, Mass Media, and Democracy,* 112.

2. Ibid., 122 (*Business Week* quoted on 122).

3. Harold A. Lafount quoted in ibid., 123.

4. Craig, *Fireside Politics,* 25.

5. Smulyan, *Selling Radio,* 118.

6. Ibid., 118–19.

7. Sterling and Kittross, *Stay Tuned,* 108.

8. Quoted in McChesney, *Telecommunications, Mass Media, and Democracy,* 35. On Robinson, also see Slotten, *Radio and Television Regulation,* 59–60.

9. Eugene J. Coltrane, "Radio in Modern Life" [unpublished essay], folder 1033, box 54, Payne Fund Records.

10. "Minutes of Conference on Radio Education, Chicago, Illinois," June 13, 1929, folder "Conference on Education by Radio—Oct. 15, 1930," box 1, entry 60, OffEdu; McChesney, *Telecommunications, Mass Media, and Democracy,* 40–41.

11. "Meeting of the Advisory Committee on Education by Radio," November 6, 1929, folder "Report of the Advisory Committee on Education by Radio, Commissioner Cooper," box 3, entry 60, OffEdu.

12. Armstrong Perry to J. L. Clifton, August 21, 1929, folder 1068, box 56, Payne Fund Records.

13. McChesney, *Telecommunications, Mass Media, and Democracy,* 38–39.

14. Ibid.; Levering Tyson to Benjamin H. Darrow, June 20, 1932, folder "Ohio School of the Air," box 3, NACRE Records.

15. McChesney, *Telecommunications, Mass Media, and Democracy,* 39–40.

16. Armstrong Perry to J. L. Clifton, August 21, 1929, folder 1068, box 56, Payne Fund Records.

17. Ibid.

18. Olive M. Jones and B. H. Darrow, "Report of the Preliminary Committee on Educational Broadcasting," n.d., folder 981, box 51, Payne Fund Records.

19. McChesney, *Telecommunications, Mass Media, and Democracy,* 40.

20. Levering Tyson to James L. Fly, September 30, 1940, folder "Federal Communications Commission, box 15, NACRE Records.

21. Levering Tyson to T. Harvey Searls, October 13, 1925, folder "Miscellaneous Memoranda," box 2, entry 58, OffEdu.

22. Levering Tyson to Frederick P. Keppel, February 2, 1925, folder 240.12, box 240, Carnegie Files.

23. Levering Tyson to T. Harvey Searls, October 13, 1925, folder "Miscellaneous Memoranda," box 2, entry 58, OffEdu.

24. Levering Tyson to Frederic A. Willis, July 2, 1935, folder "Columbia Broadcasting System," box 10, NACRE Records. On the importance of Pupin's involvement with AT&T, see Levering Tyson to David Sarnoff, October 27, 1936, folder "Radio Corporation of America," box 14, NACRE Records.

25. Levering Tyson to T. Harvey Searls, October 13, 1925, folder "Miscellaneous Memoranda," box 2, entry 58, OffEdu.

26. Levering Tyson to Frederick P. Keppel, February 2, 1925, folder 240.12, box 240, Carnegie Files.

27. Levering Tyson to James L. Fly, September 30, 1940, folder "Federal Communications Commission," box 15, NACRE Records.

28. Levering Tyson to James L. Fly, September 30, 1940, folder "Federal Communications Commission," box 15, NACRE Records.

29. Levering Tyson to Norman H. Davis, July 7, 1931, folder 240.14, box 240, Carnegie Files.

30. Levering Tyson to Frederick P. Keppel, February 2, 1925, folder 240.12, box 240, Carnegie Files.

31. Levering Tyson to Norman Davis, July 7, 1931, folder "Keppel, F. P.–1930," box 2, NACRE Records.

32. Levering Tyson to Frederick P. Keppel, December 4, 1929, folder 240.12, box 240, Carnegie Files.

33. Levering Tyson to James L. Fly, September 30, 1940, folder "Federal Communications Commission," box 15, NACRE Records. For the "Dean" reference in correspondence, see Levering Tyson to "Dean," May 19, 1940, folder "Carnegie Corporation of NY (1937–39)," box 15, NACRE Records.

34. Levering Tyson to John C. W. Reith, April 20, 1931, folder "British Broadcasting Corporation," box 1, NACRE Records.

35. Henry Suzzallo to Frederick P. Keppel, July 7, 1931, folder 241.1, box 241, Carnegie Files.

36. "Minutes of Conference on Radio Education," June 13, 1929, folder "Chicago Conference (Minutes) June 13, 1929," box 1, entry 60, OffEdu.

37. Levering Tyson to John C. W. Reith, April 20, 1931, folder "British Broadcasting Corporation," box 1, NACRE Records. On the effort to avoid duplication, see "Meeting of the Advisory Committee on Education by Radio," November 6, 1929, folder "Report of the Advisory Committee on Education by Radio, Commissioner Cooper," box 3, entry 60, OffEdu.

38. McChesney, *Telecommunications, Mass Media, and Democracy*, 41.

39. "Report of the Advisory Committee on Education by Radio," February 15, 1930, folder "Report of the Advisory Committee on Education by Radio, Commissioner Cooper," box 3, entry 60, OffEdu.

40. "Meeting of the Advisory Committee on Education by Radio," December 30, 1929, folder "Report of the Advisory Committee on Education by Radio, Commissioner Cooper," box 3, entry 60, OffEdu; McChesney, *Telecommunications, Mass Media, and Democracy*, 41–42.

41. Untitled document beginning "The Advisory Committee on Education by Radio, appointed," June 26, 193[0], folder 1070, box 56, Payne Fund Records.

42. "Memorandum of Conference with Mr. Perry," July 23, 1930, folder 1352, box 69, Payne Fund Records.

43. McChesney, *Telecommunications, Mass Media, and Democracy*, 42–45.

44. "Memorandum of Conference with Mr. Perry," July 23, 1930, folder 1352, box 69, Payne Fund Records.

45. "Memorandum Re: Conferences October 9 to 12, 1930," folder 1352, box 69, Payne Fund Records.

46. McChesney, *Telecommunications, Mass Media, and Democracy*, 46.

47. Ibid., 46.

48. Armstrong Perry to Ella Crandall, April 15, 1930, folder 1070, box 56, Payne Fund Records.

49. Charters quoted in "Memorandum Re: Conferences October 9 to 12, 1930," folder 1352, box 69, Payne Fund Records.

50. "Memorandum of Conference with Mr. Perry," July 23, 1930, folder 1352, box 69, Payne Fund Records.

51. Ibid.

52. Secretary, Association of College and University Broadcasting Stations, to FRC, January 14, 1928, box 1, folder "Association of College and University Broadcasting Stations," NACRE Records.

53. McChesney, *Telecommunications, Mass Media, and Democracy*, 63–72; Godfried, *WCFL*.

54. McChesney, *Telecommunications, Mass Media, and Democracy*, 128.

55. Armstrong Perry to Ella Crandall, April 15, 1930, folder 1070, box 56, Payne Fund Records.

56. Ella Crandall to Armstrong Perry, December 23, 1930, folder 1071, box 56, Payne Fund Records.

57. "Memorandum Re: Conferences October 9 to 12, 1930," folder 1352, box 69, Payne Fund Records.

58. Bolton to Morgan quoted in McChesney, *Telecommunications, Mass Media, and Democracy,* 51.

59. "Memorandum on Discussion between Miss Crandall and Mr. Perry, 11 Aug. 1932," folder 1075, box 56, Payne Fund Records.

60. On the establishment of the NACRE, see Minutes, Executive Committee, NACRE, April 23, 1930, folder "American Association for Adult Education," box 1, NACRE Records.

61. Levering Tyson to W. W. Charters, July 18, 1930, folder "Charters, W. W.," box 1, NACRE Records.

62. Ibid.

63. "Memorandum Re: Conferences October 9 to 12, 1930," folder 1352, box 69, Payne Fund Records.

64. Levering Tyson to C. M. Jansky, June 1, 1932, folder "C. M. Jansky Jr.," box 3, NACRE Records.

65. Levering Tyson to Benjamin H. Darrow, June 20, 1932, folder "Ohio School of the Air," box 3, NACRE Records.

66. For the first quotation, see Levering Tyson to C. M. Jansky, June 1, 1932, folder "C. M. Jansky Jr.," box 3, NACRE Records. For the second quotation, see Levering Tyson to Arthur S. Garbett, November 1, 1930, folder "National Broadcasting Company–San Francisco," box 2, NACRE Records.

67. J. C. Jensen to Willis K. Wing, February 14, 1927, box 1, folder "Association of College and University Broadcasting Stations," NACRE Records.

68. Levering Tyson to T. Harvey Searls, October 13, 1925, folder "Miscellaneous Memoranda," box 2, entry 58, OffEdu.

69. Henry Suzzallo to F. P. Keppel, July 7, 1931, folder 241.1, box 241, Carnegie Files.

70. Armstrong Perry to Ella Crandall, October 24, 1931, folder 1073, box 56, Payne Fund Records.

71. Quoted in McChesney, *Telecommunications, Mass Media, and Democracy,* 48.

72. Armstrong Perry to Mrs. Chester C. Bolton, March 5, 1932, folder 1074, box 56, Payne Fund Records.

73. Armstrong Perry to S. H. Evans, January 6, 1931, folder 1071, box 56, Payne Fund Records.

74. Quoted in McChesney, *Telecommunications, Mass Media, and Democracy,* 232.

75. Ibid., 224, 260.

76. Ibid., 128–30.

77. Ibid., 146.

78. Ibid.

79. Crandall quoted in ibid.

80. Ibid., 140–41.

81. Graham Spry, "The Canadian Radio Situation," in *Education on the Air: Second Yearbook of the Institute for Education by Radio* (Columbus: Ohio State University Press, 1931).

82. Armstrong Perry to Walter V. Woehlke, November 28, 1932, folder 1167, box 60, Payne Fund Records. For a general analysis of Davis's role, see Jennifer M. Profitt and Michael Brown, "Regulating the Radio Monopoly: Ewin Davis and His Legislative Debates, 1923–1928," *Journal of Radio Studies* 11 (2004): 100–115.

83. McChesney, *Telecommunications, Mass Media, and Democracy,* 124–27.

84. Walter V. Woehlke to S. Howard Evans, October 2, 1931, folder 1163, box 60, Payne Fund Records.

85. "Proceedings of Radio Session of the Fifteenth Annual Meeting of the American Association of Advertising Agencies," April 15, 1932, 5, folder 1159, box 60, Payne Fund Records.

86. Armstrong Perry to Walter V. Woehlke, November 28, 1932, folder 1167, box 60, Payne Fund Records.

87. See especially McChesney, *Telecommunications, Mass Media, and Democracy,* 124–27.

88. Evans quoted in ibid., 145, 152.

89. Ibid., 194–95.

90. Ibid., 188–98.

91. Ibid., 198–99.

92. Ibid., 199–200.

93. Ibid., 200–206.

94. Ibid., 181–83, 200, 208.

95. Quoted in ibid., 107.

96. Ibid., 107–14.

97. Ibid., 107–9.

98. Armstrong Perry to H. M. Clymer, January 12, 1931, folder 1071, box 56, Payne Fund Records.

99. Florence Hale to Levering Tyson, January 11, 1932, folder "National Education Association," box 3, NACRE Records.

100. "Memorandum Re: Conference, October 1, 1932," folder 812, box 42, Payne Fund Records.

101. Armstrong Perry to Ella Phillips Crandall, May 11, 1932, folder 1075, box 56, Payne Fund Records.

102. McChesney, *Telecommunications, Mass Media, and Democracy,* 147.

103. Armstrong Perry to Ella Phillips Crandall, February 17, 1930, folder 1069, box 56, Payne Fund Records.

104. R. S. Lambert, "Report on Educational Broadcasting in U.S.A." [unpublished paper], July 1930, folder "Lambert, R.S.," box 2, NACRE Records.

105. "Some Notes on the Trip to University of Kansas, Kansas State Agricultural College, State University of Iowa, Iowa State College, University of Minnesota, University of Wisconsin, University of Chicago," n.d., folder "Russell, John," box 2, NACRE Records.

106. Ella Crandall to Armstrong Perry, December 2, 1930, folder 1071, box 56, Payne Fund Records.

107. Armstrong Perry to E. G. Lancaster, May 25, 1933, folder 1131, box 59, Payne Fund Records.

108. "Report of the Service Bureau: June, July, August, September 1931," folder 744, box 39, Payne Fund Records.

109. "Statement of Progress of the National Committee on Education by Radio," April 4, 1933, folder 904, box 47, Payne Fund Records.

110. "Report of the Service Bureau, October and November 1931," folder 744, box 39, Payne Fund Records.

111. "Essential Don'ts for Broadcasting Stations," n.d., folder 744, box 39, Payne Fund Records; "Report of the Service Bureau: June, July, August, September 1931," folder 744, box 39, Payne Fund Records.

112. "Crusade," n.d., folder 1336, box 68, Payne Fund Records.

113. Tracy F. Tyler, "Observations in the Field," folder 744, box 39, Payne Fund Records.

114. "Crusade," n.d., folder 1336, box 68, Payne Fund Records.

115. Higgy quoted in "Statement of Progress of the National Committee on Education by Radio," April 4, 1933, folder 904, box 47, Payne Fund Records.

116. "Crusade," n.d., folder 1336, box 68, Payne Fund Records.

117. Don E. Gilman to Roy C. Witmer, March 22, 1937, folder 9, box 57, NBC Records.

118. McChesney, *Telecommunications, Mass Media, and Democracy*, 101–2.

119. "The Hook-Up: A Round-Robin Circuit Linking Farm and Home Broadcasters, January–February–March 1936," vol. 1, no. 2, folder "The Hook-Up-By John Baker," box 7, Entry HRTB, USDA.

120. McChesney, *Telecommunications, Mass Media, and Democracy*, 228–29.

121. Levering Tyson to Robert M. Hutchins, January 14, 1933, folder "Hutchins, Robert M.," box 5, NACRE Records.

122. Levering Tyson to John F. Royal, June 1, 1934, folder "National Broadcasting Company," box 8, NACRE Records.

123. McChesney, *Telecommunications, Mass Media, and Democracy*, 230–31 (quotation on 231).

124. Levering Tyson to Richard C. Patterson, November 29, 1932, folder "Patterson, Richard," box 4, NACRE Records.

125. Levering Tyson to David Sarnoff, October 27, 1936, folder "Radio Corporation of America," box 14, NACRE Records.

126. Levering Tyson to Martin Codel, December 3, 1936, folder "Co," box 12, NACRE Records.

Chapter 6

1. Edward Lane Burrows, "Commercial Radio at the University of Florida: WRUF—An Historical Overview" (M.A. thesis, University of Florida, 1974), 88–89.

2. Cedric Cummins, *The University of South Dakota, 1862–1966* (Vermillion, S.D.: Dakota Press, 1975), 196.

3. B. B. Brackett to Tracy F. Tyler, May 19, 1933, folder "KUSD–correspondence/Misc. 1927," SDPB.

4. "Educational Broadcasting Stations–1941," microfilm reel 1, KOAC Records.

5. "Station WILL, University of Illinois," in *Education on the Air: Eighth Yearbook of the Institute for Education by Radio* (Columbus: Ohio State University Press, 1937), 70.

6. Moran, "From a Toy to a Tool," 35.

7. "Annual Report: Radio Activities of Broadcasting Station WOI, year closing December 31, 1940," WOI Records.

8. WOI station director to President Friley, June 9, 1945, folder 8, box 20, Ralph Kenneth Bliss Papers, ISU Archives.

9. W. L. Kadderly, "Radio Station KOAC," in *Education on the Air: Fourth Yearbook of the Institute for Education by Radio* (Columbus: Ohio State University Press, 1933), 265.

10. Ibid., 265.

11. "Educational Broadcasting Stations–1941," microfilm reel 1, KOAC Records.

12. Ibid.

13. Harold B. McCarty, "WHA, Wisconsin's Radio Pioneer: Twenty Years of Public Service Broadcasting," 202, 204, folder 7, box 1, Engel Papers.

14. Harold A. Engel, "Wisconsin State Station Completes New Studios," *Education by Radio* 5 (September 9, 1935): 45, folder 2, box 1, Engel Papers.

15. Ibid.

16. Harold B. McCarty, "WHA, Wisconsin's Radio Pioneer: Twenty Years of Public Service Broadcasting," 204, folder 7, box 1, Engel Papers.

17. Harold A. Engel, "Wisconsin State Station Completes New Studios," *Education by Radio* 5 (September 9, 1935): 46, folder 2, box 1, Engel Papers.

18. Penn, "Origin and Development," 449. On the completion of the mural, see "Document 691–December 1943: Annual Report of the University Radio Committee," 9, WHA Subject Records.

19. Untitled document beginning "Less than handsome," n.d., folder "WHA-Historical," box 49, McCarty Papers.

20. Josef F. Wright to Griffith et al., January 23, 1934, folder 5, box 1, NAEB Records.

21. John W. Dunn to Frank, March 20, 1946, folder 1, box 4, NAEB Records.

22. "Mr. Educational TV: He Got Involved When It Was Just a Twinkle in the Eye of the FCC," folder "WHA History–Xerox 10/14/84," box 34, McCarty Papers.

23. "Biographical Notes: Zelta Feike Rodenwold," microfilm reel 2, College of Science Records, record group 24, Oregon State University, Corvallis.

24. "Application for Radio Broadcasting Station Construction Permit," November 20, 1933, p. 22, folder 7, box 3, Engel Papers.

25. "State Radio Station in a Time of Depression," folder 2, box 2, Engel Papers.

26. A. Lee Henderson, "The Ohio Emergency Junior Radio College," in *Education on the Air: Fifth Yearbook of the Institute for Education by Radio* (Columbus: Ohio State University Press, 1934), 156–65.

27. Moran, "From a Toy to a Tool," 56.

28. Harold B. McCarty to Lyda Shay, December 6, 1932, folder 16, box 2, WHA Subject Records.

29. Harold B. McCarty, "The Wisconsin Plan for State Radio Service," in *Education on the Air: Fifth Yearbook of the Institute for Education by Radio* (Columbus: Ohio State University Press, 1934), 126.

30. "Oregon Poets over Radio Station KOAC," August 18, 1932, microfilm reel 1, KOAC Records.

31. "Oregon on Parade: Condensed Report for the Period June 10 to September 10, 1940," microfilm reel 57, Pres/Oregon.

32. "'Oregon Parade' Has Wide Field" [newspaper clipping], September 21, 1941, microfilm reel 2, KOAC Records.

33. Moran, "From a Toy to a Tool," 25, 78 (quotation on 25).

34. Carl Menzer to Harold McCarty, December 3, 1936, folder 1, box 2, NAEB Records.

35. Moran, "From a Toy to a Tool," 46.

36. Ibid., 46–47.

37. Director to Charles L. Hill, January 30, 1939, folder 6, box 3, WHA Subject Records; "WKAR Radio, 1922–1998," 8, MSU Archives.

38. "Station WOSU, Ohio State University," in *Education on the Air: Eighth Yearbook of the Institute for Education by Radio* (Columbus: Ohio State University Press, 1937), 76.

39. Ibid., 74.

40. Edgar H. Felix, "Recent Developments in Electrical Transcription Broadcasting" [submitted to the Federal Radio Commission], June 17, 1931, folder 1047, box 55, Payne Fund Records.

41. Josef Wright to President Kinley, March 6, 1930, folder "Radio, WILL, 1928–53," box 112, AgrSub/IL.

42. Carl Menzer to Mac, December 3, 1936, folder 1, box 2, NAEB Records.

43. Carl Menzer to Armstrong Perry, April 26, 1935, folder 1080, box 56, Payne Fund Records.

44. Josef F. Wright to Rogan Jones, April 13, 1931, folder "J-Radio, 1930–36," box 2, Pub/IL.

45. "Electrical Transcriptions" [extract from writings of Peter Dixon], n.d. [before 1935], folder 1047, box 55, Payne Fund Records.

46. "NBC Electrical Transcription Service: Its Growth and Volume," May 11, 1937, folder 44, box 92, NBC Records.

47. Frank M. Russell to M. H. Aylesworth, April 13, 1934, folder 53, box 90, NBC Records.

48. M. H. Aylesworth to R. C. Patterson Jr., June 24, 1935, folder 41, box 91, NBC Records.

49. "Annual Report: Radio Station WSUI, Year Ending June 30, 1941," subject file "Radio-WSUI-1920s-1940s," UofIowa Archives.

50. W. T. Middlebrook, "Educational Sponsorship of Radio Programs," in *Education on the Air: First Yearbook of the Institute for Education by Radio* (Columbus: Ohio State University Press, 1930).

51. Josef F. Wright to F. O. Holt, November 27, 1933, folder "W-Radio, 1927–36," box 5, Pub/IL.

52. Untitled document beginning "KOAC, the state-owned educational station of Oregon, holds a unique and available position," n.d. [probably 1938], microfilm reel 7, KOAC Records.

53. On KWSC, see Glenn Jones to A. James Ebel, February 2, 1945, folder 3, box 2, NAEB Records. For KUSD, see "Report of the Committee on Radio Broadcasting to the National Association of State Universities," November 8, 1940, folder 4, box 3, WHA Subject Records.

54. I. D. Weeks to Harlan J. Bushfield, April 17, 1943, folder "KUSD," box 26, Papers of I. D. Weeks, SDPB Papers.

55. McCarty, "Wisconsin Plan for State Radio Service," 127.

56. "Annual Report: Radio Station WSUI, Year Ending June 30, 1941," subject file "Radio-WSUI-1920s-1940s," UofIowa Archives.

57. Program Director, KOAC, to Levering Tyson, December 30, 1929, microfilm reel 7, KOAC Records.

58. Quoted in Moran, "From a Toy to a Tool," 40.

59. Harold A. Engel to Charles E. Coughlin, January 3, 1932, folder 12, box 2, WHA Subject Records.

60. Harold A. Engel, "WHA, Wisconsin's Pioneer," August 10, 1936, folder "WHA-Historical," box 49, McCarty Papers.

61. McCarty, "Wisconsin Plan for State Radio Service," 127.

62. Harold A. Engel, "A Story of Public Service Broadcasting," December 1, 1936, folder 2, box 1, Engel Papers.

63. Ibid.

64. "Application for Radio Broadcasting Station Construction Permit," November 20, 1933, folder 7, box 3, Engel Papers.

65. For the Oklahoma example, see John W. Dunn to Frank, March 20, 1946, folder 1, box 4, NAEB Papers. For the WOI example, see Moran, "From a Toy to a Tool," 96.

66. "Application for Radio Broadcasting Station Construction Permit," November 20, 1933, folder 7, box 3, Engel Papers.

67. "Report for the Year 1931–1932: College of Engineering Radio Broadcasting Committee," Engineering Experiment Station (WEAO and WOSU): Logs and Programs: 1931, 1955, WOSU Records.

68. Josef F. Wright to David Kinsley, n.d., folder "Kinsley, President David, 1919–1930," box 2, Pub/IL.

69. W. I. Griffith to Members of the Faculty, November 30, 1929, folder "WOI Policy and Organization," box 1, WOI/Griffith Records.

70. [Unknown author] to J. W. Studebaker, February 3, 1936, folder "KUSD," box 26, Weeks Papers.

71. Untitled document beginning "Broadcasting hours," folder "Corresp.–Misc., 1936–37," box 19, McCarty Papers.

72. Minutes of the Quarterly Meeting, Advisory Council on Radio Policy, Oregon State College, November 30, 1945, folder "Advisory Council on Radio Policy," box 5/1/10/41, KOAC Records.

73. On WOI "Fiddle-Fests," see Harold A. Engel to V. M. Jacobs, April 14, 1933, folder 13, box 2, WHA Subject Records. On Viking Accordion Band, see WOI Program Guide, September 1939, box marked "640 on Your Dial," WOI Records.

74. W. I. Griffith, "Annual Report: Radio Activities of Broadcast Station WOI, Fiscal Year closing December 31, 1934," n.d., WOI Records.

75. Josef Wright, "Statement for Board Regarding Radio Station Activities," 1937, folder "Public Information," box 30, Willard Papers.

76. George D. Stoddard to Bruce E. Mahan, October 27, 1936, folder "WSUI Aims and Functions," box 1, WSUI Collection.

77. "A Few Suggestions for Preparing Radio Talks," folder "Radio Programs–Advisory, 1936–43," AgrSub/IL.

78. "Techniques the Thing Says Baker," *KSAC Pick Ups* (newsletter) 1 (March 1939): 1, KSU Archives.

79. F. J. Keilholz to H. W. Mumford et al., December 23, 1937, folder "Radio, 1924–1953," box 112, AgrSub/IL; "Helps in Building Radio Programs and Script and Talent Requirements for Broadcasting over WSM," folder "Radio, 1924–1953," box 112, AgrSub/IL.

80. "Exhibit III: 'Radio News Service for KSAC Broadcasters,'" January 6, 1931, folder 1138, box 59, Payne Fund Records.

81. "Brief of Arguments Presented before Examiner E. W. Pratt of the Federal Radio Commission re: Application of WSUI for Unlimited Time on Present Assignment . . . December 10, 1930," folder "WSUI Hearing 1931," box 2, WSUI Collection.

82. "Station WNAD, University of Oklahoma," in *Education on the Air: Eighth Yearbook of the Institute for Education by Radio* (Columbus: Ohio State University Press, 1937), 75.

83. "Tips for Radio Speakers," n.d., folder "KUSD," box 26, Weeks Papers.

84. "The Music Program: Round-Table Discussion," in *Education on the Air: Eighth Yearbook of the Institute for Education by Radio* (Columbus: Ohio State University Press, 1937), 99.

85. H. W. Mumford to E. C. M. Case et al., May 26, 1937, folder "Radio, WILL, 1928–53," box 112, AgrSub/IL.

86. H. Umberger, "The Influence of Radio Instruction upon Farm Practices," in *Education on the Air: Third Yearbook of the Institute for Education by Radio* (Columbus: Ohio State University, 1932), 283.

87. Moran, "From a Toy to a Tool," 43–44.

88. Curtis quoted in ibid., 44.

89. "Annual Report, Station WOI," December 31, 1939, WOI Records.

90. Moran, "From a Toy to a Tool," 61.

91. See comments about how WHA evaluated different kinds of letters in "Letters from Listeners," n.d., folder 4, box 3, WHA Subject Records.

92. Meyer quoted in "Oregon State System of Higher Education: General Extension Division" [Annual Report of W. L. Kadderly, July 1, 1932, to June 30, 1933], 70, microfilm reel 57, Pres/Oregon.

93. Mrs. Glen De Haven quoted in "Report on Response to Recent KOAC Announcements," n.d., microfilm reel 1, KOAC Records.

94. Jones and Mooney quoted in "Oregon State System of Higher Education: General Extension Division" [Annual Report of W. L. Kadderly, July 1, 1932, to June 30, 1933], 74 (Jones) and 78 (Mooney), microfilm reel 57, Pres/Oregon.

95. Mrs. Fred Lang quoted in ibid.

96. Mary Butts to Mr. McCarty, March 19, 1935, folder 1, box 3, WHA Subject Records.

97. "Bouquets from Listeners," n.d., folder 2, box 3, WHA Subject Records.

98. Lucina Averill quoted in "Oregon State System of Higher Education: General Extension Division" [Annual Report of W. L. Kadderly, July 1, 1932, to June 30, 1933], 73, microfilm reel 57, Pres/Oregon.

99. W. L. Kadderly, "Radio Station KOAC," in *Education on the Air: Fourth Yearbook of the Institute for Education by Radio* (Columbus: Ohio State University Press, 1933), 270.

100. Anonymous letter quoted in "Oregon State System of Higher Education: General Extension Division" [Annual Report of W. L. Kadderly, July 1, 1932, to June 30, 1933], 78, microfilm reel 57, Pres/Oregon.

101. A. G. Woolfries, "Lifting Listeners' Appreciation Levels," in *Education on the Air: Seventh Yearbook of the Institute for Education by Radio* (Columbus: Ohio State University Press, 1936), 38.

102. Ibid., 38–39.

103. Excerpt from W. I. Griffith, "Annual Report—Radio Activities of Broadcasting Station WOI, fiscal year closing December 31, 1935," folder "Not Used 1930s," WOI Records.

104. A. G. Woolfries, "Lifting Listeners' Appreciation Levels," in *Education on the Air: Seventh Yearbook of the Institute for Education by Radio* (Columbus: Ohio State University, 1936), 39–44 (quotation on 40).

105. "WOI Policy," May 8, 1943, WOI History File, ISU Archives.

106. Morris, *Remembered Years*, 31.

107. "Minutes of the Quarterly Meeting Advisory Council on Radio Policy," April 16, 1943, Office of the Chancellor Archives, Oregon University System, University of Oregon, Eugene.

108. Grace C. Stanley, "Radio in Rural Schools," *Sierra Educational News* 21 (November 1925): 598.

109. G. T. Hankin, "Mechanical Aids to Education," *New Era in Home and School* 12 (August 1931): 261.

110. "Classroom Education by Radio," *School and Society* 31 (March 8, 1930), 327–28.

111. See, for example, Garland Powell to John J. Tigert, September 13, 1945, folder "Group Corresp. WRUF Radio Station 1945," box 54, Tigert Papers.

112. Robert B. Brodie, "Fitting Radio into the School Program," *Nation's Schools* 15 (February 1935): 56.

113. "Classroom Education by Radio," *School and Society* 31 (March 8, 1930): 327–28.

114. Virgil E. Dickson, "Radio in Oakland Schools," *Journal of the National Education Association* 13 (November 1924): 279.

115. Margaret B. Harrison, "Survey of What Is Being Done throughout the Country in Radio Education," *Junior-Senior High School Clearing House* 7 (October 1932): 83–84.

116. "Music on the Radio," *School and Society* 40 (October 20, 1934): 517.

117. "Radio in the Rural Schools," *School Management* 7 (February 1937): 160.

118. "Radio Challenges the Schools Today," *School Management* 7 (November 1937): 93.

119. "Alabama," n.d., folder 1361, box 69, Payne Fund Records.

120. Perry quoted in discussion of paper by P. O. Davis, "A Centralized Unit in Educational Broadcasting," in *Education on the Air: First Yearbook of the Institute for Education by Radio* (Columbus: Ohio State University Press, 1930), 76.

121. Rosene, "History of Radio Broadcasting," 82.

122. John L. Clark to John F. Patt, August 12, 1931, folder 890, box 46, Payne Fund Records.

123. B. H. Darrow to Arthur G. Crane, February 23, 1937, folder 889, box 46, Payne Fund Records.

124. S. Howard Evans to B. H. Darrow, February 25, 1937, folder 889, box 46, Payne Fund Records.

125. "KOAC Progress Report," June 10, 1936, microfilm reel 1, KOAC Records.

126. "Survey of School Broadcasting Questionnaire: Radio Station KOAC," n.d., microfilm reel 2, KOAC Records.

127. "Report of a Field Trip for WHA," January 16, 1936, folder "WHA Scripts: Wisc. School of the Air," box 19, McCarty Papers.

128. Moran, "From a Toy to a Tool," 71–72.

129. "KOAC Listening Groups in Oregon," n.d., folder 914, box 47, Payne Fund Records.

130. "Education by Radio—1936," included with letter, Franklin Dunham to John F. Royal, July 30, 1936, 3–4, folder 6, box 92, NBC Records. On the use of group listening in other countries, see British Institute of Adult Education, *Group Listening: A Report Prepared for the National Advisory Council on Radio in Education, Inc.* (Chicago: University of Chicago Press, 1934).

131. Radio Advisory Committee to H. W. Mumford, September 20, 1937, folder "Radio Programs–Advisory Listener Groups, 1937," box 27, AgrSub/IL.

132. "Some Achievements of WBAA an Educational Broadcasting Station," 1932, folder "Radio Educational Programs: Purdue University, 1930–32," box 4, Pub/IL.

133. "Annual Report: Radio Station WSUI, Year Ending June 30, 1941," subject file "Radio-WSUI-1920s-1940s," UofIowa Archives.

134. Charles H. Brown to Jerome O'Connor, January 28, 1941, WOI Records.

135. Jerome O'Connor to Manager Station WOI, January 24, 1941, WOI Records.

136. W. I. Griffith to B. B. Brackett, January 26, 1934, folder 5, box 1, NAEB Records.

137. "Statement of Policy Relative to the Use of the Radio Broadcasting Channels Licensed to Agencies of the State by the State Radio Council," December 6, 1938, folder 13, box 1, Engel Papers.

138. Untitled petition from Josef F. Wright et al., n.d., folder "Radio Committee," box 2, WSUI Collection.

139. Luke L. Roberts to Alfred Powers, February 25, 1938, microfilm reel 1, KOAC Records.

140. James M. Morris to Mr. Herman, October 14, 1946, microfilm reel 1, KOAC Records.

141. "Governing Policies of Station WILL," pamphlet, folder "1939–75," box 1, DeptJrnlsm/IL.

142. "Annual Report: Radio Station WILL, Year Ending July 1, 1940," box 1, DeptJrnlsm/IL.

143. Moran, "From a Toy to a Tool," 76–77.

144. "Wisconsin State Broadcasting Station: A Summary of Facts and Figures," 1933, folder 2, box 1, Engel Papers.

145. Penn, "Origin and Development," 362.

146. Harold A. Engel, "The Wisconsin Political Forum" [unpublished paper], n.d., folder "Radio 1943–45 Examine!" box 49, Engel Papers.

147. Harold A. Engel, "WHA, Wisconsin's Pioneer," December 1, 1936, folder 2, box 1, Engel Papers.

148. Unidentified proceedings involving discussion between Wright and McCarty, folder 17, box 2, WHA Subject Records.

149. "1939 Broadcast Series by Wisconsin's Congressional Representatives," n.d., folder 5, box 2, Engel Papers.

150. Letter from unnamed WHA staff member to a friend, August 10, 1932, folder 13, box 2, WHA Subject Records.

151. John B. Chapple to Harold A. Engel, November 2, 1938, folder 3, box 2, Engel Papers.

152. Burrows, "'Super-Powered' Goodwill Ambassador," 159–80.

153. Acting President to W. J. Bivens, June 26, 1928, folder "Corresp., 1928 A–F," box 1, Office of the President, James M. Farr Administrative Policy Records 1928, series P6, University of Florida Archives, Gainesville.

154. B. C. Riley to W. H. Lighty, December 9, 1927, folder "Correspondence 1927, Dec.–n.d.," box 30, Lighty Papers.

155. Burrows, "'Super-Powered' Goodwill Ambassador," 159–65 (attorney general Fred H. Davis quoted on 165).

156. John J. Tigert to Armstrong Perry, April 4, 1933, folder "Group Correspondence WRUF Radio Station 1933," box 53, Tigert Papers.

157. Garland Powell to John J. Tigert, July 31, 1933, folder "Group Correspondence WRUF Radio Station 1933," box 53, Tigert Papers.

158. H. Harold Hume to Garland Powell, November 14, 1932, folder "WRUF, 1930–47," box 3, AgrExp/FL.

159. Garland Powell to H. Harold Hume, November 16, 1932, folder "WRUF, 1930–47," box 3, AgrExp/FL.

160. Burrows, "Commercial Radio at the University of Florida," 63–64.

161. Wilmon Newell to Garland Powell, November 26, 1932, folder "WRUF, 1930–47," box 3, AgrExp/FL.

162. Wilmon Newell to J. J. Tigert, January 13, 1934, folder "Group Correspondence WRUF Radio Station 1934," box 53, Tigert Papers.

163. W. A. Burk to H. B. McCarty, January 3, 1933, folder 17, box 2, WHA Papers.

164. Ibid.

165. Harold Ellis to Tracy F. Tyler, December 7, 1934, folder 873, box 45, Payne Fund Records.

Chapter 7

1. "The Serious Side of Radio," *University of Chicago Round Table* promotional brochure, n.d., folder "Current Additions," box "Radio and TV Office," GenFiles/Chicago.

2. Allen Miller, "Broadcasting at the University," *University of Chicago Magazine,* March 1930, 243–44, reprint in folder "Radio Correspondence, 1925–30," box 3, Pub/IL.

3. On Harper and adult education, see untitled document beginning "Early in 1931 . . .," February 3, 1938, folder "University of Chicago Roundtable," box 1, Miller Papers; Thomas Wakefield Goodspeed, *A History of the University of Chicago: The First Quarter-Century* (Chicago: University of Chicago Press, 1972), 136, 150, 210.

4. Miller, "Broadcasting at the University," *University of Chicago Magazine,* March 1930, 243, reprint in folder "Radio Correspondence, 1925–30," box 3, Pub/IL.

5. F. W. (President Frederic Woodward), n.d. [probably 1925], folder 15, box 69, Pres-Papers/Chicago; "Meeting of the Radio Committee," February 19, 1926, folder "University of Chicago Radio Committee," box 1, Miller Papers.

6. "Meeting of the Radio Committee," April 13, 1926, folder "University of Chicago Radio Committee," box 1, Miller Papers.

7. "Meeting of the Radio Committee," June 10, 1926, folder 15, box 69, PresPapers/Chicago.

8. Allen Miller to Frederic Woodward, April 13, 1929, folder 18, box 69, PresPapers/

Chicago; Miller, "Broadcasting at the University," *University of Chicago Magazine,* March 1930, 242, reprint in folder "Radio Correspondence, 1925–30," box 3, Pub/IL.

9. On the chapel service being broadcast, see Miller, "Broadcasting at the University," *University of Chicago Magazine,* March 1930, 242, reprint in folder "Radio Correspondence, 1925–30," box 3, Pub/IL. On early public-affairs programs, see "University Radio Activities in 1925–26," *University of Chicago Magazine,* March 1926, reprint in folder "University of Chicago Radio Committee," box 1, Miller Papers.

10. Thomas Vernor Smith, *A Non-Existent Man: An Autobiography by T. V. Smith* (Austin: University of Texas Press, 1962), 62.

11. Allen Miller, "Radio Broadcasting at the University of Chicago," August 1930, 1–2, folder 18, box 69, PresPapers/Chicago. The university considered establishing its own station during the early 1930s, but budget problems made this impossible. See "Radio at the University: A Resume of Growth of Reputation and Expansion of Programs," April 28, 1935, 1–11, folder "University of Chicago Radio Committee," box 1, Miller Papers; Robert M. Hutchins to Harold L. Ickes, January 13, 1933, folder 20, box 69, PresPapers/Chicago.

12. Miller, "Radio Broadcasting at the University of Chicago," August 1930, 2, folder 18, box 69, PresPapers/Chicago.

13. Allen Miller to R. C. Higgy, February 16, 1931, folder 921, box 48, Payne Fund Records.

14. Smith, *Non-Existent Man,* 62.

15. Allen Miller to Charter Heslop, July 15, 1963, 1–6, folder "University of Chicago Round Table," box 1, Miller Papers. Smith described himself as a "specialist-in-things-in general" in his autobiography: Smith, *Non-Existent Man,* 63.

16. S. G. Reynolds, "Construction Plans of the University of Chicago Round Table," January 6, 1941, microfilm reel 7, KOAC Records.

17. Allen Miller to Charter Heslop, July 15, 1963, 2, folder "University of Chicago Round Table," box 1, Miller Papers.

18. George E. Probst, "Round Table Memorandum," 1948, folder "University of Chicago Round Table," box 1, Miller Papers.

19. Allen Miller to William Benton, February 22, 1938, folder 15, box 69, PresPapers/Chicago.

20. Allen Miller to Charter Heslop, July 15, 1963, 5, folder "University of Chicago Round Table," box 1, Miller Papers.

21. George E. Probst, "Round Table Memorandum," 1948, folder "University of Chicago Round Table," box 1, Miller Papers.

22. Allen Miller to William Benton, February 22, 1938, folder 15, box 69, PresPapers/Chicago.

23. Charles A. Siepmann to William Benton, April 10, 1941, folder 15, box 18, VicePres/Chicago.

24. Sound recording, *Town Meeting of the Air* radio program titled "Has Twentieth Century Civilization Improved Mankind: Are We Better; Are We Happier?" February 16, 1939, SoundDiv/LC.

25. Sound recording, *University of Chicago Round Table* radio program titled "Problem of Propaganda in the United States," August 14, 1938, SoundDiv/LC.

26. On Hutchins wanting NBC to absorb the costs of programs, see "Special Meeting of the Radio Committee," February 13, 1932, folder "University of Chicago Radio Committee," box 1, Miller Papers.

27. "Meeting of the Radio Committee," February 1932, folder "University of Chicago Radio Committee," box 1, Miller Papers.

28. "Meeting of the Radio Committee," November 1931, folder "University of Chicago Radio Committee," box 1, Miller Papers.

29. "Meeting of the Radio Committee," February 1932, folder "University of Chicago Radio Committee," box 1, Miller Papers.

30. W. G. Preston to William Benton, April 10, 1941, folder 11, box 18, VicePres/Chicago.

31. John F. Royal to William Benton, April 8, 1941, folder 7, box 18, VicePres/Chicago.

32. "Meeting of the Radio Committee," February 1932, folder "University of Chicago Radio Committee," box 1, Miller Papers.

33. "Meeting of the Radio Committee," June 8, 1933, folder "University of Chicago Radio Committee," box 1, Miller Papers.

34. Sydney Hyman, *The Lives of William Benton* (Chicago: University of Chicago Press, 1969), 69, 126, 158–93; William Benton to James Angell, December 8, 1937, folder 15, box 69, PresPapers/Chicago.

35. For the 1937 statistic, see Sherman H. Dryer to Robert M. Hutchins, July 1, 1939, folder 15, box 69, PresPapers/Chicago.

36. W. B. Benton to James Angell, December 8, 1937, folder 15, box 69, PresPapers/Chicago.

37. Hyman, *Lives of William Benton,* 132, 143.

38. For the first quotation, see Hyman, *Lives of William Benton,* 177. For Benton's views about "good broadcasting" practices, see William Benton to James Angell, December 8, 1937, folder 15, box 69, PresPapers/Chicago.

39. William Benton to Miller et al., February 18, 1938, folder 15, box 69, PresPapers/Chicago.

40. For the first quotation, see William Benton to Robert M. Hutchins et al., November 10, 1944, folder 6, box 14, PresPapers/Chicago. For the second quotation, see John F. Royal to Lenox R. Lohr, August 8, 1938, folder 21, box 65, NBC Records.

41. Allen Miller to William Benton, February 22, 1938, folder 15, box 69, PresPapers/Chicago.

42. Allen Miller to Robert M. Hutchins, February 18, 1938, folder 3, box 86, PresPapers/Chicago.

43. Miller's reluctance to support Benton in his attempts to get NBC to change the time for the *Round Table* was another source of friction. See William Benton to Charles Newton, August 30, 1938, folder 3, box 86, PresPapers/Chicago.

44. Judith Waller to Niles Trammell, January 5, 1938, folder 21, box 65, NBC Records.

45. John F. Royal to Lenox R. Lohr, August 8, 1938, folder 21, box 65, NBC Records.

46. William Benton to Niles Trammell, November 6, 1944, folder 2, box 14, PresPapers/Chicago.

47. On the importance of increased attention to developing station relations, see Sherman H. Dryer to William Benton, June 27, 1939, folder 15, box 69, PresPapers/Chicago.

For the number of stations, see Sherman H. Dryer to Robert M. Hutchins, July 1, 1939, folder 15, box 69, PresPapers/Chicago.

48. Benton to Trammell, November 6, 1944, folder 2, box 14, PresPapers/Chicago.

49. John Howe to D. F. Cameron, May 25, 1940, folder 12, box 11, VicePres/Chicago.

50. Hyman, *Lives of William Benton,* 203–4.

51. George E. Probst, "Round Table Memorandum," 1948, folder "University of Chicago Round Table," box 1, Miller Papers.

52. William Benton to John Howe, January 20, 1939, folder 15, box 69, PresPapers/Chicago.

53. Sherman H. Dryer to John Howe, July 9, 1941, folder 15, box 69, PresPapers/Chicago.

54. William Benton to Robert M. Hutchins et al., September 1940, folder 9, box 14, PresPapers/Chicago.

55. John Howe to William Benton, December 3, 1937, folder 9, box 1, VicePres/Chicago.

56. Alfred P. Sloan to William Benton, June 19, 1945, folder 1, box 44, VicePres/Chicago.

57. Arnold Zurcher to Neil H. Jacoby, November 9, 1945, folder 6, box 14, PresPapers/Chicago.

58. Zurcher to Jacoby, November 9, 1945, folder 6, box 14, PresPapers/Chicago. On Dryer's background, see Sherman H. Dryer to Charles Newton, n.d. [probably May 1938], folder 17, box 8, VicePres/Chicago.

59. Zurcher to Jacoby, November 9, 1945, folder 6, box 14, PresPapers/Chicago. Howe admitted that Merriam uncharacteristically interrupted Hayek too many times during their program, but he claimed that Hayek said he enjoyed the experience and that before the program when they played recordings of other *Round Table* programs Hayek had criticized participants for being too polite.

60. On the uncertain relationship with the foundation, see George Probst to Ernest C. Colwell, January 14, 1946, folder 5, box 33, PresPapers/Chicago. On the Sloan Foundation being satisfied with the Round Table, see George E. Probst to Ernest C. Colwell, April 2, 1947, folder 4, box 33, PresPapers/Chicago.

61. Sloan's views related in Sherman H. Dryer to William Benton, July 24, 1939, folder 9, box 10, VicePres/Chicago.

62. Comments reported in John Howe to William Benton, June 22, 1945, folder 3, box 14, PresPapers/Chicago.

63. Virginia Hawk to William Benton, April 10, 1945, folder 15, box 41, VicePres/Chicago. Reports from the station relations director who visited individual stations found that this economic motivation was the major reason local stations did not take the program from the network. See, for example, Virginia Hawk to John Howe, June 11, 1945, folder 15, box 41, VicePres/Chicago.

64. Robert M. Hutchins to Judith Waller, June 25, 1931, folder 18, box 69, PresPapers/Chicago.

65. Allen Miller to Robert M. Hutchins, April 13, 1934, folder 17, box 69, PresPapers/Chicago.

66. Preston quoted in John Howe to William Benton, February 18, 1939, folder 3, box 86, PresPapers/Chicago.

67. Judith Waller to Sherman Dryer, October 25, 1940, folder 7, box 18, VicePres/Chicago.

68. Sherman H. Dryer to William Benton, October 3, 1940, folder 35, box 17, VicePres/Chicago.

69. Judith Waller to William Preston, May 12, 1939, folder 39, box 73, NBC Records.

70. Sherman H. Dryer to William Benton, June 28, 1939, folder 32, box 73, NBC Records.

71. William Benton to Niles Trammell, June 30, 1939, folder 32, box 73, NBC Records. On Dryer's advice about the title for the program, see Dryer to Benton, June 28, 1939, folder 32, box 73, NBC Records.

72. John F. Royal to Niles Trammell, July 6, 1939, folder 32, box 73, NBC Records.

73. Royal to Trammell, July 6, 1939, folder 32, box 73, NBC Records.

74. Niles Trammell to John Royal, July 17, 1939, folder 32, box 73, NBC Records.

75. Sherman H. Dryer to William Benton, February 1, 1940, folder 7, box 10, VicePres/Chicago.

76. Mary Ann Dzuback, *Robert M. Hutchins: Portrait of an Educator* (Chicago: University of Chicago Press, 1991), 160.

77. Hyman, *Lives of William Benton,* 238. On Benton denying that he or Hutchins belonged to the committee but acknowledging his connection to Bowles, who was a member, see William Benton to Paul S. Mowrer, December 16, 1940, folder 2, box 7, PresPapers/Chicago.

78. William Benton to Sherman H. Dryer, February 28, 1940, folder 7, box 10, VicePres/Chicago.

79. John Howe to William Benton, June 14, 1940, folder 18, box 9, VicePres/Chicago.

80. Richard W. Steele, *Propaganda in an Open Society: The Roosevelt Administration and the Media, 1933–1941* (Westport, Conn.: Greenwood Press, 1985), 127–46; Gerd Horten, *Radio Goes to War: The Cultural Politics of Propaganda during World War II* (Berkeley: University of California Press, 2002), 27–40; Hilmes, *Radio Voices,* 230–33.

81. William Benton to John Howe, May 21, 1940, folder 9, box 14, PresPapers/Chicago.

82. Ibid.

83. Sherman H. Dryer to William Benton, October 24, 1941, folder 26, box 25, VicePres/Chicago.

84. Sherman H. Dryer to William Benton, May 24, 1940, folder 9, box 14, PresPapers/Chicago.

85. Ibid.

86. Sherman H. Dryer to Mr. Lewis, n.d., folder 6, box 14, PresPapers/Chicago.

87. Ibid.

88. Sherman H. Dryer to William Benton, December 15, 1941, folder 25, box 25, VicePres/Chicago.

89. Hilmes, *Radio Voices,* 236–44.

90. "Notes on Meeting of the Faculty Advisory Committee on Radio," January 29, 1943, folder 3, box 33, VicePres/Chicago.

91. Sherman H. Dryer to William Benton, February 12, 1943, folder 25, box 32, VicePres/Chicago.

92. Excerpt from *This Is War!* quoted in Horten, *Radio Goes to War,* 45. Sherman H. Dryer to William Benton, March 23, 1942, folder 24, box 25, VicePres/Chicago.

93. John Howe to William Benton, May 12, 1942, folder 5, box 25, VicePres/Chicago.

94. Sherman H. Dryer to Albert W. Sherer, March 6, 1942, folder 24, box 25, VicePres/Chicago.

95. Sherman H. Dryer to William Benton, May 12, 1942, folder 5, box 25, VicePres/Chicago. On the federal government's efforts to deal with race using radio broadcasting during the war, see Barbara Dianne Savage, *Broadcasting Freedom: Radio, War, and the Politics of Race, 1938–1948* (Chapel Hill: University of North Carolina Press, 1999); Hilmes, *Radio Voices,* 238–64.

96. Sherman H. Dryer to William Benton, May 29, 1942, folder 23, box 25, VicePres/Chicago; Savage, *Broadcasting Freedom,* 200.

97. For other programs broadcast during this period that addressed the issue of racial discrimination, see Hilmes, *Radio Voices,* 256–59.

98. William Benton to Sherman H. Dryer, April 9, 1943, folder 25, box 32, VicePres/Chicago; Dryer to Benton, April 2, 1943, folder 25, box 32, VicePres/Chicago.

99. Savage, *Broadcasting Freedom,* 200.

100. Sherman H. Dryer to William Benton, April 2, 1943, folder 25, box 32, VicePres/Chicago.

101. John Howe to William Benton, June 30, 1943, folder 7, box 14, PresPapers/Chicago.

102. George E. Probst to David Englestein, November 12, 1946, folder 18, box 69, PresPapers/Chicago.

103. Howe to Benton, June 30, 1943, folder 7, box 14, PresPapers/Chicago.

104. There is evidence that Waller did not personally find prejudiced views of African Americans a particularly troubling matter. When a participant expressed extreme embarrassment after he unintentionally used the phrase "nigger in the woodpile" during a *Round Table* discussion on China, Waller tried to reassure him by expressing her own view that "it is such a common term that it is not as offensive as some other phrases which might be used." Waller is quoted in George E. Probst to Ernest C. Colwell, December 17, 1945, folder 6, box 14, PresPapers/Chicago.

105. Waller quoted in John Howe to William Benton, June 30, 1943, folder 7, box 14, PresPapers/Chicago. On Waller's threat to cancel the program unless they included a southern white, see Sherman H. Dryer to William Benton, July 7, 1943, folder 7, box 14, PresPapers/Chicago.

106. Dryer to Benton, July 7, 1943, folder 7, box 14, PresPapers/Chicago.

107. Sherman H. Dryer to William Benton, July 15, 1943, folder 27, box 36, VicePres/Chicago.

108. Eddie N. Williams, "Foreword" to unidentified document, 1–3, Round Table folder, GenFiles/Chicago.

109. George E. Probst to Benton et al., October 4, 1949, folder 3, box 33, PresPapers/Chicago.

110. George E. Probst to R. M. Hutchins, February 17, 1950, folder 2, box 33, PresPapers/Chicago.

111. John Howe to William Benton, January 19, 1944, folder 15, box 36, VicePres/Chicago.

112. George E. Probst to Benton et al., October 4, 1949, folder 3, box 33, PresPapers/Chicago.

113. Sterling and Kittross, *Stay Tuned,* 331–33.

114. Harold D. Lasswell, "University Policy and the Round Table," n.d., folder 11, box 37, VicePres/Chicago.

115. Slotten, *Radio and Television Regulation,* 113–88.

116. George E. Probst to E. C. Colwell, April 4, 1950, folder 2, box 33, PresPapers/Chicago.

117. BofTM/Chicago, April 14, 1955, 64. After helping to pioneer a noncommercial educational television station for Chicago, WTTW, the university resurrected the *Round Table* as a television program beginning in December 1967.

Epilogue

1. Robert J. Blakely, *To Serve the Public Interest: Educational Broadcasting in the United States* (Syracuse, N.Y.: Syracuse University Press, 1979), 77–78. The first real success with gaining frequencies for educational radio occurred in 1938 (77).

2. Ibid., 79. For the "renaissance" quotation, see Ralph Engelmann, *Public Radio and Television in America: A Political History* (London: Sage Publications, 1996), 86.

3. Blakely, *To Serve the Public Interest,* 124.

4. Engelmann, *Public Radio and Television in America,* 86.

5. Blakely, *To Serve the Public Interest,* 124.

6. Jack W. Mitchell, *Listener Supported: The Culture and History of Public Radio* (London: Praeger, 2005), 25–26.

7. Blakely, *To Serve the Public Interest,* 9–10.

8. Engelmann, *Public Radio and Television in America,* 86.

9. Blakely, *To Serve the Public Interest,* 10–11.

10. Ibid., 102–14.

11. Ibid., 85–103, 169.

12. Engelmann, *Public Radio and Television in America,* 86–87 (quotation on 87).

13. Blakely, *To Serve the Public Interest,* 134–35.

14. Mitchell, *Listener Supported,* 26–28.

15. Ibid., 28.

16. Blakely, *To Serve the Public Interest,* 167–69 (quotation on 169).

17. Carnegie Commission on Educational Television, Summary, 1967, Public Broadcasting PolicyBase, *Current* Newspaper, http://www.current."rg/pbpb/carnegie/Carnegie/Summary.html (accessed March 20, 2008).

18. Quoted in Mitchell, *Listener Supported,* 28.

19. Ibid., 30–33 (quotation on 33).

20. John Witherspoon and Roselle Kovitz, *The History of Public Broadcasting* (Washington, D.C.: Current, 1987), 16.

21. Mitchell, *Listener Supported,* 34.

22. Ibid., 33–37; Blakely, *To Serve the Public Interest,* 185.

23. Blakely, *To Serve the Public Interest,* 148–49, 185.

24. Ibid., 149.

25. Quoted in ibid., 150–51.

26. Land Report quoted in ibid.

27. Land Report quoted in ibid.

28. Carnegie Commission on Educational Television, Summary, 1967.

29. Historical Note on Samuel Holt, Finding Aids at the University of Maryland Archives, http://hdl.handle.net/1903.1/1557/ (accessed March 20, 2008).

30. Mitchell, *Listener Supported,* 33–37.

31. Ibid., 43–48 (Gunn quoted on 45).

32. Ibid., 46–47.

33. Ibid., 48–49.

34. Ibid., 49–52.

35. Engelmann, *Public Radio and Television in America,* 94.

36. Mitchell, *Listener Supported,* 55.

37. Engelmann, *Public Radio and Television in America,* 129.

38. Ibid., 116–17.

Index

Note: Italicized page numbers indicate illustrations.

programming; political programming; public-affairs programming; religious programming; sports programming; women's programming

propaganda: academic fears of, 237; dangers of, 91; FRC prejudice against, 137–39; political, 75; public-affairs program on, 220; use of term, 5–6; wartime dissemination of, 87–88, 232–33. *See also* special-interest or "propaganda" stations

public-affairs programming: broadcast practices in, 205–8; civil rights issues and, 228–29, 233–34; differences in, 220; economic discourse in, 225–26; funding dilemma and, 208–9; nonpartisan approach to, 74–79; political education commitment in, 207–8. *See also* political programming; *University of Chicago Round Table* (program)

Public Broadcasting Act (1967), 7, 241–46

Public Broadcasting System (PBS), 3, 7, 245–46

public broadcasting system (radio and television): emergence of, 4; federally defined form of, 7, 242; oversight and funding for, 2–3, 245–46; radio vs. television in, 243–44; seminars on, 240; television emphasized in, 241–43. *See also* National Public Radio (NPR); noncommercial radio stations; Public Broadcasting System (PBS); public radio; public television; university radio stations

public-interest standard: antipathy to propaganda stations unspoken in, 137–39; definition of, 3, 105; FRC hearings and, 121; FRC principles of, 127–30; in granting licenses, 118; in Radio Act of 1927, 109; rationale for, 4–5. *See also* educational programming; public-affairs programming

publicity: records in exchange for, 77–78; redefinition of, 118; university radio's role in, 26–27, 147, 186–87, 217; value of radio's, 220. *See also* advertising

public radio: motivation underlying, 33–35; use of term, 99, 176–77. *See also* noncommercial radio stations; university radio stations

public-service ideals: agricultural connections in, 28–29; of amateur operators, 18–19; articulated in objectives, 187–89; congressional debates underlying, 5; ethics of, 52–53; Hoover's support for, 102; of

post office radio stations, 89; public discourse on, 6; of university radio stations, 23–27, 41–42, 150, 183–84; value placed on, 93. *See also* commercialism vs. public-service ideals; public-interest standard

public-service programming: as absent in commercial radio, 57; commercial compromises of, 76–79; license based on providing, 94–95; models of, 150, 183–84, 213–14; musical broadcasts as, 57; obligations of commercial stations in, 6–7; role of university stations in, 23–27; use of term, 188. *See also* educational programming; public-affairs programming

public television: use of term, 243. *See also* Public Broadcasting System (PBS)

Pupin, Michael, 11, 157–58

Purdue University: continuous wave transmission and, 11; faculty and amateur cooperation at, 19; radio experiment at, 97–98; radio operators trained at, 29; radio station of, 35, 77, 180, 205

radio: commercial vs. home-built, 30–33; competing meanings, 9–10; dual system of, 93–94; emergence of, 3–4; as essentially commercial, 192; intrinsic qualities of, 193–94; "party line" telephone model for, 25–26; point-to-point model of, 10–11, 18, 20–21, 81, 87; power of, 153–54; private vs. public ownership, 159–60, 166; proposed tax on receivers, 278n77; public vs. educational, 176–77; transformation in 1920s, 1–2. *See also* broadcast practices; commercialism vs. public-service ideals; land-grant universities and colleges; network radio and broadcasting; programming; public-interest standard; radio policy; radio stations

Radio Act (1912): impact on amateurs, 18–19; impetus for, 84–85; legal case concerning, 107–8; on types of licenses, 19–20

Radio Act (1927): authors of, 168–69; context underlying, 103–8; Davis Amendment to, 123–26, 127, 130–33; description of, 108–11; FCC and language of, 166; passage of, 5. *See also* Federal Radio Commission (FRC)

Radio Book Club (program), 74

Radio Broadcast (periodical), *90, 93*

radio broadcast reform: commercial station-university experiments in, 157–59;

WPSC (Pennsylvania State University), 35, 143–44

WRC (Washington, D.C.), 99

Wright, Josef: on equipment costs, 64; in NAEB "brotherhood," 181; on objectives, 186–87, 190–91; on program funding, 57; on shared recordings, 185

WRUF (University of Florida): advertising on, 53, 210–11; announcer of, 178, *191*; funding dilemma of, 209–10; importance of, 35; musical programming of, 77, *191*

WSBT (South Bend), 136

WSUI (earlier WHAA, University of Iowa): audience letters to, 61; broadcast practices of, 193; in community of stations, 181; controversial topics avoided by, 205; earlier call letters of, 260n19; educational programming of, 50; hours of, 175; im-

portance of, 42; license of, 17, 180; musical programming of, 56–57; objectives of, 186, 188; programming philosophy of, 57, 184; program recordings by, 185; sports programming of, 26, 65; studio of, 74

WTAW (Texas A&M University), 35

WTTW (Chicago), 303n117

WUOA (University of Arkansas), 113

WUOM (University of Michigan), 244

WWJ (Detroit), 67–68

WWL (Loyola University), 211–12

Yale Sheffield Scientific School, 11

Yale University: commercial radio station used by, 42

Young, Owen D., 171

Young Aviators (program), 203

HUGH RICHARD SLOTTEN teaches at the University of Otago in Dunedin, New Zealand. He is the author of *Patronage, Practice, and the Culture of American Science: Alexander Dallas Bache and the U.S. Coast Survey* and *Radio and Television Regulation: Broadcast Technology in the United States, 1920–1960*. His articles have appeared in *Media History,* the *Historical Journal of Film, Radio, and Television, Technology and Culture: The International Quarterly of the Society for the History of Technology,* the *Journal of American History,* the *History of Education Quarterly,* and *Isis: The International Journal for the History of Science.*

The History of Communication

Selling Free Enterprise: The Business Assault on Labor and Liberalism, 1945–60
  Elizabeth A. Fones-Wolf
Last Rights: Revisiting *Four Theories of the Press*   *Edited by John C. Nerone*
"We Called Each Other Comrade": Charles H. Kerr & Company, Radical Publishers
  Allen Ruff
WCFL, Chicago's Voice of Labor, 1926–78   *Nathan Godfried*
Taking the Risk Out of Democracy: Corporate Propaganda versus Freedom
  and Liberty   *Alex Carey; edited by Andrew Lohrey*
Media, Market, and Democracy in China: Between the Party Line and the
  Bottom Line   *Yuezhi Zhao*
Print Culture in a Diverse America   *Edited by James P. Danky and Wayne A. Wiegand*
The Newspaper Indian: Native American Identity in the Press, 1820–90
  John M. Coward
E. W. Scripps and the Business of Newspapers   *Gerald J. Baldasty*
Picturing the Past: Media, History, and Photography   *Edited by Bonnie Brennen
  and Hanno Hardt*
Rich Media, Poor Democracy: Communication Politics in Dubious Times
  Robert W. McChesney
Silencing the Opposition: Antinuclear Movements and the Media in the Cold War
  Andrew Rojecki
Citizen Critics: Literary Public Spheres   *Rosa A. Eberly*
Communities of Journalism: A History of American Newspapers and Their Readers
  David Paul Nord
From Yahweh to Yahoo!: The Religious Roots of the Secular Press   *Doug Underwood*
The Struggle for Control of Global Communication: The Formative Century   *Jill Hills*
Fanatics and Fire-eaters: Newspapers and the Coming of the Civil War
  Lorman A. Ratner and Dwight L. Teeter Jr.
Media Power in Central America   *Rick Rockwell and Noreene Janus*
The Consumer Trap: Big Business Marketing in American Life   *Michael Dawson*
How Free Can the Press Be?   *Randall P. Bezanson*
Cultural Politics and the Mass Media: Alaska Native Voices   *Patrick J. Daley and
  Beverly A. James*
Journalism in the Movies   *Matthew C. Ehrlich*
Democracy, Inc.: The Press and Law in the Corporate Rationalization of the
  Public Sphere   *David S. Allen*
Investigated Reporting: Muckrakers, Regulators, and the Struggle over
  Television Documentary   *Chad Raphael*
Women Making News: Gender and the Women's Periodical Press in Britain
  Michelle Tusan
Advertising on Trial: Consumer Activism and Corporate Public Relations in the 1930s
  Inger Stole
Speech Rights in America: The First Amendment, Democracy, and the Media
  Laura Stein

The University of Illinois Press
is a founding member of the
Association of American University Presses.

———————————————————————

Composed in 10.5/13 Adobe Minion Pro
by Jim Proefrock
at the University of Illinois Press
Manufactured by Thomson-Shore, Inc.

University of Illinois Press
1325 South Oak Street
Champaign, IL 61820-6903
www.press.uillinois.edu

DATE